A Buckeye Abroad.

Engraved by Robt. Hinshelwood.

MOUNT BLANC. FROM St. MARTINS. Pag: 311.

A BUCKEYE ABROAD,

BY SAMUEL S. COX.

THE DRACHENFELS & NUNNENWORTH.

on the RHINE. page 341.

New-York. G.P. Putnam.

A BUCKEYE ABROAD;

OR,

Wanderings in Europe, and in the Orient.

BY

SAMUEL S. COX.

"The Utopians imagine that HE, as all inventors of curious engines, has exposed to our view, this great machine of the Universe, we being the only creatures capable of contemplating it."—*Sir Thomas More's Utopia.*

NEW-YORK:
GEORGE P. PUTNAM, 155 BROADWAY,
MD.CCC.LII.

JOHN F. TROW,
Printer and Stereotyper,
49, Ann Street.

PREFACE.

A Book of travels is no longer a book of marvels. There remains but small portions of *terra incognita*. Asia and the Americas are pouring in their tributes to the curiosity of this locomotive age. Africa, even, in the page of Cummings and others, peers from behind her veil of mystery, and the Arctics are melting their frigid bonds, to flow in the channels of literature. The only merit reserved for a volume of travels is, either that the ground is untrodden, or that the mode of observation is new and peculiar. The author can lay no claim to the former. Something may be conceded to him, from the fact imported by the title—A Buckeye Abroad. A native of the west, and of that part, familiarly known as the Buckeye State,—may be supposed to look upon the scenes and mingle with the throngs of the Old World with new and peculiar sensations, which may find sympathy, if not with the general reader, at least with readers in Ohio. Indeed it was such an interest at home that called for the revision and the publication of these passages of travel. They embrace a tour through France, Italy, Germany, Belgium, Scotland, England and Ireland; delightful sojournings at Rome, Naples, Malta, Venice, Athens, Smyrna,

Constantinople, Geneva, and amid the Alps; and observations along the Mediterranean, amidst the isles of Greece.

The pleasure of travelling was enhanced by companionship. We numbered four in our company, two ladies and a gentleman, Mr. Philo Buckingham, and myself—just the number for convenience and unity of movement, as well as for pleasure. The time, too, was propitious. The year 1851 may be truly called *annus mirabilis*, at least so far as travellers were concerned. The Great Exhibition—that novel phaze of our civilization—was enough to entitle the year to the honor, as a special wonder.

Each observer is a type of a large class of observers, mankind generally; and it is not to be accounted egotistical that the writer perpetually speaks of himself. Of necessity he must use his own senses and reason; but through these, others, especially if educated and governed by similar influences, may perceive and reflect, by virtue of the common vinculum, which binds mankind together. The impressions herein recorded were mostly taken upon the spot, and the allusions, historical, classical, or otherwise, were not sought for, but sprung out of the time and locality. Each lineament of each form in Nature or Art, each custom and characteristic were daguerreotyped, though somewhat rapidly, if not imperfectly, from the original, as it appeared in itself and in its environment. Well knowing the inferior rank in literature to which a work of this kind is entitled, I reluctantly commit it to the public, trusting that it may be read as it was written, more for enjoyment than *profit*.

S. S. C.

ZANESVILLE, OHIO, *Jan.* 1, 1852.

CONTENTS.

A BUCKEYE ABROAD.

I.

Over the Sea and Rail to England.

"Hey boys! she scuds away, and by my head I know,
We round the world are sailing now,
What dull men are those who tarry at home,
When abroad they might wantonly roam,
And gain such experience and spy too
Such countries and wonders as I do."

Cowley.

NO one can contemplate a long sea voyage to distant lands without foreboding. To a native of the west, unaccustomed to the ocean, and only glancing at its terrors, through a dim and often distorted medium, a journey over its troublous bosom is trebly fearful. Pluck up what courage he may, yet the heart will quail when the hour approaches, in which to sever connection with the stable earth. Upon this merry May morning, as we are preparing to board our steamer, there is a sort of "fearful looking for" the terrors of the deep. This is entirely unnecessary, at least for the first *three* hours. Yet I would not be deprived of this semi-melancholy and this semi-terror which enshroud the mind before a long sea voyage. Madame de Stäel has remarked, very truthfully, that it is a great trial to leave one's country, when one must cross the sea. There is such solemnity in a pilgrimage, the first steps of which are on the ocean. It seems as if a gulf were opening behind you, and your return becoming impossible. How can it be otherwise to us western folk, whose visions have been circumscribed by hills and forests, rivers and plains? The round "dim inane" of the ocean horizon already, to the mind's eye, fills the imagination with the terror which springs from vagueness. In such a stretch of the sight, not only the eye, but thought even is lost. Suggestions, connate with those which the idea of death prompts, arise in the soul.

And yet, for all these imaginary as well as real experiences of ill, what a compensation has the traveller, in the anticipation of standing upon the shores of the old world, with its scenes of renowned enchantment and heroic deeds, with its very dust golden with historic memory! It is well to be shut out, as if by a wall of brass, from old and familiar things, to enjoy such hallowed and hallowing scenes.

Severed from familiar objects by an abyss of water, more formidable than brass, it will be mine to transcribe the observations and thoughts which these scenes inspire.

The contrasts which a sea voyage present are not unworthy of some note, especially as we have not the opportunity, as yet, to tread in the path of antiquity—to gather moss from its ruined monuments and crumbling towers—to forget the ordinary experiences of every-day life, and to wrap ourselves in the shadowy mantle of the past.

We left the dock at Jersey City upon a fine day. The sun shone mildly. A light breeze, which had not power to curl a single snow-wreath, played in the harbor. All aboard. The deck was thronged with passengers and their friends to bid them "good bye." The boat is cleared of all save the passengers, and we move out, how proudly, from our mooring. The crowd on the dock cheer us; our guns answer with a quiver and a report. Away we dash—past the Battery and down the bay!

A few tears from the ladies; a few farewell wavings of handkerchiefs, and New-York begins to die away in the distance. The Battery becomes an indistinct clump of foliage. The forest of masts becomes pencilled so fine as to seem but one mark; the land soon fades into a blue sky, and we are afloat!

For the first few hours the fresh air of the salt sea and the novel situation, afford agreeable excitement. The frame quivers with a new-born delight. The soul sweeps the horizon with a larger circuit and a bolder wing. The Old World already looms up in the East, a glorious promise to the Eye of Hope!

Soon we hail a vessel, and let off the pilot. The little boat drops astern, amid the foam of our wake, and the steamer again throbs on its way. We had not gone far before a singular phenomena—singular at least to our Buckeye eye—appeared. There was a something spouting salt water against the sky! It proved to be a *whale*—a live Jonah-swallowing king of the deep! We lingered upon deck to watch the sun sink in splendor. The process of setting sail began, with the cheery songs and cries of the sailors. A west wind is coming along to add to our velocity and give exhilaration to our spirits.

Exhilaration? If you could only have seen your new-fledged traveller, from that time forward up to the time when he first seized this pen, you would have found him a perfect embodiment of *inverted* exhilaration. He began to experience all the seven-fold horror of the sea. Oh! this rolling, rolling, straining, creaking, pitching, and tossing! all day—all night. When will this voyage end? He begins to count the hours, and measures them by groans. Eating? Horrible! All that he can do is to take down beef-tea, porridges and soups, and such other watery aliment, only fit for the spectre of Melancholy. Old Burton must have been upon the sea, when he wrote the couplet:

> "All other griefs to this are jolly,
> Naught so damned as Melancholy."

"Have any thing to-day, Sir," says our excellent servant John:—"No!" is the unmannerly retort. Imprisonment in the meanest county jail, on bread and water, with whippings hourly, would be heaven to this. And then the idea of coming back. I lay whole days thinking of it—wondering if there could not be found some short-cut over Bering's straits. No matter for bad roads and cold weather, so it is mother earth—give us EARTH, Zealand or Greenland. Only let this heaving instability cease.

Washington Irving never said a truer, yet in some respects a less true thing, than when he called the Ocean a *blank page*, separating two worlds. It may be blank; but like the pages between the Old and New Testaments, it affords a resting-place for the mind, wherein to contemplate the wonders and majesty of the Creator. It affords, too, a space for the solemn records of "Deaths," and sometimes of "Births," of which latter, our good ship received an addition when three days out. But to my thinking, this page is written all along significantly. I do not mean to say that I have been gazing out into the ocean, drinking in its roar and its sublimity; though I confess to drinking, in certain peculiar moments, divers quantities of the beverage it affords—slightly warmed. To come home to our subject, I have been a *victim*, by no means a solitary one, to the god of the Trident. I will not say, that he has used me peculiarly unkind; for daily, since my body assumed its perpendicularity, have I seen others coming from their berths,—pictures of Spencer's Image of Despair, or rather, resembling rats emergent from holes into which young Nimrods had been pouring warm water. For over a week has my poor system experienced what never before it experienced, and (how I fear!) may again experience. But this is a part of the royal game of travel. It is this experience which is written in illuminated characters all over Irving's blank page.

I would advise every one who thinks of crossing the sea, to provide a cast-iron stomach; or else procure some preparation, by which that sensitive part of our organism may be rendered *ex tempore* insensible. I am aware that there is, on land, some strong prejudices against sea-travelling, on account of sea-sickness. I had some misgivings myself. They fell so far short, however, of the reality, as to work great injustice to the power of Old Neptune.

I would not undertake to tell precisely the treatment which Dr. Atlantic prescribed. The day after I came aboard, I inadvertently caught him assuming the office of Æsculapius, taking a diagnosis of my case, and pressing home the remedy with a summariness not exceeded by the sharpest practice of another learned profession. The unremitting vigilance and care of my "big medicine-man" cannot, in my present state, be too highly lauded. That he has suffered me to sleep—a little, almost suffuses my eyes with gratitude. Dr. Sangrado prescribed a remedy for all diseases, so simple as to have become classical—blood-letting and warm water. Our Doctor disdains the former. The latter, I am pleased to say, has been adopted in these latitudes (with an addition of the *saline*), with good effect. The fact that I am able to write on this eighth day out, is evidence,

——Clear as a fountain in July,

that a searching potency has been exercised, which places Medicine upon the topmost sparkle of the wave of science.

A person after emerging from the Hades of sea-sickness, is for ever after a privileged community in himself. He has certain irrepealable franchises, among which are freedom of speech, I wish I could say "free soil." FREE SOIL! I am a great free-soiler, just now. Give me soil, that is all I ask, whether it be the veriest rock upon which a lichen would starve, let it be stable—only still—rocky, but not rocking. No one can appreciate the merits of that much-abused party who has not been sea-sick. You might as well attempt to master the Integral Calculus, without a knowledge of algebra, or to read Shakspeare without a knowledge of the alphabet. It is a *sine quâ non.* Each particular fibre in my body would quiver, if it were only placed upon an immobile element—upon free soil.

One thing I have learned within a week, and that is, fully to understand the merits of Christopher Columbus and Captain Cook. Even in my most pluckless condition, pale, haggard and hirsute, I could have performed a genuflexion, with the ardor of Carlyle himself, to these heroes of the sea.

I have wondered how any soul could feel grand or sublime upon the ocean. Lord Jeffrey has demonstrated that beauty and sublimity are subjective, not inherent to the objects seen, but depending upon the mind of the person seeing. The labyrinth of forms which emanate from the painter's pencil and distil upon the canvass the freshness of Nature's Beauty, are first pictured in his soul. The warm breath of enthusiasm passes over the gross materials of earth, solves them into the refinement of thought, and then the "imprisoned splendor of the soul" bursts forth to beautify and bless. If, therefore, there is to be found beauty or sublimity upon the ocean, the mental tentacula must reach out and find it. But when they are paralyzed and shrunken by this everlasting sea-sickness—where is the sub——, I beg pardon. Eureka! It is the sublimity Burke discovered in Spencer's Cave of Error,—the *nauseate sublime!* Its monosyllabic expression, is simply—*Ugh!*

On Sunday we passed amidst six icebergs. They were said to be beautiful. No doubt. But if each iceberg had been as radiant with gold and orange, green and violet, and prismatic generally as Trinity church windows, with a Polar bear surmounting each glittering pinnacle, the scene could not have aroused my sense of the beautiful. I did not even go on deck to see them. The beautiful was drowned fathomlessly in the ocean of sea-sickness.

These British vessels run up north and over the Newfoundland banks. They thus save upwards of 300 miles. We have passed very few vessels. It is not the route for sailing vessels. During the rough time upon the banks, we ran by a little schooner, with no sails set, dancing away 1500 miles from either hemisphere—playing "hide and go seek" with the billows, as if it were in very deed, the fairy gondola of Phedra which passed on its way, unharmed, without oar, sail, or rudder.

We also passed the U. S. steamship Humboldt, upon our fifth day out. It is her first trip. She had, however, only seven pieces of canvas spread, while we had ten. Our American ladies did not like the idea of having Uncle Sam thrown behind in that way. I am free to confess that not a sentiment of patriotism disturbed my sea-sick heart. I was helped on deck for a view of this strange meeting of the steamers in mid-ocean. We ran along side of her, only distant one half mile. We saluted with cannon, and she returned it gallantly. How finely she dashed the waves from her black prow! What a thing of life is the proud, throbbing steamer, conscious of dignity, sinewed with brass and iron, with a viewless power mocking human might, beating in its iron heart! This gigantic power has been evoked into being, by the genius of this latter time, the distinguishing feature of which, *above all others*, is expressed in Wordsworth's lines:

——— An intellectual mastery exercised
O'er the blind elements; a purpose given,
A perseverance fed; almost a SOUL
Imparted to brute matter.

I would not decry the British because we are her rivals in this race of material progress. Let honor crown the Anglo-Saxon of both continents. These petty irritabilities which have sprung out of this oceanic rivalry, and which have even poisoned the sociality of our voyage, are beneath the dignity and generosity of our countrymen. For safety and speed, for careful management, good servants and skilful officers, the "Asia," at least, cannot be rivalled. We shall try the American line on our return, and may then express our preference. Until then,

God speed the noble steamers of both nations upon their missions of interchange!

My first nautical observation on deck was that of a little bird "all alone, all alone," seemingly exhausted, yet still flying in its own element. What a lesson does this äerial pilgrim teach us. We who are continually passing the "flaming bounds" of worldly wisdom, and striving for the unknown and unapproachable mysteries of God and of the spirit world—does it not teach us to be content in our own sphere of knowledge? How beautiful would be the song of that little chorister,

——"Upon a bough high swaying in the wind,"

in some sequestered nook, surrounded by leafy prospects and smiling cultivation! How like a hymn to its Creator would go up its carol to the All Audient One; yet, here it is, with fagged wing and panting breath, contending with harsh, cold blasts, just able to overtop the snowy spray of the mid-ocean; deluded from its greenwood home by the persuasive mysteries of the unknown; a thing of song in a sea of chaos, soon to be whelmed for ever. Is it not an epitome of man, when he breaks the golden chords of that harmony which bind him to his God?

As my strength increases, the sea grows on my esteem. The warmer air detains me above, where the employment of the eye gives relief and delight. The sailors are putting up their ropes into snaky coils. The sound of dish-washing unromantically mingles with the "profound eternal bass" of Ocean's roar. French fops and English cockneys (we have a motley crew) puff the light cigar vapor. It darts away to blend with the blue, that bends above us like an unbroken canopy, embroidered with a few fleecy clouds. What a circle the horizon describes in the clear air! I do not know whether it pleases most from its perfect geometry or its bewildering extent. The waverings of the water are softened by the distance. It seems as if GOD, as he sits upon the circle of the heavens, had by his power carved out a vast liquid gem, variant with lights and shades. The sea, as your eye approaches the edge of the horizon,—that mysterious and ever-changing line bounding the visible sphere and dividing it from the invisible,—grows darker, until upon its rim, where it clasps the sky, it is black; the result of perspective, heightened by the contrast between the dark water and the fair sky.

What an infinity of angles the wind makes the sea make! Like the agitation of one overmastering thought upon the world of mind. Each medium reflects it similarly, yet with a marked difference. One, like a Bacon or a Newton, heaves it heavenward, flashing it white and beautiful. Its very foam attests the strength of the billow. Another receives the power, and with docile humility, projects but a tiny drop—it may be, but a drop from the spray of the mightier wave.

The officers are accustomed every log, to drop a bucket, and take the temperature of the water. This is reported, perhaps to Greenwich; and there the immense repertory of isolated, meaningless facts is put into the crucible of generalization, and comes out vital principles of navigation. So much for a bucket of salt water, and the Baconian system of induction.

We are almost to Cape Clear, the southern point of Ireland. I am a living witness that the account Tacitus gives of these parts is an unmitigated fabrication. Thule, Ultima Thule, is generally acknowledged to be Ireland, I believe. Tacitus says, that the seas around Thule were a mass of sluggish stagnation, hardly yielding to the stroke of the oar, and never agitated by winds and tempests. About as authentic and probable as Juvenal's poetic account of the sun, which he affirms could be heard hissing in the waters of the Herculean Gulf.

Audit Hercules stridentem gurgite solem.

All on the look-out for land! Man at the mast-head and officers with glasses! The hour of enfranchisement draws nigh. Wearied with gazing into the dim distance, I went below, to return on deck at dark. Clambering up the taffrail I saw—

horror of horrors! within twenty-five yards of us, a huge black rock, rising up in the gloom, like the back of Leviathan! I involuntarily dropped. We were in sight of land with a vengeance. This rock is within a few miles of Cape Clear. The light-houses showed that "sweet Ireland"—(sweet indeed to the longing eye), was on our left. The next morning confirmed our locality. It found us pushing up the Channel between Wales and Ireland, not far from Braichen Point. We moved in a direct line to Holyhead. Away to the west, in dim, graceful limning, float, cloudlike, the cerulean mountains of Ireland. The low coast cannot be seen. "*Heavy a port!*" growls the officer at the wheel-house. "*Heavy a port!*" echoes the mate at the compass. "*Heavy a port, Sir!*" drawls out the man from the tiller, and the deflection eastward continues.

I observed an oval line of a most ethereal fineness upon the right. It grew, with our panting steamer's progress, into form, grand and palpable, until Holyhead burst upon us. With a glass we viewed the immense work begun by government here. A harbor is being built for the Cunard and mail steamers. Already it is connected with Liverpool by cars. As we hove in sight, we ran up signals, which were carried to Liverpool before us,—as was indicated by the line of steam which began to flow throughout the distant landscape.

We took a pilot aboard and received from him one newspaper, which was cut into shreds and devoured by fourteen passengers at once. The breath of the fresh landscape is around. Now I can write like a native of this round earth; for land is all about us. The cliffs of Old England stand out in definite outline. Light-houses and mansions attest the presence of a superior civilization. How many thronging associations flit through the mind, as I recall, that here, not in fancy's eye, but in reality, stands the little isle of power—the home of OLD COKE and CROMWELL, of SPENCER and COWPER, of CHATHAM and CANNING, and all the host of glorious minds with whom so much of life has been passed. Aye; in very truth, my eye has greeted the land of William Shakspeare and Guy Fawkes, John Milton and Titus Oates; the ideal realm of John Falstaff and Little Nell; the theatre of Roundheads and Cavaliers. Yonder, verily, just over to my right, actually grew into life that vigorous feudalism out of which rose the fabric of our own common law. These remembrances come over me wildly and strangely. Old England! Yes; God bless her! With ears in my eyes, I beseech Heaven's best benison upon her. I forget her, as the land of ruth and wrong; I remember her only as the land of noble deeds and generous hearts. Her literature, from Chaucer's first uncouth song to D'Israeli's last sarcasm, floats through the memory like a vivid power, transforming every prejudice into praise, and even wrong into glory.

But I am ahead of my reckoning. I am not yet done with the Ocean. Such an event as crossing the Atlantic by a backwoods Buckeye, deserves a fuller treatment. Of course, in this gossiping of mine, you will not expect me to confine myself to any system. I reproduce only hasty impressions hastily; pretending to no *in*sight, simply to sight; to no profundity in reading character and discussing vital principles, simply to superficial glances and occasional hearings.

Now that the horrors of sickness are over, the ocean presents itself under another sky. I have spoken of our "volant home," the noble steamship. Ours was not tested very strongly by Neptune; yet not a fear as to the result intruded itself into our minds. It requires a good share of confidence in a vessel, to step from the firm set earth upon its fragile planks, which are to be upborne by so unstable an element. It instils a thrilling awe, to feel yourself moving away to some mysterious realm, the existence of which seems to hang only upon the prompture of Faith. The divorce from the old and familiar has begun. Day after day, you are

——— "Borne darkly, fearfully afar,"

reaching no shore, and night after night, you hear, by your very pillow, the

"Ever drifting, drifting, drifting,
Currents of the restless main."

Yet to know that the potent water-breath, we call *steam*, can mate the Ocean in his wildest Saturnalia, gives all the joy of security, while it does not rob us of the vague mystery. Let the Sea King try his strongest, to crack our vessel's joints and sinews—cheerily sing the sailors, and merrily laugh and skip about the boat the frolicksome children. No drifting at the pleasure of the elements, with our vessel; but a straight path and a steady one. Vulcan, amid his coal smoke below, is the controlling spirit; and reeling Neptune drops his trident in the fire.

Can it be that here indeed is the rock-ribbed coast of England? Yes; for the tokens are evident. The rocks are all fissured, and gray as the hoar-frost with salt. Irregular masses seem to have been heaped ashore. No footing is found upon which to stand. The rocks impress one strangely, not alone because they form an outline of the isle of our ancestors, but (we must own it) because that isle affords our poor physical frames a steady foothold, and an uninterrupted appetite. How much of the crockery ware is burned into this human "wessel of wrath," along with the exquisite porcelain?

We are about to turn up the Mersey, and to leave our open seaward for a narrower path. Perhaps from this point one may fully appreciate the glories of the ocean; for its roll no longer disturbs the mind. CAMPBELL has embalmed in the splendor of his verse, more of the beauty and sublimity of the sea, than any other poet, BYRON not excepted. He loved to retire from the bustle of London, Edinburgh, or Glasgow, and from the height of St. Leonard's (on solid ground—mind you!) listen to its murmurs, which to him were dearer than all the applause of the world. He found peacefulness in its din, and repose in its restlessness. He looked out upon the depths, amid the storms, and saw the lightning sink half way over the main, like a wearied bird too weak to sweep its space. He saw it in the calm, when the firmament of stars found in it a gorgeous mirror for their Infinitude! What a fine thought is that of his, which calls the sky the mistress of the sea, giving from her brow his moods, morning's milky white, noon's sapphire, and the saffron glow of evening. So beautiful did it seem to his poetic eye, that he wondered not that Love's own Queen was fabled to have come from the bosom of the sea! He likens it to creation's common (a purely Anglo-Saxon metaphor), which no human power can parcel or inclose. This idea is akin to that of MADAME DE STAEL, which Byron engrafted upon his immortal Apostrophe. "Man," she says, "may plough the earth, and cut his way through mountains, or construct rivers into canals to transport his merchandise, but if his fleets for a moment furrow the ocean, its waves as instantly efface this slight mark of servitude, and it again appears as it was the first day of the creation." Or, as Byron phrases it,

> "Time writes no wrinkle on thine azure brow,
> Such as creation's dawn beheld, thou rollest now."

The figure, however, which pleases my taste most is that of the mirror. It has been used by BAILEY, in his "Angel World," to illustrate the most stupendous truth which the human mind may entertain; the mysterious combination of the Eternal Father with the everlasting Son, the union of Infinite Justice with all-gracious Love,—

> "The unseen likeness of the INEFFABLE ONE,
> Each like the other, as the *sky and sea*,
> Imbosoming the Infinite."

Material though the ocean be, it has a power to penetrate into the mind's immaterial recesses, to inspire it with Beauty, and elevate it with the emotions of Religion.

Have I written too much upon this theme? My Jeremiad on sea-sickness required an antidote to do justice to the element which has borne me over its bosom so safely.

II.

The Commercial Metropolis and Rural Scenery.

"All that Nature did thy soil deny,
The growth was of thy fruitful Industry;
And all the proud and dreadful sea
A constant tribute paid to thee."

HERE we are upon substantial soil. Liverpool! How languidly the word melts in the mouth! My partiality for steamships and big ponds could not restrain the outbreak of joy with which we pressed the solid land. The effects too of our experience, though sad at first, have resulted in a bound of animal spirits almost inconsistent with sanity.

At the mouth of the Mersey we took a pilot aboard, and with our "starboard, sir," "port, sir," and "steady, sir," we reached Liverpool at 11 o'clock, upon the night of the 17th of May, 1851. It was some recompense for missing the green, bright green banks of the Mersey, with its cottages and residences, that we passed up amid a galaxy of many-colored lights, which, reflected upon the water from Birkenhead on the one side, and Liverpool on the other, almost transformed the scene into one of fairyland. Our guns boomed; mails were taken; and after the custom-house proceedings, by no means vexatious, we were permitted to land. The first person that spoke to me was a little imp, modelled after the exterior of Oliver Twist. A police officer touched him with a bâton. He was *non est* in a jiffy.

Our first impression of the population here was not very favorable. True, we saw the fag-end of humanity in the shape of beggars and loafers at the landing. We had no sooner taken up our march to our hotel, preferring to feel the delight of a walk, after so long a ride on the billows, than a fellow who said that he was a servant at the Waterloo, offered himself as our pilot. I suspected him, but thought that we would use him, as it was nearly two in the morning. We had not gone far before we were saluted with, "Which hotel, sir—which hotel?"

"Waterloo!"

"Sorry—very sorry—can't accommodate you, sir—I'm boots at the Waterloo, sir—all full, sir. Three ship-loads just arrived, sir—very sorry—Victoria Hotel near by—few minutes walk, sir —own sister of the Waterloo keeps it."

He had said too much. We marched on, heartily laughing at "Boots!" Saint Somebody's church illuminated the hour of two, and it was nearly daylight—a phenomenon belonging to this northern clime which considerably bewildered our Buckeye experience. We found the Waterloo open, and the lady at the door with her servants, ready to take down our names. I introduced our pilot as their servant. They, of course, disclaimed his acquaintance. "You are a pretty specimen of human veracity."

"Yes, sir, I am obliged to you, sir."

"But I suppose we ought to pay you for your guidance?"

"Oh yes, please you, sir, you are very kind, sir."

I gave him a shilling, with a caution about lying, which he, with a rub over his red nose, and a low bow, acknowledged.

We had scarcely appeared this morning at our window, when that extreme of English civilization called "starvation" was seen in the shape of a young urchin, whether boy or girl I could not discern, for the dress consisted of only two rags. He stood bobbing his head and whining, while I sketched him. His counterfeit presentment followed us, as soon as we left the hotel to take a stroll; and the little gipsey had the same monotone of grief. He was joined by another; and thus marshalled, we had to pass the agony of some squares. It was not until a fretful threat to "cut his weazand," that he cut our company, which he did with the remark, "they won't pay any more."

How comfortably every thing is conducted in these English hotels. We have our own parlors, and our own meals. It looks so cosey to see our own good company presiding at the tea-urn, and dispensing the Johnsonian beverage.

Of course, the modes here strike us strangely. But as we started out to admire all that is admirable, we must commend the English mode of hotel keeping, with its private parlors and private meals.

Every object, even the go-carts, strike a stranger queerly at first. Omnibuses, with nobody inside, and crowded a-top, dash past our windows. Cabs as big as our carriages, like a streak of lightning, dash by with one horse. Horns musically quiver in the fresh morning air. The tall dark houses and clean white paves of Liverpool surround us, while on every side green foliage and twittering birds betoken that love of rural life which the English bring even into their cities. One thing in-doors is noticeable. The sedulous zeal displayed in curtaining out heaven's sun light. It would seem that, with the prodigality of gloomy weather in this isle, as much of the light as possible would be admitted, more especially as a heavy window tax is assessed. But no such thing. Why? Is it a phase of that habitual exclusiveness and love of domestic ease which form so prominent a trait in the English character?

We have viewed the city. Its Corinthian elegance of architecture, illustrated especially in the Exchange; excellent police; above all, its magnificent docks, by which the shipping is brought into the city and preserved aflōat, notwithstanding the tides—bespeak for Liverpool the encomium of the traveller. There are two provisos. The first, beggars, I have named. The other is, the apparent sacrilegious treatment of the buried dead. Would you believe it? The pave to several of the first churches here is over and upon the tombstones of the buried. The inscriptions are being effaced by the feet of the passenger. Nurses with children, men, women, and boys, indiscriminately, tread over the ashes of the departed.

In our walk, we noticed *Roscoe* street—a reminder that Liverpool was the home of the Historian of the Medici. It recalled his splendid descriptions of that age, when Scholarship and Art were beginning to burst the barriers of the dark ages, to herald the new-born civilization which is ours to-day. It also recalled Irving's elegant tribute to the merchant litterateur. You remember how Irving first saw him, entering the Athenæum, with his venerable air—a fine illustration of "a chance production" disappointing the assiduities of Art, and working out of the busy mart of traffic the glory and the genius of the great Tuscan era. You remember, too, how nobly he bore the loss of his books, and what a noble consolation he found in the closing words of his sonnet,

> "Mind shall with mind direct communion hold,
> And kindred spirits meet to part no more."

The country lying adjacent to the great railway between Liverpool and London, presents a perfect succession of rural beauties: one sweet continuous garden, divided off into elegant compartments, and dotted with residences of the most exquisite taste. After passing out of the tunnel from Liverpool, which is cut through the solid rock, and which we performed for a mile and a quarter up an inclined plane, drawn by a stationary engine; after we struck the daylight and the country, a bright greenish green, so green as almost to be yellow, saluted our eyes, albeit unused to any other than sea-green. The meadows all along seemed indeed a carpet, into which were inwoven snow-flakes of daisies, buttercups in profusion, and pansies large and plentiful! Yet the land here is naturally sterile, having a reddish tinge, and as we approach nearer the great metropolis it displays a chalk formation. We are at one moment moving in sight of a beautiful tower upon the hill, surrounded with walks and embowered in leafiness; then past a succession of ivy-covered cottages, thatched with straw, and in themselves, with their streams and parterres, forming a rural landscape. The high gothic chimneys, and the very red of the bricks, give to the towns along the way a very picturesque effect. Nature seems like Cowper's rose, as if just washed in a shower; and so bright, yellow almost, and many-shaded, is the green, that it pleases the eye like an autumnal forest in Ohio. The churches are all perfectly neat; some, elegant gothic buildings. Now and then, a still, hallowing sense of antiquity hovers around these churches and their grave-yards, which we look for in vain at home. How pleasing to see, peeping from their verdurous coverts, these little minsters of heaven! From these, notwithstanding the marriage of Church and State—which cannot be too much abominated—have emanated those salutary influences which are illustrated by the surrounding practical works. From these chapels, honored by a LATIMER, a JEREMY TAYLOR, a HOOKER and a BERKLEY, in the elder time, came forth the power which has transformed the naturally poor soil of England into a garden of cultivation. They have made the ever-sweet hedges, and have constructed these roads which seem like elegant winding garden paths, extending as far as the eye can penetrate, like lines of light in a vast panorama of verdure.

We did not observe in all this journey a single sign of poverty. *Comfort* is impressed every where. In every village and cottage, Plenty appeared rejoicing in her stewardship. In the manufacturing districts through which we passed, the same rural air of neat exactitude and repose was apparent. You could only distinguish these districts by huge piles of coal near the railroad, and the tall chimney stacks lifting themselves out of the level against the sky, and topped with wavy streamers of smoke, which in the distance reminded us of our Liberty poles and flags. Each railway station is a pretty piece of architecture, with its elegant surrounding grounds. There does not seem to be a thing neglected or out of place. As the car dashed from point to point, our surprise was increased. Never through our minds played the like. It resembled a fairy dream, in which each scene seemed "picked out as an example for the best."

But while lost in admiration, I have forgotten that the cars have been ruralizing toward the valley of the "royal toward Thames." Our outstretched necks have discerned its winding mist already. Already is the eye peopled dim, with figures of Westminster, the Tower, the Parliament Houses, and above all, the Palace of Crystal!

Sure enough here we are in the Depot; and not yet out of the country;—in London, but still it is *rus in urbe.* We are flanked by terraced gardens and foliage. Robins and thrushes make music, while we rumble to our stopping point. The charms of the day cling like good genii to the last: as if determined to impress into our deepest hearts the adoration of England's Bard of Olney, who attuned, years ago, our own spirit as he sung of him, who looked abroad upon the varied fields, the mountains, the valleys, and the resplendent views of Nature, and by virtue of his filial confidence in the Creator of this delightful scenery, could call it all his own, with a propriety which none could feel, but he who could

———"Lift to heaven an unpresumptuons eye,
And smiling say, 'My Father made it all.'"

III.

The Brittle Wonder, and a Royal Chase.

" A wilderness of building, sinking far
And self withdrawn, into a wondrous depth,
Far sinking into splendor—without end."
Wordsworth.

THE morning of the 21st of May found us in London, amid its coaches, drays, dog-carts, phaetons, choked roads, its whirl of wheels and its war of confused noises. Never was there such a horse and vehicle-loving people as the English; judging by the manifold and multiform vehicles which crowd and clog the thoroughfares. Not alone in Picadilly, the Fleet, Cheapside, and the neighborhood of St. Paul's, where streets have recently been cut through great blocks of houses to give passage to the throngs; but in the less compacted parts of the city, and just now in the neighborhood of Hyde Park, near the Crystal Palace, is there to be found involutions of wondrous perplexity, consisting of cab and carriage, horse and footman, go-cart and poney; but all moving and winding with the precision of machinery, under the unostentatious power of an efficient police.

Without that power, what a complexity would London be to a stranger? With it, access is made easy to every point worth seeing. Our first venture abroad was toward the Crystal Palace. Upon our way thither, we passed the famous Apsley House of Wellington, and the great equestrian statue of the Iron Duke.

But the one great ornament;—the desire to view which, prompted our journey hitherward, was the Crystal Palace. Well,—our eyes have seen it. But how shall we reproduce its wonders for the eye of others? Never since "Dardanian hands," at the command of King Brutus, began this town of *Londinum* has there been such a rare and glorious spectacle as that which now glitters under the May sunshine in Hyde Park! This is a bold saying; but the documents, in the shape of royal catalogues and colored engravings, lie around my table, and they afford most practical proof. Our verdict, by actual inspection, has also been rendered, but not reduced to writing. This latter is most difficult. I have been afraid to undertake to tell how my senses have been raptured. After loitering amidst the manifold splendors and intricate complexities of this "industrious" world, the mind has become benumbed, and refuses to officiate but tardily. It seemeth as if a "star had burst within the brain," and that the rockets and pyrotechnic beauties were still going off in the chambers of imagery.

Nathless I essay. The reader who undertakes to form an idea of this crystal structure of wonders, from these feeble limnings, might as well judge of the palace visually by one pane of glass, or of its contents by the India-rubber trowsers in Uncle Sam's department.

When the palace burst upon our view, which it did as we approached the transept on the southern side, all was intense eagerness; every hand went up, but not a word was said!

There it stood—the cynosure of industry! How fragile, yet how substantial; so gorgeous in its colorings; with the flags of all nations playing in the breeze; its guard of majestic trees about it; extending nearly nineteen hundred feet, and running back one-fourth of that distance; with its six thousand iron columns, painted blue, red and white, in grateful variety; covering nearly thirty acres in a magnificent park, and radiant and glowing, yet transparent under the mellow shine of this May morning! Where under heaven was ever raised such a structure of beauty and magnificence? We have read of glittering ice turrets among the Alps, with pillars pellucid, and "glorious as the gates of heaven beneath the keen full moon." Imagination has penetrated the earth with her fires and illuminated grotto within grotto, embossed and fretted, and reflecting and refracting the light into manifold splendors. We remember the famous ice-palace of the Russian Queen—that Northern wonder which Cowper illumined with his fancy,—built without forest or quarry, whose marble was the glassy wave, whose cement was water, and which, when lighted within, gleamed a clear transparency. Somewhat thus, though far otherwise, gleamed this structure of JOSEPH PAXTON—this palace of Industry.

> So stood the brittle prodigy, though smooth,
> And slip'ry the materials: yet fast bound,
> Firm as a rock. Nor wanted aught within
> That regal residence might well befit
> For grandeur or *for use.*
> ————Mirrors needed none
> Where all was vitreus.

In the evanescent glory of the ice-palace, the poet saw an undesigned severity in imagining the cold, yet glittering, the durable, yet transient fabric of human grandeur and courtly pride. How is it with this Crystal Palace, wherein is really seen, not fantastically imaged, the fruits of human progress, resulting from the common labor of all men, springing from the germs implanted within our common nature by our Creator, and by Him, in his own good pleasure developed into forms as exquisite as they are beautiful! Yonder, before our rapt vision, stands no ice-frolic of haughty power; but a glowing enshrinement for the objects of mingled beauty and utility, which Thought has produced in every clime. It is no pyramidal monument to Pride, no classic temple for Beauty to linger under; but a form in which is sanctified the loveliness of that religion which would cultivate the amenities of good will, peace and purity! I devoutly thank God, that He has permitted me to view this common shrine among the nations—this brittle, yet firm bond of brotherhood,—this crystal medium through which a better day doth glimmer.

To have stood the half hour we were compelled to stand, before the arched centre, awaiting the hour of admission, and to have enjoyed the vision, were worth a pilgrimage around the world, including several sea-voyages.

We pay and enter severally. Only one can enter at a time. Our first step is marked down by a machine, which tells the number who visit here daily. These numbers average from thirty to fifty thousand.

It was no sinecure office to make an inventory of the immensity of the minutiæ here collected. But no description, however minute, can give the effect of the first view from the centre down the four aisles. But before you reach that centre, you pass the equestrian statue of Victoria, flanked by two pieces of statuary, —groups of Amazons,—and Zephyr and Aurora. Then bursts upon your view the far-famed glass fountain, under the dome, flinging not only from its five tons of flint glass every hue of the prism in a flood of beauty, but a graceful jet of water which rivals the crystal in purity, as it curls in a smooth sheet and branches into a myriad of lesser prisms. As you gaze on it, surrounded by palm trees from Madagascar, and overshadowing foliage with flowers,

> The growing wonder takes a thousand shapes
> Capricious, in which Fancy seeks in vain
> The likeness of some object seen before.

Thus has British Art worked as if to mock at Nature. To my eye, each radiant point of this fountain gleamed more gorgeously than the great diamond "Koh-i-Noor," or Mountain of Light, which, as the Queen's contribution, and standing near the fountain on the right, deserves high honor in the catalogue.

We have you at the fountain. Before you, gush and bubble two other fountains, interspersed with tropical plants and every variety of flowers. Each one of these flower groups would reward an hour's view.

But the eye, fond of the garish, espies above, the carpets of the Orient and English oil cloths—immense and beautiful, and the hangings of a tall and superb pagoda—richer far in colorings, and much more varied in forms, than even the flowers of Nature. Far down the hall flame gorgeous gallery hangings. In the centre, on the right and left, are lifted above the other objects, the combat of the horse and dragon, the Duke of Rutand, Godfrey de Bouillon, the Bavarian lion—all in bronze or laster, very much magnified, gigantic and imposing! Do not let your eye be distracted by the birds in the large glass cases, though gorgeous and glittering. Do not stop to listen to the live birds which are flying and twittering about the palace, and amid the large trees at either end of the transept. Another caution—do not let your senses be ravished by the organ and harps which, from the galleries, have broken forth into melody, vibrating, strangely mild and sweet against and along the vitreus corridors. But let the eye, like the gallant Knight of Courtesy, Sir GUYON, pass through the Bowers of Bliss, untempted by the "silver sweet sound." Let it take in the lofty summer-house of bronze, in which Appollo matchlessly stands, after sending his arrow through the eagle above; then, the fur trophy, the Ross telescope, the marble pillars, the chemical monuments of alum, spermaceti, Rochelle salts, tartrate of potash and soda, illustrations of Nature's geometry playing into utility! Nay, go on! See the rich tracery, the superbness and elegance of that altar screen of oak; then the bird trophy, carved by machinery, with deep under-cuttings. Passing by the Elizabethan fountains, what strange array of glass is that beyond? What lenticular arrangements could produce half the effect? What is *their* use? They are model light-houses, revolving and breaking and casting out the light, not for the view of beauty, but for the glass and eye of the navigator amid the perils of the deep!

Remember that we are passing over the heads of many objects in the west half of the building—and these, too, in the midst of the aisle. I have not dared to look galleryward. Neither dare we go, as yet, into the compartments of British industry, which lie on either side in great alcoves. At the far west end, duplicating the whole exhibition, is the largest mirror in the world, 18 feet 8 inches by 10 feet! There are other mirrors nearly as large, with frames, some gilt, carved into every sort of beasts, birds, creeping thing, flower and vegetable; to say nothing of little Cupids and angels inhabiting the involutions which in every part attest the consummation of art.

This end we have reached by slow procession, moving around each department, itself a world's fair in itself, and decorated with striking elegance. Here the cool atmosphere enters. No oppressive sense from heat, or confined air, disturbs the uniform comfort of the building. Although fifty thousand people are within, yet there is no jostling, no disturbance. The police with their blue coats, brass buttons and glazed hats, are distributed, with a few red coats, around; and these, without other aid, keep the vast mass in order. The English mostly compose the mass. A few Chinese, some negroes, French in plenty, and some other foreigners—I could not determine what part of the world they came from—were mingled with the mass.

The observations we have hitherto made have been confined exclusively to her majesty's dominions. Neither have we deviated into the apartments, wherein the products of English industry are systematically arranged. Systematically; because it was found, upon consideration, that the materials operated on, and the results, could be comprehended in thirty classes. Grouping, therefore, as to Great Britain, was regulated by the character of the productions, while in the east half of the building, and in the colonies, they are arranged according to their districts.

We began our examination, and the best could be but slight, by proceeding round the western end and down by the south wall. Mineral productions and mining, and the agricultural implements, we passed by hastily; then came the splendid assortment of woven materials, London, Manchester, and Glasgow, vieing with each other in this generous rivalry. Woollen and mixed fabrics, and Irish flaxen fabrics, with a loom of exquisite construction ready to show how the fabrics are woven; these, in all their wondrous variety of figure and style, riveted the attention of our ladies, while the gentlemen preferred seeing the smooth and intricate machinery in the northeast of the palace. Oldham and Manchester, with their cotton works, are here reproduced with most pleasing effect. The great business of England is, at a glance, observed in motion.

To depicture the furniture, some elaborately carved and gilt; some formed of peculiar woods and arranged in perplexing uniformity and variety; to reproduce the papier machè tables and ornaments, with their gorgeous hues and dazzling beauties; to write down—no! no! It cannot be done.

In passing through one part of this department, we were astonished to find the British Bible Society represented by one hundred and fifty-eight copies of the Word of Light and Life, each in a separate language. There they stood, all opened, with their mysterious symbols,—pervaded by the holiest of inspiration,—cloven tongues of fire, yet dove-like as the Holy Ghost which has baptized the zeal and energy of this noble Society, preparatory to a new Pentecostal day. Each Bible had its peculiarity of impress. The very characters indicated, as plainly as the diverse features of the human face, those national diversities and antagonisms which can only be harmonized by the spirit enshrined within these Bibles. To my mind, this peculiar exhibition was the crowning trophy of English Industry and Genius. The wood and metal trophies from Canada are massive evidences of English empire over deep mines and great forests; the India room over the way, lined with gold cloth, filled with the furniture of the sumptuous Orient and dazzling with jewels from Lahore, in the midst whereof is lying, in humble subjection, three strange-shaped diamond-and-gold crowns of Hindoo Kings and other tributes from the proud sheiks of the land which Alexander and Bonaparte could not comprehend in their conquests, however much they dreamed of the glory,—is another trophy of English potency in Central and Southern Asia, godless and cruel though its exercise has been; those Kangaroo skins and coral beauties, jaspers and agates, copper and gold,—do they not tell of English rule over antipodal realms in the mid-ocean? English home-produce, from the circular comb for carding wool up to yon splendid steam-ship enginery, from that beer-barrel machine up to yon process for engraving on steel by electricity, from the rudest implement of primitive husbandry up to the highest refinement of modern science,—all demonstrate a power to dignify ornamental forms by *use*, and to raise merely useful forms into beauty, which should be the great ambition of Art; but all this is powerless and puny beside the triumph which radiates from those Bibles, with their lips of fire, this moment regenerating the kingdoms of the earth, and pouring abroad that light of life

——"which never was on land or sea."

England, say what we will, stands confessedly *the* Christian realm. Her history, from the time at least of Elizabeth, is full of her influence upon the policy of the world, in opening the way for the gospel. True, her rapacity has been unbounded.

"Heav'n, Earth and Ocean plundered of their sweets,"

is well attested by this Exhibition. But if China was compelled to take opium, she had to take the Bible. If Turkey looked to England for aid against the Russian domination, free toleration to Christians was consequent.

With the increase of Anglo-Saxon power, there has been spread, along with the practicalness of the age, a spirituality more divine than the soul, with all its power, hath yet been gifted to imagine.

There is one article in the furniture list which elicited a spontaneous burst of admiration from us all, especially the ladies, who have been used to seeing homely wooden cradles, if not sugar troughs. It is called the "Regia Cot," I believe, and is thus described:

A cradle carved in Turkey boxwood, symbolizing the Union of the Royal House of England with that of Saxe Coburg and Gotha. One end exhibits in the centre the armorial bearings of her Majesty, the Queen, surrounded by masses of foliage, natural flowers and birds; on the rocker beneath, is seen the head of Night, represented as a beautiful sleeping female, crowned with a garland of poppies, supported upon bats' wings, and surrounded by seven planets.

The other end, or the back of the head of the cradle, is devoted to the arms of H. R. H. Prince Albert; the shield occupies the centre, and round it, among the arabesque foliage, the six crests of the Prince are scattered, with the motto, "Treu und Fest." Below, on the rocker, is discovered a head of "Somnus," with closed eyes, and over the chin a wimple, which, on each side, terminates in poppies.

In the interior of the head of the cradle, guardian angels are introduced; and above, the royal crown is imbedded in foliage. The friezes, forming the most important part of the sides of the body of the cradle, are composed of roses, poppies, conventional foliage, butterflies and birds, while beneath them rise a variety of pinks, studied from nature. The edges and the inside of the rockers are enriched with the insignia of royalty and emblems of repose.

Have done quick with this royal baby nest! Quick! There is a crowd across the aisle among the paper articles. Sure enough, there is a curious contrivance! What! An envelope maker! folding by one click of a machine an envelope, and passing them out by hundreds. Only a little boy attending it. Now that we are over, we may observe the sea-weed arrangements. How snugly they lie in their little baskets! Euclid illustrated and illuminated; a model of St. Paul's cut with a pen-knife, and consisting of over 50,000 pieces. Nay, do not start; there is an article in Spain, at the other end of the palace, with three millions of pieces of inlaid wood! Most elegant landscapes made in this way upon the tables and other furniture, are common.

Here we are amid the models again. Castles overhung with ivy, houses in the old style, complete within and without. Even Shakspeare's house is perfectly represented, and the room where he was born, *just as it was.* Now we have the model of a tournament, now of Knox's house in Edinburgh, now of flower gardens in every variety, now of a scene upon the Danube, now the projected pyramid, in which five millions of coffins may be preserved; now we are among the medals, needle-work, pianos, porcelain, chandeliers, stained windows; and now, do take breath to look at the Shakspeare "Jubileum." Jubi—what? Here is dramatic unity for you! Here we have the heart of the English mind in all its windings and off-shoots. Hazlitt has said, "that the drama is a root growing through its own age, out of the Past into the Future." We have the Jubileum as one of its stray blossoms. Upon it is represented every play of Shakspeare, from old Sir John in the basket to Richard in his tent of terrible dreams. A strange medley!

Before we leave this end of the building, which we do under oriental umbrellas with long silver handles, it would be well, simply to glance at those ox-horns eight feet from point to point, from Good Hope; those wild beast skins above, those sleighs and furs from Canada, that Indian riding gear, jewelled saddles, elephant accoutrements and some other trifles from the British Colonies.

Arm in arm, let us quit this minute examination of articles piece by piece, and proceed up the palace and around the galleries. We are anxious to see what the United States has contributed. Softly there. To tell the truth, we are rather a negative quantity in this exhibition. Passing by the exhibition of the European nations, we reach the end set apart for the United States.

Plenty of room was allotted, and the most conspicuous. The American eagle "spreads herself" in the west end, over—little or nothing. Punch could not help but catch at the idea. "No eagle," he says, "asking of itself where it should dine, and hovering in space without a visible mouthful, could represent the grandeur of contemplative solitude better than is shown by the United States' eagle in the firmament of Mr. Paxton's Crystal. This is the more to be lamented, inasmuch as a very little consideration might have given us the American eagle, with the treasures of America gathered below its hovering wings. Why not have sent some choice specimens of slaves? We have the Greek captive in dead stone—why not the Virginian slave in living ebony?"

The satire is well pointed. We feel it abroad. The thing above all others which I was proud to see in that palace—the nonpareil "Slave" of Powers, becomes the occasion of bye-word and reproach. The most refined company in the palace were gathered about this offspring of our Ohio sculptor, admiring in—silence. After passing through the heavy sculpture and garish display of the world's art; after the sense ached to faintness with the violence of the colorings of luxury's trapping, it was a sweet and cordial relief to stand before the matchless form of the pure and simple Greek girl, mourning so deeply, yet so subduedly, at her fettered destiny. And as we thought of the genius of the sculptor, the lines of Shelley glided into the mind,

> "It was for thee, yon kingless sphere has long
> Swung blind in unascended majesty."

An iron safe is also here, so constructed, that no person but the inventor can open it. It is the same owned by Hobbs, who is called at home the great lock-king. At a meeting to-day of Americans at Trivort's, I met the genius. He has put all the lockmakers here to the blush, and beat Chubbs himself. By a little instrument which he carries in his vest, he picked the best lock of England in a few minutes. He stated that £10,000 forfeit could be raised by Englishmen alone, to put up against the big diamond, provided they would give him a night to pick for it, through any lock in England.

Various excuses have been made for our country's defection at this exhibition. Tardiness in the governments, distance from the Exhibition, and bad arrangements here, have been offered as excuses. We trust that it is not owing to a want of the materials to exhibit. Had the last Ohio fair been culled a little, it would have been a proud exhibition compared to this. One item; why was there not a model of the Burnet House—a standard hotel—sent on here? It would have been quite a specimen even among the glorious architecture of the Past. And let me delicately hint, that a real Burnet House would have been an acceptable refuge to us Americans.

Let us ascend the galleries and take a farewell (for to-day) of this "brittle wonder." From a seat near the transept, the eye may gather in glorious unity the thousandfold spectacle. Look up and down as far as the vision can distinctly reach, and you will see but one moving river of humanity, flowing amid margins of paintings, hangings, and architectural display; and around isles of fountains, towers, statues, barges, and trophies of every color and form; and under a net-work of silver lucency, seeming to be hung in air! Music mingling with the hum-hum-hum of the rustling, eager throng, and with the tinkling of the fountains; birds carolling in the trees before and behind you—temples and booths, flags, organs, and segments of churches—not severally (for you cannot find the prominent object where none has its parallel), but all together strike your bedazzled view as a

"Glory beyond all Glory ever seen."

Can ye not believe in something transcendent, as the effluence of this universal jubilee of Industry in its crystal home? Hear ye not prophetic harpings weaving their spell of enchantment, while genius paints undying pictures of that promised day, when "war shall cease and conquest be abjured," when garlands from every clime shall be brought to deck the Tree of Liberty!

The eye would fain close on the scene and commit it to the more facile play of the imagination. To attempt to delineate it, so that he who reads may see, is as vain as to attempt to "paint chaos, make a portrait of Proteus, or to fix the figure of the fleeting air." We must only attempt in our further acquaintance with its contents, to select isolated objects, with their several utilities.

Our jaded spirits were revived by a little incident upon the street, as we drove homeward. There is no particular harm in an American getting a glimpse of a Queen; as, happily, Queens are such rare birds in our land. Let no harsh Republican mistake the motive which prompted the exploit, which issued in a full view of royalty. We left the Crystal Palace, about six P. M. Our minds were completely wearied with the vision of the glorious structure and its splendid contents—the array of diamonds and gold—India riches, French elegance, German ingenuity, and British 'all sorts.' Pondering these things, yet with eyes about us for the *mirabile* of the metropolis, we drove down Green Park (these London parks, oh! but they are emerald gems in their rough setting of aristocratic mortar!) and into famous Oxford street;—When lo! a couple of outriders dressed in red—then a splendid open carriage (it was a bright day), drawn by six horses with red riders, then—(keep cool!) two other riders with livery; and then—(steady sir!) two other red fellows, with canes and on horseback, who looked as savage as catamounts at a hack driver that did not give way immediately. This unexpected array rather beclouded our senses, already intoxicated with the sights of fountains, gold cloths, pagodas, carpets, trees, Hindoo rooms, statuary, and every thing else conceivable in the world. It was a theatrical show in every deed—a dashing splendor!

What can it mean? My head goes out inquiringly. I see hats going off on both sides. Drivers give way. "I say driver—isn't that the *Queen* herself!" "It's 'ur zur." Hurrah! "Then drive after—give chase—extra shilling—crack up—all right!

we're sovereigns ourselves, sir; give us an equal chance to the pave!" Away dashed royalty in her elegant coach! away dashed—we, in an indifferent four-wheeled cab! I noticed as we passed a little fellow dressed in a silver-laced cap—a handsome little fellow, and quite a pretty little girl on the front seat; and behind, the Queen, an ordinarily dressed and tolerable good-looking woman—not unlike Mrs. A., Mrs. B., or Mrs. C., of our humble vicinage.

We sovereigns of America gained on her of England. The outriders did *not* look savagely around at us; but as we got pretty close, to our utter amazement and mortification, the Queen herself turned round, and gave us a good-natured look and a full view. We had a hearty laugh at our good fortune, and came home full of the Exhibition, and feeling quite royally.

IV.

An English Saturnalia.

"Away they go! One retires to his country-house, and another is engaged at a horse-race; and as to their country ——!"

Junius.

WHO has not read Oliver Goldsmith's "Citizen of the World?" The remarks of his Chinese pilgrim in London seem to be applicable to myself. He felt himself as a newly created being, introduced into a new world in which, although every object strikes with wonder and surprise, yet the imagination is still unsated. Although the world has passed through it in exhibition; and London with her majestic architecture, regal parks, and soul-thrilling historical associations has been around and within, still imagination seems to be the only active principle of the mind. The most trifling occurrence gives pleasure until the gloss of novelty is worn away. When I have ceased to wonder, I may possibly grow wise; I may then call the reasoning principle to my aid, and compare those objects with each other, which were before examined without reflection.

It is a beautiful May morning. Birds are singing. Their shrill sweetness rises even above the "London cries." To me it seems strange that the painters upon the building opposite, do not start or tumble down, at the unearthly whoops, groans, yells, and yawns below them, which announce the vender of something. I could only distinguish one vegetable in the medley,—"*Aws-pawr-goose!*" If Bedlam were out a-Maying, it would do justice to these 'cries'—to my novel hearing.

In these transcripts from the eye, I know that I am unable

to disseminate any useful principle, or afford any useful instruction. Beautiful parks and lofty monuments pass so rapidly in view, that my stare at them is almost vacant. The highest part of our human nature is not exercised. There can be no communion of soul with them as yet. We might gaze for ever and gratify the pleasure-loving propensity, and return home no wiser than we departed. But when one goes out into the English country, as I did on Thursday to Epsom, on the great Derby race day, the scenes of nature, with their hedges and vistas of trees, their meadows and cottages, all assemble upon the threshold of the mind, and many—very many, of these beauties enter into the internal economy of ideas and sentiment, there fadelessly to bloom—there continually to awaken something correspondent to their hue, form, and grandeur. I might reproduce these descriptions; but there is so much of *human* nature to commune with on this Derby day, that I forbear. Besides, as Dr. Cheever has well said, mere descriptions, be the scenery ever so grand, are cloying and tiresome. It is like living upon pound-cake and cream, or rather upon whip-syllabub.

A Derby day awakens more interest in London, than any other day in the Calendar. Every vehicle, from the splendid coach of Royalty and *Dukery* to the humble dog-cart and pony phaeton of the mechanic and shopman, are in requisition. Five thousand pounds is the stake, and millions more in the shape of bets are in the scale. The "nobs" (as the nobility are familiarly called), with their four-in-hand coaches, are the prominent actors in the day. They own most of the race-horses.

But we will start ourselves. Lunch being prepared, and a vehicle entered, we hurry by the gorgeous array in Oxford and Regent-streets, pass the parks, those green metropolitan lungs, and give a hasty glance at the statue of Canning. Now Trafalgar square appears, and the Nelson monument long detains the lingering sight. It is the finest place in London for a monument. The column and statue are 177 feet high. The statues of the Georges III. and IV., are near, and serve to show off this splendid monument to England's naval glory. The National Gallery is opposite; but the Nelson pillar detracts from every other object. Its bas-reliefs represent the famous battle of Trafalgar. How the eye swims as it upward gazes at the figure. A coil of rope relieves the pediment upon which he is placed.

> Up in the broad day's lustre doth it stand,
> A column raised to dear and dazzling fame,
> Mounting with pride the bosom of the land,
> And stamping glory there with Nelson's name.

And yet methinks, that face lifted up so prominently in the "bosom of the land" doth blush, if not in the broad day's lustre, yet at evening's reddening glow, when contemplation delights in pure thoughts and virtuous actions. Read Nelson's private life. Doth not the sea through which he sailed become incarnadine with shame?

How much of debauchery and wretchedness has been caused by the force of that splendid example which the monumental structures of England have illustrated, can only be known in that day, when the Judge of all shall winnow the purity of a heart from the glory of a name, and leave the latter as chaff for the fire.

Soon we came in sight of old Westminster. How streaked and blackened with age look the old towers! How the heart swells with the vast proportions! Tracery, towers, niches, statues, frieze, and every other architectural appliance which render the Gothic a wilderness of arching foliage, "star proof" in its woven web of beauty, are here in profuse variety. And the Abbey—the most interesting place in England—the urn of her greatness—the treasury of her genius—the Conqueror of Time;—does it not shut out all other objects? But we must reserve our thoughts until we go within.

The Derby will start before we run over our 20 miles to the turf. Now we dart down toward Vauxhall, and "Father Thames" is emptying his pitcher beneath us. How many reflections seem cast in his waters. How splendid he seemed to the imagination, before we looked down upon his familiar face. The English poets had never seen our western streams—the magnificent Mississippi and the beautiful Ohio, else they would not have extolled so highly the charms of this little river. True, grandeur hath gathered many monuments of fame and pride upon its banks, and Art hath created landscapes which "peep into its tide;" but Nature was never less prodigal than in her decoration of the Thames.

We saw St. James's palace beyond the Green Park, with the royal arms floating in the sunshine, a sign of the presence of the Queen. It was a scene thronging with recollections. There once stood the hospital dedicated to St. James, for the reception of the fourteen leprous maidens.—What tales could those old stones tell!—There Charles the First attended divine service, before he walked through the Park to his scaffold at Whitehall. In that very palace, MONK and Sir JOHN GRANVILLE planned the Restoration. There, within our vision,

——"through the towers, amidst his ring
Of Vans and Mynheers rode the Dutchman King,
And there did England's Goneril thrill to hear
The shouts that triumphed o'er her crownless Lear."

Yonder, old HARRY the Eighth chuckled at the jokes of his witty Chancellor, SIR THOMAS MORE, to say nothing of the vile pranks of that pure "Defender of the Faith." There WALPOLE practised his shameless venality, and BOLINGBROKE (Pope's Mæcenas) lounged up to see the queenly Anne. Now, amid the whirl and stir, the present usurps the past, and St. James's becomes the home of the little VICTORIA and her numerous family, the sight of whom, as detailed in our last chapter, tickled our democratic feelings.

Five bridges span the Thames, over one of which, Vauxhall, we ride toward Epsom. Granite and iron make Vauxhall only second to Waterloo bridge. From it we have a view, as yet a little misty, of the most splendid architectural display in Great

Britain. I mean the new Houses of Parliament. They front the Thames, and extend to the water's edge. It is ower true, as one of England's poets has said, that the Thames does not resemble any of those streams whose foam is amber, and whose gravel, gold. Dirty-looking, even to the depth of filthiness, is her appearance. Can she be the same crystal mirror in which Eton and Windsor dress themselves every day in their Gothic costumes? Her "oozy bed" is no doubt full of argosies which contain the riches of the Indies; but there are some riches there imbedded which are neither beautiful nor fragrant. The river is washed out by the tide twice a day—quite a consolation to the nose-possessing and water-drinking community.

Now we are fairly over into Surrey. Vehicles are beginning to close in. We are compelled to walk, and even to stand still. Three abreast, yet packed close, and not within seventeen miles of Epsom. Does it not beat every thing? It is the English Saturnalia. Every body is privileged to joke every body. 'Nobs' joke 'snobs;' and donkey carts sauce 'Hansom cabs.'—Club men in their coaches halloo to pretty boarding-school misses, peeping over their green walls, which line the pike, who snicker and chuckle. Old Johnny Bull, red with jollity, rides along, "holding both his sides." Now and then a smash and curses announce something serious. We ourselves had the honor of being bumped by Lord Strathmore's carriage, and took the license of the day to caution his Lordship.—Toll-gates and hiring taxes (?) are collected. Stopping and walking, we finally pass through the last gate, and dash away over the furzy Downs.

The prospect from the Downs is magnificent. Far below, and very distant, is seen the elements of English civilization—rail-cars puffing, roads lined with hedges; farms laid out like gardens, and gardens like paradises; towers standing upon high points, and, as we turn about, we see the stand and turf of Epsom!

Although we were a long time getting to Epsom, we are glad to find the "Derby" is not run. Let us mount upon the top of the vehicle and look around. For miles, right and left, are the people. The best part of a million are here assembled; among them are the royal house of Prussia, with their cream-colored team, as well as the poorest ragamuffin, just discharged from Old Bailey, with his stick and *crownless* hat.—The track is upon a side-hill turf, and is in excellent order. It is a hundred feet wide, but hardly distinguishable in the mingled mass of men. There is a little valley between us and the turf. A continuous rise is used, which affords a fine prospect of the race. The stand is on the other side, and its adjacent booth is perfectly black with heads. All around it for acres is the same phenomena. Now a bell rings. The police march up the track to clear it. Every body is opening baskets. Wines and sodas pop; sandwiches and shrimps appear; pies and birds are demolished, amid cries of "water," "oranges,"—"who wants a card of the races?" Fiddling and horn-tooting all around,—a fool dancing in woman's clothes, with a red calash on his head, and a parasol, mimicking fine ladies, while the fine ladies in lordly carriages are looking on laughingly; gipsies, wild in look and with eyes dark and sinister, are roving about.—See, they have that young man! "Tell your fortune, pretty gentleman? You *will* be fortunate, oh, yes! only leave a gipsy a sixpence, sir; will be a lucky one in the race, sir," and with other like remarks, she hangs on like a snapping turtle. All these scenes are transpiring, while an enormous shout and laugh go up from the crowd along the ropes. The police had cleared the track—it is only a dog or a loafer trying to run across, with a policeman after. Away they go in a mimic race!

The coast is clear. With a glass, you may see the many colored jockeys mounting. Now comes the preparatory galloping to loosen the horses' joints. Up they ride, and bets begin to run by colors. All now is still. We cannot see the start. The cry rises, "they're off!" The black heads in and around the stand have become a sea of upturned faces. We hear the tramp of horses on the distant turf. Horsemen ride over the hill to catch the sight. Now the race-horses appear around the hill nearly all together; yet so far distant, that they seem to move slowly; soon they begin to be clearly distinguished. "Hurrah for the blue-cap!—hurrah for the red!—black cap and pink ahead!" In fine style they dash between the anxious heads. The tug is between the black cap and pink, and blue. Thousands are staked upon the result. The cry is, now for one—now for the other! On they all "bicker and burn to gain the expected goal." In a twinkling they dash home. The number is run up, and the welkin rings and re-rings with the shout of immense multitudes. The track is soon broken over. The throng rushes toward the stand. The Derby is done and won! Millions have been lost and gained. Freely pop the wine bottles of the victors; merrily ring their laughs! Up rise thousands of carrier pigeons to announce the result abroad!

Now comes a scene which carries us back to the good old days of Queen Bess—such as Scott describes in his Kenilworth—the days of the tournaments. Rings are formed. Circus sports are going on upon the turf; dancing girls are soon transmuted by some magic from ordinary females; magical gentlemen begin to throw up rings, butcher-knives, etc.; music breaks out from all sides; gipsies burst anew from their tents; and—hark!—"'ansum and hinteresting presents for hinfants! only a penny! 'ave one sir?"—"'Ere's silver-tipped buttons for 'olding coats together—made out of coal!" "Sody-water! Ginger-beer-r-r!" and a hundred other cries. Beyond the turf, the manly sports are going on, such as firing at targets, pitching at points, and divers other things to me unknown. The turf was cleared again—another race—the same excitement; the air is again filled with pigeons, who dart around for awhile uncertain where to go; then off with their news.

Again, we are upon the road homeward, amid the flowery meadows, and the hedges or walls of ivy, and sometimes of flowers. The trees look so trim and perfect. Each for itself seems "dressed in living green." As well attempt to separate color from the rainbow, or extension from matter, as Beauty from these vistas made by the lines of elm, flowering chestnut and birch, filled with their little winged singing people. The leaves will grow in freshness, and the robins, thrushes, and larks, like Jenny Lind, must, although they know not why—be "singing."

On our road to London, we find every body out to see the "Derby" return. It sometimes comes home boozy. Long arrays of Charity scholars in their uniforms, and boys from school are out, under the charge of masters. Policemen are stationed all along. Within five miles of London, the road is lined ten or twenty deep. Punch and Judy, negro singers, dancers, bag-pipers from Scotland, are mingled with the throng, performing. Every body is privileged to say what comes uppermost. Although an entire stranger amid this crowd of myriads, I drank several imaginary healths from off my seat, to gentlemen with mugs on the top of the walls; exchanged spunk with the spunky, laughs with the good-natured, words with the familiar, and altogether felt at home. Wit and humor followed us through the large commons into the very city. We thought we had left London at Epsom, but the million seemed to be waiting for their horse-racing brethren to return.

The moral effect of these vast assemblages, patronized as they are by royalty itself, (for the Queen has her stand,) it is not for me to speak of. The Englishman prepares his "book of bets" a year beforehand, and comes up yearly to offer his incense to his favorite racer. We have in America very few of these sportive gatherings. Some regard it as a great defect in our social organism. Let such remember that the sun, which by its genial heat promotes the growth of vegetation, produces also by its heat the poisonous vapor.

We have lost a day from the Exhibition, but we were compensated by many insights into English manners and character, which long months of ordinary residence could not give. We saw a nation forgetful of itself, its dignity, its glory, and the "relict radiance of its past ages," besotting itself with the enthusiasm of beast-racing, and the intoxication of gambling. Can this be the England whose abbeys, monuments, and palaces of stone and crystal, rise so proudly in her metropolis? Strange and uncouth, sounds this revel of racing, amid these hallowed localities, where Antiquity is a presence and a power; as strange and as uncouth as would a vacant laugh or a squeaking fiddle amidst the diapason and "*Te Deum*," which rolls and swells along the fretted roof of the cathedral!

V.

The Commons.

"Yet who not listens with delighted smile
To the pure Saxon of that silver style."
NEW TIMON.

THROUGH the kindness of our Minister, Mr. LAWRENCE, I received a ticket for the House of Commons. By its potency, I found myself at five last evening occupying (perhaps by mistake) a seat in the little lobby, connected with, and reserved for the House of Lords. The galleries above were pretty full, mostly of Americans; for strangers from the Continent seldom visit the 'Commons.' My company was rather more aristocratic than I had been accustomed to. However, taking a stranger's privilege, I learned from my right-hand man, whom I afterwards found out to be Lord LYNDHURST, the late Lord High Chancellor, and from those in front, one of whom was the Earl of Minto, late Ambassador to Rome, and father-in-law of the Premier—all I wanted to know as to the rules and constitution of the House, repaying them in kind, by answering their queries as to *our* legislative assemblies. Let me here say, that however exclusive the English nobility seem in the streets and in their houses, there is a perfect courtesy and urbanity among those whom I here observed. There was a full attendance of the Commons, and a large number of the upper house present to hear the discussion on the Catholic bill.

The House is opposite Westminster Abbey. You reach the Hall through long passages guarded by several porters. It is not much larger than our Senate room in Columbus, rather longer, not so wide. There is but one desk under the speaker's chair, in which three wigged gentlemen sit scribbling. The speaker is gowned and wigged. He is a large, red-faced, thick-tongued, old Saxon, full of verbosity and consequence. He is the only member who has his hat off. It strikes an American strangely, to see the deliberative gravity of the greatest power in Christendom, sitting ranged in seats, with their hats on. This custom will, perhaps, account for the number of bald heads among the English. You cannot see their eyes or faces except when they arise to speak. At first blush one is apt to condemn the assembly, as a convention of stupidity and carelessness. Yet there is an agreeable surprise, in finding so much ease, and compared to my previous fancy, so very little formality in the arrangement and conduct of the House.

The preliminary business being over, a Quakerly dressed man (you might know that it is BRIGHT, Cobden's free-trade, right-hand man!) rises to complain of a trick of the Secretary of the Treasury, and is responded to by the Speaker. By his gestures you may discern where and how parties are arranged. On the left, upon the lowest bench, sits Lord John Russell, his hat down over his head, as Punch caricatures him. Upon the left-hand side and near, are the supporters of the Government. Opposite you may see an intelligent-looking, black and curly-haired, neatly dressed gentleman. That is D'ISRAELI, the author of "Tancred," and the conservative leader. Just above him is Mr. WALPOLE, a rising man, who (as I was informed by a noble Lord) would be the conservative Attorney General in case of a change. This is the Tory, Protection, or Conservative wing. At this end, near where I sit, are the Irish members, most of them in opposition just now to the Government, on account of the "ecclesiastical titles' bill," which is the theme for to-night's debate. Still, the Irish members do not act together against the Government, as is indicated by the position of John O'Connell, that red-faced, good-natured, stumpy man just facing the Speaker, on neither side. He is on the fence. You may tell the Irish members by their faces, without hearing a word of brogue.

My impression, when first looking upon this scene, was one of deep disappointment. It is cruel to have one's anticipations crushed so suddenly, when there is crushed with them so much of greatness, splendor, and ability, which have ever been associated in the mind with the English Parliament. I said to myself almost bitterly, "Is this the famous Parliament wherein SIR EDWARD COKE, SELDEN, PRYNNE, HARRY VANE, PYM, HAMPDEN, and 'OLD NOLL," battled the kingly prerogative of the Tudor and the Stuart; declaring by charters and bills of right, 'Apologies' and remonstrances, that there was no other source of legislation or revenue, than this their own Commons, one of the estates of the realm, whose laws could brook no 'dispensing' from kingcraft? Is this stupid-looking, hat-wearing, vociferating body, the same ordeal through which ST. JOHN, by the persuasion of his eloquence, and the force of his invective, and through which the young cornet PITT, by the command of his eloquence entered the portals of power, to lose it by becoming respectively Bolingbroke and Chatham—lords yet more than *peers* of the upper house? Is this the forum where EDMUND BURKE displayed the riches of his lore and the glory of his imagination—where SHERIDAN electrified the house with his wit? where NORTH, the Palinurus of the State, slept through the assaults of the best genius of England, leaving his haughty solicitor and attorney to pilot his sleeping course and defend his waking course? Is this the theatre where GEORGE CANNING, whose statue I just passed in the twilight, starred his short season of ministerial power—where the younger PITT, by severe and never-failing logic, held so long the rule of British politics during its severest storms—where Fox "graced the fervor" of the hour, by winged words which bore the spirit of great deeds? Can it be that in this assemblage there still lives a single breath of the old vitality, which made, to my mind, the English House of Commons the finest arena for intellectual tilting the world has witnessed, since Athens boasted her Agora with her Pericles and Demosthenes; or Rome her forum with her Tully and Hortensius? Is this the scene of WILKES and his agitation? Was it here that the proud shade of JUNIUS hovered, to collect the rays of that reason and indignation wherewith to illumine the English constitution and consume its enemies? It was here that my throbbing heart expected to find fulfilled Burke's graceful idea of sovereignty, "*modest splendor, unassuming state, mild majesty, and sober pomp.*"

Scarcely had the debate on the Popery bill began, before all these reflections were put to rout by a movement of the parliamentary appetite. There was a rush after—supper. An Irish member, Mr. REYNOLDS, formerly Lord Mayor of Dublin, hit the incident off very happily. He arose, as Ireland generally does, amid groans of "Oh!" He perceived that some Hon. members were anxious to dine. A celebrated English poet had said that "wretches hang that jurymen may dine."—Now he would not assert that some Hon. gentlemen would hang the Pope "rather than eat their mutton cold," but he believed they would not hesitate to make short work in passing a bill of pains and penalties rather than incur that misfortune. (A laugh.)

I was however doomed to be disappointed. My first impressions proved erroneous. It was my good fortune to hear what my informants denominated their "*cleverest*" men.

The motion pending was that of TOM DUNCOMBE, as he is familiarly known—a Radical, and a genuine trump, besides being a handsome, black-eyed, black-haired, graceful personage. Mr. Duncombe had moved that the first clause of the bill, punishing those who take titles under the Pope, be postponed until the House should be in possession of the brief, rescript, or letters apostolical, upon which the enacting clause was founded; and he proceeded to make what was called a decided hit, between wind and water.

He poured hot shot right over the heads and into the eyes of the ministers charging them with deserting the principles of the Emancipation Act of 1829, and denouncing the Preamble to the present bill compared with that of 1829, as miserable, wretched, narrow-minded and pettifogging. The speech was directed to the subject of the motion. He contended that mere public notoriety, or "common clamor" (to use the Saxon) was not the evidence for grave legislation. This speech called out the legal advisers of the government, who played the game of stave-off nicely. The Solicitor General is a tall, white-headed, good-natured man, of imperfect enunciation. Indeed, I noticed that very few of the speakers failed to stutter a good deal.—D'ISRAELI was a perfect stammerer throughout. What he said was pointed, but his manner was very indifferent. The most graceful elocution was that of Mr. WALPOLE, whose finely woven words trilled musically upon the ear, as he tendered the conservative force to the government, by which they are enabled to pass their bill. But ROEBUCK is the Slasher of the Parliament. He does not mince matters quite so much.—Every other member has his "right honorable and learned friend from so-and-so," over twenty times in a ten minutes' speech. Roebuck cuts to the marrow every thrust. His under lip curls over in scorn; but he met more than his match in the tall, gray-whiskered, courtly, precise and business-like Home Secretary, SIR GEORGE GREY. He looked to me the ablest man in the Cabinet. Lord John Russell made a short and very pointed speech, displaying both tact and good nature. He always comes in to the help of his adjutants when they are pushed to the wall, and leads them off. The Premier of England, whom I had a good opportunity to see, is a little man with a high forehead, bright eyes, and hair somewhat minus, but straggling over his face. He sits perfectly quiet, with his countenance under deep shadow, so that it is impossible to tell whether the arrows strike home or not.

Let me not fail to commend the brevity and pith of the English speakers. Up they start in a twinkling, the hat coming off simultaneously. They preamble little, but shoot right at the white; reserve their antithetic brilliance for the conclusion, which is hardly uttered, before the hat is on and they drop! If you should put a pistol ball through the heart, you could not bring them down quicker. There is no loud bawling in speaking, save among the Irish. But the cheers, cries of "*hear*," and at times the perfect Babelism of the House, is as comical as it is novel to an American. Tittlebat Titmouse, when he imitated a menagerie, was accounted, for that purpose, an efficient M. P. I can now understand the eloquence of Tittlebat's zoological demonstration. When his untimely groan caused a ministry, in the full tide of power, to resign, he reached an eminence of parliamentary celebrity wholly unprecedented; because no one but Tittlebat could ever have had the insensibility necessary to the occasion. But the clamor is soon over. The member either takes advantage of the cheers and interjections, or never heeds them.

The Irish members seemed anxious to find out if government intended to put the Popery bill in force in Ireland. The bill is general, and includes Ireland. They could get no direct response; although Mr. KEOGH, a witty and able speaker, pressed them closely.

During the debate I was startled by a cry from one of the wigs, of "strangers, withdraw!" Then, just as we were about to leave, the cry was "order," and the first command withdrawn. Directly on finishing the debate on Duncombe's motion, the command was repeated. We all went into a lobby, while a division of the House was called. It was a novel procedure. As it was explained to me, the members all march out, then march in; while at two points their vote is registered. This process lasted about a half an hour, the bell in the mean time ringing in absentees. I undertook to commend our plan of taking the ayes and noes; but I believe that even our plan has been improved by a Yankee.

During the discussion an odd procedure took place. A wig and gown appeared at the door of the House, accompanied by a lawyer. His queue trembled with conscious importance, as it moved up the aisle. Out jumped from a large chair, a little man in black tights with a big sword! Pretty soon, down marched an officer with a large gilded instrument:

"May I be permitted to inquire, sir, if that—that—stick yonder, is—Cromwell's bauble—the mace?"

"You're quite right, sir. It's the bauble—ha! ha! You Americans don't pay much respect to such legislative symbols!"

The man with the mace and sword marched the others up to the Speaker, who mumbled over something. It was doubtless a message from the upper house. I could see in it, though disguised, the original of our own modus operandi. The mace was carefully laid out of sight, and I much edified.

From the vote given, one may see what the Parliament of England is about. For some months past they have debated, and for some months to come they will debate, a measure of penalty, which a new rescript of the Pope may avoid; and which, when enacted, will serve as an excellent mode of persecuting into the Catholic Church a goodly number of Her Majesty's loyal subjects. It sounded strange to my ears, to hear the old statutes of *premunire*, and other obsolete enactments of the time of Richard II., quoted in this English Parliament and in this nineteenth century, as precedents for present legislation against Pio Nono Papa! Titus Oates is not dead yet. The Premier lately declared his belief in a Popish plot to subvert the liberties of the people; and upon this belief, and a harmless letter making Dr. Wiseman an ecclesiastical officer of an English locality, is to be based a law of intolerance, which even James II. would have been ashamed to sanction. When will England learn the beautiful truths of free toleration? When will she leave accountability in spiritual matters to God alone? When will she learn the significance of the first Amendment to the Constitution of the United States, in its application to human societies of divers religions and sects: "Congress shall make no law respecting an establishment of religion, or prohibiting the free exercise thereof."

But we would not judge her harshly from whom we have received such rich legacies of political wisdom. Well we know that the ecclesiastical polity of England has been growing for ages, and intertwisting its fibres with her civil polity. To pull it down, both must be uptorn. For that event England is not yet prepared. Time is the innovator in England. With a Queen so young and popular, and to whom we may almost apply the adulatory poetry of Lord COKE (the only poetry he ever committed,) to Queen Elizabeth, that, as the "rose is the queen among flowers, and smelleth more sweetly when it is plucked from the branch, so I may say and justify, that she, by just desert, is the queen of queens, not only by royal descent, but by roseal beauty also,"—with such a Queen the loyal spirit of England is blindly enamored. The disfranchised and tax-ridden millions, and the poor, who also number by millions, must still cry to Heaven for relief; for England's hat and hurrah will go up for Victoria so long as she wields the sceptre. This loyalty operates to stem reform.

Give England an unpopular head, such as she had in the time of JUNIUS, and Truth and Justice will no longer become hollow words to "make earth sick and Heaven weary," and religious toleration may ingraft some of our own features upon the Constitution of England.

VI.

Under the Crystal and in the Park.

"The life of man is much beholden to the mechanical Arts; there being many things conducing to the ornament of religion, to the grace of civil discipline, and to the beautifying of all human kind, produced out of their treasures." *Bacon.*

AFTER the rural racing jaunt of yesterday, we are again on our way to the Great Exhibition. We pass the barracks, around which we see red-coats keeping sentinel. On the walls is written, in big letters of chalk, so that the wayfaring man, though a fool, can read; "*You bloody Saxons;*" and directly under it; "*No* bloody popery!" Thus do the chance scribblings of the "vulgar" show the effervescence of the public mind. These two signs upon the house of Force—do they not state the question which was debated the other night by England's best minds? Write that debate out, and boil it down, and it is still "bloody Saxon" and "bloody Popery."

We should be, indeed, culpable, if before we reach the palace, we failed to notice the elegant gates and delightful gardens which adorn Hyde Park. This Park is 360 acres, or more, in area. It has many gates. The most costly and beautiful is the principal entrance. It cost over seventy thousand pounds alone. It is of the most exquisite carving, and forms a fitting portal to so spacious and inviting a spot. Nearly all of this part of London has been built within ten years. Lofty mansions, cities of squares, crescents, terraces, noble streets and avenues, fine churches and great gardens, are all about us. Lots of land which, in the early part of the last century, brought $60 rent per year, now bring $60,000.

But the Exhibition opens. We enter at the east entrance, finding the United States at work fitting up its department. We trust in the end our Union will make a fit and appropriate show. The Times, in speaking of our meagre collection, makes this remark: "They don't 'whip all nature hollow,' but they have several very interesting machines, and the useful character of their display as a whole, forms a really striking contrast to the showy attributes of the national industries developed around them." It is true. There is not so much to catch the eye by the gairish display of our contribution. While crowds surround the Queen of Spain's crown and bracelets, with their jewelled splendors—while the Indian elephant-saddles have their hosts about them—while the French silver and porcelain tea-service, wrought into every modification of beauty, catch the sight—while the great English carpet, woven by the fifty loyal ladies of London for the Queen, has its throng of admirers—while the Tunissian pack-saddles and brocade costumes, the Milan sculpture, the Wurtemberg stuffed animals, the French tapestry, (oh! how magnificently regal!) each and all are cynosures for eager gazers, our American collection boasts of the *utile, non dulce.*

I spoke of Hobbs, the lock king, in a former chapter. I met him to-day, and he explained his lock, which is on exhibition. It is a permutating lock. The key makes the lock. The modifications which may be made in it are only 1,307,654,358,000! It would take a person more than a Methuselah's age to use these mutations. He opened the lock and explained its intricate complexity. It is a wonder, and excites attention in the United States department only next to the Greek Slave.

Upon this day we began to visit the nations in the east end of the building, skipping Russia, whose articles are detained by Baltic ice, and commencing with the German states under the Zollverein. A fine piece of statuary representing the Bacchantes, attracts our attention, while, as if firing at the tipsy followers of the vine-god, is pointed a splendid gun, glittering like a mirror. Next comes an exact imitation of the towers of

Heidelberg, complete to the smallest rock. We have a model of Niagara Falls here, but it is a miserable one, affording no adequate idea of the extent of the fall. It is spread over some miles, consequently the cataract looks puny enough.

Prussia has one of the most entrancing rooms in the palace. It is lit with colored glass, all figured richly with recesses around, wherein is arranged statuary, paintings, and porcelain frames. We noticed a chess-board, costing $15,000, carved out of silver, set with jewels, and each knight, king, queen, and bishop, a perfect gem of carving in itself.

Prince Albert's birth-place, Rosenau Castle, in Saxe Coburg, had its model—a most bewitching piece. The German lasses were waltzing upon the green sward, while a German holiday had gathered its thousands about the castle. While seeing so many fine representations of scenery, and knowing how munificent nature has spread her beauties in my own American land, could I help wishing for some of Cole's landscapes of Hudson or Susquehanna scenery? Could I help wishing for a faithful portrait of that nature which Bryant, in a sonnet to the painter, reminds him before going to Europe, to bear uppermost in his mind:

> "Lone lakes, savannas where the bison roves,
> Rocks rich with summer garlands, solemn streams:
> Skies where the desert eagle wheels and screams,
> Spring bloom and autumn blaze of boundless groves."

Instead of these, the observer meets with model towers and ruins, churches, and opera houses, and even models of Swiss scenery. How we longed to see the lofty originals of the latter.

I observed in a large glass case, a magnificent representation of Alpine scenery, wherein at a glance was combined every form of sublimity and terror, of loveliness and beauty. The proximity is singular. Upland valleys of softest verdure repose sweetly at the foot of the eternal glacier. Huge snowy peaks, ready for an avalanche, frown over delicious spots of pastoral quietude, while horrid gorges yawn with silence and desolation, near the flowery marge of meadows.

Leipsic, with her books, Saxony, with her wool, and long courts of velvets, cloths, and satins, must lead us out into the nave again. Perhaps in the multiplicity of German infinity, you may notice that button trophy, with 21,300 varieties glistening like a miniature universe under the clear light.

We are called to refreshments by the whispers of the tired body. That finished, can you help stopping a moment to look at those Indian ivory chairs, that couch of gold, that Eka, or one-horse chariot? Shall we not wonder at the Sancsrit literature in Persia—venture within that Turkish canopy of blue with another tent within, filled with its long hangings of silver laces?

The Mosaic of Italy, is certainly one of the most wonderful things in the Exhibition. Large centre-tables are thus formed, with landscapes and figures, whose perfection shames the pencil. The Coliseum, Romulus and Remus, the Forum, and other classic memories and scenes, are thus preserved in undying freshness of beauty. I know there is no great utility in these costly Mosaics; but taking this branch of labor, at its lowest value, as a mere source of pleasure from the love of imitation or representation of agreeable objects, it nevertheless becomes the remembrancer of scenes of thrilling interest. It is the elegant accomplishment, by which homes are embellished. It enters into the sisterhood of arts, bound by a common bond—the culture of the human, through the influence of the divine, which ever dwelleth in the pure, the fair, and the beautiful!

What object is that upon the point yonder, which requires a glass to perceive it? Ha! ha! Can it be? A cherry-stone with twenty-five portraits on one side, and St. George fighting the dragon, sculptured on the other! "'Tis sure as any thing most true." Look for yourself! Italy has at least the palm in microscopic beauty, although yon Herculean Godfrey, from Brussels, in the nave, bears away the guerdon for muscular might!

We might fill pages thus depicting each object—which in itself perhaps was a study of years for the artist—but to which we do not give as many minutes. Passing by the statuary of Hero and Leander, which the mournful music from the gallery seems to render more sad, we enter the French tapestry room. There is the French trophy! That hanging, so dazzling in color, so striking in design, at which the eye blenches—cost twenty-six men eight years' labor. That is an object for an industrious exhibition! It is of course from Gobelins.

France is not alone *la belle France.* The finest collection of philosophical and surgical instruments are hers. False legs and arms, and every aid to injured humanity is hers. Not alone does she excel in Lyons silks and laces, but in kitchen ranges and physical sciences. Like her character is her exhibition of industry. Confectionaries of rarest temptation sweeten near "drums, guns, trumpets, blunderbusses, and thunder." Steam engines revolve in beauty, whose polish almost emulates that of her dazzling mirrors! Wigs, in profusion, are within hearing distance of harps, fiddles, flutes, and pianos. A very medley is France, a serious comedy, a laughing tragedy.

We have done for to-day; yet much of the Eastern entrance and galleries are not glanced at. We go away stunned, as before, at the immensity of this exposition of toil. Truly the dwarf man, "behind his engine of steam, can remove mountains." What a mine of meaning is there in the remarks of Lord Bacon, which we have prefixed to this chapter; yet even his comprehension, which almost became prophecy, could not grasp such a stupendous illustration of their truth as is here enshrined. What an ingathering of the world's daily experience is here! Even so feeble a sketch as this will enable the intelligent reader to form some idea of the wondrous world we live in.

Again, we visit the home of industry. It is Saturday, and ingress cannot be had until noon, by which time a great concourse has collected. A rush is made, during which examples of English rudeness, especially toward the gentler sex, is so common, as to excite the remark and contempt of every well-bred stranger.

The palace is filled at once, as if from a hundred sluices, with all kinds of people. Invalids, even, in their conveyances, are drawn through the courts. Painters and drawers are perched here and there, copying the articles and scenes. Policemen are taking their stations. Red coats are brushing off the dust from the articles. Paxton was at a loss for a cleaner to the building, and invented, at great expense of time and money, a hundred-housemaid-power-broom for the purpose. He found, after the first day's experience, that the long sweeping trains of the ladies performed the office to a nicety.

I began to-day with France, on the southern side. Amid the jewelry, which shone as "from a sky," we discerned some clocks, fashioned curiously out of trees, in the branches of which chirped, fluttered, and leaped from bough to bough a choir of birds. There were some pecking at beetles, others in the nest, but all pervaded by a vivacity which, at first glance, made the illusion perfect.

Here, too, we saw the rarest fruit-piece of porcelain painting which ever delighted the vision. The grapes and other luscious fruitage hung from a golden frame-work, while tulips and garlands of every flower seemed to hide an angel, of form so ethereal, and with shading so softened, and light so mellowed, as to enthral the fancy. Tapestry overhung all. Further down, and into the nave, is a fine piece of statuary, representing Love scizzoring off the claws of a lion; allegorizing the French sentiment:

> Amour, Amour quand tu nous tien,
> On peut bien dire—Adieu Prudence.

Silver service, pictures raised, and interminable vistas of dry goods, we fly from, to find refuge in the arms of Belgium, which are spread just above the next department. Here are chimney pieces, with carvings exquisite. Nests of little Cupids and flower bas-reliefs surround us. On move we with the crowd, until the Austrian statuary room receives us. What a sweet piece is that nun, veiled with marble, and in very truth realizing Wordsworth's line,

———— breathless in adoration.

The effect of a veil of marble, dimly showing the beautiful cast of countenance, is indeed a triumph of the chisel.

The machinery department has been slighted. My foolish eye has been caught by gauds, as "larks by looking-glasses." Imagine a vast vista of convolving, revolving, intertwisting, gyrating, perpendicularizing, horizontalizing, and whirlygigging generally; yet all playing as silently as polished steel, well oiled, can go, and as gracefully as the stir

"Of a swan's neck among the bushes;"

and you have a glance at the engine-room with its contents. Here on our right is a new locomotive runnning by atmosphere; there is, also, an improved "feather" paddle-wheel, with two shafts, one within the other, the inner one a screw; the set of paddles, as they rise out of the water, turning so as to find no resistance, and presenting their edge to the air. Miniature engines of every form, are in motion, and the machinery so bright as to reflect, in itself, its own motion. A steam engine with a moveable cylinder seemed a singular piece of adaptedness of means to end. Needle machines were at work, washing and drying machines, hydraulic pumps, machines for dressing stone, (from Bosting!) diving-bells, already in the bottom of the mock sea, and, last, printing-machines of many kinds, all in operation. The "Illustrated News" is struck off at the rate of over 5,000 to the hour. From four points the paper issues. The exhibition is thus rapidly illustrating itself to the wide world. But to my unpractised eye, the looms and mules and the other machinery for weaving, are the most wonderful. Large laces and splendid table-linen, costly cloths and cheap cottons, alike come forth from the swift-flying shuttle, amid a maze of rotation, driving and springing, the machinery performing every motion and intricacy from which power is evolved and comforts multiplied. This, amid the roar of water-falls, the buzz and hum, the click and clatter, the throbbing, glittering and dancing of wheels, is all dependent upon steam power, which is hidden from the eye. Is there not here a magic beside which Aladdin was a dunce, and the old enchanter, Merlin, a booby? Hurrah! for the age of steam wonder! Pyramids and Pantheons, Gothic buildings and Babylon gates, should sink into oblivion beside this steam-century, with its palace of Industry.

The west end, in the gallery, to which, with the help of fancy, you are transported, is now filled with prisms flung by the colored glass between you and the setting sun. You have passed royal couches, with Aurora and Somnus carved and painted, all golden and glittering. You have passed intricate mazes of food, seeds, woods, and fabrics, from Scotland and other parts of Great Britain. You glance at the naval glory of Britain, represented by her innumerable models, with the Battle of Trafalgar to top the group. You observe that centrifugal machine, illustrating the planetary motions completely. At last, relieved, you stand upon the threshold of—start not! It is only the organ, near which you are unconsciously standing. It strikes up, with four men to blow, and three to play. As I am a living soul, its thundering sound made the—yes, believe it, Rochester-knocking credulity—it made the UNIVERSE tremble!! I have told some things which unsophisticated Buckeyes rarely see, and can hardly imagine; but I was not under oath then. Now I am. I distinctly swear that I saw Jupiter quake amid his satellites, Venus tremble in her sandals, and Mars in his boots, Saturn shake in his ring, and the Sun itself start from his sphere, as the flood of sound rolled out of the organ and upon the—orrery!

While observing this phenomenon, which Herschel must explain, the organist struck up Yankee Doodle! My heart beat hot and queer. I felt the Declaration of Independence and a couple of Bunker Hills rising in my bosom. As such feelings were inconsistent with this temple, dedicated to peace, and as I was a delegate from Ohio to the World's Peace Convention, I prudently retired out of the British domain and seated myself again at the transept, to take a last look before going to the Continent.

At the four corners there are crowds, looking down on throngs beneath, moving in and out under canopies, and into the courts. Opposite is a large glass chandelier, almost the counterpart of the fountain, which, with its sisters three, are making melody by graceful water jets amid the palm and flower groves below. The sight woos the thirst, and the hum almost sinks one in a "swound," like a murmur of bees. White as ghosts, the long lines of statuary guard the little apartments, with varied hangings suspended from their roofs. Away down on either hand is seen one living stream moving amid gorgeousness, and under glancing sunlight.

How many hearts beat within those vital frames, the mechanism of which, comparable with nothing in this vast theatre of ingenuity, is hidden from the eye! How many immortal souls are here intent on seeing—seeing—seeing; forgetful of every thought as to the wondrous mind-mechanism which evolved all these wonders. "Ye fools and blind! for whether is greater, the gold, or the temple which sanctifieth the gold?" The gold must perish, the temple and its spirit survives.

Wrap those moving bodies in the silks of yon pagoda; or bury them amid the glitter of those Indian gold cloths, but they will not stay. Those flowers may be renewed by the genial breath of spring; those bodies, of form so radiant, must lie in "cold obstruction." Surround their tombs with the bronze and stone which line the nave; their memory is soon erased by the footstep of time. Yet this undying mind is perpetual. It lives through its creations. Nation to nation, man to man, hands down the results of the vigilant life. Who can tell what thoughts have been here developed to bless the race? What ideas of beauty suggested, what cordialities cultivated to decorate this world of tears?

Behold below, a world's representatives interlacing themselves. As Shakspeare has it:

> ——— "No man living
> Can say *this is my wife*, there; all are woven
> So strangely in one piece."

Listen to the hum of speech; look to the produce of thought. Hear ye not therein the shuttle of kindness flying from heart to heart, weaving its viewless warp and woof into one sublime fabric, many-hued as that tapestry, intricate as that mechanism; a fabric fit to be hung from the battlements of heaven, between the sins of man and the majesty of God!

The sun is sinking toward America. Its slanting radiance kisses the concave crystal. The statues in the transept fling long shadows down the nave. The thousand glitters of the glass are reflected from jewels and glass within. What if all the minds here represented by their results were gathered into a common mental palace, so transparent that the most profound thought of each and all could be perceived; the astronomer sweeping the sky with that telescope, down to the humble African who made yon miserable human image; the genius of the sculptor bodying forth his exquisite ideal in stainless Parian, embracing the tiny thoughtlet of him who mechanically turns a machine which thinks for him; could we not then approximate toward the idea of an Omniscient Reason, in the largest sense of that term? Yet these—all these—are the varied product of His hand, modified through the contaminated reason of man!

With such reflections half saddening the spirit, and with a curiosity to see the delightful environment of Hyde Park which surrounds the palace, I am led to the open air, to be freshened into new life by the side of a river of beauty—the Serpentine, set in emerald. A massive stone bridge arches it, over which are passing crowds from the exhibition, horsemen practising in the park, and coaches drawn by blooded horses. Soldiers and policemen are around here, as they are everywhere in London. Before us spreads the stream, with its water-fowl, ducks and swans. Sharp-pointed boats dart from under the bridge, and skim away as gracefully as the water-fowl themselves. A few sail boats shoot in and out, as if playing amid the splendid elms which line the stream, and which in clumps all through this park throw their shadows deep and inviting. Walks are distributed about in negligent precision. Boys with water spaniels and mimic ships are laughing away merry May hours in their pastimes. But these elms, how perfect each one appears! It is remarkable to one used to seeing nature in her unpruned, careless dress, how much like leafy architecture a noble tree may be made.

A perfect study for the Painter is each old elm, its long branches intertwisted neatly and gracefully; its shadows and lights conspicuous as those in a Gothic Minster; bending over to its sustaining mother, the earth, with a freight of foliage, and bestowing upon her verdurous bosom a rich gift of shade.

Far off, before me, yet clear as if in reach, stands the Duke Wellington in bronze, upon his lofty steed against the blue sky. Here come some of his class—a troop of soldiers in hats nearly as big as themselves. The lofty towers of Apsley House, the Duke's residence, are about his monument. Let the eye skim around to the right, until it meets between the trees the glittering palace, full of its throbbing life and myriad illustrations of life-results. At least tenscore of flags—white, blue, red and variegated, waver to the mild wind; while the transept at both ends is surmounted proudly with England's ensign 100 feet above the concave! The colors of the iron work are but dimly seen from here, yet most gratefully do they task the eye. The Park is speckled for miles with gayly-dressed women and soldiers.—Sheep, too, lazily lie about the lawns. Just behind yon trees, shut in by a gate guarded by soldiers, are at least count, 500 carriages and their liveried attendants, awaiting the pleasure of their masters and mistresses.—"Thank God," I mentally ejaculated, "I am no man's man." Could we not put these tight-legged, gold-tipped, hat-laced, powder-headed, bow-scraping, velvet-pawed footmen and drivers to a better account in Ohio? Make men out of them, albeit apparent manikins now? They do not know any better. If they could only *feel* what it is to have a free heart beating beneath the meanest vesture—but Pshaw! Velvet Paw must needs be Velvet Paw; else England's aristocracy would have to wait on itself, a degradation which would knock the underpinning out of one branch of the Constitution, and perhaps out of another. Look from the ignoble growth of men, to the noble growth of those old knotty, shaggy, twisted, Elms—Centuries of storms they have stood. They have been like true men, gnarled into greatness!

But we must be going homeward. Having bid farewell to this glorious Park, those graceful swans, whom I have just called to the bank and fed; to the Crystal Palace, in which a whole education has been mine, I strike for Victoria gate, thence through Sussex to Hampstead road. The scenes, however, in this English Park must remain written *here* forever. Our only drawback is that no more of our friends are along, to see the same beauties and enjoy the same delights which we have, in this Park. Would that my descriptions could convey one tenth of the satisfaction to my readers which I have felt within its bound.

VII.

Westminster and Dover.

——— "Traveller!
Remember these our famous countrymen,
And quell all angry and injurious thoughts."
Southey.

THERE are two spots to be visited before leaving England, that deserve especial mention. They have often been described; but every traveller observes them under peculiar circumstances. Westminster Abbey and Dover Heights—classic in association; do they not thrill to the inmost heart?

On Sabbath we went to Church in Westminster. It was a rare moment when we passed beneath that crumbling arch, and entered that venerable pile. Black and streaked with age; with the tracery and sculpture corroded by time; the very image of venerableness and awe, Westminster Abbey stands confessedly before the eye, the selectest spot of interest upon English ground. We stood in the midst of the consecrated fabric.—aisle opening within aisle, niches around, and the sculptured forms erected near the tombs of the buried great, lifelike, standing and reposing about us, and all richly painted with a dim and mellow lustre from the lofty circular window before us. The Abbey within is in the shape of a cross. From one branch came the organ tones and the singing, responsive to the service at the opposite end. All around were seen the trophies and arms, the scrolls and images, with their Hebrew, Latin, and English inscriptions.

We were compelled to stand during service. However much I wanted to hear a specimen of English preaching, yet I could not tear my eyes from the inscriptions around. We stood near the poets' corner. I turned about, and the first name I saw was GARRICK. There he stood, the English ROSCIUS—parting the marble tapestry, revealing the bust of Shakspeare; while below him are female figures, one of Comedy, fitting on the sock; the other of Tragedy, with dishevelled hair. It was a fine piece of sculpture; but it could not detain the eye long. Next I saw the name of CAMDEN; then Sir GEOFFREY KNELLER; then the monument of MAJOR ANDRE; then that erected by Massachusetts Colony to GENERAL HOWE. From my position, I could not see much of the poets' corner, although standing near. But whose monuments are those, heavy with dust, their images in repose, apart from the ordinary tombs of knights and abbots? These are the royal line of England.

Service over, which was performed by a large, hearty minister, who apparently enjoyed a fat living, and who preached about making self-sacrifices and cross-bearing—we leave. We are permitted to pass out along the damp, cold tombs, beneath and around us. Here lie abbots buried in the tenth and eleventh centuries. The statue of Charles James Fox reposing, with certain forms about him, is conspicuous. These forms are intended to be emblematic of his services in the cause of negro emancipation. They represent negroes, with all the appurtenances of curly hair, flat nose, large lips and low brows; but they are in *white* marble! They kneel at the feet of Fox, raising the whites of their eyes (done to the life) in thankfulness to their benefactor. The taste, thus developed, is questionable. Indeed, it almost confirmed an idea long pondered, that the province of the chisel lies exclusively in the Ideal realm. The pure forms of the stainless marble seem to require a spirituality, such as speaks from the lip, and in the mien of the Apollo Belvidere, or such as dwells in the gentle melancholy of the Greek Slave.

The panting heart left the immense repertory of the glorious dead, thrilled to its minutest fibre. The long corridors open before the eye, displaying monuments that defy the tooth of Time, but in vain. Every where you see its crumbling, corroding power. The very birds, as if in mockery of man, have built nests in the streaked and dark walls, and sing amid decay.

When we return to England, Westminster shall be again visited and fully described. Our route is now directly for Paris, by way of Dover. Let the traveller remember to arrange his time of leaving London, so as to come down to Dover by day, and remain some hours before the boat departs for Calais, if he would fix in everlasting freshness the incidents of "Lear," of which the white, tall cliffs of Dover formed so prominent a part of the tempestuous scene.

Before we were ready for it, our cars dashed into the bowels of Shakspeare's Cliff, and, after rumbling awhile, darted out again into the sweet May-shine. Behold! the sea speckled with vessels, and the dim whiteness of the French coast in the distance. Again we turn; and now that we are shut out from that fine view, let us look upward. There indeed is the glory of Kent, the place where good old Gloster is alleged to have stood. Although we cannot stop our swift rushing car to say, "Here's the place, stand still!" yet we can truly realize Shakspeare's description of the fearful, dizzy height; so high that the crows showed scarce so gross as beetles, and the sapphire-gatherer seemed no bigger than his head. We saw persons on the cliff's fearful edge (how fearful to poor, blind Gloster!) whose Lilliputian size brought back the poet's description most vividly.

Under the direction of our host of the "Gun," we traversed the ground where poor Tom was "a-cold," and where Cordelia redeemed the woman-nature of the olden British time.

Dover lies under the frown of the blanched cliffs in a semicircular form; her bay surrounded with boats, and the beach lined with bathing wagons. The town is not large, but looks neat. Long paved walks, made of a composition of coal, tar and sand, (quite an idea!) are in front of the beach, along which seats are ranged. The shore is yet faithful to the description of

Shakspeare; for I wandered along it, to verify that the "murmuring surge on the unnumbered idle pebbles beats." And as the surge rolls up its tribute of water and thunder, and recedes, the tiny multitudinous pebbles rattle away most distinctly and musically. It could not "be heard so high" as old Gloster stood.

We went upon the cliff, between Dover Castle and Shakspeare's cliff, by a tunnel and stairway. There are three stairways leading up to the fort on this hill, which could empty a goodly number of men in case of invasion. Indeed, Dover is perfectly prepared for that event. The Castle is the highest point, and within the bosom of that cliff, are trap-doors, stairways, and divers other arrangements to decoy an enemy in, then topple it over, or stifle it with poison. The face of this cliff looks like a great prison; its huge towers rising in the upper air, and its iron-bound windows in harsh contrast with the white beauty of the surface, which white beauty, is not unadorned with yellow and white flowers, as well as with green foliage. Little houses hang upon its sides like nests; and talking of nests reminds me of the birds. If there were no other feature in the scenery of England than these feathered carollers, it would entitle her to the appellation of "merry England." Where do they not sing? In the green lanes towards Epsom, in the depots of the Liverpool railway, in old Cathedral towers, in the Crystal Palace; all

> "O'er royal London, in luxuriant May,
> With lamps yet twinkling,"

they sing their matin; and here at our departing point, high aloof upon the Castle cliff, ring their merry twitterings, without the fear of big fort-cannon and gruff soldiers before their eyes.

The top of the cliff is a green plot finely laid out; but the fortifications lie higher. We ascended only to meet the challenge of a soldier to "*stand*," which we laughingly did. "*You must obtain a pass.*" "But, my good sir, we are strangers."

"*Must obey orders, sir.*" "Is your gun loaded?" "*No, sir.*" "Then I think we may say what we please and scale the ramparts." He turned out to be a good-natured fellow, and obeyed orders like a machine, as all good soldiers are. We therefore lost the best view. After gazing off towards the home of Fenelon, Rousseau and Chauteaubriand, and trying to conjure up Shakspeare amidst the old cliffs, albeit inhabited by unpoetical locomotives, we departed.

Dover is a point, in travel, to hang many a wild wonder upon. But, most, it is the point upon which hinges the greatest tragedy of the greatest Dramatist. Here the foulest ingrates that ever fleshed their teeth in the heart of paternal kindness, received an embodiment; and here, Cordelia, the brightest spirit that ever shone in upon the dark depths of Despair, received a local habitation and a name. Thank England's muse for linking such lessons with such localities!

You may be sure, that the enjoyment of travelling has begun, when we can take to our feet, and ramble amidst these grassy mounds covered with May flowers, and look out into the straits, and even catch in the sun's glancing, the white coast of France; when we can feel the fresh air blowing high and aloof from the city's dust and smoke; when we can find in the localities around, something which speaks of literary association and the olden time.

The ride down was of a piece with all of the other travelling into the English country—a rural prospect of rare beauty from Surrey to Dover. Tunbridge furnished a fine old ivied tower. Another loomed up near Dover—strange old milestones down the road of time.

The hour is rung, and our little boat made "the fire fly" in phosphorescent sparkles out of the straits. From certain recollections of salt water, I kept very mouse-like, until our vessel was moored between the long line of piles at Calais.

VIII.

France.---An Entry and an Exit.

> "Rattle her chains
> More musically now than when the hand
> Of Brissot forged her fetters, or the crew
> Of Herbert thundered out their blasphemies,
> Or Danton talked of virtue?"
>
> *Coleridge.*

IT was a moonlit midnight of the latter part of May, that found us landing at the pile-driven harbor of Calais. We walked into the Custom House of France, between cloaked and curly grey-whiskered and mustachioed old soldiers, and amidst cries from baggage-men, of "prénez garde, Monsieur!" Well, the officer having examined my passports, and hastily inquired after my family (very kind of him), most of whom (to wit, my wife) were named in the passport, he signified, by some outlandish gibberish, that I was free to roam in the new Republic.

We took the cars instanter. As soon as it became light, we found ourselves in foreign parts indeed. The houses looked small and old; the ground was divided into little patches, and there was wanting the neat air of English rural life. There were few hedges. The "lay" of the country resembled our prairies very much. The fruit trees were in bloom. The dress of the peasants was generally blue short coats. They looked quite picturesque in the early dawn. We observed many large peat beds, and quantities of that essential to caloric piled about. Wood seems to be a scarce article. The tall, straight, Lombardy poplars begin to appear thick and fast. And now we see soldiers, and priests, too. Next, windmills not a few. All these impressed us strangely. The houses, with their earthenware roofs and old walls, had an antique look, and these, with the jabber of talk among the French, told us that we were pilgrims indeed.

Not so when we reached Paris. Not having our tongue in as yet, to the little French we knew so imperfectly, we were compelled to address ourselves to the railroad agents, who spoke English. There we first began to realize the *fact*, and not the *form* only, of French courtesy. As soon as we let the officers know that we were Republicans from America, and not English, how they hopped about to show us our baggage, and even accompanied us to our hotel. Let American travellers in France not forget, to dispossess the minds of those who have charge of them or theirs, of the idea that they are British. You ought to see a Paris cabman take off a gruff John Bull, with his churlish crossness, and his shrug of discontent.

Not expecting to remain in Paris longer than was necessary to prepare our passports for Italy, we took but small and imperfect glimpses of the capital. But such as we took rewarded us well. How proud the French are of their capital! and they have reason to be. Not of their long and dirty streets, with little or no pavements, of which a great part of the city consists; but of their Boulevards, the Luxembourg, the Champs Elysées, the gardens of the Tuileries, and other spots which we visited.

We needed no guide. Our company being inside, I mounted the cab, and with a modicum of bad French began the duty of guide and interpreter, as well as of learner and teacher.—The shrewd cabman could readily understand me. He drove us to the famous Arch of Triumph, from which we took a view of the city. The arch itself is worth a visit to Paris. It is erected to honor Napoleon, his soldiers, and his victories. It is replete with carving, representing every variety of prowess by arms, and every mode of its consequent glory. From such a point I could not dwell upon detail.

Buy a medal, or give the old lady at the entrance a gratuitous franc, and you may ascend the Arch. What a glorious prospect is here on every side! You will, with the aid of Gallignani's map, or with the aid of some Parisian, perceive the principal points of interest in the throbbing life of gayety and glory below. In front are the Champs Elysées, with their fine walks, seats and shades; and throughout, are scattered stalls, booths, and circuses, together with thousands of human beings. Indeed it is no uncommon thing, of Sundays, to see at least two hundred thousand assembled in these retreats. That place of fountains before us, is the Place de la Concorde. You will rcognize one of the fountains as the original of one in the French department of the Great Exhibition. Still in front are the gardens of the Tuileries the Place du Carousal, with its fine arch, and the Louvre.

But we have not time even here for particulars. Let us walk about the arch, to find how Paris looks generally, with its roads leading back to Versailles and St. Germaine, its chateaux and its forts.

Then again for the cab and a minute inspection of the Luxembourg. There we confess that even Hyde Park is beaten. Its long rows of statues, its elegant flower-plots, its terraces, its splendid fountains, its urns, its delicious umbrageousness, its glorious palace, and above all, its thrilling associations with the great names of France, render it, thus far, the prominent object in our travels.

But what shall we say of Nôtre Dame, whose superb architecture calls for the best and loftiest sweep of the vision? We drive round to wonder at the work of man in rearing such a pile, and at the work of Time in touching its stone with decay. We enter. Hushed is the air! "Peace, be still!" the spirit of the place seemeth to say. One or two figures are in prayer at the other end of the Cathedral; all else seems a SPIRITUAL PRESENCE! How high, how deep—*deep*, is the air above! Move slowly and solemnly along, and gaze upon the master works of sacred painting to your right and left, until you stand before the altar! Then look upward. What a Tabernacle, Great God! is this for THEE?

In such a temple, the ALMIGHTY, if ever shrined visibly, would appear! What mellow splendors from the many-colored windows meet each other midway under the dome, and shower their united flood of rainbows on the scene below! Here is a place where His Presence may be felt, even to the renewing of life, to the brightening of heavenly Hope, and to the antedating o. celestial felicity. Would that we could here linger, until the sacred atmosphere of the temple should purify our souls, and create a new and holier essence for the cycles of eternity!

We almost forget that human greatness, "only not divine," was here enthroned, amid the pomp and circumstance of power, in the person of Napoleon. What songs, what breathings from yon old organ, what display of insignia and ceremonial observances, what an array of military valor and pride, what crowds of expectant spectators then made Nôtre Dame the shrine of earthly ambition in its proudest worship!

But we pass to another scene, where an ambition and a greatness of another mould is celebrated. Not in loud murmurs. Oh! no—the tombs beneath the Pantheon weep eternal silent moisture over the remains of the truly great of France. "La Patrie," hath remembered them by a most fitting, a most tear-compelling, a most magnificent tribute.

Thus has France, while erecting her memorials to victory all over her capital, not forgotten the immortalization of Thought, which endlessly wings its way down to the latest generations, through the works of her scholars and literary men! No one can fail to observe, even without visiting France, the intense feeling constantly flowing out in honor of her great men. Persons, rather than principles are reverenced. Immortalization of renowned names has superseded the immortality of the soul. The latter is almost an obsolete, if it ever were a prevalent idea. All classes of the community unite in homage to the hero. The very churches are built to honor humanity, not Divinity. The names of the citizens who fell in July 1830, are engraved upon splendid shafts; but the principles which prompted the revolution and which lie at the root of all popular sovereignity, were as evanescent as last Sunday's gala. Dynasties may be overturned, barricade-war be declared biennially, the vivas of the people changed weekly; yet the great citizens of France will ever receive apotheosis. The seven millions who have in December 1851, sustained the coup d'état of a BONAPARTE, have been mostly moved by the *name* upon the bulletin.

However fickle the populace of this city may be, it is cerain, that for all the revolutions of France, her Pantheon, to the truly great, will remain as everlasting as their fame. "Art," it has been well said, "is dependent on the tone of the public mind, as the more delicate plants on atmosphere and weather." It needs a general enthusiasm for beauty and sublimity, like that in the time of the Medici, to call forth a host of great spirits. No less it needs the same enthusiasm to erect monuments to their memory. France has had her era of enthusiasm. Indeed, it is an element which never subsides in her bosom. We may well rely upon it to protect the monuments it has reared.

Tired, but not sated with Parisian spectacles, we wended our way to the hotel, there to experience a new mode of life, wherein the café is united to the lodging-place, where the garçon plays the part of the English John, and the fat fellow with a white sugar-loaf cap, presides over cutlets and omelettes, the very Zeus of Olympian cookery. You know French cookery is as world-famous as Yankee notions. Did you ever hear it accountde for? *You did not?* Here it is, from *Savarin* himself. "When the Britons, Germans, Cimmerians, and Scythians broke into France, they brought with them a large voracity, and stomachs of no ordinary calibre. Hence Paris became an immense refectory." Is not that a perfect *sequitur?* At any rate, we blessed those hungry heathen, and felt one more of the glories of the French capital, with an intensity, quickened by exercise and seasoned by novelty.

Every body has heard of a French diligence. To my imagination, it always had a piratical cast of countenance. It swelled up in my fancy as a huge, lumbering, lazy, wallowing, unwieldy, rickety vehicle, requiring as many guards as passengers. Either this impression was erroneous, or else vehicles have improved rapidly in France. Look at that huge mass in three parts, with a loading that would do honor to a regiment of donkeys, or a patient road-wagon in Pennsylvania. It does at first sight look gloomy enough, yet in every thing it seems comfortable. Start off; and away we rattle, amid the hallooing of boys, the gaze of women, with the crack of the whip, (how the French do eternally snap their whips!) and the merry blast of the horn.

Dr. Johnson thought that one of the greatest exhilarations of life, was a start of a pleasant morning upon an English coach. He might have enlarged the remark so as to comprehend his French neighbors. Rattle-rattle—amidst the narrow lanes of the merry Parisians—down one rue, up another, past this column, near that image—and at last we find the open air and a splendid railway station. Soon our diligence is hoisted upon the cars—an odd-looking genius of steam; and without change, we are dashing by gardens with stone circular wells, surrounded by flowers, and little tracts of land cut up into smaller ones, all smiling with cultivation.

Let me remark that the land here is owned or leased in little *tractlets;* which are subdivided into as many plots as will raise wheat, barley, rye, oats, grass, and vetches (a red flowering grass for horses, similar to our clover). They also sow tares, to cut them up while green, for cattle. Their stock is all confined, so that even fences are dispensed with. Prominent among the divisions of the tractlets are the twisted grape vines, trimmed closely, and just now tufted with verdure. The hills are staked plentifully for their aid. Flax, mustard, and turnips, some of them in flower, are also distributed. The price of ordinary peasant labor, as I learned from our conductor, is only about one franc at best (19 cents) per day; and when the laborers broad themselves, upwards of five francs; so that you may see that provisions are as high as wages are low.

To any one used to the big, fenced fields of the West, these little divisions of a tenth or twentieth of an acre, which appear even to the summits of the highest hills, in oblong form, and many-colored, present a strange appearance, and remind one of the patchwork quilts made from calicoes or silks.

As we rattle through the beautiful valley of the Seine, variety adds to the natural loveliness of the landscapes. Windmills fan the air, and tall Lombardy poplars, with their tops plumed like soldiers, stand in battalions, almost as plentifully as the soldiers themselves.

From the first moment we touched France, at every point, we have seen men in glazed caps, with their handles turned up, indicating as a Western boy would express it, "Corn for sale;" with violent red pants and long surtouts; profuse hair, over a pinched, ochre countenance, with sensual, petty-larceny looking eyes, and with little swords dangling to their sides, or muskets on their shoulders. This is a republic too. God save the mark! Why even in the walled city of Avignon, with its forty thousand inhabitants, there are eight thousand soldiers—one-fifth of the population. At Paris every turn shows a soldier. "Liberté, Egalité et Fraternité," is inscribed upon all the monuments and public property. The commentary is near by in the shape of a bayonet. The Hotels of Ministers, and the Chamber of Deputies, as well as hospitals and barracks, have a parading musketeer before their doors. The gardens and walks are thronged with military locusts. Why this spectacle, so strange to a transatlantic republican? It is because France fears herself; because a strong government is needed to suppress internal revolt, because a large class of her population must be vagabond, and society is relieved by putting them under military subjection; and lastly, because Louis Napoleon would perpetuate his power, and France must be ready for intervention in Italy, or in other nations on the continent. Already great preparations are being made to send troops to Rome. Large numbers are leaving Paris daily for that city, to suppress an expected revolt. They will be needed at home, soon, no doubt. France has had a taste of republicanism. She cannot remain as she is, so long as her present laws remain. Since the law requiring three years' residence for the voter, disfranchised three millions of her people; since the law in harsh restraint of the press, requiring editors to sign their articles, and holding them responsible for every criticism upon the government; and with 346,000 soldiers, and 87,000 horses feeding at the public crib, how can she be stable or free? The alteration of the Constitution, by which Louis Napoleon may be made Emperor, or (so called) President for life, is the prominent political question. We hear it discussed on boats and in cars.*

But we are ahead of our journey. The Lombardy poplars were our theme. These seem to be the only wood here. They are raised for the lumber. We saw persons with hand-saws at work in this age of steam, and within fifty miles of Paris, making boards out of them. The limbs are stripped, and out of the bushes are made faggots, which are tied in bundles, and used for firewood.

The women do the greatest part of the field labor. Our ob servation of them may be summed up thus: the young are vivaciously pretty, and the old are horribly ugly; but both are extremely polite and unexclusive in their communication. But one should be chary of criticism upon the women of France, among whom are numbered Joan of Arc, Madame de Stäel, and the little wife of the great Condé, who was fighting her husband's battles while he watered pinks in prison.

One feature of the landscape we should not omit. It is the donkey, almost hid though he be, under the weight of harness. Along he trudges, jingling his bell, and his little feet in strange

* The reader will remember that these pages were written in France, before the coup d'état. Political prognostics for a country, like France, is at best but wild guessing.

contrast with the heavy burden he bears. He called for more sympathy than any other part of the population. COLERIDGE must have travelled here when he wrote his plaintive ode to that languid animal, and "meek child of misery." I can well understand how the poet's sensitive soul trickled with pity as he contemplated the young foal's prophetic fate, under the thousand aches which patient merit from the unworthy takes; but if I should live until the star of empire should set, I could never understand how a poet even, as Coleridge did, could find in the harsh, dissonant, prolonged, agonizing, choking, desperate bray of the donkey, a spirit and a tone more musically sweet than warbled melodies that soothe the aching heart to rest! But there is a second sight, I suppose, allowed to the poet, which the *profanum vulgus* must not seek to attain.

Alternating between diligence, cars and steamboat, we pursue our way. We left the cars at Tonnêre, not far from which city is a queer old ruined castle, one of the finest of the middle ages; passing Dijon, we reached Châlons, where we took a long, narrow, low steamer, about as wide as one of our canal boats, and twice as long. The Saone is a clear stream, perhaps one hundred yards wide, and walled almost all along. Its banks are green and low. The country, unlike other parts of France, seems to be improving. The towns through which we passed before we took the boat, are of stone, and rapidly dilapidating. The streets are all well paved, however, and the accommodations good.

It would have made you laugh to have peeped in upon us while at supper in an old half-castle, half-stable, of an auberge, in one of the towns before we reached Dijon. About twenty French men and women, all jolly, sat around us Buckeyes. Away they gibbered, and directly we became acquainted. Different persons, who knew as little English as we did French, undertook to speak for us; and while the wine went round, and the dishes were passed, laughing and joyance followed. Such a glee we never saw; we knew they were not laughing at us, for the French *never* do this. Every attempt at French was *très bien.* Every successful attempt at bad English by the French, we received with "*bon, bon.*" They acknowledged we spoke better French than they English, and with mutual gratulations to the two great republics, we again resumed our way. That scene can never be pictured. If you would illumine Babel with a few gleams of sunshine, and set out in it a creaking board of supper, you might allegorize it somewhat. We knew just enough of French to make the perplexity efficiently comical for a good farce. The stamp of an awkward man upon a gouty toe is not half so comically embarrassing. The perfect understanding we all had, when it came to the language of spoon, knife and fork, heightened the scene. The French gesture, not alone with fingers, hands and arms, but on this festal occasion eyebrows, eye, nose, mouth, whiskers, and head entire, were called into use to give significance to the tongue. I do not wonder the French boast of the first comic writer, Molière.

What fine bridges span the Saone! They are very low; but a tinkle of the bell lowers the pipe of the steamer, by hand, and we dart between the piers, when it is raised by steam. The freshly-ploughed hills on the right swell up, and smile to the very clouds with the evidences of industry. How they will bleed with the wine in October!

We soon arrived at Maçon, near which Lamartine was born, and the scene of much of his "Confidences." The pensive beauty of the surrounding scenery might well develop so melancholy and tender a Muse as his. Half in shadow, and half in sunlight, hung the long line of hills, sentinelled here and there with the poplars, and all overarched by a soft, clear, blue firmament. Well might they infuse into his soul that intense feeling of the lovely and ecstatic, which distinguishes Lamartine.

Soon we leave the stone quays of the wine-trading town of Maçon, where we were met by a host of women, with baskets of edibles on long poles, who poked them under our noses from the banks. A few hours more, and our boat is approaching the silk and velvet metropolis. You may know Lyons by the splendid pallisades, upon which frown rare old legendary towers, round and grim; the rocks surmounted with elegant residences; terraces of green and flowers beautifying the gray and dark rocks; statues adorning arches and gateways, and every where the contest of haggard, petrified Nature, embracing, but subdued by the gentle influences of leafy groves and artistic monuments. The isle Barbe here was once a favorite residence of Charlemagne, and is even yet a spot of rare beauty in the Saone.

Below in the river we pass a fleet of river craft, laden with hay and straw. Bell ringing, military music and noise, usher us into our pier. Lyons is throned among hills, and looks imposing.

It is hard, after looking upon and describing such spectacles as the Luxembourg, the Pantheon, Nôtre Dame, and other places in Paris, to find adequate admiration in language for other less attractive scenes. There is a "joyful amazement" that entrances the traveller, which is not dependent merely upon relative beauty, but which belongs to the *spirit*. As he passes from novel enchantment to even a less enchanting attraction, that amazement increases in intensity and refinement The eye becomes able to see all beauty, the ear to hear inexhaustible harmony, and "the senses to drink in the balmy and bracing air."

Just as the evening of Thursday was dying away, our diligence abruptly turned from its direction down the Saone, into a valley of exquisite beauty, which yet lingers about my mind as a dream of heaven. I thought at first it must be the far-famed valley of Vaucluse, opening to us its world of witchery. But no; as we learned very soon, it was near Vienne, the ancient capital of the Allobroges,—a ville between Lyons and Avignon.

Let us look around. Upland slopes rise one above the other, high as the eye can see without pain, and cultivated to the very summits with the vine. An infinity of stakes set for the vine multiply before the eye; while terraces relieve the rocks of their barren appearance. Skirting our road are huge rocks upon which cling yellow, purple and red flowers. Wild roses hang over their edges, and form natural tapestry. The meadows below, are spangled with unromantic poppies; but they look beautiful in their wild, bright-red dress. A stream of water flows far below the meadows, making the air musical with its falls. Groves of the Lombardy stand unconcerned about the hills; while as we advance, mulberry-trees, upon which boys are gathering leaves, goats feeding upon the side-hills, and the little earthenware roofs of the vine-dressers, appear.

Now a factory for silk gives the *idea* of utility to the view, and we meet crowds of pretty girls in caps, and with flowers, passing and repassing, as well as boys with their fishing-poles, returning home to Vienne. Far over beyond all this realm of beauty, is a huge range of rocks, in which are carved houses. Now splendid châteaus, with vineyards and flower-gardens, leap as if by magic, from behind hills, in the very bosom of the valley. Soon we pass stone fountains, and all at once the "arrowy Rhone" bursts upon the view, red and golden in the sunlight. What strange old pillar is that we saw in one of the meadows of the valley—towering up seventy or eighty feet? It cannot be French, for it is too old. I learned that my surmise was correct, that it was a Roman monument. Somehow or other the French make their roads, so as to run near any monument of beauty or of antiquity. In America, we scarcely deviate from a graveyard for a railroad. As the sun went down, it glanced through cloud-bars with a brilliancy that sparkled in the glistening air. Surely we must be approaching a sunnier clime, where Beauty reposes in the lap of a lovelier nature.

Scarcely had we reached Vienne, before the sound of music and the appearance of a dance, down the street, about a half square from the diligence-office, riveted the ear and eye. Young men and maidens were moving "right and left," crossing over and all around,—embodiments of happy hilarity. But where we stopped, there was found a contrast to this gay scene. A crowd of beggars, consisting of cripples of all twists, shapes, some circular, one-legged, armless, and otherwise deformed, crowded around us. A regular fight ensued, as to who should obtain precedence to the diligence. What a commentary! It completely unveiled Charles Lamb's humorous sophistry in his plea for beggars, wherein he demonstrates the unenvied contentment of the beggar's lot, above all strifes, suits, fashions, chances, bankruptcies and ills which fortunate flesh is heir to—the only absolute monarchs and independent citizens! In France, even beggary fights for its caste, as well as whines for its sous. Yet there was bread (large circular rolls or loaves, about three feet round, in the French style) hanging within reach, at a baker's shop.

The silk-worm and the grape-cluster—how simple in themselves; yet how many millions in France depend upon them for life. How strange, too, it was, to see those beggars in that beautiful valley, where one might imagine the fruition of Milton's idea of a perpetual feast of nectared sweets. After having gathered flowers by the hill-side, as souvenirs of this enchanted spot, we courted the influence of the poppy, which by a curious *lucus a non lucendo* seems to be the most plentiful flower in this *unsleepful land.*

The next morning, our conductor gave me a seat by his side, and with my little French, which is daily improving of necessity, I learned every thing of interest in yesterday's ride. What strange appearance is that in the east, away off among and above the dim hills? Can it be solid earth, with clouds below it? "*Alp montaigne*," says our conductor. A long range of the Alps followed us during our ride, at times white-topped with snow. Soon we entered upon the valley of Vaucluse, so famous in the songs of the Troubadour; so famous as the locality of the tombs and fountains of PETRARCH and LAURA; so famous for its beautiful heaven and unrivalled scenery; and so famous for its Roman ruins. But, above all, to my mind, it was the home of PETRARCH. The Abbe de Lille touches the right strain when he sings,

"Ces eaux, ce beau ciel, ce vallon enchanteur
Moins que Petrarque et Laura interressoient mon cœur.
La voila donc, desors-je, oui, voila cette rive
Que Petrarque que charmoit de sa lyre plaintive."

We passed crosses at the road-side, hung with chaplets, peasants driving homeward the early harvesting of hay, and auberges with their signs of holly over their hospitable doors. Soon the old ruins begin to appear. I called all my poor French into requisition. How it brings one out, this curiosity. The most prominent ruin was called the Château de Mont Dragon. It was a high, long palisade, built by Nature for a stronghold. The walls ran up in solid masses 175 or 200 feet high, and upon these the old Roman caution had built towers against the Allobroges. All around the hills were the ruins of the Roman. Here the eagles of Cæsar and Marius played with the wind.

After having passed the Château de Mont Dragon, which is in Vaucluse, we glided between tiled houses and willows, which line the road-side, until Orange gleamed in the sun. Here is a grand amphitheatre of the Romans; and the relict ruins of the Princes of Orange, above it upon the hill. As we passed very near, we had a good opportunity to see the outside of the amphitheatre. Its concave was turned to the hill, consequently we could not see its interior. It was not until we passed, and that my neck had been stretched some feet out of the diligence, that I caught a view of the seats. It is not broken and ruined, like the Coliseum. Its semicircle is perfect. It looked the *old Roman* in every stone. Here, doubtless, were the Gallic prisoners of war sacrificed to grace a "Roman holiday." Many a noble Allobrogian struggled in the ring with the wild beasts of his native forests, and died amid the shouts of his victors. In glancing at such and similar scenes, how often recurred to my mind the verse:

"What tales, what morals of the Elder day,
If stones had language, could that pile convey."

A poet has said that there are *sermons* in stones; and verily, that solemn, gloomy vestige of the mighty power of the olden time, is more eloquent in its silence than a great many sermons which I have heard.

A splendid arch appears! And now, as we approach it, snakes, shields, battle-axes, and other figures, all in ruins, yet sufficiently solid and distinct, while crumbling, to tell us that Marius was here with his legions of Victory, and that this is his memento of the battle with the Allobroges. But how much brighter is the triumphal arch to Napoleon at Paris! Cæsar himself pales before Napoleon's blood-red glory. But we have more marvels in this valley of Beauty. Avignon, our dining-place, appears, not by itself, but by its splendid representative, the palace of the Bishop, whose lofty turrets and gray old towers, massive and substantial, are lifted high above the surrounding country. This view gives place to the high wall, not without a certain rude ornament, and not untouched by Time, which with its towers and deep moat surrounds this city of forty thousand people. An old aqueduct crosses the Rhone here; or rather has crossed it once. Now it has broken down in the middle. Its windows and arches look mournful and dreary beside the new, prim, and saucy suspension bridge, which, just below it, leaps the stream, as if the effort were of little consequence. Here, too, we see a splendid depot, and locomotives puffing over the iron rail. The old and new civilizations meet together. The middle and later ages kiss each other.

You remember that there was an ancient tradition among the Romans, that when their Capital was founded, the god Terminus refused to yield to Jupiter; and hence, the boundaries of Roman power never would recede. Vain and delusive prediction! Had there been no other Jupiter to subdue their Terminus, steam would have become the "Father of gods and men." The thunder of Jove must have succumbed to the lightning of Morse. Steamboats and locomotives would have driven Terminus to his seven hills. In this interior city of France is an epitome of the *great* past, and the greater present; the one splendid in decay, the other wonderful in its active energy. Upon this energy hangs the future fate of Nations. Iron, not gold, is the metal to be sought for, whose subtle power, alchemy in its most potent form, under the spell of its old enchanters, RAYMOND LILLY and ROGER BACON, could never rival.

Over hills and down dales, amid mulberry groves and silk factories, and everlasting soldiers, we find the open country, and with the speed of a locomotive we dash away in our diligence towards this my present locale of Avignon, where at the National, late royal (?) Hotel, strawberries and cherries blush to be seen in luscious prodigality.

Two things yet deserve mention. Before we reached Avignon, the castle called the ruins of the Baron d'Ardret appeared. It towered upon high battlements, filled with port-holes. Art had been aided by Nature to construct one of those illustrations of strength, which, after repulsing many a gallant foe, has even bid Time defiance. The legend connected with this castle, as I gathered it from our conductor, is briefly, that the Baron whose name it bears, upon the breaking out of the French revolution in 1789, good-naturedly, no doubt, hurled four of his domestics over these terrific heights. That places it conspicuously upon my list of ruins.

We dashed under the arched gateways of Avignon and into a courtyard; and really the scene came over me like a romance of the middle ages. We entered a fine hotel, kept in a sort of old castle, yet fixed up most comfortably. All the houses here have stone or marble floors, and although these do not coincide altogether with our ideas of comfort, yet the romance of the thing—you know—makes up. We wished for a longer repose than two hours at this beautiful city; but no! down we dash towards Marseilles. What towns we passed—what olive orchards, what black and gray old rocks, what vineyards and terraces, before our cars entered that three-mile tunnel, dark and damp, under the mountain, are all too common by this time to be particularized. At last, through a mountain gorge appeared the Mediterranean, with its bosom of blue, speckled with its sails of white. A summer storm came up as we drew near our destination, a storm of rain, sunshine and rainbows. I saw one column of a beauteous bow coming out of an old tower, and gradually moving into the Mediterranean. It arched us so completely that we may truly say, that we entered this 'Queen city' of the Mediterranean, upon the last day of spring, under a bending heaven of prisms! As it cleared away, the air was filled with a rich, interpenetrating lustre; and the sun went down under a golden canopy which only hangs in a southern sky.

Marseilles is a gay, godless, and not a very cleanly city; soldiers fill every part of it. Its promenades are fine. We visited the Château of Flowers, which is the favorite resort on Sundays, of the population. It was well named. Flowers of every hue, beds laid off in every form, places for amusement and exercise, lakes with boats and swans, hills, grottoes, a circus and fountains, all unite to make it a place of pleasure, a favorite resort of the gay French.

We went upon a high point near the sea, overlooking the city, to take a farewell of it, as well as a complete glance. We were not disappointed in our view. But we met three odd, turbaned human beings upon the lofty promenade, seated cross legged, and smoking as composedly as Mahomet amid a heaven of houris. I supposed they were Turks. They nodded. We nodded. The chief had, strangely enough we thought, a very long white beard (albeit a young man), a very fair complexion, and very light eyes, which he twisted very remarkably. Finding I did not advance in conversation, he inquired in French if we were not strangers, then if we were not English. '*Non Non!*' rather emphatic. I asked him, in return, if he and his compatriots resided in Marseilles? '*Non*, *Non*.' Once more—delicate question to such a queer heathen, 'If he did not reside in Turkey!' '*Moroc*, Monsieur.' Whew! perhaps the Emperor of Morocco himself. He gravely pulled out his snuff box, and I, with a grand flourish (I hate snuff as bad as brandy), took a tremendous pinch; and with the most approved Oriental sweep of the arm, applied it to my nose. Before the first explosion took place, I was behind the bushes. 'Oh—Ah—Chee—Whoo-o!' six times sonorously loud. The Emperor roared. Our party roared; and I described space, aided by gravity, remarkably rapid. Snuff is a miserable practice. None but heathens use it.

I must bid farewell to France. She has been a garden of delight to me. Never was I so beholden to Nature and Art for enjoyment.

I write amid the discussions of some six or eight white-robed Capuchin monks, whose sweet Italian (Tuscan it is), ravishes my ear, while it disturbs my pen. We are aboard of the Sardinian steamer Languedoc, bound for Leghorn and Naples. I cannot but look upon these strange monkish men with a sort of reverence. Sacrificing the world and its pleasures, continually engaged in spiritual or mental exercise, they do deserve the regard of every tolerant Christian. Whatever of abuse may have been by them perpetrated and perpetuated, I never can forget them as the preservators of the classics and the regenerators of the Arts. The Benedictines first penetrated the chilly north of Europe and christianized it. From them sprung the infinite beauty of the Gothic architecture, and the entrancing sweetness of Music. The Augustines built fine Cathedrals, and attracted the untutored mind to the service of the God of Mercy.—The mendicant friars founded hospitals. As architects, as glass painters, as mosaic workers, as chemists, as carvers in wood and metal, the Benedictines were the first and almost only artists of the middle ages. St. Francis, when he wooed and won his bride, *Poverty*, in his brown sack and cowl, at the same time, gave the hue and tone to that mystic school of painting and poetry, which has ever been the greatest attraction to the loftiest genius. Giotto in painting, and Dante in poetry,—are they not offspring, noble enough to justify our commendation? In all, these poor monks worked not for themselves; but for the glory of God!

And now as they, with their clear dark eyes and lofty brows, are retiring to their berths, my eyes follow them as strange relics of an earlier day, lost to the active world and busy with scenes of the past and of the future. Sleep on! Ye have no illiberal, harsh Protestantism following ye to your lonely pillows. May God reward your zeal in his service, by the fruition of your happiest hopes!

IX.

The Home of Columbus.

"Italia! that thou wert in thy nakedness
Less lovely or more powerful, and could claim
Thy right, and awe the robbers back who press
To shed thy blood, and drink the tears of thy distress."

BYRON.

I HAD scarcely written the word "Genoa," in my journal, before the evening gun from the fort was fired, the report of which startled a thousand echoes. Never did I hear such a fine succession of iterated sounds. Of course we rushed to the window; but only saw the smoke rising and beclouding the young crescent moon. The light-houses are gleaming around another crescent which the harbor of Genoa forms, while including in it the masts of a thousand ships. The long promenade of marble, which forms the roof of the Porticato alla Piazzo, whitens beneath us, in the warm atmosphere; and the sound of singing, of merry bells and of voices rise, forming a rare medley of music.

Were I to select a word descriptive of this city, which is called the "superb," I would select the above—*medley*. Not only is it a medley in its people, its palaces, and its poverty; but in its cathedrals, its cafès, and its scenery. As we approach the city from the blue sea, which we did in the morning, it seemed one compact mass of marble, cut out in semi-circular form for a harbor. It lies upon a high hill-side,—one street of palaces rising above another, in close proximity. To all appearance, there is not much to be seen here. But judge not too quickly. You may find much, even in the little walk from the boat to the hotel, to reward your observation. No doubt, you will be first caught by the graceful and peculiar costume of the ladies. They are exceedingly well dressed, and walk nearly as easily and as finely as our own American women. They wear a white veil, which being confined with a silver pin in the back part of a fine head of black hair, neatly braided, flows in the most elegant, wavy lines imaginable. It is disposed in handsome folds over as handsome dresses. If you would go down the Strada Nuova, as we have to-day, the first idea would be—"why, can this be real—is it not a general bridal-day? How happy and spruce dance the merry brides along this palace-street!"

The other part of the population do not dress peculiarly. They have a harsh language, however, even though it be Italian. Indeed, it is as different from the sweet Tuscan or Neapolitan, as I am from Hercules. The Sardinians cannot be understood at Naples, any more than a Pottowattamie by a Flathead.

Upon entering our boat at Marseilles, where we spent a delightful day, we found three Americans, Mrs. Stephens, the authoress, and her company, with whom we formed a delightful acquaintance. She has been travelling in Europe for more than a year; passing, by virtue of her talents and reputation, among the best and noblest of Europe. And let it be remembered too, that wherever she has been, she has not forgotten that she was a plain-spoken American lady. The reader may remember the cavalier manner in which she treated the Queen of Greece, who insulted our consul, by refusing to permit him to present them. It was capital. She told us the story with great éclat; while we young embodiments of American grit and spunk, cheered it most joyfully.

I had no idea that Genoa was of such consequence. She has not lost her commercial power since the days of Columbus. Others have excelled her—that is all. One hundred and fifty thousand people mostly depend on her commerce. She is the outlet in the Mediterranean, for Switzerland, Lombardy, and Piedmont. Her silks, velvets, and damasks, to say nothing of her filagree work in silver, which our ladies have been handling to-day in the famous Goldsmith-street, are prominent objects of manufacture.

The first thing which strikes a foreigner here, is the narrowness of the streets. Indeed, there are very few over which you cannot step from roof to roof. Carriages are rarely seen. Mules are the only living objects visible, beside human beings. The streets are not gloomy, however. They are lined with fine houses, built when the maritime splendor of Genoa was at its zenith. These houses are all called palaces. They have been such, but from the poverty of the nobles, or from some other cause, they have been leased out. I saw a blacksmith shop in the lower story of one of them; and little stores are not uncommon in some of the largest class. These palaces looked worn and tired; their painting spoiled, and not unlike a fine lady jaded after some grand ball. The paintings on the marble walls are rubbed and dim. The statues, almost all of them, have their noses knocked off. The fine stair cases, with their guardian marble forms, look dirty and neglected. Yet Genoa is—superb; every body says so. It would not do for us to say nay, to such a community of affirmation.

I do not mean to say that there are not exceptions, though few, to this untoward appearance of the palaces. Nor would I thus depicture the inner appearance. Our visions to-day forbid. There is an air of massiveness and *stoneness* about the edifices, which is as striking as it is comfortless. This is as apparent in the old as in the new part of the city. The best of the palaces exhibit to the gazer moving past, a large hall, supported partly on columns, leading to an alcove, or court, surrounded by arcades, the arches of which are supported upon columns. Flights of marble steps lift themselves far up; and above and beyond is a great stair-case rising on each hand, and frequently further beyond is a small garden, shaded by oranges, and sprinkled with the spray and voiceful with the music of fountains.

We have not as yet visited the interior of any palace, though we have of some of the churches. Our first visit was to the Duomo, or Cathedral, built in the eleventh century. How different are these churches in Italy, from Westminster or Nôtre

Dame. These latter seem to be mouldering. Owing to the softer material and a northern clime, they must of necessity first yield. To all appearance, the Duomo is as young as ever. It is of black and white marble, and is altogether out of shape. Only one tower is built where the taste calls for two. Throughout the church there is illustrated the Genoese *medley*. The aisles and naves are separated by fine Corinthian columns, connected by pointed arches of Gothic, and bearing a horizontal entablature; above which is an arcade supported by columns and piers. The same black and white marble appears within.

We are allowed to go within the choir. The seats are finely inlaid with musical instruments. A bronze Madonna and child, by BIANCHI, decorates the altar. After examining the two finest paintings (for in such a display of canvass and configuration one must select), we did not enter, and did *not* see the remains of John the Baptist, which are contained in the chapel dedicated to him. The chapel is elegant enough, with its four porphyry pillars, and a sarcophagus to contain the relics; while a splendid shrine of Gothic panels, tracery, and finicals of the most exquisite kind, is inscribed with his history.

There are several apocryphal relics in this church, as in most of the Italian churches. The prominent one is the *Catino*, a vessel said to be a gift to Solomon by his ancient admirer—she of Sheba; and also said to be the dish which held the paschal lamb at the last supper; and also, to be the identical dish which Joseph of Arimathea used to catch the blood from the bleeding side of our Saviour. This relic was never permitted to be seen. Some sceptical Germans, however, got access to it, and discovered it to be, instead of a single emerald, as was told, a dish of ordinary glass!

But we cannot enumerate the items of interest, sacredly hoarded up in these churches. One old relic—which I could swear to—is a rescript in almost illegible Latin, to Constantine the Great, which is inlaid in the wall, and is no doubt coeval with that monarch.

We leave the Duomo with its niches, twisted columns and mixed architecture, black and white marble, with not one idea of unity and order. It has not the simplicity in variety, which in the Gothic so charms the senses and awes the soul, by the association with Infinity. The other churches are less medley, but somewhat the same impression is left. On our first entering the ungainly-looking church of Saint Sira, a perfect blaze of painting and richness arrested our sight. It seemed thronged with great masses of the pencil's populace. Angels and saints in white marble relieved the eye below; and after ranging up over the frescoed vaults, the sight found relief in a huge dome, still painted, but which opened to another dome, through which seemed hastening up to heaven the winged aspirants to the upper air, bearing through it a garlanded cross! The conception of this group, with its upward flight surrounded by forms of beauty all too lovely for earth, was only rivalled by the genius which executed it. Forty marble columns, and all the apostles and prophets in marble, gave us the idea of profusion without beauty, and maze without form. The associations connected with this church are the best part of it. Here in the fifteenth century was Boccanegra created the first Doge of Genoa, amid cries of "*vive il popolo.*" Here the eternal right of popular supremacy was asserted and embodied in him, whose fine form we just witnessed in the Ducal palace. The Genoese treasure his memory. Indeed foreigners who think the Genoese have no liberty, or resemble the other Italian cities, greatly err. I do not wonder that in the beginning of the present year (1852) Austria has made the insolent demand to have troops stationed in the arsenals of Sardinia. Sardinia is a constitutional monarchy to be sure; but her councils represent the people and control the State. Books of the republican class are unrestrictedly circulated and sold here; while at Naples all books, from the Bible and Shakspeare down to the latest French squib, are forbidden. Education in Genoa is a high object of public interest. I asked a merchant to-day in Goldsmith street, how it happened that so many of the people spoke English. He responded that the course of instruction in the public schools was most thorough, including French, German and English. It is getting to be a great mark of nobility on the continent to speak English. We are in for that rank, finding it more easy than French. Custom is mighty.

We visited the Ducal palace and the chamber of the grand council. It is pillared and frescoed off finely; while ranged around, are the casts of statues which formerly stood in marble in the same niches, but which during Bonaparte's time, were thrown from their pedestals. The city has not yet lost the traces of the French. It was held by Massèna for a long period, while besieged even to the starvation point by the Austrians.

We also visited other churches in Genoa. They bear the same general appearance as the Duomo; a style resembling the Arabian, or Saracenic commingled with the Gothic. In all, there is the same blaze of fresco, which, owing to the peculiar manner of the incorporation of the color with the lime in its wet state, gives out a lustre more brilliant than oil. The columns are of marble—red, white, and spotted; some of them spiral. The Church of the Annunciation gleams with fretted gold. We noticed there, a fine painting of St. Francis dreaming of his Bride, Poverty, with the angels surrounding the slumberer. Also, a painting of the Last Supper. We could not begin to describe or criticise the paintings. Our only mode is to fix upon a few gems and study them. To run the eye over fine paintings, as we must do, is but to tickle the optic nerve for a moment. It leaves no impress upon the memory. After going through the Church of Santa Maria—which is unlike all others, being purely white within and without; after passing through the Church of the Jesuits, wherein fresco and tracery, substance and shadow, are intermingled so as to be confounded; after listening to the monotone of the chanting Franciscans, seeing the strange confessional with its penitent trembling at the ear-hole of the Father; after being shown about by sly Italian priests, until seeing and hearing became a burden, we ascended the hills and found, oh! how grateful a relief, in the promenades and villas above the city.

Let me give you a single description. *Uno disce omnia.* A long promenade hedged with telio, and winding about orange groves and fountains, led us to a flight of steps. Having ascended we were immediately in the midst of numerous fountains in artificial grottoes. Above, are clinging to the rocks and bared to the sight, the smooth twisted roots of the fig-trees. We ascend at this vestibule of verdure, through arched grape vines, and with the walls skirted with roses up—up—past terraces wherein are growing orange trees, full of golden fruitage, and exceedingly tempting to larceny. Here we stop upon a variegated pebble pave, while before us rises a yellow and white marble palace. Herein resides the poet and owner, the Marquis De Najora, whom we are informed is not yet arisen from his slumbers. Oh! luxurious idler and dreamer. All this paradise surrounds thee, but to woo thee to repose in that closed chamber. But it is of no use to moralize. Ethics must bend to beauty; subjectivity to objectivity.

All around the palace, amidst the foliage, are busts of the celebrated Genoese, among whom "COLOMBO" claims my first regard. Around, too, are cool, large grottoes made of shells, mirrors and spars. Other grottoes are frescoed upon the walls in mockery of the cool originals near. Paths lead through them and up to a higher vantage ground. Can it be possible? Must there be a higher heaven yet? Stay! Here is a name that rivets the attention, and there is a bust familiar as an American landscape. Under it is inscribed,

"ALLA MEMORIA DI WASHINGTON."

Canova stands near. Below his bust is a billiard room. Farther on is a seat, at least 300 feet above the city, from which we may grasp Genoa in one glance. Near by upon another hill is a large fortification in ruins,—the result of the popular commotions of 1848. Below are walks and trees of all kinds. The pepper-tree near the japonica; alche trees embracing the cypress and olive, lemons and figs; the cerino full of berries, and the umbrageous fraschino. Scattered among them are tall, rare Egyptian palms.

The fresh air comes up freighted with a rich burden of fragrance. All around the bay are arranged the pyramidal roofs of the superb city, varied by the towers and steeples of the churches; while the bay itself, fretted by a breeze ever so light, emulates the cerulean of the sky, save in that deep ribbon of blue which separates the rarer from the denser element. Up rises with the sound of voices and bells, and mingled with the song of birds (we mnst be faithful), the horrid, infernal music of unhappy donkeydom!

We had better seek another spot. If you are dainty about treading on lizards, you may let me lead. Here, upon the north-east, we have another view—a full sweep of the valley beyond Genoa. Yonder in that grove is the house where Byron lived for two years. It might well awaken the poet's soul to gaze up and down this valley of terraces and palaces. Beneath us is the plash, almost roar of waters. It is the aqueduct, so constructed as to empty its silver vein into a basin below, and apparently out of a grove. Trembling in its spray are oranges. Far above us even, rise other gardens and palaces, similar to this; and far above them are the eternal hills bare and comfortless. Now we may descend among flower vases, gum-elastic trees and roses, into the open street, to meet again the everlasting beggar of Italy. Whine away, poor human nature! it is your brother, made of the same mortal clay with yourself, who holds that regal palace, adorned with art, and garnitured by nature. False to the memory, and recreant to the hope of Italy, he sleeps in ignoble ease, while the garden of Europe holds within its enclosure a degraded, begging and outcast population, whose rulers are serfs to Austria, or puppets of France.

There are at least two thousand people now in the public

poor-house of Genoa, and God only knows how many more ought to be thus provided for. If beauty and art must flourish in these palaces and gardens at such an expense of misery, let the axe fall at the root of the poisonous tree, that its exhalations may no longer taint the mild air of this heaven-kissed clime. Let your marbles be overturned; your Correggios and Guidos be cut into ribbons; your frescos be whitewashed, and your soil of beauty indurated for ever.

But this, we thank the Creator of the Beautiful, is not the sacrifice required. He who made the fair so near akin to what is good; who gives immortality to both by the same law of his will, requires only the sacrifice of lustful power and absurd pomp.

We spent the last few hours of to-day in passing through some of the superb palaces, whose outside we yesterday saw. The Salle palace is perhaps the richest in its collection of paintings, although it had no golden room like another we visited. Vandykes, Rubens, De Vincis, Paolis, Guidos, and others, line the resplendent walls; while the never-failing fresco and statue meet you at every side-glance. One painting among them all I now remember distinctly. It is here for ever engraved. It is Tasso in the mad-house, at the foot of Rubens, while Montaigne, the French philosopher, stands near. The expression of the pale, woe-stricken poet, with his lofty sorrow and half maniac glare, as he kneels to be released by his visitors, has the very soul of Melancholy, not yet lost to Despair. It seemed to me, that in this picture I beheld the fate of Italy. Images of poetic grandeur surround her; the Past beckons, and invites her to search its repository for the influence of Example; the Future is lit up with hopes as beautiful as the angels which float upon her painters' canvass; but the spell of Despair hovers near where Melancholy is already seated. Oh! that the glorious soul of Massini might be created under the "ribs of death," which are even now visible beneath the rich vesture that nature has bestowed upon Italy!

X.

Rome,—Living and Dead.

"Hail to the great Asylum!
Hail to the hill-tops seven!
Hail to the fire which burns for aye!
And the shield which fell from heaven!"

Macaulay's Lays.

I.—LEGHORN TO ROME.

AFTER leaving Genoa, we resumed our career over the deep blue of the Mediterranean and touched at Leghorn, where we left our good company, Mrs. Stephens. We delayed long enough to see all that Leghorn could show, which is little more than a statue with four ugly pirates chained—a local monument, representing an incident in the history of the city worthy of the best Roman days. The son of a Doge was sent after a Corsair, whose piratical adventures were the scourge of the sea. He was victorious, and in the flush of success, hesitated not to break the quarantine laws of Genoa, by entering port in disregard of their provisions, the penalty of which was *death.* He suffered the penalty. The Doge's justice did not yield to the paternal yearning. The monument supported by four pirates attests at once the valor of the victim and the impartial rigor of the law and its executive.

We visited, pioneered by some whole-souled American officers of the U. S. steamship Mississippi, which lies here, the grave of TOBIAS SMOLLETT, the Novelist and Historian. It is a simple pyramid in the Presbyterian burying ground, enclosed by iron, around which flags and flowers grow, and snails crawl.—We then went aboard the noble steamer; and truly we were proud of our country and its foreign service. We were so fortunate as to visit the Mississippi, during a visit of the Commodore (Morgan), and were received most cordially by all. The ship was about to proceed—where no one knew but the Commodore and Captain; but it was generally thought that Kossuth and his companions were the object of the voyage East; and then (how they gladdened at the thought!) for HOME!

At Leghorn there is little to be seen. It is a large trading port. There is here little of Art or Beauty. The city is of recent origin, having been founded in the fifteenth century. Ferdinand the first, one of the Medici, encouraged Moors, Jews, persecuted Catholics from England, and others to come to Leghorn, where he granted them the equal privileges, which their descendants now enjoy. Leghorn is a free port; by which is meant a port where the custom-house bleeds you *freely;* even charging heavily for the privilege of landing.

We met on board the Mississippi steamship, which was lying here, Powers, the sculptor; and had the delight of his acquaintance, with a promise of its continuance at Florence. He had come down for the purpose of sending off his son to West Point. He was carelessly dressed, and hid beneath a "round-headed" felt, a rotund, pleasant face, and an intelligent, large eye of rare brightness.

A lady companion not unknown in the literary world, whose opinion is generally entitled to authority in matters of art, does not (as do most Americans, and all Italians) rank Powers as the equal of many other American sculptors, and simply because his chief work, the Slave, does not express the high-souled indignation and flashing scorn, or the exquisite distress which a female, situated as the slave is supposed to be—should exhibit. In this criticism, the most beautiful and truthful principle is disregarded, not alone in my humble judgment, but in that of the best writer upon æsthetics known in the realm of criticism, the German Lessing. In his "Laocoon," he seems to have had in his eye, the very form of the Slave, with its noble simplicity and sublime patience under indignity, and to have answered just the objection above made. "As the depth of the sea remains *forever quiet*, however the surface may rage, so the expression in the figure discovers in the midst of Passion a great and calm soul." Is not this the attitude and expression of the Slave? Where, in all the array of art in that Crystal Palace, can be found such quiet grandeur, such nameless simplicity of distress? —After the eye had palled with gazing on the gauds of the Indies and the south of Europe, I invariably found the heart (which has a reason of its own) impelling me toward the Slave; there to dwell in silence upon the beautiful result of that genius which gleamed in the piercing eye of our *American* POWERS. The idea of the sculptor is not, as the objector must erroneously assume, to follow nature; but his ideal projected from nature into the plastic air of his imagination. The Slave, if it were distorted with distress or wrought into an agony of indignation, would lose its auriole of calm glory, which ever shines in the subduing influence of the soul over the body.

We saw and passed the Isle of Elba, only notable for being the prison of greatness; and the morning of the 4th of June, found us in the harbor of Civita Vecchia, surrounded by massive walls. The place is distinguished for nothing except that it is the gate to Rome. The vexations of the custom-house are not so terrific as is imagined. We have found gentlemen in the officers. Let the traveller remember, especially if a lady, that the want of baggage is the greatest relief. Our ladies absolutely left all their trunks at Paris, and with a carpet bag apiece, have passed easily all barriers, and penetrated into the Eternal City.

2. APPROACH TO ROME.

The road from Civita Vecchia, which we traversed by a diligence conducted by a bob-coated bandit of a postillion, lies mostly along the sea. The country resembles Ohio in its rolling hills and wheat covered fields. Harvest time on all sides made the country seem busy. The road was lined with great loads of hay moving to Rome, drawn by beautiful cattle, with long polished horns and distended nostril—worthy to be sacrificed to Jupiter himself. We passed several old ruins, and among the rest the Egyptian tumuli, at Monterone, which were opened by the Duchess of Sermoneta, in 1838. They are now closed again. Vases were found ornamented with the lotus, and painted ostrich eggs were not wanting. We also passed the Cæritis Amnis, rendered classical by Virgil, as well as other places of historic interest. The rich twilight of antiquity began to gloom about the old towers and castles, which ever and anon we perceived upon the sea-coast. Especially should be remembered, the polygonal walls of a Pelasgic temple, near the picturesque fortress of Santa Sevaia, which was once the head-quarters of the Tyrrhenian pirates.

As we approach Rome, these interesting relics increase. The very dust which flies in our faces is without doubt as sacred as it is unpleasant. For the distance of twenty miles before we reached Rome, St. Peter's lofty dome hung its conspicuous architecture in mid air; and what was so strange, although we saw it, as it were a half mile off, we did not approach seemingly any nearer. Indeed we never suspected it to be the marvel of Michael Angelo, until within a few miles of Rome, when the certainty flashed upon us, that it must be *St. Peter's*. We had thought it a church of some village near; but the dome of the "Pantheon hung in air" became more apparent, and by this great demonstration, we were assured that it was Rome itself we saw! I doubt if there can be any feeling more tumultuous and grand, than that which ushers Rome into the chambers of the vision! It was sunset as we approached the Cavalleggieri gate; and before we entered it the moon had assumed her mild sway, casting over the palaces and vineyards which lined the Aurelian way, her

———"wide and tender light
Which softened down the hoar austerity

> Of ragged desolation, and filled
> As 't were anew, the gap of centuries;
> Leaving that beautiful which still was so,
> And making that so, which was not, till the place
> Became religion, and the heart ran over
> With worship of the great of old."

Can this *be* the fountain of Power, almost supernal? Power, secular in the past, which still rules our spirits "from its urns;" Power spiritual, in the Present, which gives the canon to more than the half of Christendom!

We passed St. Peter's, with its colonnades, and its deep shadows, swelling vast and beautiful in the silver sheen of the moon. Driving down the piazza of St. Peter's, we recognized the lofty and lonely Castle of St. Angelo, and in a twinkling we were on its bridge, the old *Pons Aelius*, and the Tiber rolled beneath! We could not discern the color of the classic stream. The statues upon the bridge looked grim and majestic! This is ROME! Not the foster child of the she-wolf; for ancient Rome lies at the extreme south. *This* is Rome of modern days, whose apostolical rescripts have engaged the British parliament for months. This is the powerless-powerful Pontificate, whose thunders may be hushed by the French cannon the next hour, but whose silent authority is ministered unto by thousands of handmaid churches and millions of devotees, throughout the world!

After passing through some dirty, miserable streets, we emerged into the region of palaces, darted down a dark avenue, and drove under the old forum of Antoninus, upon whose high, massive roof there is a building and a profusion of verdure,—and which is now used as a custom-house. While undergoing the customary search, we observed the eleven Corinthian columns of Greek marble. Some of the old architraves are preserved; but the bases and capitals are gone.

3.—French Soldiers.

The eternal city has so often been described, and its every column numbered, that it would be gratuitous in me to attempt any thing of the kind.

Thus far we had found our own way, without the aid of swindling guides, but here they are necessary. Not only guides in the human shape become essential, but Murray himself began to compensate us for lugging him about. In the latter is found every spot of classical association; and to undertake, even upon a small scale, to enumerate these, would be as foolish as it is impossible. A few general views will suffice. These shall be taken without pedantry and without color.

There is one object connected with Rome that intrudes itself at every step. It is the French soldier. The sound of brazen martial music now reminds me of him. Pope Pius sleeps sweetly, no doubt, under the everlasting marching, fifing and tooting of the soldier. I understood that some time ago he sent word to the French commandant, that the city was in good order and quietude; but France was as obtuse as an adder to the hint. Why? Austria was pouring her soldiers into Tuscany, and it was feared that Rome was their final destination. The Pope and Cardinals, it is said, even second the efforts of the Republicans in order that they may be free from the French rule. There are now in this city over eight thousand French soldiers, and ten thousand more are expected. They infest galleries, churches, gates, villas and palaces. Rome seems destined by the Almighty to answer for her past sins in the triple exactions of a military, ecclesiastical and civil domination. It was here that the nations of old, including ancient Gaul, lost their liberty, and it is here the nations, including present Gaul, now appear to enslave Rome herself.

4.—The Capitol View.

Passing through long lines of soldiery, we direct our course to Capitol Hill. From its tower, the general survey of the city should first be made. It stands between the new or Ecclesiastical Rome, and the old or Pagan Rome; between the living and the dead. This point is peculiarly appropriate and thrilling for a first view. It was here that Gibbon sat, when he contemplated the august relics of former glory; and saw starting from behind each fragmentary pillar or arch, the mysterious influence of Deity, writing the history of the nations. It was here that he first conceived the idea of writing the "decline and fall" of that city, the closing scene of whose magnificent career he describes as the "most awful in the annals of mankind."

At the base of the hill, on either side of the long flight of steps which have often been ascended by kneeling friars, is a fountain. The colossal Gemini are at the top of the flight, and a colossal bronze of Aurelius, on horseback, in the centre. On your left is the temple of Jupiter, which, like most of the ancient ruins, is *converted* from Paganism to Christianity. You find yourself, after many windings, in the tower. From the eastern view, immediately below, is the Forum, the spot which was once the heart of ancient Rome. The artist, upon the subsequent page, gives some idea of its position and appearance. It was here that Hortensius and Tully spoke, and winged words flew to the hearts of thousands through the same blue atmosphere which now surrounds these broken columns. Even yet,

———"The immortal accents glow,
And still the eloquent air breathes,—burns with Cicero!"

The temple of Vespasian, now only three columns; the arch of Septimus Severus, with its strange configurations; the temple of Jupiter—the Thunderer—are seen; and further on, down the Sacra Via, on every side are irregular piles of ruins; tow-

THE ROMAN FORUM.

ering up sublimely among which, like a crown upon the hoary head of antiquity, is the Coliseum. On the right, the eye is absorbed by the immense ruins of the palace of the Cæsars, utterly misshapen and haggard, clothed with rank grass, and opening by damp vaults underneath. It is not unworthy of the description of Byron, who saw it covered with cypress and ivy matted together; with hillocks heaped upon what were chambers, with its arches and columns crushed into fragments, and nothing left but the name—"Imperial Mount"—to tell how human greatness can fall.

As we stood looking upon the scene below, the eye ever and anon glancing toward the Tiber upon the right, and passing in one sweep its valley of relics, we could repeat almost in mockery the gratulations of Macaulay's lay, at the head of our chapter.

Mockery indeed, if we recur to the present. What a miserable set of people—what "a rakehelly rout of ragged rascals"—are those below; some laying in the shadow of the Arch of Titus; some pitching coppers near Constantine's Basilica; some digging fishing-worms near the Appian Way; others driving miserable donkeys and ox-carts; others working in the ruins for relics; and others making ropes upon that pathway where the spoils of the extremest east and west were paraded, where legions of victorious braves marched under the potential eagle, where Sallust and Livy, Virgil and Horace (jolly old Satirist!), Marcellus and Cato, all walked and talked, and where the fluent sonorousness of the Latin rung upon the enchanted air and made Oratory immortal!

The men of might rise from these gloomy vaults and pass again beneath these crumbling arches and pillars—an exceeding great army. History gives up its dead, even in the midst of temples desecrated by the smell of fish and the meanest of offices. Theatres loom grandly, even though converted into stables; and mausoleums and palaces rise far into the glistening air, although Stefano has therein a blacksmith shop, or Michael sells in them cabbages to poor Franciscans. What are all these sacrileges? Are we not in the proud capitol of that metropolis of which Julian said—"All the inhabitants of the (known) earth belong to her;" and of which Claudius could truly say, that she was the fountain of all laws? Was it not here that the Northern conquerors of Rome placed supreme power in the hands of a poor pastor, whose prerogative grew so glorious and powerful, that Charlemagne ascended the steps of St. Peter's to acknowledge it; and which seemed in outward splendor, as it was in real power, the visible vicegerency of God upon earth? Can we not discern, in the present abasement of that power, the hand of Him who is the author of all history; whose arm overturns the proudest steeds of Pompey and the columns of Trajan, the finest marbles of Aurelius and Augustus, and the most magnificent arch of the greatest Cæsar? It is worth while to come from the Western world, to see how GOD ALMIGHTY writes history, in which nations come and go, as rainbows. Truly, Italy is a conspicuous chapter in that momentous history; but is it all written? Would that her people could obey the inspiration of Massini:—"Give to Italy your thought, your counsel, and your blood. Raise it up great and beautiful, as foretold by your great men.—*Let it be one, as the thought of* GOD! You are twenty-four millions of men, endowed with active, splendid faculties, with a tradition of glory—the envy of the nations of Europe. Your eyes are raised to the loveliest heaven, and around you smiles the loveliest land of Europe. You are encircled by the Alps and the sea—boundaries marked out by God, for an army of giants. And you must be such, or—nothing!"

Shall it be nothing? When such sentiments can be thus uttered, is there no hope? Is man here but the insect caught in the unyielding amber of an infallible theocracy? Shall Popery, the joint tool of France and Austria so long, and soon, we trust, to be the tool of neither, for ever crush the energies of myriads of human beings? We will not cease to hope for the people. The reign of Injustice is not eternal—it feeds upon its own black heart. Dark though seems the prospect, we will strike up the cheering song:—

"When wilt thou save the people?—
Oh God of mercy, when?
Not kings and lords, but nations—
Not thrones and crowns, but men?
Shall crime breed crime for ever?
Strength aiding still the strong—
Is it thy will? Oh, Father!
No! say the mountains; No! the skies;
Man's clouded sun shall brightly rise,
And songs ascend, instead of sighs,—
God save the People!"

5. Our Consul and the Villas.

There is no keener delight while travelling abroad, than that which follows a meeting of friends and Americans. Especially is it the case, when these friends have opportunities of unfolding the mysteries which perplex the sojourner. Our Consuls have it in their power to endear themselves to their fellow-countrymen, in a peculiar manner. Not that they all do this; by no means. As to our chargè at Rome, Mr. Cass, we cannot refrain from expressing publicly the gratitude of our hearts, for the urbane and cordial manner with which he has received and aided us. He is well beloved at Rome by all. Even now at his house there is a young American from Georgia, who has returned from Syria with the fever, receiving the last kind offices to the dying from our warm-hearted Consul. The foreign officers of our government should all be such. I regret to say that, at some points, some of these offices are filled with foreign upstarts, who know just enough of English to treat you cavalierly, and who, in comparison with our good Consul at Rome, deserve no mention, unless it were a rebuke.

Mr. Cass has a fine gallery of paintings and sculpture. During the troublous times of 1848, he alone, among the foreign Consuls, remained. As money was scarce, and gems of Art plenty, and every thing precarious, he had the opportunity of purchasing the works of the masters at the most insignificant prices. He showed me a Guido, for which he paid five dollars, and for which he could now obtain hundreds. Works that he gave hundreds for, would now be fortunes to him, were he disposed to sell.

Through his kindness we obtained access to two of the best villas near Rome, that of the Borghese, and that of the Albani family.

The Borghese was formerly the great promenade of Rome Its park was even superior to Hyde; superior because it was every where adorned with statues of the finest mould. The commission of defence against the French, thought proper to upturn and destroy some of the finest parts of this villa; but the works of Art in the long galleries remain untouched. These galleries are entailed and descend with accretions from age to age in the same family. The park is but the wreck of what it was before the Revolution; but even now it is a miracle of a cool and beautiful retreat. One peculiarity of these villas is, that in their walls are placed the old fragments and inscriptions which once adorned the ruins about the Capitol. They are rare and weird in their potency over the mind; lulling it into a sense of the hallowed past, and making it contemporary with the great which they commemorate.

6. Italian Art.

Every where in these villas is seen *form;* here, minute and graceful; there, colossal and awful; yonder, fragmentary and mournful. But every where is *form.* Why—(for the mind must repose amid this continuous range of painting and statuary to ponder general principles), why this idolatry of the Italian mind, to form? In itself, it is but the quality of a material object. It cannot be destroyed, however, without destroying the individual subject to which it belongs. Matter, circumscribed and limited, is form; and to be beautiful it must wave or curve. To be beautiful in the highest spiritual sense, there must emanate from that form the passions of life in all their multiplied variety. The highest expression of passion may be represented in the human countenance, and this expression is beautiful in a threefold sense; physically beautiful, that is, independent of any expression of character; beautiful in the expression of some permanent and distinctive disposition; and beautiful in the expression of some emotion which we love or approve. The union of all produces that perfection of beauty, which to-day we have admired in the Curtius leaping into the Gulf; in the Venus of Canova, for which Pauline Borghese, the sister of Napoleon, sat; in the celebrated Apollo Sauroctones of Praxiteles, considered by connoisseurs the most exquisite bronze statue in the world, and in the ever young and seraphic Antinous, crowned with lotus, which, next to the Laocoon and the Apollo Belvidere, is the most beautiful monument of the Elder Art. This last gem, although it is over two thousand years old, glances in its white radiance, as if just from the hand of Grecian genius. These last two pieces are in the Albani galleries, intermingled with a host of lesser beauties, and surrounded with landscapes, urns, and marble pillars. In viewing them, you tread over mosaic paves of delicate workmanship; while above you, look down multiform beauties in enduring fresco! Out of the fine windows are leafy prospects and embowering glades, down which the white forms of Numa, Minos, Virginius, and Scipio, "move to your pausing eye." Fountains playfully burst into the warm air, and tinkle softly and melodiously.

We depart with a wondering, almost bewildered mind. How many throbs, wild and great, have followed the million pencil-touches and chisel-strokes, which have here imaged thought, to vivify the future! How many scenes of joy and sorrow has genius embodied, not of the ideal only but of the real,—"all compact;" for the ideal in its first prompture bounds from the *ovum* of the real, not at once full-fledged, but with the elements of aerial life, to be cultivated by classic myth, historic deed, and the "aims and triumphs of a hero's life." The material leaps docile into the arena of beauty, under the idealizing power of Art. The stony crypt of the gray past is penetrated, and becomes a star-strewn vault where imagination may gaze into the Infinite, and by gazing, learn to decorate life with forms of dreamlike softness and heroic grandeur.

With what endless repetition does beauty enshrine herself along these corridors of Art! Here all Homer is embodied; there the Æneid; and further on, the long line of Roman Cæsars shine upon their pedestals. As all the gods of all nations came to Rome and were absorbed in her Mythology, so they were all represented with their various attributes, acting in the sullen stone, and speaking from the dumb canvas. The phase of Beauty here

——— "repeats itself for ever,
And, repeated, ever pleases."

There is one statue which stands in the loftiest niche of my memory. We went to the Church of St. Peitro to see it. It is the MOSES of Michael Angelo! It is colossal, and was intended to form a part of the tomb of Julius II. Although it is not surrounded as the artist expected, yet its commanding expression and majestic mien make it more than Olympian. It is the leader and lawgiver of Israel. He has seen the Ineffable One upon Sinai! How awful and sublime is that terrific front! How meanly and indifferently are all the other niches of the church filled, beside this great work of the greatest of Artists! The beard and horns have rendered it obnoxious to criticism; but they give the air of the demi-god to the majestic marble. It may be that they are blemishes. There are spots even upon the sun.

Must Genius and Poverty ever go hand in hand? In the literary world it has ever been thus. In a national point of view Italy illustrates it. It was through suffering, that the brightest sons of earth were educated into the priesthood of power. The same enthusiasm which worshipped the charms of the Virgin soul—the " Perfume of Paradise,"—yet lingers here about its old haunts. It is seen upon the veriest ox-cart, whose figure-head is a beauteous Madonna. It shone in the filagree and mosaic of Italy at the World's Fair. It stares you in the face at every corner, where prints and paintings are exposed. It is carried upon the cane-heads of the merchant. It flows in the fleecy veil of the lady. In fine, is not Italy happily likened to the magic gift possessed by the girl of the fairy story, who dropped pearls and diamonds at every opening of her mouth, to the sad detriment and loss of her teeth, those homely but very needful functions of speech and mastication !

In these poor ideas about Art, I do not mean to be critical. I have neither the disposition, nor the ability, to criticise the great works, which are seen but to be admired without question. Universal taste has stamped its signet upon them, as infallibly as upon the Iliad or Æneid ; and though a thousand connoisseurs should " peep at them with the rounded hand," they would still shine peerless in their perfections, and permanent in their beauty.

7. Coliseum and St. Peter's.

The finest contrast which Rome presents is the Coliseum and St. Peter's. The one is at the nadir, the other at the zenith ; the one was dedicated to the destruction of that religion which now is enshrined in the other. The one is the marvel of antiquity ; the other is the wonder of modern time. One was used for the gratification of the meanest passions ; the other as the temple of Him who taught Peace and practised Benignity. Indeed the contrast might run on, until comprehended at last, in this, that the one was the offspring of Pagan power ; and the other the result of Christian power.

There are no two spots upon the round earth so full of interest It may, perhaps, be a matter of pleasure to my readers to hear from one who has been surrounded by influences common to both writer and reader, about these spots of celebrity, and the emotions they awaken.

Before reaching the Coliseum you pass through a long line of ruins, the columns of which are still standing, and out of the crevices of which long tufts of grass and flowers grow. The greatest part of the ruins is, however, fifteen feet below the ordinary level; and large excavations were made, in order to reach the marble floors. Many of the columns only show the capitals. This void has been filled simply by the crumbling of the walls. In the ruins of the huge arches of Constantine's Basilica, great fragments have fallen some two hundred feet from the roof, and have been moved aside to accommodate the goats and cows which herd there.

We entered the beautiful church of Santa Francesca, which is built upon the temple of Venus, and examined the floor. It is the same exquisite mosaic which was trod by the devotees of the myrtle in the time of Roman luxury.

Our eyes take in the old sites of at least fifty temples and theatres, as we look down the sacred way between the arches. On the right hand is the palace of the Cæsars, now owned by an Englishman, Mr. Mills, (Oh! Cæsar, where are your wounds now, and where is your Mark Antony to preach their woe?) who has torn down the little shops which once lined the way. Workmen are engaged in levelling the ground, and in breaking stone about the Coliseum. Their song really enlivens the dread desolation of the scene. An old fountain called *Meta Sudons* is near, wherein the gladiators were wont to refresh themselves after the labors of the ring. It was an important appendage to the Coliseum,—that splendid pile of irregular, circular, columnal ruins, which stand out the most perfect of the relics of Old Rome! The Coliseum is full of holes, out of which metals have been extracted; and its windows serve to relieve its dim arches with wild and broken light. As we approach it, we pass the Appian Way, the only refreshing street in Rome. Its long vistas of trees betoken the march of improvement in that direction. We approach the old structure. The warder unbolts the heavy gate. We pass under the arches, past a strange fresco of Jerusalem and Calvary, and enter the interior; and lo! tier on tier of heavy stone, covered with green, patched with brick work, and rising up into a huge oval, carved out from the clear vault of heaven, a great sapphire irregularly round! Birds are flying about the old walls, fig-trees grow here and there; a cross stands in the middle of the arena, and fourteen statues of our Lord's passion are placed around it. Deep, dark dungeons, in which the early Christians, prisoners, and wild beasts were kept, gloom about the place.

The amphitheatre is built principally of travertine. The external elevation consists of four stories. The area was once nearly sixty acres. There were four tiers of seats corresponding with the external stories, and these would hold 87,000 spectators! More than two-thirds of this immense building has been taken down, and now forms part of the palaces of Popes and Cardinals. The Coliseum was built by Vespasian in the year A. D. 72. Nearly 400 years saw it the scene of barbaric spectacles. At its dedication, 5,000 wild beasts (heavens! what a howling there must have been!) were slain. St. Ignatius here met the death of a Christian martyr; and how many more suffered in this same den of devils, history amply records. It has been used as a fortress, a woollen factory, then as a saltpetre factory, and finally sanctified with the "Pon. Max" upon it, and consecrated to the memory of the martyrs.

A stair-case led us up through the galleries to the summit. The view from one of the "rents of ruin" is fine. The temple of Nero, and a large garden of flowering pomegranates, almonds and figs, fill up the foreground; while the hills of Tivoli are spread out under a delicate haze of blue in the distance. The splendid Basilica of St. John Lateran lifts its fine proportions between. In front, we look across the Tiber to the green hills of the Janiculum, where Oudinot and Garibaldi contested for the city, and left the marks of the Vandal upon the beauty of Art.

Byron describes the Coliseum as he saw it by moonlight, and his description I read to our little company, from off a broken seat of

"That noble wreck in ruinous perfection."

We expect, if we can venture out under these delusive moon lights, to enjoy the dark waving of the trees in the blue mid night, and the shine of the stars through the rough old windows and recall the touching pathos of that marble gladiator of the Capitol, which personates the prisoner from the Danube, leaning upon his hand in the bloody circus, while his dizzy brain reels with the death dance, and he thinks of his hut upon his native stream, and his Dacian wife and young barbarians at play! The shout of thousands rings again from side to side, in this vast arena, as in fancy I see the gladiator sink beneath the blow of the kingly beast. Rome had here her holiday; what recked the poor slave's life?

Ah! different—far different—is Rome now! To-day I heard before the assembled Cardinals and Pope, a dark-skinned Abyssinian—a student of the Propaganda—grow eloquent in classic Latin, over the mercy and love of that Saviour whose precepts teach the equal right of all to live, and that—for ever.

I am now called away to see the Coliseum by moonlight. My heart bounds to behold the soft radiance of Dian flinging its lustre of beauty amid the rough and broken shadows, and among the enormous crevices and flaws.

We are returned. The dream is over. *Dream?* How else could float in the soft light of an Italian moon such a stupendous miracle of beauty. How lonely in their loveliness the surrounding ruins sleep in the mellow lustre!

On our way, we stopped a while before the column and forum of Trajan, to admire its rounded shaft, with its colossal figure and its broken columns, standing like sentinels about the monuments of the Past. The arch of Severus, the temple of Jupiter Stator, and the "nameless pillar with a buried base," stood silent as the tomb. What are they, but the *tomb* of buried power? Their gestures point backward to the abyss and rearward of time, to show what was, and what must be. The moon breaks through the arches of Constantine's Basilica, and glistens below upon the fragments which have fallen from the aperture. Now we pass under the arch of Titus; and the seven golden candlesticks are lit by the soft luminousness, and reflect evidence strong as holy writ, of the identity of the arch as the memorial of the conqueror of Jerusalem. Blot out all other records, and leave these candlesticks and this moonlight, by which they are made visible; and the greatest prophecy of old is proven by stone!

And now the Coliseum stands confessed in her garment of moonlight, *the perfect ruin, the sublimest structure in the world!* How its round walls glisten! Is it not perfect? Show flaw or rent or breach *now?* Doth not the clear shine, wall up, with its crystal architecture, each crevice, each window, each rent? Is not this material of richer lustre than even those rare gifts of the Pasha of Egypt to the Pope—the alabaster pilasters and columns which to-day we saw at St. Paul's? How full does the night scoop out of the huge circle its arches of darkness! Hundreds of these arches repeat the gloom around the vast circumference. The great area is chequered with irregular lights and shades, playing among every form, and rising tall and dreamlike, against a star-strewn and a moonlit heaven.

Within that circle, covering six acres, how much has been enacted; of sportive savagery and noble martyrdom, how much? Can it be that but one-third of what was the Coliseum only remains in that vast pile? Yes; for we have passed to-night, palace after palace, constructed out of its material; and we can see that the outer arches have been peeled off (as it were) time after time; yet so much remains that the imagination reels under the vision.

We drove around, taking in, with some few hundred yards, a small segment of the circle, when the glisten of a bayonet,

6

with a challenge in French, "*Stand!*" reminded us that even this pride of Rome was humiliated by the guard of foreign soldiery. Once it was not so. Gods! If the old Scipios, within whose dark tombs we were to-day, could only "revisit the glimpses of the moon" to-night, it would make their ghostly teeth chatter with rage, to see their seven-hilled city under the control of the descendants of those barbarians who formed part of their triumphal marches, and who, perhaps, to grace a Roman holiday, fought the beasts of that Coliseum which their descendants now guard.

We turned about. Finally we found admission to the building. The walls loom up much higher than they seemed in daylight. They seemed now close against the sky. A white fleecy mantle of cloud streams from the moon, and hangs over the jagged edges and outer rim of the theatre. The verdure is all silvered; and upon the north side, where the full radiance falls, looks like thin mist. The arches, doorways and crannies, are black upon that side, in bold contrast with the other, where they are lighted up. The stars glimmer down aud overpeep the horizon of stone—innumerably; spangling an awning of blue, richer than ever was spread at the royal tournament of old. A solitary bird startles the echo—so melancholy, from the darker side of the ring. This is the only sound heard amid the desolation. Shouts no longer crack the welkin; the roar of beasts no longer answers the greeting of the populace. Yet through these old walls, the storms of nearly two thousand years have whistled, and roared, and beat; yet it stands, the monument of Rome, and the everlasting testimony for that Christianity, whose early apostles met Death and gained the Victory in its inhospitable embrace.

We drove home past a temple in front of which are great piles of rocks. Among them, are water-gods, tritons, and horses colossal, around and out of which gush, in every direction, streams of water, falling into beauteous basins, clear as the moonlight which flashes against it, and musical as the birds which sing near its natural fountains among the hills of Tivoli. This is the sweet "virgin" fountain. It takes its name from an ancient story, which in bass-reliefs is told upon the lofty temple's face.

Why have we nothing like this in America? Why is Art so slow? It is because Time has been so brief with us. Nothing can make an American abroad feel how much his country has to do, as to see what strides others have made, who have been even less favorably placed. Ours is a struggle yet for the material—the needful. The Ideal will succeed, as the rainbow doth the sun and shower. We are following the true order of nature. With our Religion and Liberty we shall not have Coliseums, to remind future nations of any departed barbaric glory. Nobler temples will be dedicated to nobler purposes.

It remains for us to exhibit the contrast of the Coliseum,—St. Peter's; and to recall the reflections which that celebrated pile and the Vatican aroused.

Three visits to these spots have given me some familiarity with them; but it is not the familiarity which ceases to wonder, much less that which creates contempt. Neither is it that pompous procession of religious association, moving down the corridors, the aisles, and through the wilderness of stone, called St. Peter's, which excites so much admiration and wonder. It is the untold magnificence of Art, which on every side bursts upon the unaccustomed mind of an American. We have seen exhibitions of art at every step throughout Rome. Sometimes in the churches, it is in exceeding bad taste, and even disgusting. I do not remember, however, to have seen any thing *quite* so bad as a picture of the Last Supper, of which I have read, and which, I believe, was found in a church in Mexico—where the Cherubim and Seraphim act as cooks and scullions; one scouring a dish; another blowing a fire; a third frying eggs; while in the background, with head and wings prominent, others are passing round the edibles. But this specimen of Art will serve as a comment on a great deal of the worst Art to be found in Roman churches.

Its tendency is to unspiritualize every spiritual object—to *earthify* it, so to speak; to make it sensuous and tangible. Even in St. Peter's, where the boldest genius of his time, Michael Angelo, has represented God himself hurling the sun and earth into existence—this tendency is apparent. The culture of humanity is the prime object of Art. Is this effect produced by unsphering from the lofty temple of the soul those objects, which to be rightly influential, must be spiritual, and by degrading them to a niche in a human temple made with hands—temporal and not eternal?

The approach to St. Peter's is imposing. A great circular piazza opens before it, surrounded by three hundred and sixty large columns, gracefully surmounted by an entablature, upon which statues glisten in the sun. Stand upon the steps of the Basilica. The great circle of columnal grandeur bends about the high obelisk and the twin fountains. On either side, at right angles with the church, are the vaulted pathways, leading to the chapels. Upon the left rises the Vatican, with its intricate complexity of palaces. The crows, high up among the carving of the capitals, are rearing their young, and cawing like a company of Frenchmen. The plash of fountains hushes into Sabbath silence the air around. The colossal figures of St. Peter and St. Paul stand guardians of the place. Turning around—the eight huge columns which hide in their shadows other columns, lift on high the mighty temple of Catholic Christendom. The jutting cornice and tracery gracefully hang under niches and over windows, in and around which are figures with scrolls, sceptres and crowns. Far out in front (for the eye leaps about as if a strange spell were upon it) gleam white in the sun the angles and curves of the fine walks. No verdure relieves the extensiveness and massiveness of the view. Bass-reliefs, inscriptions, bells and clocks, furnish lineaments for the church's countenance of stone. As the eye ranges upward, covering the vast expanse of architecture, we may well exclaim with Gibbon: "*Here is the most glorious structure that ever has been applied to the use of religion.*"

Upon this spot where we now tread, scarcely a century after Christ, an oratory was erected by the Bishop of Rome, to honor the place where St. Peter was interred. Here Constantine worshipped the cross he saw in the heavens, and built the great Basilica. Here pope after pope added adornment to adornment, until the finishing genius of Michael Angelo completed the structure, by crowning its sublimity with the ever-during beauty of the Pantheon. What expense, what labor, what genius has been here expended upon a few acres! Indeed the expense of the additions to the pile were so great—extending over the reigns of forty-three popes—that the sale of indulgences was resorted to for the purpose of meeting it. This resulted in the Reformation. At the close of the 17th century the expense amounted to $46,800,498—exclusive of the sacristy, models, and mosaics, estimated at $900,000.

One is staggered which to wonder at—the power that can levy such contributions upon the labor of the world, or the genius which transforms rough masses of rock, cragged logs and trees, and even the mire on which we tread, into palaces, spires, temples, and forms of every variety of beauty and sublimity! Aladdin's lamp was a wonderful instrument in its day. It converted stones into gold, and carpeted the earth with velvet for the tread of kings and queens. The human mind far exceeds its magic power. At the bidding of Mind, this immense structure stood unrivalled and alone,—the towering grandeur of all time;

> "Worthiest of God, the holy and the true.
> Since Zion's desolation, when that He
> Forsook his former city, what could be
> Of earthly structure in his honor piled
> Of a sublimer aspect. Majesty,
> Power, glory, strength, and beauty,—all are aisled
> In this eternal ark of worship undefiled!"

When first I looked upon St. Peter's I confess to a keen disappointment. Its size seemed flattened, and its dome insignificant compared to the fancy of it I had indulged. No doubt the colossal size of the human forms about it, contributed to this effect, by giving a false standard of measurement. Indeed, it is so immense that the mind is bewildered in its huge details, and loses the sense of the immense whole. Byron accounts for the same impression, not by the lessening of the pile, but by the expansion of the mind under the genius of the spot. The church is about 806 feet long. The transepts from wall to wall are 450 feet. The diameter of the cupola is 195 feet, being a little larger than the Pantheon. The height of the cross upon the cupola from the pave is 435 feet!

But how can I paint with indigent ink the interior? At first sight, as I looked down the vaulted roofs and long nave, and up its swelling dome, I felt no holy awe, such as hushed the soul into stillness in Westminster and Nôtre Dame. The statues of popes, the paintings of saints, the sacred canopies and shrines, the presence of lesser *form* in its endless variety, attracted the attention, and disturbed the aspiration of the soul towards the Infinite. The Baldacchino, or grand canopy, cast into spiral columns out of the bronze taken from the Pantheon, and garlanded with gilded flowers and foliage, stands over the grave of St. Peter. The eye swims as it gazes upon it. This beautiful object breaks the awe-inspiring impression of the dome under which it stands. Over one hundred lamps burn around it, while below, is a shrine and the kneeling statue of Pius VI., by Canova. The concave of the church is ornamented with stuccoes and mosaics, while at the further end is the apostolic chair in bronze, lifted aloft under such a variety of ornament as can only be seen, not pencilled. Among the various statues is the monument to the Stuarts, by Canova. The outcast Royalty of Britain is here entombed in more regal state than Westminster could bestow. The gazer is informed, by an inscription, that James III., Charles III., and Henry IX., *Kings of England*, here repose! Some one should forthwith advise Macaulay of this large gap in his history. There is certainly one chapter omitted, if this inscription be true. Why will men for ever use the memorial of the dead as the instrument of lies? Shakspeare exaggerates but little when he says, that there is

> ————"On every grave
> A lying trophy: and as oft is dumb
> Where dust and damned oblivion is the tomb
> Of honored bones indeed."

But we will let the exiles of England sleep. Their arrogance no longer tramples upon the necks of our good Puritan ancestors. Their monument rises beneath a dome as glorious as the highest ambition of their God-anointed heads could imagine.

By the kindness of Mr. Cass, we procured a ticket of admission to the *Grotte Vatican*, the subterranean chapel, for our ladies; as ladies are excluded therefrom without a special permit from the Pope. This chapel is a part of the old Basilica, which yet stands over the tombs of the early martyrs. The original floor is still there, and there, too, is the tomb of St. Peter. As we passed it, with our torches and our company of priests, we observed before its secluded shrine a solitary monk, saying mass. Our guide and the priests dropped in adoration, while we stood involuntarily bowing before the strange spectacle. Around were the graves of the dead. The spectral shadows upon the mosaics and bas-reliefs peopled the narrow chambers; while gloom seemed here to linger as if in her own dark home. Our breathing grew short and our step fearful, as we wandered amid this home of departed priesthood. At last we emerged again into the nave of the church, with the prayer that our last repose might not be in such a corridor of stone and darkness; but under the pleasant light of heaven, amid the beauty of nature, where birds might sing, and in the place where affection should prompt and love to linger.

Having viewed the depth, we could not refrain from visiting the height of St. Peter's. A broad paved spiral staircase leads by gentle ascent to the roof of stone. One might easily drive up with horses and carriage. The top would form, also, a pleasant drive. On the walls are the names of the sovereigns who have been up to the cupola—a long list. This list might be increased considerably, if the American sovereigns were added. The roof seems to be a city in itself. Upon it are belfries, domes, houses, and other appendages of a city. Rome begins to grow small below. The head grows dizzy as the eye dares to descend—but we are not half up. The Pantheon stands before us upon the roof, surmounted by the brass ball, which seems some two feet in diameter, and into which it is said sixteen people may be stowed. Through winding stairs, by tugging and resting, and gazing out of the windows, we reached the top of the dome; and walked out into a balcony, whose railing is invisible below, and into the open air some 400 feet above the city. Below us are the flowering orange trees and gardens of the Pope; far to the south-east, the Coliseum and its brother-ruins fling their broken shadows to the earth; still further beyond, under an exquisite web of mist, lie in quiet beauty the hills of Tusculum, Viterbo, Tivoli, and the chain of Apennines. To the left, old Mount Soracte, of classic memory, whitens its top in the sky. Monte Mario relieves its baldness by a green summit, nearer to our view. Between, in dead long levels, the freshly-mown Campagna spreads its great carpet about the seven hills,—the dim blue fringe of which carpeting is none other than the Mediterranean, visible in a long line upon the left. The birds chirrup among the fragrant gardens, and fountains endeavor to climb upward, only to curl in beauty and murmur their music. The Tiber, seemingly a little run, plays awhile amid the foliage, glances, winds here and there amid the roofs below, and under the Angelo bridge, and then darts away towards the horizon, to mingle its thread of yellow in that fringe of blue.

Can we ascend higher? Try that perpendicular iron ladder,

and follow it upward through that long narrow neck, and you are in the ball itself! One of our ladies even dared it. The atmosphere was a little tepid to be sure, owing to the proximity of the ball to its solar companion. The echo of our voices clinked so fearfully on its sounding metal, that—yes—it was really fearful. The sense of being so high, worse than the sight through the little chinks, made me feel more indescribably queer and qualmy than ever I felt before. The trembling knees almost refused the rapid descent, while pespiration dropped beads from the brow, like Oriental trees their "medicinal gum." My second ascent in company was much more pleasant. Our guide told us a good story of an obese Frenchman, who, the other day, squeezed through the neck and found himself puffing in the ringing ball. He illustrated the old Horatian fable beautifully; for he could not take the back-track. He was too, "Oh, call it not fat—*oleaginous*," to return. There he remained between heaven and—earth, half a day, all the while dripping like a fountain, or like Falstaff, "larding the lean earth," until the profuseness of the perspiration had somewhat diminished the rotundity of his corporosity, when he descended from his oven, a sadder and a thinner man!

On our return down, we saw the lamps with which St. Peter's is illuminated on festal days. Boys are tied in strings (like Wethersfield onions), and hung down in great garlands along the lamp lines. Three hundred and eighty-two men are also on hand to assist in the lighting. Every column, cornice, and frieze, and all the details, even to the summit of the cross above the ball, are to be lighted. In eight seconds, at a given signal, 6,800 golden lights leap into being, and burn against the gigantic architecture—a firmament of fire!

The sun dial, upon the roof, points to the hour of ten minutes after *thirteen!* which is *our* ten minues after nine. Another singularity as to time in Rome is, that at noon a gun is fired, a black ball rises over the college, and every bell rings the time. It produces quite a startling effect on the stranger.

8. The Vatican.

Our visit to the Vatican occupied two days, and then it was but a hurried glance at this great repertory of art, learning, wealth, and power. We democrats from the land of home-bred simplicity, and brick and mortar unadorned, were completely confounded by the constant succession of splendors. Here are the spoils of Time as well as its trophies, arranged amid the museums and libraries, and long—long—galleries. Here learning and taste have added building after building, so that the appearance of the whole from St. Peter's cupola, is that of a long parellelogram of stony fabrics, with squares between, wherein are gardens of rare exotics in great urns, together with fountains of clear water. Long arbors of boxwood, and high impenetrable hedges of living green, spread around the palaces, upon which we may look, as we stroll through the long corridors, filled with busts, statues, sarcophagi, and old inscriptions inserted in the walls. To compute the extent of these halls, miles might be used. The number of apartments may give some idea of its extent. It has eight grand stair cases, 200 smaller ones, 20 courts, and 4,422 apartments.

The wonders from Etrusca and Egypt form separate museums, and speak an earlier civilization than that of the elder Romans. In the cabinets, relieved by porticos, were the choice statues of antiquity, some greatly mutilated. We had many opportunities of applying the principle "*ex pede Herculem.*" Here were statues of every animal, as well as every variety of men and divinities.

Separate and apart from all others stood the great group of the Laocoon. The greatest offspring of the chisel stood before us, in his torture dignifying pain,

> "With an immortal's patience blending."

Oh! what a clench was that old man's; what expiring sadness upon that young brow, and what speechless, anxious agony upon that other! For two thousand years that "long envenomed chain of living links" has wound about the father and his sons, awakening the deepest sympathy of the soul, while it illustrates the power of the Rhodian sculptors over the passions of man.

What a contrast to this is the APOLLO BELVIDERE, which is near. Light enshrined; every dignity personified; Love deified; Beauty, Manliness, and Genius, encased gracefully in the white marble; all that rivets admiration in the fair, or awakens awe in the supernal, stand

"Starlike around until they gather to a God!"

Raphael's "Transfiguration," which we afterwards saw, could not compete for the guerdon beside these marble marvels of antiquity. The stone has no peer in the canvass, in the highest heaven of art.

It would only weary, to tell our visions of beauty and uniqueness, which every where gleamed from niche, ceiling, wall, and floor; throughout library, portico, museum, and cabinet. Here were the maps of all Italy, worked in the wall. There, the mosaic manufactory, where all the saints and popes are starting a new race for immortality in the panels of St. Paul. There, the richest tapestry of Gobelins, with the Bible illustrated by a strange order of art. Every where the same impression is produced, of endless variety, in the mazes of which the mind is almost lost, like a child amid a wilderness of foliage and beauty. Yet out of all these endless varieties and "brotherly dissimilitudes, arises the goodly and graceful symmetry," that speaks the common reason and nature which we all wear under God, our Maker. Through manifold phases and turnings the mind ascends to that apex of generalization, where Unity kisses heaven and is embathed in its pure light; where the greatest as well as the least obey that common law, whose seat is in the bosom of God.

9. The Pope at Service.

Yet one may wander amidst all these magnificent results of Art in the Vatican and St. Peter's, yet fail to catch the spirit that breathes throughout them. The actors in this splendid theatre should be noted, as they move in full costume to fill the swelling scene. This was our object upon the first Sunday morning in Summer, as we drove toward the piazza of St. Peter's. The Pope was to officiate in Sistine Chapel. Our ladies had doffed the gaudy-ribboned bonnet and donned the simple black veil. We had, according to the rule, put on dress-coats. The crowd increases as we drive within the enclosure. Following our guide along the straight corridors, and through files of the Pope's Swiss guards, dressed in fantastic yellow and black, with Turkish pants and long spears, we were ushered by soldiers (one of whom valiantly siezed my cane and straw hat and bore it away in triumph) into the chapel. The ladies we leave seated, looking through great gilded bars, while we pass in among Austrian soldiers, Franciscans in their brown robes, and a goodly variety of other holy orders.

While waiting the entrance of His Holiness, the mind can find delight in examining the "Last Judgment" of Angelo, frescoed upon the wall of the Chapel. Every variety of Hope, Doubt, Despair and Beatitude, beam upon us from the figures upon the wall. Within a sacred enclosure, over which tip-toed curiosity can barely peep, is a green-carpeted floor and tapestry hangings, with an altar and a throne. Seats are arranged for the Cardinals, who soon begin to pour in, dressed in great red gowns and skull caps, attended by servants in purple. After bows and crosses, the servants proceed to unroll the trains and seat the Cardinals A very hearty array of old Romans they seem, with their arms under cover, their gray hair shining, their lofty brows and intelligent faces bespeaking good living as well study and reflection. Most of them kept up an inaudible prayer.

One fine, old, tremblingly fat gentleman seemed to be beyond the age of piety, but his habitual prayerfulness still played upon his lips. He reminded me of Chaucer's monk, who repeated all his terms,

> "That he had learned out of some decree,
> No wonder was, he heard it all the day."

Directly, buff soldiers, with gilt helmets and drawn swords, rush in to guard the door. I thought, at first, that there was a sudden insurrection, knowing that in matters of power, as poor Pius has learned, "there is but one step from the Capitol to the Tarpeian Rock." But no—the choir strike the high notes; the doors beyond open, and—"Voila!" the Vicegerent of God appears in his tiara and cloth of gold! Around him swarm ministers of every degree and shade of color. He kneels: the rustle of red Cardinals shivers in the hallowed air, and all kneel. Then he ascends to the throne—a fine-looking, full-faced man, graceful and dignified in his bearing. Power he seems to wear as a familiar garment. How graciously he extends his hand to the Cardinals, who severally leave their seats, attended by their attendants in purple, carrying their trains. They, bowing, kiss the hand, or, as I was informed, the diamond brilliant upon the Pope's ring, as a token of reverence. An inferior order prostrate themselves, and tip their labia at the shoe of His Holiness, upon which is a cross of silver. In the mean time, seraphic music from the Pope's select choir ravishes the ear, while the incense titilates the nose. Soon there arises in this chamber of theatrical glitter, a plain, unquestioned African, and he utters the sermon in facile Latinity, with graceful manner. His dark hands gestured harmoniously with the rotund periods, and his swart visage beamed with a high order of intelligence. He was an Abyssinian.

What a commentary was here upon our American prejudices. The head of the great Catholic Church, surrounded by the ripest scholars of the age, listening to the eloquence of the despised negro; and thereby illustrating to the world the common bond of brotherhood which binds the human race. I confess that, at first, it seemed to me a sort of theatrical mummery, not being familiar with such admixtures of society. But, on reflection, I discerned in it the same influence which, during the dark ages, conferred such inestimable blessings on mankind. History records, that from the time when the barbarians overran the Western Empire to the time of the revival of letters, the influence of the Church of Rome had been generally favorable to science, to civilization, and to good government. Why? Because her system held then, as it holds now, all distinctions of caste as odious. She regards no man, bond or free, white or black, as disqualified for the priesthood. This doctrine has, as Macaulay develops in his introductory chapter to his English history, mitigated many of the worst evils of society; for where race tyrannized over race, or baron over villein, Catholicism came between them, and created an aristocracy altogether independent of race or feudalism, compelling even the hereditary master to kneel before the spiritual tribunal of the hereditary bondman. The childhood of Europe was passed under the guardianship of priestly teachers; who taught, as the scene in Sistine Chapel of an Ethiop addressing the proud rulers of Catholic Christendom teaches, that no distinction is regarded at Rome, save that which divides the priest from the people.

The sermon of the Abyssinian, in beautiful print, was distributed at the door. I bring one home as a trophy and as a souvenir of a great truth which Americans are prone to deny or contemn.

I had seen the successor of Hildebrand and the tenth Leo. I had seen the head of that anti-Christ which Luther fought, with so much rancor and heroism. I had seen the visible impersonal power, which in former times had made Henry the IV. stand for days bare-headed under the blasts of an Apennine winter, praying admission to humble himself; which in the person of Alexander III., whose tomb we saw, placed its foot on the neck of the haughty Frederick, with the expression, "*Super aspidem et basiliscum ambalabis.*"

Glitter and pomp greater than what I had seen, could not surround the human form.—Homage such as could only be shown to the representative of the SAVIOUR, was here exhibited; but one could not help feeling that the mighty heart of Popery as it once throbbed, was not here. Whether there be only one more niche in St. Peter's for Pius Nono to fill, and thus end the long line of the Holy Fathers, I did not observe; but this I did feel, that in Italy and in Europe, the *people* had become alive to the compact of tyranny between the Church and State. To borrow the biting sarcasm of a Westminster Reviewer of last January; "Even the most superstitious have had their faith terribly shaken, and have seen the infallible successor of St. Peter ignominiously kicked out of his apostolic chair by his own children, and ignominiously kicked back again by a French army. Heaven had no thunder to hurl destruction at the impious republicans; and neither virgin nor saints were in the clouds arrayed in their best clothes to give honor to his return. His exit and his restoration were both vulgar, and the poor old man is forcibly held in his uncomfortable seat by his masters in Paris, Vienna, and St. Petersburg, trembling every inch of him, lest the whole machine should again be blown to shivers, and he *himself be snuffed out like a candle that is no longer wanted because daylight is come.*"

The weakness of the pontificate does not spring from any peculiar corruption such as formerly severed the best part of Germany and Switzerland from its influence. Children no longer sing, as they did in Melancthon's time;

> "Of all foul spots the world around,
> The foulest spot in Rome is found."

That weakness springs from the increased light of the age. The holy wicks only shone awful and potential in the dim twilight of ignorance; but then they were the only lights a misguided world possessed. Pius is well meaning enough. His countenance bespeaks a quiet and tender heart. He lacks decision of character. He fears to take a step that will end disastrously to the people. Let me illustrate by an incident that occurred the other day. Some French soldiers were stilettoed a few nights since, apparently for smoking, which the Italians detest. Some six Italians were arrested and condemned to death. The Pope, as it was in his power, reprieved them. The French Commandant sent Pope Pius word, that if he were not permitted to execute the sentence he would resign and go home; thereby intimating that difficulty would follow. The Pope timidly yielded; and the six men, who are now in the Castle of St. Angelo, are to be shot.

This state of things cannot last. Secret societies bound together by sacred oaths, and resolved for republicanism, are known to exist here. They comprehend the greatest part of the people. Silence—which seems as "harmless as the rose's breath to a distant passenger" is the result of secrecy, and betokens, in fact, the hushed breath of that liberty which, as Grattan has it, will not die with the PROPHET, but survive him!

What reflections ensue upon leaving these vestibules of Power and Splendor? Do they humiliate the poor and humble wanderer from the distant shores of the Western world? Thank God, No! Under our own *free* sky, we have a temple of worship, whose pillars stand upon no slavish foundation, and whose dome was reared by no traffic in sin. Jewels we have, sown every dawn upon the fertile earth, well worth whole satrapies of power; tapestry dyed in sunsets of gorgeous glory; and forms of freemen—"lords of the lion heart and eagle eye"—every one a POPE,—moving in individual independence—accountable to God alone! And as we take a last look at the gorgeous interior of St. Peter's Basilica—at the vast fabric, with its vistas and aisles opening on every side—as high thoughts lift the soul upward to its fount—as the rich light streams in, through and upon dim religious forms—as we feel the blest effluence from God,—half lost in the contamination of man—as the idea of Eternity grows upon the soul with the eye moving upward and upward within the swelling dome; still—*still*, the home of the loved and the free land of our birth is ever the prayer and the burden of the full heart.

10.—The Cardinals and Politics.

It was a wonder to my unsophisticated mind how these Cardinals here, were supported in their stately pomp. I wondered no longer when I learned some of the secret springs which political churchmen have the opportunity and the will to touch. You may see their carriages rolling by, adorned with arms and liveried servants. They live in sumptuous style in splendid palaces. When elected, a salary of about four thousand dollars is attached to their office, as well as the tribute of some foreign Bishopric or ecclesiastical establishment. They are the sources of power, and this affords them an immense revenue. With very few exceptions they are said to be profligate and corrupt; and this they are, without the mitigation which the warm blood of youth and ignorance might furnish.

The prominent cardinal is named, I believe, Antonelli. He was formerly a Bandit, and condemned as such. Gregory XVI. found in him, a shrewd, ingenious, gifted mind, and attached him to his household. He rose rapidly in the priesthood, and now exercises the controlling power in these States. The Pope has more heart than sense. He is a kind, generous, tender-hearted old gentleman; exceedingly fallible in judgment, and weak in decision of purpose. He has qualities which fit him for the head of a church, but not for the head of a troublesome civil organization. He has been so keenly reproached for bringing all the trouble of the Revolution, by his liberality, that he has committed to others political matters, and now concerns himself simply with the affairs of the church. If he could only dissever the civil from the papal power, he would give Popery a tremendous influence which it now has not, throughout the world;

especially in the United States, where the democratic principle can brook no constraint from any other influence.

What I have said and shall say about the Catholic religion at Rome, has reference simply to its connection with the state; which unholy alliance, ever fraught with corruption to both, whether at Geneva, at Canterbury, or in Rome, must be deprecated by every American who is proud of his own Constitution and who loves its liberal principles.

What I have said in relation to matters here, might well be said by any intelligent American Catholic. God forbid that a single blot of intolerance should blacken my poor pages. I have studied with too nice a heed the human heart, and its relations to man and to God, ever to color facts or aggravate prejudice, where conscience is the arbiter of conduct, and God alone its Judge. I have remarked, too, with pride, the great difference between the Catholic religion at home and abroad. As well accuse Protestantism of the absurdities of the Shakers, as Catholicism of some of the absurdities I have seen practised here in the churches. *Churches?* Not so. Only one church, that of St. Augustine, and called the church of the common people, was the scene of what in America would be called, or would seem, idolatry. We entered the church to see its singular *bedizenment.* The pillars were hung with silver ornaments as high up as you can see. The church was darkened; only lighted by candles, whose glare made it glitter like a hall of flaming diamond. Some say the silver and jewels are bogus and paste. Of that I am not able to speak. It would be no marvel if they were all genuine. The prime object in the church, is a large image of the Virgin, holding the Son. It occupies a niche near the door. It is decked out in all the beads, tinselry and gaudiness of an Oriental Indian Princess, while the environment is one blaze of jewelled light. Neck, arms and shoulders, are hung with necklaces and bracelets. The figure of the child was quite encased in the glittering splendor. Lights burn before the altar continually. Around this altar, are numbers bowing and crossing; while every moment some one passes up to the image, and wiping its silver foot, kisses the toe once, sometimes twice,—crosses, and retires to give place to another. While we stood there, perhaps five minutes at least, a dozen devotees performed this ceremony. The richly dressed lady enters, and with lace handkerchief wipes the sacred foot, kisses it, and is followed by a beggar in tatters, whose sleeve and lip answer the same office. And yet, as we look around and see the pious, upturned, happy faces of the worshippers, seeming to be gladdened by the radiance of the Virgin, as they repeat their Ave Marias; as we remember that from childhood these habitudes have been forming, and as we recall the tremendous power of religious emotion, we cannot but sympathize with the devotee, who seeks the intercession of the sweet Virgin to save from sin and woe.

Far otherwise is our regard toward the pampered Cardinal of Rome, if I am to believe what comes to me upon the best authority. Let me give you a fact. During the Revolution, our Chargé had access to many places which upon ordinary occasions were barred. In one of these penetralias of power, he read, in Latin, a law by which if any one, dying, signified to the attendant Cardinal his wish to leave him his estate, all that was necessary upon the death of the person, to obtain the estate, was for the Cardinal to proceed to the Sistine Chapel and make oath to the bequest, when all other wills were set aside, and the Swiss Guards were ordered to put him in possession. The Cardinal, at the dying hour, had the power to command all out of the presence of the dying man. You may thus see what a handle of iniquity is this statute. Well may it be kept close. "*But is it ever put in execution?*" Listen! The head of one of the oldest of the noble families of Rome, named Franjapanelli, was about to die. His friend, the Cardinal (I cannot spell his name), called to "see him off," and administer the holy wafer. He had before solemnly disposed of his immense property among his children; the greater share to his eldest son, who had *mar-*

ried an American lady, and the rest of his estate satisfactorily. He died at night. The next morning the Swiss Guards put the Cardinal into the family palace, and into all the other possessions, and the family out upon the world penniless. This was just before the Revolution. The eldest son became a Republican and died in defence of the city. His widow is pressing her suit in the ecclesiastical courts, but without hope. The court is made up of Cardinals or Priests, who are without soul or sympathy. Not having families, they know no tender ties of father or husband. They sit in frigid iceberg dignity, in the large marble palaces, and never warm except in the lust of power or profligacy. Yet the only tribunals of Rome are constituted of such. They have no record. They have not even that respectable appendage of a Court, termed *lawyers*. Bribery is their argument, and corruption the conclusion of their justice. We may truly say, that to press a suit in that tribunal, would be to appeal to sullen stones. Here, if any where on earth, the " learned pate ducks to the golden fool." The English chancery is beatitude to litigation in such a place.

I hope the Pope will create no Cardinals for America. It was rumored that Bishop Hughes was to have a hat. The ill success attending the Wiseman experiment in England will prevent Papacy from creating any Cardinals in Protestant countries. His Holiness, who seems to fancy our Chargé here sufficiently to consult with him, informed him that there was no foundation for the rumor of an American Cardinal. Mr. Cass rather advised him against the step; although he explained how perfectly easy the matter would be received in our tolerant country.

Mr. Cass trims his diplomatic sails very neatly, and has run between Scylla and Charybdis without so much as a single leak. While he explained to Mazzini and his friends the operation of republican institutions, and loaned them our constitutions, he protected Cardinals and Priests in his house from popular fury. He has been well repaid for the latter services

He showed us two Bibles which he received the day before yesterday, one in manuscript, *one thousand one hundred years old, illuminated on parchment!* The other in print, being the first edition of the Bible in 1440. The former was presented by a monk from the convent of Mt. Sinai in Egypt, and the latter by priest from the monastery of Vallambrosa, near Florence. He afforded protection to these priests during the siege. Poor fellows! He could not persuade them to sleep *in* his bed, but they would sleep under it, in humiliation and fear. The first Bible is one of the rarest things of the kind known. One of the capital letters was under process of illumination it is said for a year. No one but an old cloistered, patient monk, could have made it. The Vatican boasts of but one more ancient than the above manuscript Bible. It is a Bible in the capitals of the sixth century; but it does not compare with this, as a specimen. The Secretary of State offered $800 for it, to place it in the Vatican.

Priests meet us on every hand. Rome is thronged with them. As I write long processions of monks in black and white crape, and in brown robes, move under our window, chanting for the dead body which they bear. Some rich man has died, and left a paul a piece to these poor monks, to sing his soul out of purgatory.

I passed upon the Corso one of a fraternity composed of the noble and rich, completely hid in a rough sack, with two holes in it for his eyes. He was on a mission of mercy, begging for the poor and afflicted. It was one of the peculiar sights of the Catholic metropolis. A procession of similar penitents, guarded by soldiers with lighted candles, passed yesterday up to St. Peter's.

A brisk correspondence has been lately going on between the Papal and Austrian ministers, in relation to the troops of Austria. Austria had quartered in the States of the Church 30,000 men at an expense of over $100,000 per month. The Papal Secretary wrote to the Austrian, that at the present, circumstances and the budget demanded a reduction of the troops to ten thousand. The Austrian replied, that the present posture of affairs required the presence of all. The Secretary rejoined that the Papacy were the judges of that. The matter has been left to the arbitrament of the French minister, who will certainly side with the Papacy, and then look out for squalls in the camps. Austria cannot yield her influence at Rome. France is keenly jealous of hers; and it is shrewdly suspected. in more places than in England, that her policy is to colonize Rome with French, and reduce the Eternal City to a dependency upon herself. And so they play the game—knocking Popery, as boys do a ball at "two-hole cat," between them. I would like to remain here a little longer to see the sweetness of this union of Church and State in other phases.

Two cases illustrative of the nature of this government have come under my eye. We found our Minister yesterday in hot water over the case of a lady from America, who was about to be imprisoned by the police, because her villainous servant had run up bills which she would not pay. A servant at the Hotel, Dominichino Pollano, who is a Piedmontese and speaks English, just received a passport to leave Rome in three days—why? He was a Republican. We intend to 'annex' him to our company, and take him to a land of liberty.

How beautiful and benignant seems our own Constitution, which holds aloft from the power of priest, whether in surplice or white neckerchief, the Palladium of our liberty. We had Lord Baltimore and Roger Williams, early in America, while in Europe, contemporaneously, persecution wielded the sword of the magistrate, and even gloried in indiscriminate massacre.

By the way, that reminds me of the settlement of a question, long mooted by the Protestant and Catholic reviews. The former contended that the Pope had a coin struck in honor of the massacre of St. Batholomew. It was denied strenuously by humane Catholics. Last week, Mr. Cass found at the Papal mint, one of the coins with symbols upon it, representing the Destroying Angel vindicating God's church.

Far better were it, if such illustrations of human depravity were always as rare as that long questionable coin. Even in this little squib theological about a coin, we see the greatest passions of mankind in the arena. One side is ready to believe all wrong, the other all right. From opposite sides they approach human nature;

> "And would have fought even to the death to attest
> The quality of the metal which they saw."

Between all extremes, few look for truth in the middle; yet there it lies all golden in its neglected placer. Men move over it for centuries, too proud to stoop down and winnow, with the purity of reason, the rich ingot from the dirt and dross.

11. Palace of Nero and the Church of Lateran.

The palace of Nero, which we first visited yesterday, lies beyond the Coliseum, in the southern part of Rome, amidst the arches of triumph, and the ruined aqueducts. We pass to it, down that sacred way, which Horace was accustomed to walk, *meditans nugarum*, he did not know what. We did not follow his example. These scenes were *not trifles* to us; but stern mementoes of fallen might.

The custodian, who is ever ready when a few pauls are to be made, lighted his torches; and we began to descend through those chambers wherein dwelt the worst of men, and the most brutal of Emperors. The rubbish and dust had been removed from the damp cool vaults; and by our torches we could discern upon the faded walls the ancient paintings, and beneath our feet splendid mosaics. Nero's "Corridor of Thought" was shown us, where the fell monster was accustomed to aggravate his hellish deeds by meditation. We were shown his old bath-rooms. These were all filled up by Titus, who built a palace above them. The caterpillars and lizards abounded in every point where light could penetrate. It was in this place that the famous statue of Laocoon was found.

How strange is it, that all these ancient sites can be determined with even more certainty than the corners and monuments of our quarter sections. Not strange either, when I remember that I saw to-day, at the Capitol, inserted in the walls of the old Senate House, a great number of stone tablets, or plats of the ancient city, which were dug up in a perfect state; and by means of which, one point being given, all may be determined.

The money of princes and nobles has been prodigally expended in excavating and disinterring; so that the floors of most of the ancient temples have been reached, and something confirmatory of their identity has been found. The Roman villas, the palaces and the Vatican, abound in inscriptions and monuments dug from the various structures of antiquity.

We went to the Basilica of St. John Lateran, farther out to the southeast. This is the oldest Christian church, and takes precedence even of St. Peter's. Constantine founded it. It contains some precious relics. It ought to, as it is over fifteen hundred years old. While the monks were chanting under the lighted candles, we looked at the colossal marble statues of the Apostles; were shown the *same* table upon which the last supper was taken; the stone upon which the four soldiers cast lots; the broken pillars of the temple; the impression of the Saviour's feet when he appeared to St. Peter, to warn him of his approaching death; the well of the woman of Samaria, with some *crosses* (?) on it; the slab under which the Saviour stood to measure his height; and a hole in a board made by the miraculous fall of a consecrated wafer, from the hand of one who doubted the real presence! "Can such things be, and overcome us like a summer cloud, without our special wonder." I had the audacity, lawyer-fashion, to cross-examine one of the monks as to the identity of the relics. A seraphic smile of pity for my incredulity broke over his Italian visage, as he assured me, that there was no question as to the authenticity of these marvels. The vault of this church is gilt with the first gold brought by Spain from Peru, and gleams finely from the lofty ceiling.

After visiting the sacristy, we emerged again into the region of ruins; in which men in long gowns were sweating under loads of hay, raising it aloft among the chambers of ancient power. My risibles were excited by a strange-looking set of little trotters, over which was a load of hay, a man, and behind a boy. The animal was the patient donkey; about the size of a good dog. He does most of the work here. I noticed that the wheat harvest had already begun, although it is about the first of June, and Rome is farther north than Ohio.

I never saw such a collection of lassitudinous mortality as lay, about noon, under the shadow of the wine shops near the Tiber. Some were prone and asleep upon the soft side of a marble slab, with, very likely, an ancient pillar for a pillow. Some hung their unshaven faces and uncut heads upon their breasts—pictures of the last Romans!

12. The Capitol and the Tarpeian Rock.

After examining various ruins, we again ascended Capitol hill, through the forum; and began our examination of the fine collection of antiques, pictures, sculptures and frescoes. The buildings on the Capitol piazza were designed by Michael Angelo. Like most of the present buildings, they are so built, as to include a part of the old buildings, upon whose sites they are erected. We first entered the senate-room of old Rome. The temple of Jupiter stood here. Its pillars, however, are now to be seen adorning numerous churches. The battle pieces illustrating Roman history gleam from the wall. Laws, written upon marble, and from which Rienzi demonstrated the ancient popular rights of Roman citizens, are inlaid upon the walls of the staircases. The busts of the Emperors and of the philosophers are separately congregated. Chambers are set apart in good taste, for statues of particular classes, among which is the splendid collection of Canova's busts. In one of the rooms we found the famous bronze wolf, a monument of early art, which has given rise to many learned disquisitions. It was found under the rubbish of the Capitol. Cicero and Virgil have rendered it classic in Latin; and Byron has given to its honor, one of his rich stanzas, which I read to the old animal, charging her to

> "Guard her immortal cubs, nor her fond charge forget."

Romulus and Remus are drawing from her kindness the milk of conquest. One of her legs is torn by lightning, by which she has been recognised as the thunder-stricken foster-mother of the babes.

Paintings from the finest masters allure the eye, but their number renders it impossible to describe, or even to remember them. The celebrated 'Hope,' by Guido, is here. A fine copy of it attracted our attention, and we succeeded in obtaining it. Passing through the hall of bronzes, glancing at the colossal and miniature forms of gods and heroes thick as autumnal leaves on every side, we are at last ushered into the room of the "Dying Gladiator." It is not alone immortalized by its perfections of form, attitude and expression, but by the touching pathos of Byron's description. *It is a wounded man, dying.* This idea is written in every lineament. No one can meditate upon the image, without a feeling of melancholy, even tearful. The posture is so graceful, yet so gently yielding to the languor of Death, that all nature seems to have been invoked by the artist, to give unity and expression to his idea.

> "He leans upon his hand—his manly brow
> Consents to Death, but conquers agony."

A nobler idea could not be more beautifully carved. It is the highest attainment of that Art, which would give to Soul, the supremacy over the marble as well as over pain itself! This image is well associated in our minds with the grandeur of the Coliseum—that glorious pile wherein gladiatorial strength and brutal cruelty met so fatally and so frequently, and where the patience of heavenly martyrdom shone resplendent in the agony of Death.

Down through dirty streets, out of whose high windows clothes are drying, we pass to the Tarpeian Rock! An old woman, in a big straw hat, answers our bell. We pass into a garden of flowers and fig-trees. Far down the yellow waters of the Tiber, not so large as our own Muskingum, wind under a slight scarf of mist, while on the left, beyond those great piles of massive ruins, known as the baths of Caracalla, and between them and the blue, but dim hills of distant Frescati, sweeps the Campagna. We approach the precipice, "whence the Traitor's leap cured all ambition." It was some seventy feet in height. It consists of a mass of volcanic tufa. But it is greatly filled up now. Beneath us are the crockery roofs of little houses. The rocks, like most of the ruins, are terraced off and used for raising vegetables. Where the great criminals of Rome received their punishment, a few old women, with knitting needles at play, guard a wooden door. We plucked a few flowers as souvenirs of this remarkable locality.

13. Graves of Shelley and Keats.

We should not forget our visit to the temple of Bacchus, which was a preface to our tenth day's experience in Rome. While looking at the strange wine-jugs and mosaics, we were compelled to listen to the clucking of frightened chickens and the gobble of unromantic turkeys. We saw where the Horatii and Curatii fought, and we threaded the great halls of Caracalla's baths, in which large numbers of peasants were making hay, amid ruined walls. Here Shelley used to wander and clamber, while he composed his "Prometheus." That noble poem was chiefly written upon what he called, from its magnitude, the mountainous ruins of Caracalla, and among the flowery glades and thickets of odoriferous blossoming trees, which are extended in every winding labyrinth upon its immense platforms and dizzy arches suspended in the air. The bright blue sky of Rome, and the effect of the vigorous awakening spring, and the new life with which it drenches the spirit even to intoxication, he says, were the inspiration of the drama.

Alas for poor SHELLEY! Rome was to him the scene of a sadder drama, in the last act of which, the drapery of the life he so earnestly dedicated to Beauty, was dropped for ever. We visited his burial-place in the old English grave-yard. We found the "cors cordium" engraven with his name, and the verses which symbolized his change "into something rich and strange,"—upon a plain, flat, almost black marble slab. A few tall cypresses wave above it, while near and almost covering it, is an old ruin above the wall. The snails and caterpillars lazily crawl over the memorial. Near it, is a proud monument to some Englishman, killed in hunting over the Campagna. Around, are graceful stones and elegant monuments to the unknown, as far eclipsing the humble slab of SHELLEY, as his name does theirs. Chaplets hang on theirs. None on his. No flowers decorate the spot, where the heart of SHELLEY sleeps from its fitful throbbing. The wind moans piteously in the funereal cypress above him. Joy seems to hover over every other grave. Neat box-wood hedges surround other stones. Even the great pyramid of Caius Cestus upon the right, is decorated with green and flowers. But the narrow home of SHELLEY's heart is bare and flowerless, black and gloomy. Can it be that this apparent neglect springs from prejudice against the young skeptic SHELLEY? Is the grave of him who wrote "Queen Mab" to be slighted, and shall no flower grow over that heart that sang the "hymn to intellectual beauty?" Ye birds that charmed so sweetly the soul of poetry in SHELLEY living, have ye no carols for his repose? Yes, yes—before we can leave the spot, or brush the tear from the eye, a blithe spirit, bird-shaped—but

"Bird thou never wert—"

with the gush of melody such as SHELLEY's own sky-lark carried up to the gates of heaven from her dell of dew, began a song of rare music from the heart of the cypress, relieved the sombre gloom of his tomb and kindled rapture in the soul!

Plucking a twig of cypress, we passed into the other graveyard, where the body of JOHN KEATS lies. The yard is grassy, surrounded by and surmounting old Roman streets. No trees shade the small upright marble which tells so sadly of him, whose name was not writ in water. A few poppies and yellow flowers, emblematic of his "Sleep and Poesy," grew from the sunken mould. A short inscription told of the bitterness of his critics and the sensibility of his heart. But we feel that the fine Grecian soul of KEATS lingers not about this resting-place of his mortal remains. Doth it not burn where SHELLEY saw it through the inmost vale of heaven?

> "The soul of Adonais like a star
> Beacons from the abode where the eternal are."

We leave the graves of SHELLEY and KEATS with a mournful step. The place of their repose, amidst the relics of Roman glory; the similarity of their genius and destiny, and the companionship they bear in the neglect of their countrymen, make their resting-place the most interesting tombs in the world. Immortality more fadeless than marble, has placed their image in its Pantheon of poetry!

The church of St. Sebastian contains nothing in itself wonderful. We visited it for the subterranean catacombs, which extend (incredible as it may seem), twenty miles around and beneath Rome. A brown-clad, red-nosed, cross-eyed, Franciscan lit our torches, and we descended with him into these receptacles of the dead. After winding where the old thieves, of which Cicero speaks, were accustomed to hide, and where the ancient Christians also were concealed, we were at last relieved by daylight. I am not partial to such underground promenades, with tallow candles and a sinister priest. Here was once the tombs of St. Peter and St. Paul. We returned home past the perfect little temple of Vesta, near the Tiber; gazed into the light yellow stream, wondered at the self-regulating fishing-net, moved by the water, a Yankee-Romanism; passed through the region of cobblers—all at work out doors, and as queer a group as ever I saw; noted the babies, whose little heads peeped out of great bundles of swaddling-cloths, looking like infantile live mummies, under manifold wrappages; turned our eyes on the numerous shrines which lined the different ways; mingled with priests in black broad brims, and with French soldiers; saw the famous arch of Janus, over 2,500 years old, running 300 yards to the Tiber, and full of crystal water from Egeria, which the poor were carrying away for its *virtue;* and with our mosaics, our flowers, our memories and wonderments, we sought repose in the hotel.

14. The Paul, and the Palaces.

The paul (a small piece of money equivalent to our dime) is a potent agent in Rome. It has magic. Prince Arthur's horn could hardly do more, as an "Open Sesame" to the portals of beauty and antiquity here. What Spenser says of the horn, we may as truly say, with little alteration, of the paul;

> "No gate so strong, no lock so firm and fast,
> But with its *jingling* noise flew open quite or brast."

The palaces of the Pope and of the nobility, the churches, the tombs, the baths, the villas and the temples,—every thing in Rome opens with the palm which clasps the paul. Whether it is the dark rooms where Nero meditated his cruelty to Christians, and Mecænas his kindness to poets; whether it is in the old church of St. John Lateran, which Constantine founded, or the temple of Bacchus, now adorned with an hundred paintings of martyrs in misery; whether the Tarpeian rock, at which the traitor trembled; whether it is Saint Sebastian with its gloomy catacombs, or its neighbor, St. Paul, about to boast the most splendid pillars of alabaster the world ever saw; whether the grounds where KEATS and SHELLEY lie in their silent homes,—even at the Capitol itself, where dignity in the person of the old Roman Senators, more potent than arms, beat back the invading Goths, —in every place of pride, power and antiquity, the obliging Italian, more courteous than the Frenchman, bows you an entrance, and gracefully takes your—pauls! Saint *Paul*—not Saint Peter, should be the presiding saint of Rome. No one can complain that his orisons are not answered with such intercession. Let it be said, to the eternal honor of the eternal city, that among its characteristics is an eternal opening of galleries, villas and palaces, and an eternal outlay of pauls therefor.

A few pauls opens for us the—palace of the Cæsars! Shakspeare, in the person of Hamlet if I remember rightly (I have no pocket editions along), made imagination trace the noble dust of Cæsar stopping the bung-hole of a beer barrel. Shakspeare did not see the *reality* of the Cæsarean humility. We felt it, as we trampled on the sacred dust of the imperial palaces, for a paul apiece. We marched over the grounds on which Augustus built; over the houses of Cicero, Hortensius, and Claudius, which Tiberius increased, to which Nero added his golden house and Titus his beautiful palace; trampling amid the cypress and rose walks, ilex, grape-vines and red flowering pomegranates, peas and beans, and over arch reared on arch, and choked up vaults, in which midnight keeps perpetual silence; and around all which creeping vines and yellow flowers cling,—and all comprising about a mile and a half in circuit—for the which we paid—two pauls! Royalty in ruins is cheap. Royalty in splendor will be cheaper than that, in the "good time." This palace is on the Palatine hill. The temple of Apollo was formerly connected with it. A very singular Chinese house, built by Mr. Mills, who "owns the fee" to the palace, is the prominent object above the ruins. Among other places of interest we were shown by our guide Stefano, the bath where Seneca bled to death. The compartments of this palace are immense. Villas and gardens spread out over them on every side: yet the position is prominent even now. From almost any part one may range in vision far to the south, from the Coliseum, the Campagna, the pyramid of Cestius, the Sepulchre of Metella, even to the Albanian and Tusculan hills. Below us—far below, are the Farnese Gardens, elegantly laid off. Under us, wherein were enacted scenes of power, whose effect flashed from the Thames to the Danube, you may find peasants in long coarse shirts, sweating under the hot hay which they are lugging into the stables! Fortune turns her ever-shifting wheel,—the king goes down, the peasant up!

15. Fountain of Egeria.

How refreshingly different in fact and association is the fountain of Egeria, which we visited shortly after. Through freshly-mowed fields of hay, over gentle undulations, and under cordial umbrage of orchard trees, we found our way into the vale of Numa's nymph. Turning around a hill, and passing down, we stand pleased to hear the dripping and gushing of water. Farther along, and we see under an overhanging hill of foliage and flowers, the classic fountain. Its presiding goddess is broken, but her reclining form is still visible. Stone paves surround her, upon which the lucid lymph gushes and sprays. Of course we drank the water. We would not show the least disrespect to the spirit of Nature, which Numa quaffed in such glorious goblets at the hands of the nymph, and from the influence of which Rome received her first great impulse. The eternal "*rub-a-dub*-DUB" of the French soldiery reminds me, as I write, for the hundredth time, that the people who stole the female Sabines, and respected Numa, have most wretchedly deteriorated.

While in Egeria's pleasant vicinage, which brings Ohio to mind at every step, we might describe Metella's tomb, so celebrated by Byron's stanzas. You know how sweetly and touchingly he puts the queries about her *incognito* as to character, wondering who she was—"the lady of the dead"—whether she died young in beauty, with the hectic light upon her cheek; or old—surviving all her kindred; and winding up with the unsatisfactory conclusion—

> "Thus much alone we know—Metella died,
> The wealthiest Roman's wife.
> Behold his love or pride!"

A conspicuous tomb, ivy-garlanded, 70 feet in diameter, solid with walls 25 feet through—it has stood stronger than the fortresses of power, for nineteen centuries!

16. The Pantheon.

You must pardon my omitting many lesser beauties, for the Pantheon is the central orb around which all revolve, and by which they all shine. But who is not familiar with the Pantheon? Eighteen centuries ago it was described with admiration. Fire, pillage, flood and rain have wasted their efforts in vain. Its beauty seems destined to be a glory for ever. So perfect are its proportions, that Pagan and Christian, Greek and Vandal, alike found in it the spirit of beauty, which is common to all God's creatures. Hence its singular preservation. It is only 143 feet in diameter, and 143 feet high. The portico is composed of sixteen columns of oriental granite, with capitals and bases of Greek marble. Each column is about 50 feet high. The great bronze doors speak of classic times. The interior of the temple is a rotunda, supporting a dome one half of the height, or 71½ feet. Niches surround, which Michael Angelo gracefully converted from places for Pagan deities into places for saints and martyrs. Only one of the old pieces of statuary remains—an ancient Vestal, now bedizened with the frippery of jewels, and answering as the presiding saint of a shrine, before which numbers bow in silent adoration. The dome rises majestically, and is divided into square panels, originally covered with bronze. Every thing in the shape of metal has been removed, save the brass ring which supports the aperture above. The effect of this rising dome, and the open space, is very imposing.

The clouds are seen floating over the miracle of architecture, like fairy ships in a sea of azure. The eye and the dome swim with them, dizzily entranced. The sunlight, spiritually thin and transparent, slants in beauty through the aperture, and down the swelling dome, illumining a shrine and a marble saint. Apollo seems enamored of the place, and fills it with his presence.

The perfection of architecture is said to consist in the ability of the columns to support the entablature; just as that wall is perfect which supports the roof. The idea of utility is connected with that of beauty. Out of their marriage, in "sweet union doubled," springs Harmony. This harmony breathes in the Pantheon. It extends from the portico to the smallest capital; from the largest niche to the nicest tracery; from the swelling dome to the majestic whole. It is the grace and charm of the Pantheon. It is the fit tomb for Raphael, whose sublime genius towered so finely to-day, as we gazed on his "Transfiguration." His remains are under one of the shrines, before which a ghostly father was saying mass. Annibal Carrachi also lies here in his company.

One of the first things which attracted our wonder was, that so large a temple *seemingly*, should be so small in fact. This is designed. Madame de Stäel says, that it proceeds from the great space between the pillars, and from the air playing so freely within, and still more from the absence of ornament, with which St. Peter's is surcharged. This latter fact will account for the seemingly small appearance of St. Peter's, compared to its actual size. But in the Pantheon *every* concomitant is present, to make it

> "Simple, erect, severe, austere, sublime,—
> Shrine of all saints and temple of all Gods
> From Jove to Jesus—spared and blessed by Time;
> *Looking tranquillity!*"

Passing out of the Pantheon, you will find the step to the ridiculous at its door, where an herb-market, a puppet-show, a crowd around a fiddler, and a "natural *panram*," as our guide

ST. PETER'S, FROM THE JANICULUM.

termed it, are presented. The hurly-burly of old women, and the chaffering of buyers of cherries, radishes, apricots, etc., rise amid the plash of fountains. Rome is never without these latter beauties. Here, aqueducts are copious and clear. After entering a palace or so—among which is the Rospigliosi, where we saw Guido's splendid fresco of Aurora being copied by several artists—we ascend, for a closing view, the Janiculum.

17. The Janiculum.

We pass by the prison wherein the Republicans are confined; we pass across the Tiber, and through the region inhabited by those who call themselves the descendants of the old Romans. I only saw one of them. He was over six feet without boots—wore baggy, dirty linen pants, and a questionable coat. His head gloried in a red cap. He moved a Roman Ichabod Crane, the ghost of Famine, Campbell's *last* man, or whatever else you please—only do not call him an old Roman. If you do, burn Tacitus and Plutarch.

We ascended into that part of the city where the French and Italians fought. Men are engaged even yet in mending the wall. We can see where it has been breached and patched. The picture which follows but faintly delineates the scene. The so-called palace of Garibaldi, as well as its adjacent buildings, are in ruins. Marks of musket and cannon balls are plenty. In the finest gallery of Rome—the marble room of the Colonna Palace—we saw a cannon ball lying upon a white step, with the marks of its ruin yet apparent in the broken marble. It had entered one of the windows. Every where about Rome, especially on the western side, are the marks of no ordinary, nay, of a terrific struggle. We drove up to the fine fountain of the Janiculum; saw far, far down, the French cavalry practising, the colonnades and Basilica of St. Peter's, the Vatican with its rich gardens and palaces, and all around us that Campagna, which seems (as has been beautifully said) to be wasted, as if the earth, fatigued by Glory, disdained to be productive. Passing down, I observed a gravel mound by the road-side, with two rough crosses of wood stuck on it. It was the grave of some four hundred brave fellows, (God bless them, for the priests did not, even refusing them decent burial,) who fell here, defending the young Republic from the invasion of perfidious foes,—foes who should have been friends. May the Avenger—No! Injustice, false and foul, is ever its own Avenger. The human heart contains the whip of scorpions. Think you, no tears water that little mound—no curses are muttered over those rude crosses!

18. Farewell to Rome.

Before leaving Rome, we visited the theatre. It is cheap in price and poor in quality. The box, to the first, is only fifteen cents. It looked odd, that theatre did, under the open sky, with the seats of stone, and a few hundred lazily laughing at a comedy which was only pantomime to us. We could see that it was a love scene, anyhow. Love knows no language, you know. For all that we could understand of what a big-whiskered servant in a Duke's disguise was saying to a pretty Baroness, enamored of his swaggering air, it might have been as well the Kickapoo.

Time gallops fast amidst orange groves and picture galleries, ruins and roses, Villas and Vaticans, music and mosaic. As yet the confusion arising from the multiplicity of objects, all intensely interesting, prevents me from giving prominence where all is so beautiful and bewitching. I could as soon tell "which nymph more neatly trips it before Apollo than the rest."

We are about to close our sojourn at Rome. Ten days were never as full of incident to us. We have mingled in every variety of life, have recognized our own kind in the smiles and woes of the oppressed and beggared, have spared no effort to renew the great scenes which were here enacted, and no pains to learn the present state of things in this anomalous government.

These ruins and temples, relics of departed power,—how boldly do they contrast with the scenes recorded in our chapters upon the World's Exhibition! What new phases have been produced by modern civilization! What strange elements of life are the offspring of Christianity!

Now farewell to Rome. Upon this Sabbath night we leave for Naples. Right sorry are we that we could not wait till Wednesday, the time fixed by the Pope for our presentation to him, on the kindly application of Mr. Cass. But no: already we are in our vetturino, parting the crowds at St. Peter's Piazza, and making toward the gate in time to be out before it should close for the night. How finely Rome, and especially St. Peter's looked at the setting of the sun, as we drove for the last time over the bridge of St. Angelo. The castle towered up round and grand against the sky, with its figure of St. Michael and his drawn sword, standing out palpably beautiful. The Basilica of St. Peter's, from which we parted with regret, looked gloomy, with its long shadows and great colonnades; but how coolly refreshing was the relief furnished by the twin colossal sheafs of water, bending over with their rich harvesting of spray.

We are on the highway. A moon of red and gold burst out of Rome, to light us over the Campagna. Hushed and stilly was the repose of Nature over these plains which once shook with the tread of legions, and which was once adorned with the splendid residences of the lords of the earth! Now and then the silence was broken by the encouraging cry of the teamsters, who were moving toward Rome with their loads of hay. We drove past old towers brightened into new life by the light. We looked timidly out for some romantic rascal of a bandit; but the Campagna disdains such puny heroics, intoxicated with its olden glory. As we passed each glen, or hill, I looked in vain for that respectable personage, who has so long resided in the covers of novels and in the brains of boarding-school misses. He was not to be seen—that deep-browed, whiskered bandit, with his blouse and sash, his sugar-loaf hat all plumed, and pistoled belt, his fore foot planted firmly, and his profile painted dimly between the eye and the sky—not he.

Now we pass a man with a sharp ironed stick, pricking tardy oxen homeward—now a diligence hurrying along, in muffled mystery. We hear a low, mellow sound, much like music heard in dreams. As we approach we see a new moon, "dipped, not drowned," in the Mediterranean ; but broken into myriad lights upon her mobile bosom. Soon we halt, to rest upon the shore of the sea, and amidst ruins upon which the silver waves dash, and over which they leap in filigree spray. Here romance may fill her goblet and drain it in gladness. We do not need the bandit, to complete the scene. A sweet voice from the auberge struck up an Italian song, while I sat upon a ruin, writing at midnight, by moonlight, in my journal ; our ladies all the while ecstatically predisposed, and ready to fall in (love with) the Mediterranean for joy!

The next night we slept upon this same sea, right soundly, in the midst of moon-lit waves, oblivious,—while our steamer was bearing us southward to the place where Beauty loves to breathe in her own selectest home.

XI.

Naples,—its Loveliness and Horror.

"Hunc igitur terrorem animi tenebrasque necesse est."

Virgil.

MY pen moves to the soft and silver purling of the waves against this delicious shore. Our hotel is upon the Bay of Naples—only divided from its cerulean waters by a garden of flowers walled in from the sea, and against which the gentle undulations sing their madrigals of sweetness. The eye wanders over the "most beautiful bay in the world," now clothed in its morning garment of transparent light; while past our window the sail-boats fly and the oars flash. Upon the right, there rises gently from the bay, hills of fruitage. Naples swings about circularly, and white as if newly washed. We begin to realize that there is a lovelier nature in this sunny land. The breeze comes gently warm and deliciously laden. The sparkle of the waters has more diamond points. The horizon kisses the heaven with a warmer blush, and the heaven bends over with the witchery of beauty.

In a land where the fruitage "drinks gold even from the mid-winter air," it might be expected that nature would be richly adorned in this middle of June. The consummation of this southern Italian scenery may find expression in the familiar hymn,

"Here *every* prospect pleases,
And only man is vile."

We woke up in the Bay of Naples; that is, our boat was therein. A band at the fort was laboring as hard as it could with brass, to destroy the soft influences of the place by their clangor. The jargon of boats assists the band. Naples lies around us; her domes swelling under the loftier hills, whose trellised terraces bespeak the favorite home of Bacchus and Pomona. White-dressed soldiers are apparent all about. The isles of the bay sleep sweetly and smilingly under their Arachne web of haze—the favorite resorts of Lamartine; Ischia, the home of Graziella; Procida and Capræ, the selectest spots wherein Paul and Virginia might fully know the "unreserve of mingled being," and where the brow of nature is imbound with the golden rigol of love! Vesuvius, twin-peaked, gracefully rises from the bay, with her slight scarf of white smoke curling from her top. Do you wonder that amid yon isles, set in the sparkling azure, and amid such a sweet circuit of beauty, the genius of the French poet, wild as that of Ossian, and tender and melancholy as that of Rousseau, dropped pearls of rare loveliness?

We are called ashore, and there, amid the police and custom-house officers, the lazaroni and hotel-runners, we feel that angels do *not* people this beautiful land. Soon the lofty window of our hotel becomes an observatory, high and aloof from all human disturbance, where the eye and the mind, wearied as it has been with the creations of art, can drink in the spirit of this incomparable scenery. There are no harsh edges or determinate outlines of things; but all is blended into soft and mellow unison —a harmonious flow of beauty. The breeze breathes over the bay in flickering shadows, as if a great spirit were moving upon its face. Within this amphitheatre of rocks and groves, there lies something deeper than mere imagery. It is the inner and tranquil *soul* of beauty—

"Deep bosomed in the still and quiet bay—
The sea reflecting all that glowed above,
Till a new sky, softer, but not so gay,
Arch'd in its bosom, trembles like a dove."

But we might for ever dwell upon these *features* of beauty, and still receive no lasting good, no joy other than that transient bound which pleasure brings. Nobler influences should emanate from such exquisite external forms. If we would feel the "passion and the life of things," we must perceive God's excellency, love and purity, enshrined, all crystalline, in the water as it rises in flowers of white and falters into music below, and in the sky which bends over in its warm livery of lustre. That soul which cannot here find new splendors in the grass, new glories in the flower, richer tintings in the fruitage, love unutterable in the landscape; and which cannot rejoice with nature in her wedding garment, and sing her epithalamium, must be "dull as the lake that slumbers in the storm." Sensation here becomes lulled, form is melted, the soul is transported, thought even dies in enjoyment; and the hymn of praise rises, without effort, to the first Good, first Perfect, and first Fair. Is it wonderful that the ancient Roman senators and citizens here expended untold wealth to make Baiæ their summer resort? Is it strange that Virgil here sought entombment by the sweet murmur of the limpid wave of Parthenope? Is it curious that Cicero here listened to the soft and sonorous lapse of the eloquent sea, curling full and graceful as one of his own *ore rotundo* periods? Is it startling that the luxurious people of Pompeii and Herculaneum lingered here under the very shadow of destruction, spell-bound by the Siren of the shore?

But stay! had we a poet's pen, wherewithal to lose oneself in labyrinths of sweet utterance, there would still remain that "drainless shower" of beauty, which again I have just seen flooding the heaven and the earth; whose element is light, whose music is the undertone of love, whose fragrance is the stilly prayer of the humble heart, and whose aspiration is to walk with white-handed Hope and pure-eyed Faith, in such soft, rich radiance, where summer smiles ever in the gardens of God! One should have the golden flush of Landon's prose, and the resources of Burke's imagery; the Grecian loveliness of Keats, and the fusing sensibility of Byron, all elevated by the devotion of sweet Jeremy Taylor; or their nearest combined approximation in the intense feeling of the mild and lovely, which drops from the pen of Lamartine, to utter the sentiment and soul of this scenery of the south !

Mr. Cass showed me a painting of Neapolitan scenery in his gallery at Rome, which I pronounced an excellent *Idealism* of some genius who had glimpses of celestial shores, where rose-tinted waters make melody on gems and gold. "You had better wait, sir, until you see such a heaven and such water at Naples, before you pronounce this ideal." So I have. I am content to believe the painter has failed to do justice to the original. I ordered, with his permission, a copy of the landscape by the same painter, to take home to my friends, as the evidence of my enthusiasm. "Oh! what a goodly earth is ours !" is the ready exclamation at each gaze from the window. There *is* music here full and tender ; but like that in Hamlet's flute, it cannot be brought out unless one knows the—stops. There *is* beauty in that bay, now glittering with pearl and ruby, amethyst and emerald, turquoise and diamond ; but like those gems in the enchanted cave, they must lie unseen, unless some genius of magic would illumine my page with Aladdin's wonderful lamp. I neither know the flute, nor possess the lamp ; still "sweet will be the dew of these memories, and pleasant the balm of their recollection."

The singular contrast to this beauty towers up above the bay, and holds within its molten heart the elements of Destruction. God has implanted amid this garden the mountain of Vesuvius, and opened to the view of the luxurious people the ruins of buried cities. Truly is it said, the dwellers here live upon the confines of paradise and hell fire ! We bear evidence of both. Yesterday we visited Vesuvius and looked down its crater and saw there —————— !

Before I tell you what I saw, my reader had better ascend with us. After engaging the good guide Antonia, and preparing a basket of lunch, we drive around the shore, hugging the bay as long as possible. Palaces alternate with shops ; fine vistas

SCENE NEAR NAPLES.

of orange gardens through high portals, succeed to dirty houses, at whose doors pigs and donkeys are tied. We pass the king's palace, well guarded and frowning. He seldom comes forth, poor prisoner; for he is afraid of being shot. Well he may be. We enter some fine piazzas with colonnades; but "none to speak of," after seeing St. Peter's at Rome. It is the hour of noon; and every body is sleeping, except the ever-laboring donkeys. We observed at the great granary, the largest building in Naples, some hundreds of workmen, all lying prone upon the stones, asleep—a strange group! Men in long brown woollen caps, driving cows, oxen and donkeys, sometimes all in one team, hold the reins—asleep; and we distinctly saw one strapping fellow, *ahold* of his donkey's tail—a common mode of guidance here, walking along—asleep. The rumbling of our carriage disturbed his dream of paradise, which consists of apricots and maccaroni. There is one portion of the population still awake, that is, the beggars. Our carriage was thronged with them when we stopped; and as we moved, they ran for hundreds of yards, holding up withered arms, opening diseased eyes, and piping their theatrical anguish most piteously. Children, dressed in no gaudy, *unnatural* way, play in the sun, in primitive, Eden style. The famous Neapolitan curriculo dashes along, loaded to the top and bottom, with dozens, though seemingly no larger than a go-cart. The picturesque costume of the people lends an air of romance to the drive. The brass harness of the donkeys, from whose backs it rises in queer shape some feet, flashes in the sun. These same donkeys perform other important functions for the lazy people, some of which are represented by our artist, in a happy style. It is no caricature either, as I can verify. Long lines of fruit venders are ranged along the streets. Still we drive and drive, occasionally looking upward, and finding Vesuvius just as near and just as distant in the clear air as ever. The city seems a never-ending one. New-York is small compared to it in length. Its population is more than half a million, it being the third city in Europe.

At last we stop, after riding long miles. Our guide informs us that we are over *Herculaneum!* A door opens, torches are lighted, and our company (eight Americans) descend. We pass into the great theatre, which is only partially excavated. Unlike Pompeii, Herculaneum is buried deep, and is not so easily displayed. The grand entrances to the theatre and niches between (wherein a marble statue was found), the long circle of corridors, the front of the stage, the place for the orchestra, the circled seats of stone, were all in perfect preservation. An impress of a mask or bust—the features finely marked in the solid lava above our heads, was seen by the aid of our torches. We passed into some of the houses, which were excavated. The old brick and mortar had withstood the besieging, burning lava, nobly; but the wood was charred. We were shown into the garden where an old palace had been dug out. The floors were finely tesselated, and the walls of yellow and red still revealed their quaintly painted figures. The walls of the city, at whose base the sea murmured as sweetly, as now to my ear it murmurs against the wall of Naples, were pointed out. Far different music it hissed and boiled, upon that fatal time, when the victorious molten elements of the mountain drove it inhospitably away. Plucking a flower from one of the gardens of the ancient city, which withered and fell, ere it could be pressed, we continued our drive through Portici, and up the mountain.

Vesuvius really extends down to the sea; but the ascent is so gradual that it is almost imperceptible. One may, however, trace the stream of lava and the stratum of scoriæ by the richness of the foliage and the sweetness of the bloom. For over an hour we wound around, amid walls overhung with fruit-trees and vines. Oranges, nectarines, apricots, big cherries, pomegranates and figs, line our upward way. What genius of cultivation could equal this mountain side in prodigality? What peculiar element of fructification dwells in this volcanic soil, and over this burning crater? My knowledge of botanical chemistry fails me in these queries. The luscious fact, however, waters most toothsomely in the mouth, as apricot, orange, and nectarine severally are victimized. The red and gold of the nectarine, and the melting glisten of its wounded side, wooing you to another indentation, brought forcibly to my mind the beautiful saying of WALTER SAVAGE LANDOR—that the best results of human thought spring from a clear head meditating over a burning heart, just as the richest fruits spring out of the sides of a volcano over its hidden fire!

We pass through a continuous succession of gardens, stopping to buy from the peasants some fruit,—meeting donkies laden with their rich burdens, going down to the city under the guidance of boys, and women with baskets upon their heads, returning from the city, their fruit all sold. As we ascend higher by the good road, the hard iron cinders begin their domain of desolation, interspersing their barrenness amidst the smiling cultivation. As we followed the zigzag course, every now and then a view would open, disclosing, on either side, gorge in gorge, and chasm fearfully hid in chasm beneath. Two or three little houses are set away up, some fifteen hundred feet above the sea, perfectly unconscious of the slumbering Pandemonium beneath. The "Hermitage,"—our carriage destination,—is still higher. It marks the summit of vegetation. Above it, there grow no more of the ever-blooming sweets of Nature. Near by, is a little cottage, prettily ensconced in the side-hill, against whose Gothic front, on which the Madonna is painted, the evening sun begins to pour his horizontal beams. Chestnuts and mulberries overhang the gorges around. We strike the level, and are in the midst of the guides and horses, and in front of the antique-looking "Hermitage." An awful and a strange scene is this, verily. Such a devilish crew—fit ministers unto such a curiosity as this of Volcano-seeing! The mountain is half-way ascended, yet there it is above us, apparently just as high as ever. Its laborious ascent is not yet begun. All is thus far a world of pleasure. If Dr. CHEEVER were writing, he would moralize this upward way into a Bunyan pilgrimage, or an allegory of some kind. We have passed through a region, upon which the Hours have pressed down to men the prodigality of Heaven. Wanton Spring and fruitful Autumn lead us with soft and downy steps so gradually upward, that we are rather allured than led by the "goodly prospect." The "Hermitage" marks the point where Paradise ends and fire begins to show its effects. It is not so bad a place either. It furnishes us a lunch of rare deliciousness and ponies of sure footing. After buying our canes, and some boxes of Vesuvian relics, we mount—a gleeful company. We ride Indian file, over and amid cragged, jagged, and ragged rocks—the result of more recent eruptions. Around and upward we wind—going over the great crater (now fireless) from whose heart Pompeii received its doom. So deep and large was its discharge, that it divided the mountain, so as to make it appear like two peaks. The right hand peak, which is nearest to the sea, is the grand one, and that which we must climb. A calcined world of desolation, with no murmur of cascades, no music of pine-trees, awaits our step. The smoke winds about its summit almost perpendicularly above us. Is the ascent practicable? Onward! The guides whip the ponies behind, steering them by their tails, and, with laugh and halloo we find ourselves at the *pedestrian* point. There are three ladies of our party, and they must mount the chairs. By the way, now that the ladies are out shopping, let me pilfer from the journal of one of them, her sensations upon the extraordinary, perpendicular, and peculiar romance of the ride. I give it verbatim: "Here, at the point of steepest ascent, were our palanquins in waiting; and then began a chattering among the guides. Some one said that they were quarrelling and scrambling to get the smallest lady. [The writer seemed to be a peculiar object of care.) Simultaneously we were hoisted on the backs of our bearers—four poles sustaining the chair in which we sat. Swart-looking fellows they were—one at each pole. L—— led the way in our horseback cavalcade, and now came my turn to swing the veil of the foremost, when—short-lived triumph!—one of my poor fellows gave way, and I was obliged to see all the others pass by. Still amid slipping rocks and sliding sand, they tugged, the perspiration rolling off in big beads. It was labor to us also, to see them, from our rocking, fearful, tremulous, dancing chair, straining and puffing with our weight. It was terrible to look below. The men seemed like little creeping things away down in the distance. I did half glance at the sun setting in the sea, and the far-off city and country. But the point of vision was too fearful to enjoy the spectacle. By dint of occasional resting and changing, our guides brought us to the top; and then such piteous grimaces and chatterings for money and drink ——." But that is a scene to be enjoyed by all. The men all walked. I seized the strap over the shoulder of my guide, who, by the way, carried the provender, and took the lead. Whether it was my light foot, or the persuasiveness of the basket, I obtained the first sight at the yellow, sulphurous, smoking, abysmal pit!

Our general guide, Antonia. was last to come up. Consequently we were at the mercy of the other guides—appropriate genii of the spot. Such a pack of imps of limbo ought only to herd about the infernal hole. My man began whimpering and hullabalooing most hideously, as he wiped the sweat from off his black face. They were paid fully by Antonia, and thought to make a speculation out of our gullability. "*Je suis fateege!*" "Me-monie!" "changez pour moi—beef stek and maccaroni!" "Oh! donnez me sum, Signor." With bad French and worse English, around the men and around the ladies, with twisted faces and devilish horror depicted on them, they danced, gestured, chattered and swore, until Antonia came up, who, by dint of wilder gestures and a greater noise, stopped them. I fixed my man's volubility by repeating the 'Declaration of Independence.' I had hardly finished one of the 'grievances' before he left me with a curse deep and strong. It made one feel queerly, to be up out of the world, after sundown, amidst these paths of fire and smoke, with only a good-sized cane, and with such a company, say twenty black-browed scoundrels to lead you within an inch of certain death. However, it was a part of the play, and along we trudged, over smoky ground and ashes, trembling and half suffocated with the fumes of sulphur, until we stood upon the brink of a visible hell. I hate swearing, but that is the only expressive word. With handkerchiefs to the noses, and eyes aghast, we looked down into the seething, smoking, blackened abyss! Here was the fountain itself of those molten streams of fire which covered the face of earth for leagues, and buried great cities! Our guides ventured upon the sides of the chasm, and rolling great rocks down, bid us list! Up, *up*, UP—comes the cracking, sepulchral noise. "Sounding on its dim and perilous way," it still rises apparently from miles below—and when it would seem that even sound, were it ever so deep, could no longer be heard, the heart would burn fearfully to hear prolonged the noise—till it seemed to expire;

> "Yet from the Abyss is caught again,
> And yet again recovered."

If one were not so horrified, fancy might picture the Devil growling below in his deepest pits, as blow after blow of the rock cracked upon his infidel head. As we looked down amidst the curling vapor, and heard the hollow sound, and inhaled the sulphurous smoke, and looked on either side at the immense gorges now emptied of their fires, we felt that for the first time, we were amid the perfection and sublimity of horror! A few steps either way, and it is certain destruction. The ground is hot. You may turn over its smoking ashes with your cane. The guide lit a torch at the fire. But even here, can we not look upward into the deep, calm heaven, with its high and vaulted boss of stars, interpenetrated with the relict lustre of the departed day? Cannot we see from this pinnacle of Dread, the beauty of that great law of Being, which is quaintly described by an old English Bard, as

A great gold chain ylinked well,
Whose upper end to highest heaven was knitt,
And lower part did reach to lowest hell!

And cannot imagination people the "deep amaze" of the starry vault with its creations of angelic beauty, winnowing the air around, and brooding over the orange groves and vineyards below; as well as the horrid mystery of Deepness and Death into which we gaze, with those ghastly and horrid phantoms, described by the Latin poet, whose tomb we are about to visit, and whose verse we have prefixed to this chapter of contrasts.

With torches bright, and hearts relieved, we took giant strides down the mountain at an angle of fifty degrees, and from a height 4,000 feet above the bay. It was tall walking—that promenade. .The space which absorbed an hour of ascent was performed downward in ten minutes. Again with horse and carriage, and moonlight, we descended into the city, whose lights in crescent beauty twinkled far, far below, displaying her as the bride of the Mediterranean recumbent and asleep,—her forehead gleaming with a coronet of gems. Soon we find as sweet a sleep as ever laborer felt. One of the biggest pile-drivers on the public improvements could not have wedged a dream into that solid sleep. I was sure in the morning, from my eyelids, that Somnus himself had been sitting on them all night. I would not perform the same operation for the reader; so I close for another theme.

XII.

Naples,—Its Gayety and Desolation.

> Audire et videor pios
> Errare per lucos, amaenae
> Quos et aquae subeunt et aurae.
>
> HORACE.

A WEEK'S stay seems but a slight taste of this Paradise. Nevertheless, the time of our visit has proved fortunate.—What we regretted to miss at Rome, and for which great preparations were making when we left, we have seen here. The festal of *Corpus Domini* is always a great gala among Italians. As we drove to Vesuvius on the first day of our arrival, our eye was attracted, at every few squares of this illimitable city, by high altars, resembling the pagodas we saw at the World's Exhibition. They consist of rough framework, surrounded by cloth of gold, gems and spangles, great stars and red tinselling. They look like large political platforms, done up in gaudy dress. Preparations were being made to illuminate the city. Lanterns of divers colors hung from garlands of green about the altars, across streets and at every door. Artificial fountains there were too, around which flowers were wreathed and paintings placed. As we returned from Pompeii, which we visited day before yesterday, we saw the illumination and the people. A gush of hilarity seemed to run all through Naples. These children of the sun,—how they do revel in pleasure upon such days as this! They save throughout the year, to eat their choicest maccaroni upon Corpus Domini. Crowds were collected about the altars listening to music. Crowds about the eating and lemonade stalls, singing and hallooing. Crowds lined the way, laughing,—as if Herculaneum were not beneath—a corpse, nor Pompeii laid bare in desolation. *Ha!* HA! Ho! in genuine fun—a language which needs no dragoman to interpret—roared around, as lantern flashed against jewelled altar, and reflected its brightness in the joyous mass. Curriculi loaded full of picturesque people, drive by—all jovial. Donkeys are piled from head to tail with human nature, the children being in baskets upon their backs, as the sketch represents them. We descended from our carriage to mingle with the mass. On every side is carelessness and mirth, and that without drunkenness. Indeed, I have seen but one drunken man, and he was a soldier, since I left England; and that although wine bleeds fresh and free from every hill-side and mountain-top. Yesterday the procession came off. Priests by the hundreds officiated. The host was elevated. The people were blessed from the altars. All shops were closed. Naples was high in her festivity. The meanest lazzarone that ever begged or stole, joined in the general joy, and forgot his condition in the glee.

In one of the churches, nuns were seen peeping through the bars, and solemn priests marched around and amidst the crowded aisle. By the way, let me tell you of a singular vegetable phenomenon which our party saw in the cloistered court of the church of St. Severino. It was a fig-tree of large size growing out of the hollow of a great oak, and bearing three different kinds of figs. Vegetable wonders, however, are as common here as the leaves upon the sides of Vesuvius. During a drive yesterday to the tomb of Virgil, we had a fine view of great fields recovered from the sea, by the labor of peasants and the money of the king, and which are covered with vineyards as far as the eye can reach, and interspersed with white houses of rare beauty.

Our visit to Pompeii will never be forgotten. Who can see and forget those long streets deserted and dead; those temples broken and robbed of their gods; those rooms with their red and yellow paintings; and those gardens with their fountains and statues, their mosaics and pillars—all, *all* speaking the great tragedy which primevally was here enacted. The forums are standing just as they stood when the lake of fire was poured upon the devoted city. The temples and their altars—strange illustrations of former worship—stand side by side with the baker shops and taverns. Barber shops and theatres, baths and tombs, are here—an unwritten history, a book of marvels, which the fire of the mountain has bound with its clasps of stone, to be pondered eighteen hundred years after by a wondering world.

The ride to this city of fire lies along the shore of the bay. The Apennines bound the vision upon the east; and between them and Naples lies the volcanic fountain. The city of Pompeii is upon the other side of the mountain, occupying a great plain. It was discovered in 1750 by peasants working in a vineyard. About one-third of it is uncovered; enough to show that the arts of painting, sculpture and poetry flourished greatly in the midst of as luxurious and wicked a people as ever were permitted to fester under heaven. *What I saw has never been written*, what I saw is evidence more than enough, even to a sense of disgust, of the deepest stains of sin, and the deepest depths of degeneracy. Sodom and Gomorrah were no doubt rank with iniquity. Pompeii, it seems to me, met with a similar fate for similar profligacy and corruption. No one (unless it be ladies, to whom such sights are not permitted) can go through these streets, look at the signs, examine the paintings and statues, without feeling that God took upon himself the office of Avenger, and used that mountain of lava as the instrument.

We entered upon our researches just outside the walls ot Pompeii near some stables and tombs. The inscriptions tell, in very plain Latin, the story of the dead. We examined wells, the stones of which are worn with ropes, as if just used yesterday. Similar appearances along the curbing of the city, indicate places for hitching horses. Ovens like our own, in which bread was found *rather* well done, and which we saw to-day at the Museum—were scattered about. The stones for grinding and working the dough were very curious. The different houses are named from some statue or bust found in them, as the house of Cicero, or of Sallust, or of Castor and Pollux. The dining rooms, as well as all the other rooms, are painted in yellow and red; and adorned with every variety of figures, mostly nude. Birds, fruits, and foliage in rare perfection ornament the walls. The rooms are all small, and *lack ventilation.* In nothing is our comfort so superior to the ancients as in this essential to health. The houses are only one story, except that of Diomede, which is two stories. The view on the subsequent page represents one of the villas near an ancient temple whose pillars yet stand. The different places of business can be told by some object found in them; as for instance, a large money chest indicates the banking house; a figure in the wall (Cupid mending shoes), a shoemaker; the chair, a barber shop, and so on. The Pantheon with its twelve gods was found in fine order, surrounded by its forum; while the Temple of Isis, with the altar for the sacrifice and even the hole for the blood, with its Egyptian symbols, and the skeleton of the priest, stands out prominent in the midst of the ruins. This last place has a peculiar interest. In it were found skeletons of priests, who had been dining when overtaken by the eruption. Bones of fowls and fish, remains of eggs, bread and wine, and a garland of flowers were found. Another skeleton leaned against the wall, with the axe of sacrifice in his hands; and still another had escaped, carrying 360 coins of silver in a cloth, but was overwhelmed near the Tragic theatre.

We lunched in a fine old dining-room, assisted by our guides, who liked amazingly to drink the health of us Americans in the Falernian. A jolly old soul was our guide. He was continually twitting us in broken French, about our love of the "*anteek.*" I tried to carry off some trophies, but his vigilance prevented me. He presented me with a big bug, and tried to catch a lizard for my pocket, remarking that they were "anteeks." Every thing was exceedingly antique to him. The very flowers and orange-peels took the hue of antiquity. He introduced me to an old gray-haired, one-eyed soldier, at the gate of the theatre near the house of Diomede, as the brother of Diomede—"*an anteek.*" The old soldier chuckled most funnily at the old joke.

We visited the amphitheatre, which you may remember was filled at the time of the great eruption, that buried the city, in August A. D. 79. Few skeletons were found in it. It is supposed that most of the inhabitants, including those in the theatres, escaped. Twenty thousand could find egress from the amphitheatre in two minutes and a half; and no wonder, with such a number of corridors and doors. There are 97 places of inlet. It seeems to me that the amphitheatre, of all other places, would receive the first warning. Open at the top—the fiery glare of the visible peak of Vesuvius would flash in upon the gladiatorial scene, while the rumble of the earth beneath would drown the loudest roar of the beasts in their subterranean dens, and startle the people from their spell of pleasure. There were about 300 skeletons found in Pompeii. Those of the soldiers in the barracks, and of seventeen persons, in a country-house whither they had fled for refuge, as well as the skeleton of the mother with her child in arms, are preserved in the studii of the Museum. As we walked upon the top of the amphitheatre, the sun of Italy was sinking in pink, orange and purple. That most beautiful of all skies seemed deep and full of the mellow lustre, weaving its witchery over ruin and mountain.

We visited another theatre. It was the favorite of the poets. It seemed as perfect as if but yesternight,

"The cothurns trod majestic
Down the deep Iambic lines,
And the rolling anapestic
Curled like vapor over shrines."

Indeed every point of Pompeii speaks of the cultivation of dramatic poetry. Paintings of masks and of actors are abun-

A VILLA IN POMPEII.

dant. But had Pompeii *one* poet, whose imagination—as it revelled in the paintings, statues and groves, the theatres and forums, the isles of the beautiful bay and the rock-bound villas of the Apennines—ever dreamed of the great Drama, whose *personæ* were the elements, and whose unity was as unbroken as its destiny was terrific? Bulwer has lifted the curtain, and displayed the scenes of that drama. Has his vivid imagination even, done justice to the awful whelming which God poured upon this seat of art and luxury?

The soft twilight breeze creeps gently over the worn and desolated streets. A trembling and a fear rustles past on its wing, as we gaze upward to the dread mount whose hidden fires may again play the same tragedy upon unconscious Naples, now decked in her festal robes and illuminated with golden lights.

While endeavoring to make out an inscription before the stage of the theatre, we were startled at a wild actor, who leaped from behind the scenes, and held us in comic wonder for some ten minutes, by some fragments of a comic play. His contortions of face, and his gyrations in the dance, added grotesqueness to the scene. It seems that our guide Antonia had slipped him in front to surprise and regale us. I never heard such a fiddling twang to a human voice before. He rung its changes oddly enough—as oddly as Punch himself. He played a mimic flute with a stick; and at the conclusion jumped into the chorus, with as much gusto as ever the Grecian chorus did under the spell of Æschylus. He danced it daintily, until a jerk of the body and a doff of the cap, which adroitly caught the expected coin—ended this specimen of the "antique."

As a lawyer I visited the tribunal, where our respectable fraternity—if any such were permitted in so wicked a place—were wont to congregate. The seat of the judges was upon a forum, immediately over the prison cells, from whose gloom the prisoners could hear their own doom. An arrangement of the kind should commend itself to our civilized communities. It would save our courts much time in sending for, and remanding prisoners.

As we wend our way homeward, a heavy cloud, betokening rain, enshrouds the apex of Vesuvius. All other parts of the horizon are clear and starry. A silence "deep as that between the trumpet summons and the judgment" sleeps in awe above. The very obscurity of the fount of fire, deepens the gloom and awe. It reminds us of the words of Festus; Obscurity hath many a sacred use. The *sacred use* of Vesuvius, I as firmly believe, as I believe in God's retribution, has been to punish godless profligacy. Is its use wholly set aside? Time may tell.

As we ride along under the illuminated garlands and altars, we perceive little shell fountains almost invisible in the foliage, out of which water is spouted of a sudden, on a crowd of laughing, mischievous rogues, assembled around the railings. Light-hearted Naples—what cares she for yon familiar fountain of fire?

We visited yesterday the tomb of Virgil. Driving down the shore on the western side of the city, we see the tomb above us upon the solid rock, overlooking the bay. To reach it we must take a longer drive. We enter a tunnel, some half a mile long, called the grotto of Posilipo,—said to have been made originally by the devil. It bears other marks, however, those of wheel-hubs, all along the sides; the grotto having been cut down time after time to its present level. It is lighted finely. Two carriages can drive abreast in it, and its height is at least 100 feet. With jolly cracks of the whip we dash by the gala people, returning to the city. The grotto rings with their merriment. Soon we are in the country, having passed under the rocky ridge which divides the city from the suburban villas. Altars of red and gold arch the streets. Chestnut venders sing their nuts; soldiers are drinking and gaming; dark-browed citizens are rolling balls on the paves; boys are driving goats into the city; the hemp is rotting in the sun by the road side after the Kentucky style; all these objects pass rapidly by,—to be absorbed in the fine view which opens upon the shore. We stand near another grotto cut by Lucullus, the wealthy Roman, in order to get to Baiæ with more facility—Baiæ, that ancient city dimly seen down the bay near the bridge of Caligula, beyond the volcanic hills of Flageria. The isles of the bay float in the distance, miles away; yet apparently very near. So clear is the air that Capræ, which is twenty-four miles from the mainland, seems not two miles from our point. The same illusion everywhere deceives the vision.

Can it be true that, upon those islands, which seem picked out for ensamples of the beautiful, the harshest rigors of tyranny are exacted? Can it be, that under this cloudless heaven, and surrounded by this delightful bay, there is at this moment, carried on the blackest system of political persecution and cruelty ever practised by despotic arrogance? It is lamentably true, as Mr. Gladstone, in his able pamphlet to Lord Aberdeen, revealed, that at least 26,000 political prisoners, suspected or convicted of liberal views, or of favoring the revolution of 1848, are chained with felons, and drudge day after day upon those isles, and in the surrounding prisons, without the hope of a hearing, or a chance of mitigation.

This is not mere conjecture, nor rumor started by uneasy Republicans. The police registers themselves show the number of political prisoners from May, 1848, to September, 1851. We append a table, which cannot record, however, the tortures and cruelties incident to their imprisonment. It speaks with no common voice, of the system of political persecution of the King of Naples.

These are the round numbers (under the actual figure), because an exact quotation might subject many Government officials to serious annoyance.

NUMBER OF NEAPOLITAN POLITICAL PRISONERS, FROM MAY, 1848, TO SEPTEMBER, 1851.

Condemned to the Ergastola, ...	36
Condemned in irons to the Bagni, ...	1,000
Condemned in irons to the Bagni, but not yet removed from prison,	300

Banished to the islands after trial, ...		800
Banished to the islands without trial, including the soldiers sent by royal authority to the camp of Charles Albert, ...		6,000
Accused, who have been, or still are, in prison, from May, 1848, to September, 1851, not included in the above, ...		15,000
Total, ...		23,136
Supposed number of exiles, ...	3,000	
Hiding from the police, ...	150	
Exiled from their native towns, but still in the kingdom,	350	
		3,500
Total number of victims of the Neapolitan Constitution,		26,636

And it must not be forgotten, that this list does not include any, from that wretched class called lazzaroni, but mostly the respectable and moneyed class, who have intelligence to know, and the will to endeavor to obtain freedom. The lazzaroni were the hired instruments of the Bourbon, who instigated them to acts of pillage, murder, rape and arson, against those, and the families of those, who favored Constitutional Reform. Even yet these fiends are the chief support of the throne. The quarter where they live is called the King's quarter. Well, like master, like man. We hope for a reckoning with both.

The best, the noblest, the brightest spirits of southern Italy, are included in the above statistics, and thus expiate what in the eye of Ferdinand II. is a horrid crime, viz., their belief in popular sovereignty. The wretched King can promise solemnly a Constitution to his people, and can deliberately perjure himself; and conservatives are ever ready to laud his love of order, and his legitimate right. But a citizen dare not whisper to his own wife hardly his hope of a better day, without being loaded with irons, chained to thieves, and sent off to one of these island prisons. The governments of the civilized world should, in the name of our common God and Humanity, protest with a vigor far different from mere diplomatic correspondence, against this wholesale abuse of power. Perhaps it would not be entirely according to international law. But is not that law progressive?

Does it not spring from the universal *reason* of men, as well as from universal custom? and where is the reason why enlightened nations should not demand the observance of humane codes? It is even alleged that the tortures of the rack are resorted to by the government of Naples, to discover the liberalists, and their designs. It makes the flesh creep to think what infamous perfidy and cruelty are known to have been here committed by the myrmidons of Power. Well; let the first overt act be done toward an Englishman or an American—that is all! People will then know how deep that moat is around the palace, and how fraternal that dear cousin of Austria is toward his ally of Naples.

Does it not seem as if Providence had ordained the inhumanity of man to be an offset against the charms of nature in this clime? But let not these things deter us from our search after the tomb of Virgil.

Driving around the bay to complete our circuit, we pass by the sweetest little nooks, hid in the coverts and inlets of the bay, the little terraces, gardens and fine houses of which are concealed, almost, amid rocks. Above and below, for hundreds of feet, is the leafy and stony architecture, natural and artificial. Luxury still is seated upon this lovely shore. Boats are plying, crowded with men and women, from the city to the booths and cafés, which line its marge. A long winding walk, up—up, amidst groves of nectarine and figs, brings us to the tomb of Virgil. On the right is the promontory of Misenum, near which Palinurus fell into the sea. Farther to the right is the ever beauteous Ischia and Procida. The ancient seats of Lucullus, Hortensius and Marius, are not far off. In this classic vicinage lies the prince of Latin poets. The inscription found here indicates, without doubt, the sacred spot. "*Mantua me geniut, Calabra rapuere, tenet nunc Parthenope, cecina pascua, rura duces.*" This inscription we copied from the stone within the tomb, which bends over the dust of the poet. Flowers bloom prodigally around. The unceasing echo of the vehicles through the grotto disturbs the stillness, not the beauty of the spot. Fancy, ranging wide for similes, likened the murmuring echo to the solemn sounding of the great epic of the bard down the long corridors of Time. The voiceful sea celebrates, in music more harmonious than his own hexameters, the undying fame of the Mantuan poet. How strange for us, from the farthest occident, to come hither looking for the mere monument of genius! Is it not true, that

> "Pilgrims come from climes where they have known
> The name of him—who now is but a name;
> And wasting homage o'er a sullen stone,
> Spread his—by him unheard, unheeded—*fame.*"

God has written all over our hearts this love of the resting-places of the great and gifted, who have inspired us by their heroic lives, or charmed us by their "tongue of subtle flame." An old writer has transmitted to us the same sentiment of veneration, for which we in turn revere him—"*Movemur enim nescio quo pacto, locis ipsis in quibus eorum, quos diligemus, aut admiramur adsunt vestigia.*" Nothing makes an American feel how much his country must achieve, as to tread in these footsteps of Antiquity, and ponder the inscriptions over the tombs of genius and heroism. Nothing makes him feel how much his country *has* achieved, as to see the operations of this present government, where every principle of civil right and common decency are sunk in the intoxication of irresponsible power.

A visit to the Museum here is a part of the performance in travel. We found it full of the relics of the buried cities, consisting of every variety of personal ornament, cooking utensils, pictures, statues, and architecture. The famous Farnese Bull, and the surrounding group in marble, are here. Next to the Laocoon, it is the most complex achievement of the chisel. Of the paintings, churches, promenades; of our visit to the opera at San Carlos, the largest theatre in Europe; of the drive we had down the Riviera di Chiaja, amidst the beauty and fashion of Naples, more splendid than Regent-street or the Boulevards; of our visit to the cemetery, whose beautiful buildings and grounds are the admiration of all visitors; of the drive to the very home of the old Siren upon the banks of the Bay, fit allegory of the paradisiacal beauty and infernal horror which dwell about us; of all these and more, are they not written upon the fleshly tablet, to be perused more at leisure?

This afternoon of Sabbath, the festival of St. Louis of France was celebrated in great parade and pomp. Long processions of priests, in white robes and with wax tapers, were flanked by long lines of soldiers, in which marched singing boys and girls bearing flower wreaths much larger than themselves. Some were dressed up as knights of the chivalric times; some in glittering costumes of other eras. Carriages, too, in long procession, in which were the *élite* of the city, brought up the line. As they marched down into the promenade, although it was the Sabbath, at least five hundred guns were fired. The promenade was crowded with the gay Neapolitans, all eager to see and hear. As the host moved by, under its golden canopy, attended by priests, or as the image of St. Louis moved along, borne aloft by priests, every hat was off and obeisance was made with humble reverence. This struck us queerly; but we are prepared for any thing. The perfect uniformity in the Catholic Church here is wonderful. Every one is a member, and pays, at least, outward respect to its ordinances.

The promenade displayed a more tastefully dressed people than London or Paris can show. The gentlemen here dress perfectly. Naples can show both extremes, the best-looking and the *worst*-looking people in the world. Our first impression was cast from the features of the lazzaroni, whose indescribable appearance is as world-wide in its notoriety as the crater of Vesuvius.

We have met many Americans at every point of our journey. They are more numerous abroad this year, than the travellers of all other nations put together. I was told by a reverend gentleman who had been to Palestine, that the Arabs were a little jealous of the Yankees. They feared the Yankees were going to "annex" the Holy Land. And certainly the reasons they give for it are ostensible, if not solid. They say that America has been sending a national expedition (Lieut. Lynch's) to survey the Dead Sea—that we follow up our government project, with droves of our countrymen, each one of which is as *curious* and inquiring after every thing, as if it were already his own. Well; who knows what our destiny may be? Palestine may in the course of time have its representative in the Congress of the United States of America and Asia; for

> "Westward the star of empire takes its way."

And if that star will *not* set, but keep moving, I do not see that we can help taking China, and so on.

Oh! for a month's annexation of Naples to our Union, that we might strike off the fetters from the thousands of Republican prisoners, who are enslaved in sight of their beautiful city, and that we might purge this Paradise of its serpents in human form, which have preyed long enough upon the anguish of the noble and patriotic.

As I write, the sound of military music mingles with the soft rolling of the waters; while every now and then a discharge of musketry announces that some procession and celebration is going on. We observe upon the piazza, and now entering the promenade, a long congregation of white priests, carrying something aloft, the host perhaps, while the people are kneeling around. What strange devotion we meet with here. We were shown in the Cathedral, forty silver images of the saints, large as life, to say nothing of mines of silver in shrines, flowers and sacred instruments. The churches do not equal those of Genoa, much less those of Rome. There is not the same Art displayed.

A week has flown here, in this other Eden, upon golden wing. It seems but a day or so, since we landed upon this shore of love and beauty. Within that time how many images of rare and exquisite form,—aye, and of rare and exquisite horror, have been painted on the memory! Some of these have been transcribed. Yet the prospect still enchants, and here I would fain linger and write about each novel phase of beauty, which is revealed under this kindlier sky and around this bay of loveliness. Here is the perfection of external Nature, where the sun,—which is the glorious source of all our joys,—warms the soil into the most fragrant and richly-colored flowers and delicious fruits, and developes a landscape that is only equalled by the water scene which goldenly glows under the "blazing Deity." The very silence is enamored of the soft plash upon the shore, as it now invades so sweetly the ear, and locks in her cell, her own "spirit ditties of no-tone." The isles of the bay loom up amidst the sea, like isles of the blest. Every thing seems to exist, to ornament a temple of Love and Purity. Surely we can exclaim with the simple-hearted Miranda in the Tempest,

> "There's nothing ill can dwell in such a temple.
> If the ill spirit have so fair an house,
> Good things will strive to dwell in it."

But look at the dwellers here—the miserable, swart, ragged, haggard lazzaroni; look at the spectacle of soldiers all about; see that great fort surrounded by a deep moat in the midst of the city, for the sovereign to protect himself from his own people; and above all, look, as I have, deep down in the great abyss of Vesuvius, walk over its smoking ashes and burning marl, inhale its sulphur breath, and tremble amid its horror; and you will find that Providence has "mingled the cup." The gold is not without alloy, the sun has its spots, the luscious fruitage hath a canker at the heart;—in fine, Naples, the home of the Homerian Siren, the seat of ancient Roman luxury, the resort of the gay and pleasure-loving from every clime, the spot chosen by Virgil for his repose; the land favored by the presence and described by the pen of Lamartine,—*Naples*—has its Vesuvius, its Herculaneum buried beneath the indurated lava, and its desolated Pompeii under volcanic ashes, partly laid bare in its garments of woe!

All these spots we have visited, alternating from paradisiacal beauty to unutterable terror. We have seen the exhumed relics of these cities in the great Museum, studied their domestic history in the familiar household utensils and personal ornaments, their pictures and statues. And, as if in mockery of these warnings, we have listened to the sweet voices of the "children of this azure sheen" swelling in mellow music and falling in tremulous cadence, in the opera; have seen them decked for the gala day, with their altars and fountains decorated as none but the Neapolitans can ornament them, and mingled with them in their joy under the very shadow of that fearful mountain, and over the very lava, under which lies stiff, and rock-bound, the city of Herculaneum.

Of all the places I have yet seen, upon which Nature has been lavish to prodigality, Naples seems the primal one. The sense aches with the continual beauty of all around. "In sweet madness" the mind is robbed of itself, and in still ecstasy it delights in the ineffable grace, music and loveliness which curls, sings and moves in the water, and is reflected in the bending blue above and the leafy landscape around.

XIII.

Sicily and Malta.

> "He pushed his quarrels to the death, yet prayed
> The saints as fervently on bended knees
> As ever shaven cenobite."
>
> *Bryant.*

FROM the sunny land of the military priesthood of St. John, my present greeting hails. Its unique and peculiar history lends a charm which would not otherwise belong to these dazzling streets and motley palaces.

We left Naples on Monday, the 23d of June, and were a long time in losing sight of the bay of Beauty. All that is magical in the combination of light and shade has been daguerreotyped by the mild sunshine upon our memory—fadelessly there pictured. We took our passage upon a French man-of-war. All went below to sleep; I alone remained above to obtain a nearer view of the Isle of Caprae, which, from Naples had slept so tremulously lovely amid her sheen of cerulean setting. We passed between the isle and Point Campanelli, leaving Sorrenta and Castel a Mare behind. The top of Vesuvius, with her flag of smoke, darted behind the point. The farewell view of evanishing Naples, becomes more and more enchanting by distance, which robes its sky and water in azure hue. Caprae looked bleak and rocky. On the seaward side, I saw an arch formed by rocks in the sea, under which undulations of light and water flashed in rivalry of beauty. The Apennines range closely to the shore—indeed, their rocky barriers here shut in the sea. Huge palisades rising 3000 feet or more, broken into promontory, gorge, bay and inlet, guard the coast. The rocks were mantled with a sort of yellow lichen. Here and there smiled spots of cultivation. We gradually diverged from these shores, leaving the Gulf of Salerno behind us, until we passed Point Palinurus, whereabouts we watched a round and golden sun roll down his disk into the waves. The waves were lit into blazing splendor by his fire. A long line of dazzling, flashing radiance, swam upon the horizon, under a canopy of cloud impurpled and red, with long illumined cords and tassels dripping with sunlight down to the water's edge. The spray made by the steamer was as royally purple as the stole of the imperial Cæsar. Soon the last tint of gold was softened into a rich mellow lustre of orange. Evening sobered down gradually into night. The flickering shadows of the air played between the eye and the distant horizon. A sunset upon the Mediterranean—is it not an object to be seen with rapture? What pen can distil its beauty into expression, or enthrall, by words, the tranquil *spirit* of the scene?

Yesterday morn I hurried on deck to see Stromboli with his column of fire, and Ætna with his pillar of smoke and his top of snow. The last was just observable above the highlands of the northeast part of Sicily. We had passed the gulfs which form the *instep* of the boot of Italy, in the night, and were now in the gulf of Gioja, approaching the veritable Scylla and the undoubted Charybdis! The land and water, too, of classic memories, begin to appear as we draw near to Hellas and her Ionian isles. Scylla is a high rock, twelve miles from Massena. Here the dogs of Homer and Virgil barked in the caverns where the waves rolled around the fabulous monster. We did not, owing to the state of the tide, see any peculiar commotion, nor hear any peculiar sounds. The waves glistened blue and bright as ever they did to the eye of Æneas. The sailors had just washed the decks, and were busy burnishing the metallic portions. The whistle of the boatswain and the bustle of the sailors, the cries of the officers to the pilots, and the additional man at the wheel, betokened that more than ordinary precaution is still necessary, even with steam, to pass this point of classic terror. Our boat moves on; but no opening appears. All is rock-bound, save a sand bank, near a fort. This soon opens and displays the channel of Massena, which divides the toe of Italy's boot from the northeast of Sicily. It seems as if some convulsion of nature had torn this channel from the rocky range of the Apennines, leaving the twin of horrors on either side to guard the shores. Massena is in sight, and Charybdis with her slight whirl of waters, some 600 feet from Massena, on the Sicilian side, attracts the eye. It is not a very great thing, although it plays such a "bloody bones" part in the hexameter. Hell-gate, at Long Island, is altogether more horrific. Indeed, since the Genoese sailor struck out into the vexed Atlantic, putting to shame the Argonautic and the Ulyssean expeditions, these old haunts of monsters look like foolishness, especially from a *steam* boat.

The head point of Sicily is a sandy beach, upon which are windowless houses, in a deserted fishing town. Massena is quite a pretty place, half hid under the shade of the rough, uneven mountains, orange-covered, yet bleak-looking, overtopping and surrounding the city.

We pass under the guns of the fort, and are surrounded with a motley crew in boats. Degenerate Sicilians! Ye who were once giants, and with your tread shook this volcanic (?) isle; ye who were once Cyclops, and with single eye glared, and with heavy arm forged Jove's thunderbolts in the depths of the fires of Ætna, Oh! how have your glories been dimmed, since they shone in the imagination of the bard of Scio!

At breakfast we were *desserted* with green almonds, yellow apricots, cherries, ripe pears and fresh figs. The latter had a mawkish sweet taste, a little like our paw-paws, which they resemble in form and color. We begin to feel in the South. Indeed, we are in Homer's "isle of the sun."

What vicissitudes, physical and historical, has not Sicily underwent! Her first inhabitants were from Spain. She was subsequently held by Saracens, Turks, Spaniards, Austrians and French. The Bourbon house was replaced upon the throne in

1820. The Revolution of 1848 extended here. The marks of it, in the ruined forts, are still visible. Successful for some months, and separated from Naples, she was again, however, reduced to the vassalage of Ferdinand II., the prince who now adorns the throne of Naples.

After breakfast, we went on deck, when, looking astern, I observed our steamer on *fire!* The sails were ablaze! I hardly knew, in my excitement, what to halloo, so I told an English friend near, whose ready French proved very serviceable. The sailors soon leaped amidst the rigging, tore the sails, and with water quenched the fire. This little incident leads me to remark upon the extraordinary safety of the boats here, compared with those at home. Human life is valued here much more than human liberty. Why cannot America at least learn a lesson in this regard from Europe?

In some respects we could well interchange some of our own manners and institutions for such knowledge. Let me exemplify. Our bankers at Naples, correspondents of Barings, overpaid us $160 in gold, while paying £125! Such a mistake at home would soon dismiss the officer. But the truth is, the Italians are utterly unfit for business Two hours will hardly answer for them to do what our brokers would do in ten minutes. Their bank at Naples was away up in the steeple of a church, not so high, quite, as Vesuvius. It was a trial to wait upon such business men. They are so absorbed by pleasure in the luxurious *now*, that providence seems wholly severed from their habits. Irresponsible, and careless even of their souls' salvation, they yield themselves to the gayety of the day, and commit their future, here and hereafter, into the hands of chance, or what is worse, of the priests, whose ready absolution is a perfect salve for every wound. The genius of the West, and of the rugged North, seems to them a wild Quixotic adventure, to end in pain and trouble. "Heart within," they have not, only as it vibrates to the music of the festival, and the garlanding of flowers. "God o'er head," what or where is He, save that He is enshrined in the visible images which are borne in the joyous procession? He breathes not in the beauteous landscape, nor liquid depths, for them. His name, is but a name—to be repeated in the prayer, and to be pulselessly dead at the heart.

Before we leave Italy, let me generalize yet further. How apparent to a student of the elder civilization does it differ from our own civilization! The old wholly absorbed the individual in the State. The new releases the individual from the State, in every country, except Italy, where the State is so intimately inwoven with religion. There, religion enmeshes the individual, and binds his energies. It absorbs the most sturdy and active in its priesthood, and hands them over to the State as curious specimens of free agents, to be again restricted and bound. The old civilization withdrew men from the home-influence to the temple, the forum, and the camp. The very construction of the domestic residences in Pompeii demonstrates how weak was the domestic tie. No such words as *comfort* or *home* are known in the Grecian or Roman Lexicon. The opposite is the case with most countries at the present day. The domestic influence in Germany, England and America, has informed the soul of the State. But in Italy the same out-door tendency pours its feeble rays of happiness, and sheds its glitter of gala pleasure. The priest stands between husband and wife, parent and child; the little orifice of the confessional becomes the medium of confidence; and even that confidence hangs by as brittle a thread as did the sword of Damocles. The State, assisted by the Church, yet binds down the energies of the mass of Italy. The artists of Naples are honored by the King, for representing by the pencil and chisel, Religion shielding and supporting Ferdinand, while Justice smiles serenely upon the royal miscreant, who is represented as triumphantly trampling Constitutionalism under his feet. May we not hope that the people will yet burst irrepressibly their iron encasement, and stand forth throbbing in the liberty of individual independence!

Naples is yet hopelessly bound. The King has his moat-surrounded forts, his trained bands, and his kind Austrian friends. These *seem* to be invincible; but another Massaniella may arise even from the humble fishermen who drag the beautiful bay, and with a surer stroke decapitate the head of kingcraft in Naples. The government encourages pleasure and priestly rule; and thus renders the popular mind oblivious of all inherent dignity and right.

We passed to-day some spots sacred to the memory of the early Christians. "Paul after having been shipwrecked" in the ship from Alexandria (see Acts, chapter 28), upon the shore of Miletus, the present Malta, landed at Syracuse, and "tarried there three days," and from thence "he fetched a compass, and came to Rhegium," which place we passed to-day. It was along these blue waves, and under the same warm sunlight, that the great Apostle followed his noble appeal unto Cæsar, even to the eternal city itself! But more thrilling still, I now write to you from the very isle of his shipwreck, and the very place where his eloquent tongue bade the inhuman sailors stay their hands: "Except these men abide in the ship, ye cannot be saved!" and he thus protected the four prisoners from death at the hands of their custodians; the very spot where the viper fell innocuous into the fire, and where the simple barbariaus proclaimed him in very deed a Deity!

Some doubts have arisen as to the identity of Malta with the Miletus of the Acts; but the place where "the two seas come together," can be no other. Controversy has settled upon Malta.

Before we left Sicily, the sun went down over distant Ætna. Cape Mirro de Porci was left behind in a haze of splendor. Shakspeare has given to Syracuse, which floats in yonder dim light, a local habitation for his muse, and mathematicians hail it as the home of Archimedes.

This morning we woke up in the rock-ribbed, trebly fortified harbor of Malta. The English flag—a relief to one's eyes—floated above us. The land of the Hospitaller and the Grand

Master was around us. This island was given to the Knights by Charles V. after they had been driven out of Palestine. From the fifteenth century to the time of Napoleon, the Grand Masters ruled here, midway between the Christian and Moslem world. We have spent the day partly in looking at the strange tombs of the Knights of St. John and the Cathedral of that name. Yesterday was his festal day. The Cathedral was carpeted over with the orange leaves which hid the rich Mosaics. The great tapestries in which shines the life of the Saint, hung splendidly from the frescoed arches. We passed into the Armory, all around which the old knights, devoid of their bodies, stiff in their armor, seem to keep guard. Curious relics were there—flags and trophies won from Saracen by Knight, and ordnance of antique mould. The keys of Jerusalem hung rusty by the side of those of Acre and Rhodes.

This city was taken by Napoleon on his route to Egypt, and the reign of the Grand Masters ceased. By voluntary annexation (a precedent for Texas) the isle was placed under British sway. But the quaint influence of the priestly soldier yet clings to each palace and church, giving strange and attractive features to each object around us. The order of the Knights was composed of persons from different European nations, distributed according to language. Their portraits in the Armory denote decision and devotion; and their arms and armor bespeak, by dents and weight, a stalwart and doughty Knighthood. Here the last rays of the orb of chivalry lingered about the gown of the churchman, long after that orb had disappeared from the horizon. Here the hardest siege of modern history was sustained by the French, who in 1799, after two years' resistance, capitulated to Lord Nelson.

The isle is barren and dry, occasionally *siroccoed* by southwest winds. Every class and every nation is here to be found; a varied assemblage;

"Long-haired Sclavonian skipper with the red
And scanty cap which ill protects his head;

White-kilted Suliot, gay and gilded Greek,
Grave, turbaned Turk, and Moor of swarthy cheek.

We cannot throw off the influence of Malta so readily. We saw so much at the famous refuge of the Knights, so much illustrative of the early struggles of the Crusaders to regain and to keep Palestine, so much illustrative of the exterminating wars between the Knights of St. John and the Templars, as well as between Christian and Turk, that it would take a long scroll to write it.

This isle of Malta seems to be well governed by the British, but it is a nest of beggary. Such a group of beggars never beset poor humanity, as clung to us when we emerged from our hotel. I had to beat them off with my Vesuvius club, so impudently daring were they to our ladies as well as to ourselves. Before we left Malta harbor, a band of four fiddlers, smoking cigars, twanged all around our boat for coppers. Although the mate gave them a few splashes with the wheel occasionally to keep them off, and although his "*Sacr-r-r-es*" rolled deep and long, still they rowed and fiddled, and fiddled and rowed, until our noble steamer drowned their harmony in its noise, as it moved out amid the eight forts of this invincible harbor. The involutions of these stony fabrics are wondrous. They were framed by the Grand Masters, one after the other, each trying to excel his predecessor, in giving strength to this last resort of chivalry against the Moslem foe. The open sea is angry and rough. Ten ships float in the offing, looking spectral and shadowy against the evening sky. They form the English fleet, which is hourly expected at Malta.

The pitching of the vessel admonishes me to cease recording, and to retire—below.

Farewell to Malta! Athens—ATHENS—the home of the spiritually Beautiful is our promise, and thitherward we shall be wending, even though unconscious, in sleep.

XIV.

Athens,---"the Eye of Greece."

"———TRUTHS serene
Made visible in Beauty, that shall glow
In everlasting freshness; unapproached
By mortal passion; pure amidst the blood
And dust of Conquest; never waxing old,
But on the stream of time, from age to age
Casting bright images of heavenly youth,
To make the world less mournful."
Talfourd's Athenian Captive.

THE heart throbbed wildly as the vessel approached the shores of Attica. Far different is its throbbing from that caused by the distant view of Rome. One was the citadel of power, physical and temporal, even in its grandest exhibition. The other is the citadel of power, intellectual and immortal. The shores of Greece as they frown upon the sea, are instinct with a genius which men will ever venerate. The general aspect of the shores of Attica is that of extreme barrenness and asperity, unrelieved by a single tree, and rarely by a shrub. There are no level lawns or beautiful groves, with which poetry would invest the land of Homer and Plato. Cicero said truly of yon island far to our northward, and of its ruler Ulysses, that he loved Ithaca "*non quia larga, sed quia sua.*" He might have extended the generalization so as to have included every Grecian; and have added, "they loved not their country because it had any attractive scenery, but simply because it was Greece." What Homer in his Odyssey says of Ithaca, may be truly said of all the Grecian coast. It is horrid with cliffs, with little or no herbage, allowing scarcely a mouthful to the mountain goat.

Greece is almost sea-surrounded. A small isthmus attaches Morea to the main land. How could such a barren soil become so great? Why do we gaze with such earnestness upon yon little neck of rocky earth between Mount Cithaeron and Cape Sunium? Why do we wander with rapture under the plane-trees, where Plato taught, or lean entranced against the Pentelic pillars of the Parthenon? Why do we listen to the subtleties of Zeno from the portico? What surrounds each statue with an auriole of light; what covers each mountain with a glory like a God? Why do nations meet here to mourn over ruins, and grow eloquent over dust? Why are millions spent here in excavating the works of the dead past? Why has an archæological society exhumed the fragmentary pillars of the temples of old? *Greece was the thinking head and beating heart of the world;* the first and brightest link in the genealogy of genius. The human mind here received its first great impulse, and it has ever since measured its advancement by the influence of literary men deeply read in the lore of Greece. The influence of letters over every other influence, is attested by every page of the world's annals; but the annals of Greece are a complete unity of evidence, every line of which is instinct with a salutary influence.

Can we help wondering that such a barren soil should have been so productive of great thoughts? Let it be remembered that the very difficulty to be contended with, "like a skilful wrestler, strengthened the nerves," and made the Spartans and Athenians, what they will ever remain, the *soul* of Antiquity.

We passed, at evening, the famous island of Cytheria, now called Cerigo. Dark clouds, with long fringes, floated gracefully over Sparta. The hills are dark, and not ungracefully pencilled against the western sky, which glows in gold, here and there dimmed by wavy cloudlets. The purple light plays upon the foam of our gallant ship How does the spirit recur to the past, and with that active race who lived upon yon shore, people the sky and earth and sea, with shapes of dreamlike beauty and austere dignity! Even there upon that bleak island, which is now used as the Botany Bay of Ionia, it is fabled that the beautiful goddess of love had her favorite resort. There where Helen, the " source of all the woe of Troy," was born, the genius of Greece imagined it saw the winged messengers of the goddess float in the purple light of love; and here, amidst this cerulean sea, it saw the goddess herself arise—the conqueror of conquerors—the charm of Mars and the companion of Jove!

As night closes over the land of Lycurgus, it seems to lie solemn and severe in thoughtfulness. No gayety or delight, such as hovered around Naples, is present to break the spell. With what longing does the mind once accustomed to ponder the thoughts that breathed and burned in the classic pages of Æschylus and Thucydides—linger about those silent hills—the home of song and philosophy.

Saturday morning found us at the Pireus. Its houses looked low and quite oriental. The stone as well as the sandy soil, was white and dazzling—the roofs are red. The most picturesque part of the view is the people in their peculiar costume. We had a fine chance to study them. They thronged about our boat, before it had fairly stopped, in their little boats, eager for the drachmas. Dressed in their long red caps, with long purple tassels; a finely-wrought waistcoat, of red or blue, very dark, over a white boddice; and a flowing skirt around the body, snow-white and sashed; together with elegant, tasselled leggings; they formed a sculpturesque and picturesque group! Some of the meaner kind were dressed in big baggy pants, which draggled in the dirt, and looked any thing but classical.

A great contest was approaching, or was going on, as to who should be No. 1, in the forthcoming spoil of passengers. All were huddled around our gangway, when splash! went the wheel of the steamboat; and away went wet trowsers, and at high tide, darted all the boats into the bay. Then came the tug of Greek with Greek, to get to the place of fortune again. A second *splash!* At last, an old Frenchman, with Madame and child, descend for a boat. A rush of boats takes place, and there follows a scene so novel in boating, to an American, that we transcribe it as a specimen of the manners of the descendants of Epaminondas and Pericles. Boat No. 1 catches Madame as she descends,—the picture of the "unprotected female" in Punch. While politely seating her, No. 2 seizes the old man, and drags him into his boat—he just escaping a cold bath. No. 1 runs up for the baggage, which Nos. 3, 4, 5, 6 and 7 have seized, amidst terrific jabberings; and which they seem determined to divide piecemeal. Madame discovers her isolated state, and reaching out her arms frantically, screams, "Papa!" "Papa!" as no one but a Frenchwoman can. The young scion adds his treble. The guns from the Greek man-of-war thundering a reception to the French admiral, who had just left the other side of our boat for his ship, join the chorus. Amid this noise and the smoke, the din of Grecian conflict continues. No. 2 quickly joins his boat, and Madame and child tumble over into it. No. 1 returns to find his prey minus, discovers the triumph of No. 2, and makes a lurch at him for the robbery. They clinch, and over they roll, perfectly unconscious of the fickle elements below; still, they somehow manage to keep in the boats. No. 3 rushes to the rescue; knocks off Madame's hat; while the disapproving scion pummels him with his little fists. Madame screams. Nos. 3, 4, 5, 6, 7, 8, &c., rush to the meleé, with oars, boat-hooks, and boots in air. The Laocoon was never so involuted as the twisting folds of these lithe Grecians. All is confusion. We stand above, laughing at the singular scene, while its objects, the passengers, crawl off into boat No. 9, and escape to the shore. Our officers are kicking at the heads of the Grecians as they approach within range. At last, our mate suggests the old expedient, and buckets of cold water are plenteously rained in upon the fighting mass. The Greek man-of-war sends a boat of sailors to aid the hydropathic expedient; and in peace we are permitted to land upon the shores of Greece.

These Greeks bear the reputation of lying, cheating rascals.

At every chance they take advantage of each other, as well as of strangers. They have a good share of enterprise. Those who come from the islands are especially sharp and active. But moral sensibility seems utterly imbruted among them. The same race who introduced by fraud the horse into Troy,—the same who pretended to leave Troy, and hid in that little isle of Tenedos, which we are approaching,—the same nation whose *faith* was a proverb for inconstancy, still people Attica. There is little to attract in the first glance at Greece. Every thing looks arid and dry. Rain they have not had for the three summer months. The olives are the only trees, and they look dusty and parched. Some few years ago the snow laid nearly a whole day upon the ground about Athens, and killed the oranges and vines, while it withered the olive considerably.

We learned at the Pireus that it would be impossible to go to Joppa before the middle or last of July, as the Austrian steamer does not leave till then. Consequently we shall have to omit our Jerusalem trip, and be satisfied with a visit to the Capital of the Ottoman.

The kind and urbane missionary at the Pireus, Mr. Buel, of the Baptist denomination, received us most cordially. We had a letter to him from our Consul at Malta. Mr. Buel offered to guide us among the ruins of Athens, which offer was readily accepted. A better guide never traveller rejoiced in. He is indeed a scholar and a Christian gentleman, and his life abroad is not without incident, which marks him as a man of earnest will and heroic devotion in the cause of liberty and gospel truth.

Our country has reason to be proud of its missionaries here. Dr. King and Mr. Hill are the missionaries at Athens; the former is of the American Board, and the latter, I believe, is an Episcopalian. Dr. King, as well as Mr. Buel, has been subjected to litigation and trouble, on account of the jealousy and intolerance of the Greek monks. These missionaries are the representatives of free discussion, guarantied by the Greek Constitution, but little known in its practical significance.* When pressed too hard by those in power, they have one argument which never fails them. It is an appeal to the "stripes and stars." The other Sunday, some of the monks of the Greek Church, wishing to embroil Dr. King in a difficulty, repaired to his church, in company with a mob of students from the University, apparently for the purpose of discussion. The Doctor had a full house. After proceeding in his sermon, he was interrupted by a monk, who wished to propound certain queries, the object of which was to draw out from Dr. King some expressions invidious to the Greek Church. The Doctor told him, that if he would come the next day he would answer him, as he did not desire a discussion at that time. But they would not be put off. Fierce gestures and threatenings followed, and they began to advance upon the Doctor. A few days before, a tin box with a flag containing quite a number of stripes, and more stars, had arrived at Athens for our Consul, and in his absence it was left with Dr. King, Consul *ad interim*. The Doctor's servant quietly slipped up stairs in the midst of the row, and while the students were advancing on the Doctor, returned with the flag, and spread it out from the pulpit! Hurrah! but you should have seen those scions of the heroes and demi-gods slink, like whipped sheep-dogs, out of the house. Not a word more, not a gesture, but a quiet sneak away from the *republican flag*, told

* Since my return to America, I have seen it stated that Dr. King had been arrested for an alleged reviling of the Greek religion; that the Court below had found him guilty, but that the case had been removed to a higher tribunal. The final hearing was had on the 18th of December, 1851, when Mr. Pilikas, one of Dr. King's lawyers, and *prytannis*, or president of the University, maintained, in an able speech, that controversy was not reviling the Greek religion; and when he took occasion to pay several handsome compliments to America, as the home of free thought and free speech. If Dr. King should succeed, of which there is small hope, owing to the corruption of the Court and the influence of the Government, it will be a triumph of civil and religious liberty worthy of that city where Socrates taught and Plato reasoned.

more of the influence of true liberty than Greece has felt for many a long year. The ancient Greeks used to imagine a Hesperian clime, beyond the pillars of Hercules, near the setting sun; and Plato organized an imaginary commonwealth, where human passion played harmoniously and subordinately for the public weal, without jar or rupture. Out of such a clime, and from such a republic, an influence emanated as ideal as it was potent upon the soul of the plastic Grecian. May we not hope that an analagous influence, as *real* as it is potent, shall emanate from our own Hesperus, to mould anew the dynasties of corrupt power in this eastern world?

When I left home I did not dream of going farther east than Rome. To be permitted to see the source of all that is beautiful in Art, glorious in Poetry, profound in Philosophy, and powerful in Eloquence, was a joy too great for my limited hope. But—I have stood upon the Acropolis! Although I had been utterly oblivious of all my voyaging hither, yet I could have told immediately, that Attic elegance, even in its ruins, environed me, and that this was indeed the marvel of Taste, the adornment of Pericles, and the eye of Greece.

Five miles through the plain, once covered with the homes of Athenians, now denuded of all save a few olive orchards and vineyards, bring us to the city from the Pireus. Formerly, the Pireus formed a part of Athens. A walled street connected them. A chariot course was upon these walls. You may remember that Socrates used to go down to the Pireus, to talk with the *unsophisticated* whom he met there, and from whom he learned many of those famillar figures of speech which convey so aptly great truths. Few ruins line the way. The Parthenon upon the Acropolis first catches the eye, and detains it to the last. Mr. Buel informed me that from his house in the Pireus, he could count its pillars, so clear is the glisten of the Pentelic marble in this transparent air. Far above the city looms up the Acropolis. From it, as from the elevated centre of a charmed circle, the eye may sweep the most soul-stirring scenery of the world, unless we except the view from the Mount of Olives.

I had been led, by hearing an Englishman expressing his disgust of Athens and its relics, to expect but a meagre view of these hallowed scenes. Perhaps I owe the intense interest I took in these associations and localities, to the intelligent and communicative missionary who accompanied us.

In ascending the Acropolis, we first stop at the temple of Theseus. It was built 465 B. C. Its parts are perfect still. The roof is modern. An earthquake has shaken it, doubtless, for the different portions of the pillars have been disturbed from their original base. Thirty-four beautiful Doric columns attest the grace and elegance of this style of architecture. On the eastern façade all the ten metopes are occupied with bass-reliefs, representing the labors of Hercules, whose friendship for Theseus is thus shown. The relics of the demi-god, Theseus, were brought here from the isle of Skyros, and interred.

The Theseum is but a stepping-stone, by which to ascend to greater beauties and more hallowed localities. What means this large area, braced around by immense hewn stones, so immense that it seems impossible that human might could have brought them here? Sixteen by ten feet in size, these stones range around the *Pynx*, so called from their pressing the earth upward. Above, as it were in the most commanding point of the vicinity, is a solid, flinty rock, carved into a platform, with seats for different officers and the orators. We can hear from the farthest point of the Bema the ordinary conversation of our French friends, who have anticipated our ascent to this massive throne of the Grecian *demus*—the throne of Oratory and Statesmanship. The *Bema* is turned from the sea to the inland. Formerly it was upon the summit of the hill, but so potent and thrilling were the allusions of the orators, as well as their gestures as they pointed out the naval scenes of triumph, that the thirty tyrants removed it further down. But it still commands a view of the Acropolis; and that view furnished

Demostenes with one of his finest allusions to the gods, who were ranged in statues above him upon the right, in his famous oration upon the crown.

We stand upon the solid platform, where Demosthenes, Æschines, and their compatriots, harangued the people. An area of 12,000 yards is about us. There is no doubt of the identity of this place, however problematical other places may be. There are two spots renowned, the one in sacred, and the other in profane history, as to the particular identity of which, there cannot linger a possible shade of doubt. One is Jacob's well—the scene of the memorable conference between our Saviour and the Samaritan woman. It is dug in the solid rock. You may be sure when you stand over Jacob's well, that you are at least within a few feet of the spot where Jesus stood. The place of the Holy Sepulchre, of the crucifixion, of the ascension, and of the transfiguration, are all in darkness or doubt. About Jacob's well, Mahomedan, Jew, Christian, and Infidel, all agree. Not less certain is the spot marked as the Grecian Bema. When you stand there, you may be certain that you stand just where Demosthenes stood, when he hurled his torrent of indignation upon his opponents, and shook, by his words of thunder, Artaxerxes' throne. From no spot in the world has emanated such winged words, freighted with so warm an enthusiasm, and so cogent a logic. It stirred the soul, to stand on this throne of oratory—to image forth the scene of that memorable day when Æschines—the polished actor of the theatre and the glosing courtier of the people, met the Prince of Orators in the question about the crown, and was forever whelmed in the popular element over which he had so often skimmed, volubly and gracefully. From that fountain sprung the mighty flood of speech, which through ages has rolled on as it began, in a channel ever full,—never overflowing. Well did it merit the eulogium of Brougham, who loved himself to quaff of its inspiring influence, "whether it rushed in a torrent of allusion, or moved along in a majestic exposition of enlarged principle, or descended hoarse and headlong in overwhelming invective, or glided melodious in narrative and description, or spread itself out shining in illustration—its course is ever onward, ever entire; never scattered, never stagnant—never sluggish." Oh! for one tone—one living breath of the old oratory from this, its early altar! Oh! for one of those vehement anathemas against Philip, which have spread the fame of Grecian oratory through the long centuries and over wide seas and continents; or even for one of his inferior harangues in favor of Rhodian liberty, or upon the Classes, on the Halonesus, or for the regulation of the State; each and all, compressed with energy and relevant with cogency; ever pervaded by prayerful devotion to the gods and to his native city! But we have no echo here of the mighty voice. Greece is pulseless, and no tone could arouse her now. With the great Past filling the charmed air, we can but stand and wonder—in silence!

Let us ascend that other hill of solid limestone yet nearer the Acropolis. The path upward is rough and uneven from the Bema; although when Paul ascended it, to gratify the Athenian love of novelty, he doubtless surmounted *Mars Hill* from the other side, where, worn by rain, yet still visible, are steps cut in the solid limestone. I sought my pocket Testament, for here was the spot of *sacred* oratory.

Boys were flying kites from its summit. Donkeys and sheep were lying lazily around its base. Burs and thistles hang to each spot where vegetation may eke out its scanty subsistence. A tall, flinty cliff rises beyond the city of Athens, which is gathered into a small space below. The long olive plains spread out beneath the eye even to the sea. A column stands on a hill upon the right, still higher than Mars, erected to Philopopus in the first century. Before us is the Acropolis—the invincible and the beautiful—whose store of relics, with their tasteful decorations, "empearl the starless ages" of the world. But here, upon this spot, first broke upon the world of philosophy, that light which alone enunciates the principle of life and immortality ; that gospel which cast into the shade all the logomachies of the schools and the discoveries of science, which reduces into nothingness even that beautiful system of unity and the highest improvement of reason, which PLATO, walking beneath those green olives upon the left, and in the mellifluousness of his divine tongue, eliminated, unassisted by Revelation. What are they all, compared to the annunciation of Paul from Mars Hill, when he declared to the men of Athens, the unknown God, and *that this God made the world and all things therein, seeing that He is Lord of Heaven and earth, dwelling not in* TEMPLES *made with hands!* To feel the force of this declaration, one must stand where Paul stood, and read it in view of the temples, gorgeous and glistening, "springing rounded to columns" from each mound and hill, and especially from that lofty hill to which he doubtless pointed, as he referred—crowned by the most splendid architectural triumph of all time! An illustration thus forcible and striking, could not have fallen upon dull ears. It had its fruit, for we read that Dionysius, the Areopagite, was converted.

There are traces of a church to St. Dionysius, below the northeast corner of the Areopagus, erected to commemorate his conversion. Upon the level of the hill, above the steps spoken of, at the southeast angle of the hill, is a bench, excavated in limestone, forming three sides of a quadrangle. It faces the south. The Areopagus sat here, it is said. Dark, dread, tribunal ; in its nightly sittings, uninfluenced by mercy, and hard as its adamantine seats to the approach of clemency!

The Parthenon rises majestically from its solid basis. Although the Venetian has been upon that basis and built his ungainly towers; although the bombs of the Turk, fragments of which we saw, have shattered many a beautiful capital and column ; although a magazine here exploded, tearing out the fine sides of this incomparable structure, yet there it stands the glory of the city, and the pride of the sea. The Acropolis itself is 150 feet above the level of the plain. Upon this is the Temple. In the temple was once the tall statue of Minerva, whose tall spear, tipped with a flag, was the first object which met the returning sailor, as he weathered Cape Sunium. The great plain of the old city spread around. Alas! but a plain compared with that Athens which triumphed at Marathon, Salamis, and Platea. But the eye may yet trace the boundaries of the Academy and the Lyceum; whose systems, false in many respects, detained, by their intellectual spell, the advancing mind of the world for fifteen centuries. The bed of the Illissus—ha! ha! what a river for an American to look at! The Sciota compared to it, is as the Mississippi to the Sciota. The classic stream is but a little dry run, shrunk into nothing, and hardly traceable. The Cephissus, which we crossed in coming to Athens from Pireus, is little larger, but rejoices in a sprinkle of water. Upon the west is the sea, with Salamis bay and isle. The Athenians could easily have seen from this point the battle of Salamis, where Themistocles covered himself with such glory as Grecians alone knew how to bestow. His tomb still looks down, in lonely grandeur, upon the scene of his triumph.

In an opposite direction rise, in serene and dim beauty, the hill Colonos, and the Pentelic mountains, both known in the muse of Sophocles. The stadium, the space over which the charioteers burned to gain the goal, is spread out between us and the distant hills. The theatre of Bacchus, in which the drama of Greece was displayed with its furies, demi-gods, and gods—lies below, marked by a few columns. Other monuments, erected by the Romans, Hadrian's amphitheatre, and such like, are in a better state of preservation.

The temple of Jupiter Olympus detains the eye longer. It was completed by a Roman emperor. Sixteen Corinthian columns yet remain to tell its superiority. Sixty feet high they tower; while anciently they performed the circuit of 2,300 feet. The whole length of the building was 354 feet, and the number of columns was 120. Now as I look at its remains, the eye finds its area covered by great stacks of wheat, in the process of threshing. Men are superintending. This process was peculiar. Imagine three *cultivators*, or corn harrows, with teeth turned backward; these chained together, and a man on each; drawn by horses trampling the straw, while men were engaged in stirring it up, and you have a very unscientific description of the threshing process. Women were riding the horses, and stirring the straw, assisting the work. A motley group that, in the temple of Jupiter! Why so much straw *here?* It is a ridiculous law, that every farmer shall bring his wheat or grain into one point fixed by the officer, there to be threshed in his presence, so that *government may take its toll!* American farmers! how would you like that? Jupiter Olympus! would you not upset such a government in a jiffy?

A Spartan band were playing most execrably under the lofty columns of Jupiter's temple. They had come as far as possible out of Athens, in order that they might not be heard. There is more harmony for the eye than the ear upon the Acropolis. The former has not yet been exhausted. The statues, fragments of tracery and inscriptions are gathered here. In each, even though broken and defaced, one may see that excellent device and wonderous slight, which formed so much to gratify the love of beauty. Many a lady at home admires an edging, or *interjects* in wonder over a figure in a fabric, whose fine original peeps out of the broken Pentelic upon the Acropolis. Many a grace has been stolen by *genius* from these rude fragments, which now shines in fresh habilaments of stone in the villas of Italy and the homes of England. All the great eras of history are distinguished by some enthusiastic sentiment as a universal principle of action. That period of Grecian glory when the distinguishing sentiment was most prominent was that of Pericles; and that sentiment was an intense love of the beautiful, not alone in form, but in idea. If a fane of alabaster rose gracefully under the enchanting sky, amid its groves of myrtles and olives, waving under the gentle breeze, there was also an answering *soul* of beauty dilating under its shadows, at the vision of truth serene, spreading graces forth, and visible in their beauty.

PLATO—all radiant and divine; what soul, unassisted by direct intercourse with its Maker, ever dared a bolder flight than his, toward that Christianity which God incarnate came to teach! Did he not dedicate his youth at the feet of Socrates, and his old age in yonder grove,—the first fruits and the latter growth,—to the upbuilding of the fairest fabric which human Reason ever reared in honor of its Maker? Where is the rule of life, the sentiment of affection, the profound thought, which he has not touched and adorned? Did he not probe the deepest truth in Nature, when he said: "Let us declare the cause which led the Supreme Ordainer to produce and compose the Universe. He was good; and he who is good has no kind of envy. Exempt from envy, he wished that all things should be as much as possible like himself. All things are for the sake of the good, and it is the cause of every thing beautiful." In one thing only did he fail. He gave no *authoritative* rule of duty, for he was not commissioned from on high. Oh! if his seraphic soul could have seen that glory which beamed in the mild star of Bethlehem, and could have listened to the eloquent Apostle from Mars Hill, as he dissipated the mists of all the schools, by declaring that "He gave to all, life and breath and all things," and that "in Him we live and move and have our being,"—what rapture would not his great mind have felt, what humility would have graced the seer of Academus!

Such reflections, and such like, have made our visit to Athens one of deepest interest. It is not the modern city—not the temples of Victory, of the Winds, of Bacchus, or of Jupiter even,—it is not the prison cut in the rock, and pointed out to us as the abode of Socrates in his last hours,—it is not the fountains and caves, not any *external* form of Nature or Art, which gives to Greece its never-dying spell of enchantment. Athens lies calmly beautiful to the mental eye, as the old haunt of Wisdom, Poetry, Oratory, Art, and Heroism. The eye seeks in vain for the "warrior's weapon and the sophist's stole;" the Grecian phalanx no longer moves to the eye, and the Orators no longer spell-bind the people from the Bema; but it is enough that here was once

> "The dome of Thought—the palace of the soul!"

After examining the singular construction of the Parthenon, in which there is not a single straight line—strange though it seem—after measuring with the eye that singular adaptation, by which part is made to lean upon and support part, thus rendering a part equal in strength to the whole,—after sweeping the horizon again and again, and standing upon that "lofty mountain thought" which rises out of the City of Minerva, we felt the spirit stretch into a view, so full of life, and splendor, and joy, that its transcript seems as impossible as its reality was sublime. One should stand upon the Acropolis, before boasting of having seen aught or felt aught elsewhere on this round globe.

But I must descend. Our guide, the kind missionary, invites us to his house. While awaiting the hospitable tea, the sun sinks in gold below Salamis, and gentle airs are wafted over the Pireus. A Grecian tea it was—dainty and elegant. With the tea is taken delicate preserves made from the split leaves from the heart of the rose, and with the water, a sweet transparent paste called *rahatlikum*, common in the Orient. But most we delight to remember the kindly grace and the genuine goodness of Mr. Buel, who saw us safely upon our boat, and regretfully left us to our eastern path. Had we remained longer with him, he promised us the pleasure of meeting Mrs. Black, Byron's "Maid of Athens," and the daughter of Marco Bozzaris (pronounced *Botezarris*), who are his neighbors, and frequently spend their evenings with him. The former is now a respectable matron of a large family. The latter is no longer connected with the Queen's Court.

Athens in itself has nothing striking in its appearance. It contains 23,000 people, but seems no larger than one of our ordinary county seats. It lies in a triangular shape. I do not see how they can pack so much humanity in it. But its streets are narrow. Men need no more house room here, however, than will serve as their couch. The shops are scanty and small. The baking is done at public ovens, on the associated Fourier principle. There are plenty of carriages at Athens, and cheap; but the roads are poor, the streets are dirty, and illy-paved and crooked. The foot-walks are about two feet wide. The people are a sad mixture of respectable and miserable; the latter predominating. They are mostly idlers; busying themselves as formerly, in "hearing and telling some new thing." Education is progressing. Many fine buildings for that purpose are being erected. The palace and its gardens stand out conspicuously in the treeless, sandy plain, upon the edge of the city. Water from the wells is constantly pumped by diligent donkeys, to irrigate the thirsty soil. The people depend on the goat for their milk and butter. Beef is an unknown luxury. Hymethus still yields her honeyed wealth, according to Byron. Perhaps it is a poetic license. There are no women apparent. It was daylight when we went through. They only appear, star-like, by night. These domestic items must now close. One should not judge too hastily of such things; but to our hasty glance, Athens modern is to Athens ancient as the poorest fragment of an old statue is to the bright and symmetrical mould of a Phidias.

The next morning found us darting around Cape Sunium, upon whose rocky steep the white columns of the temple of Minerva shine, and from which they look upon the sea. This temple was erected here to remind the voyager of the Goddess of Athens, at the very gate of Attica.

I think, with Lamartine, that a tomb or temple fills the mind with holier thoughts and purer associations, when located, as is the tomb of Themistocles or the temple of Pallas, upon a lone and rocky promontory,—"afar from the city's troublous cries,"—drawn in the clear air against the beautifully blue horizon, and rising instinct with Nature into closer communion with heaven.

XV.

Home of Homer.

"Oft of one wide expanse had I been told
That deep brow'd HOMER ruled as his demesne."

Keats.

WE are now on board the fine French steamer Egyptus, dodging, by the cunning of steam, the isles of Greece, which rise in these blue waters on all sides. We are playing between Thermia, named from its warm springs, and Zea, with Journa, the old Roman place of banishment, ahead. It will take nice navigation to extricate us from the complexity of these islands. But it is thrilling to career amidst these homes of ancient genius. They seem to have been compensated, for the bleakness and barreness of their scenery, by the growth of men in the elder day. We shall, before long, see the isles where Homer and Sappho lived and sung, and where God appeared in rapt vision to the soul of John, the seer of Patmos, and opened to him those Revelations of Wonder, Glory, and Mystery, which form the Omega of the living word.

It is verging toward midnight. I have just been on deck. The gallant steamer is shooting past the isle of Homer—the loveliest of the Archipelego—the most fruitful and picturesque of the isles of Greece—the celebrated Scio. It is called the Paradise of the Levant; and well deserves the name for its extraordinary fertility, and beautiful foliage and scenery. This isle is under the dominion of the Ottoman, and the revenues it affords are dedicated to the support of the mother of Abd-ul-Mejid, the present Sultan, who lives in magnificence upon the banks of the Bosphorus. It is in strange contrast with the other isles of Greece; which rise in rocky eminences and broken promontories from the sea. True, it suffered much in the Greek revolution. But its vineyards, its olives, its citrons and its mastic groves, then cut down, are again bespreading the island. The other isles afford but scanty homes for the goat. Man scarcely plants his foot upon the different spots we have passed to-day, but upon Scio he has revelled amidst the prodigality of Nature. The mastic is the chief object of cultivation. It is the product of the Lentisk shrub, which covers the hill slopes, and which, when cut, drops the liquid mastic. This is hardened, refined, and exported for the use of the Turkish ladies. But why speak of all this? Is not this *the* isle of Homer? Of all the claims to the honor of his birthplace Scio has preferred the best. Beside, she is rich in other names. Ion the tragic poet, Theocritus the sophist, and Theopompus the historian, all hailed from this isle. But why distinguish Scio amidst such a fraternity of isles, all rich in the associations of classical antiquity,

> "Where grew the arts of war and peace;
> Where Delos rose and Phœbus sprung.
> The Scian and the Teian Muse.
> The hero's harp, the lover's lute,
> Have found the fame your shores refuse;
> Their place of birth alone is mute
> To sounds which *echo further west*
> Than your sire's islands of the blest."

Never did bard sing more truly. Our boat is full of Greeks. I have just walked amidst them—*sleeping* upon the deck, utterly unconscious that they are passing the native spot of him, whose song has rung the name of Greece through two thousand years, and from continent to continent. The stars look down calmly and full of sparkle from their unclouded vault. The dark isle rises majestically upward, amidst their fretted fires. The Orient, with its deep and infinite splendors, fills the mind of the gazer, as he looks upward and eastward along that star-strewn path. Yonder, not far from the early home of Homer, is the ancient Troy, around whose walls the scenes of Epic glory took place, with deities for actors and witnesses, which the Bard has reduced into numbers as enduring as his own name. Fit vantage ground was Scio, whence the young poet might view the scene of his own future triumphs in Poesy; fit school wherein to nurture that imagination which dared no flight it did not attain. Perhaps from that round point of rock tufted with yellow verdure, just opposite our vessel, "he beheld the Iliad and the Odyssey, rise to the swelling of the voiceful sea." There, might have been kindled the first spark of that genius which outlives the triumphs of all Conquerors.

Thanks to thee, Old Shore! Thou who wert the parent of art, and gave that Homer to time, which time has given to our modern world! These isles while they furnished rocks and hills, bays and mountains, as the haunts of his muse; yon rocky shore which we have left behind us, while it furnished the cloud-capped Olympus towering upward amid fraternal mounts, for his heroes and gods, also cherished his minstrelsy. Athens received his Epos; her philosophers criticised it, in unity and part; her orators quoted it; her Olympic games echoed its song; her drama was moulded by it; her sculptors formed its images and her architects enshrined them in Parthenons and Theseums. Rome gave to him apotheosis, before which power bowed in wonder, love and awe. Alexandria hid his works in hieroglyphs, but at last redeemed the ancient fame of Egypt by transmitting them to us in their present form. What would painting have been without the Venus and Diana; sculpture without the Apollo and Jove; or art without the Iliad? Legislation, too, while it cherished his works, found in them the spirit of its best enactments. The literature of the world owes to them its Virgil, Dante, Ariosto, Tasso, Milton, Wieland, Klopstock, its Henriade and Auraucana!

We are apt to look upon Homer, only as a singer, whose songs have no practical bearing upon the world. To the philosophical historian, they have deeper significance. True, their first effect was the introduction of other songs, and, in time, a superior literature in Greece. But this literature proved the salvation of even Christendom. If the classics were the bulwarks around the city of God, laid by the ancients through their own history, is not Homer the strongest tower of defence upon that bulwark? The study of Platonism and of the ethics of the rival school of Aristotle, burned in the cloisters of the dark ages, when even Christian truth was almost gone out. The destruction of Byzantium scattered the Grecian literature. The key to the New Testament thus found its way into Florence under the Medici, and into Wittenberg under the elector, until Protestantism had her lion-hearted Luther, Catholicism her sarcastic Erasmus, and the world its mild Melancthon and fervent Fenelon. England had her Duns Scotus, whose scholastic learning was exhaustless, and who gathered around him thirty thousand students at Oxford, where he taught them the logic of Aristotle, with a power which drew forth the encomium, "had the genius of Aristotle been unknown, that of Scotus could have supplied his place." And it was the ethics of Aristotle, thus taught, which brightened the mind of Wyckliffe, and gave to England her first translation of the Bible, and the reformation. To this Bible and this reformation America owes her present proud position. They unlocked the prisons of power. They unloosed the disfranchised people. The individual was rescued from the congealed hierarchy. The liberties of speech; body; property and conscience were enunciated; and to Homer in the last analysis belongs a great part of the glory! Ah! if the shade of Homer could *see* (we trust his shade is better off than the original *corpus*) this steamer of ours, with its poetry of motion, parting the waves more fleetly than his most arrowy pinnace, and working more fearfully powerful than his most potent engine against the Trojan wall; if he could see this phase of a new civilization, his visions of Olympus and dreams of Divinities, would vanish before the solid workmanship of his own brother man.

What avails this pondering? Onward we move; the French flag waves in the wind; the black guns, like sleeping lions, lie about the deck; the huge pipe emits its clouds of smoke; the illuminated compass directs the silent helmsmen; the place of Homer's birth is mute and silent under the shadow of night; a small "echo further west" than even the blest isles, remembers the blind old bard in his fugitive pencillings; and we—dart away to new scenes and other shores.

XVI.

The Heart of Mahometanism.

——— " His eye looked o'er the dark, blue water,
That swiftly glides and gently swells
Between the winding Dardanelles."

BYRON.

WE have seen the Orient, if not Jerusalem. Smyrna, where one of the seven churches was located, and the point whence fruit is exported and where the camels bring the resources of Syria to market, was seen and enjoyed. Its figs and chibouques; its dirt and its dignity; its dogs and donkeys; its dreariness and picturesqueness, were all seen and felt in one day's stay; and our vessel turned her prow toward Constantinople, where Orientalism swells in complete luxuriousness under the dominion of the dervishes and the Sultan. We entered the Dardanelles about evening, having passed the isle of Mitylene, or Lesbos, (Sappho's birthplace), and having had a glimpse of the great mountain of Athos, rising out of the sea beyond the isle of Lemnos. The Dardanelles is generally as wide as the Mississippi, with a strong current toward the Mediterranean from the sea of Marmora. The land is fine, rolling and cultivated; and here and there we meet with enterprising and beautiful villages on the Asiatic and European sides of the straits. Our boat stopped some two hours at the city of Dardanelles, where there are numerous castles, as outposts of defence to Constantinople. The castles are supposed to be the ancient sites of Abydos and Sestos. A strip of stony shore, projecting between two high cliffs, furnished the European extremity of Xerxes' bridge, by which he crossed from Asia to the invasion of Greece. This part of the Dardanelles is also celebrated as the point where

Alexander's army, under Parmenio, crossed from Europe to Asia. Here, too, the Ottoman first began his inroad upon Europe, in the fourteenth century, under Sulieman. Here "Leander swam the Hellespont" to visit his Hero, and Lord Byron did the same in one hour and ten minutes, and wrote poetry to herald the feat to posterity.

Before leaving the Dardanelles, I made a singular acquaintance. It was none other than that of a Bey. He observed me examining a map of Constantinople, and politely undertook some explanations. As I could not understand Turkish nor he English, we had a pleasant time of it—very, until I got a book which contained words of both tongues, when we amused each other by reciprocating the pronunciation of words. He had a large number of servants, and sat on his fine mat, smoking his chibouque, the ashes of which were emptied and the tobacco supplied by a servant, from time to time. The tube of the pipe condescended to rest some feet from his mouth in a shining pan. The Turk always carries a comboloio, or rosary of beads, to assist conversation. What assistance these black beads, which travel over the henna-stained fingers of the lady and the effeminate hand of the gentleman of the Orient, render in the interchange of sentiment, those may understand who feel nonplussed in conversation, without the aid of a watch-key in their hands or a cane head in their mouths. The Spanish lady resorts to a similar inspiration, by the unfolding of her fan and a coquettish snap as she closes it. The Turk, however, converses but little. He prefers a passive occupation. His favorite pastime is backgammon, a board of which our Bey carried along. It is a great game with the luxurious idlers of the Capital, who stake large sums on their success. He was particularly sharp in it, as one of our ladies can testify, with whom he played. I have not seen as fine a gentleman since coming among the Turks. We gave him an invitation to America. He said he would call on us at our Hotel. Would like to have him bring a dozen or so of the Mrs. Beys along.

We found, on approaching Constantinople, many active business places, and we were surprised to see furnaces with tall chimneys, smoking in earnest. These elements of progress were soon left behind, however. Forts and walls begin to indicate that we were passing out of the sea of Marmora into the Bosphorus. We ran between the city of Scutari, in Asia, and Constantinople, on the European side, and turned around the point into the river called the Golden Horn, which divides the city proper from Para—the place for the Franks, Ambassadors, and Hotels. Our first view of this magnificent panorama was a disappointment. We had heard and read much of the view of this famous city, with its towers and domes, beaming and golden. A fog hid the city at first. Before we rounded the point, disappointment began to be dissipated with the mist. The expanding splendors opened. The minarets pointed upward, the cupolas swelled brightly amidst rising eminences of buildings stretching along the hill slopes, and unfolding brilliant involutions, as we rounded the point where the Seraglio rose, like a dream, out of the clear waters, and where Saint Sophia, the graceful Queen of a thousand beauteous mosques, gathered her cluster of minarets and domes. I have seen the vision, since, and know it to be real. Enchantment held her fairy wand before my eye at the first glance, and in the joyful amazement, I could not observe, only wonder—fearful that the dream would be dissolved, like magic views.

The green foliage of the cypress, interspersed as it always is in the Moslem cities, adds to the charm. The mirror of the Bosphorus, ranged around with the unique palaces of the pashas, and the marble, yet airy seraglio, together with royal abodes of gorgeousness, reflects three large and distinct cities, each enormous, and each divided by its own silver waters sleeping at its feet. One half of the magic ring is set within the hills of Asia, and the other half within those of Europe. Far beyond Scutari is spread the long range of Olympus, glistening under the *warm* sun, with snow, and hanging like pure clouds of white in the deep sky.

A finer harbor could not be conceived. The Bosphorus flows between two promontories, separating the Stamboul from Para, Galata, and Tophane. The largest man-of-war can here float; while around, over a space which can accommodate 1,200 sail of the line, *eighty thousand* little boats, called caïques, and resembling the canoe somewhat in its sharp point and feathery levity, dart with graceful facility. These are the hackney coaches and cabs which play over the silver limpid streets of this wondrous city of cities. These boats are called by the natives *kerlongist*, or swallow-boats, and are formed of the thin planks of beech wood. They are always dry and neat, and carved within and without. It is dainty work to ride in them, as they are as liable as a canoe to upset. Cushions upon the bottom, in Eastern style, is the mode. It is a delicious, cool ride, after threading the mazes of the dirty streets of the city, as we have had abundant cause to remember. You may fancy what these cities are, in one grand view; which requires 80,000 boats around the quays.

It would be unjust to expect a description of this city. Our stay in it must be limited to a few days; and these will be filled with laborious sight-seeing. I must leave much to your imagination, and use the suggestive style. No place can have more attractions just now for the traveller, than this half-way point between two extremes of civilization. Society is in the transition state. The old prejudices of the Moslem are giving way slowly before the progress of the age. Here, where Mahomet holds imperious sway, and where the Sovereign revels like a Sardanapalus in the most gorgeous palaces, and rejoices in his wives by the hundred; here, where the intolerant Mussulman prays five times daily, and holds his Ramazan with more than Puritan rigidity—here there is a leaven working which is destined to leaven the whole lump of that strange mixture of heaven and earth, goodness and badness, which emanates from the Koran and fills all Moslemdom.

No city has had wilder vicissitudes of fortune than this; and withstood them all. The sieges it has undergone triumphantly number twenty-four! It has been taken six times! Alcibiades, Severus, Constantine, Dandolo, Paleologos and Mahomet II., severally succeeded in entering its harbors and gates. These clear waters and swelling hills; those lofty heights of snow, and yon "golden horn" of plenty—have they not looked alike, more tolerant than its several tenants, upon the Grecian Commander and the Roman Emperor; the Persian Chosroes and Arabian Califs; Venetian Doges and French Counts; Bulgarian Krales and Avarian Chakars, Sclavonian Despots, and last and longest, Ottoman Sultans. And when Bonaparte's prophecy shall find fulfilment, and Europe shall become Cossack, may not Saint Sophia again rejoice in its old Greek worship, and that glittering Seraglio, with its golden towers, echo the iron tread of the Czar!

But this is a little too fast. Europe must play "*teeter-tawter*" over the balance of power for many a year yet, until some new Napoleon shall arise to upset all balances, or the people, the true Napoleons of the Empire, can assert their popular sovereignties, and bring government to its proper sphere, as the protector of the mass, and not the pamperer of the pride of a few.

The romance of Constantinople dies as soon as you begin to thread its dirty, splashy, bad paved, narrow, doggy, donkeyfied, carriageless, up-and-down streets. There is not a back alley in New York, which is not better than the best street here; and the comparison is an insult to the city. In going along, you cannot look at any thing, for fear of having your head cracked against the burden of some donkey, or the load of some broad-shouldered carrier; or for fear of treading upon one of the many thousand brindle dogs, who act the part of scavengers by day, and play that of howling dervishes by night. If dodging these and the innumerous criers with heads full of dainties and fruits; if missing the red-capped and brown-robed Jew; the long curly black-hatted Persian; the wily Armenian, and the turbaned Turk; if you are not run over by that mounted Pasha, attended by his slave on foot; if you do not run over those clumsy looking women in yellow boots and blue mantles, with head enveloped (save eyes) in white crape—being both black and white,—Turkish ladies and their Nubian slaves; if perchance you avoid that solitary gold-figured vehicle drawn by one horse, and called a carriage, which comes thundering along, attracting as much attention as a menagerie in High-street, Columbus; if unsplashed and with sane mind, amidst the heathenish howls and cries, and with sane body, amidst the opposing currents of the barbarous thoroughfares, you reach your hotel, you may draw a breath as long and free as mine at the end of this longitudinous sentence.

Our time, while here, has been occupied in driving about the city and environs in the carriage of our kind vice-consul, Mr. Dainese, an Italian by birth, and a noble-hearted liberal. Mr. Marsh is absent. Every possible attention, however, that we could require has been shown us. We were furnished by him with a firman and government officer, wherewith to visit the mosques, and in company with Jews, French and English, started out boldly. It was a little doubtful whether we could obtain admission or not, as it is now what is called Ramazan time with the Mahometans. This is a sacred time, which lasts for thirty days, during which all good Mussulmen are not allowed to eat, drink, smoke or snuff all day. They sleep mostly during the day, and at night begin the work of smoking and feasting. The mosques are filled day and night. It is Lent, and wretchedly do they look who keep it. It is a little doubtful whether it is kept strictly. Were it kept, you would see more miserable sights upon the Bosphorus, where the poor Moslems row all day, earning their bread by the sweat of their brow. At night the coffee-houses are crowded with Turks, who wait not to eat, before they take the chibouque, and puff away clouds of incense to the prophet.

Well, as I said, we started for the mosques. But first we were taken across the stream to the famous Seraglio. There we had to draw boots, or put on sacred sheep-skin slippers over them. A ridiculous plight we figured, slipping along the marble floors, wending our way through apartment after apartment, under roofs of fretted gold and many-shaped glass. Fountains, with golden fishes gliding in their basins, cooled the rooms. Elegant tracery and ornaments; ottomans of rarest richness; places for coffee, for smoking, for repose; a view of the Bosphorus and of verdurous gardens full of fragrance and flowers—everywhere told us of the dreamy Orient, and that here was the very select home of indolence, ease, luxury and—Eunuchs! We went into the harem; but the birds had flown across into Asia, where they were caged in one of the other (he has dozens) palaces of the Sultan. The wicker was there still; and the long gallery was hung with landscapes of every scene and clime—a gift to the harem by Reschid Pasha.—Here the Sultanas took their airings and peeped out into the free world. Poor prisoners in golden chains! Flowers bloom at your very windows, but ye cannot pluck them. Heaven arches how lovingly above you; but ye are the thoughtless slaves of the grossest sensuality, cribbed and cabined in these walls—no longer children of nature as God made ye!

Finally we came into splendid flower and fruit gardens—tastefully arbored and arched with the green architecture, in multiform beauty, on every side. The walls were tapestried and festooned with flowers and running shrubs. The Turks, more kind than the Italians, freely permitted us to carry away bouquets. We learned that the associations connected with the Seraglio, have not rendered it a favorite resort of the present Sultan; for it was here in the time of his father, that the Janizaries committed their acts of cruelty, which the lofty walls of the Seraglio were not strong enough to check. But no such associations disturbed our enjoyment. The fragrance of the mind will ever arise as each impression of these scenes of oriental and regal enchantment is renewed by memory.

After visiting the armory, we went to the Mosque of St. Sophia—the most splendid fabric (except St. Peter's) in the world. While we stood in expectancy of admission, with our slippers in hand, we were astonished at the appearance of a Nubian slave, with a whip or cane, and possessed with a devil, a shade or so blacker than himself. He was in an agony of inspiration—sent by the priests to drive the infidels away, and well he performed the office—the black rascal! As our guide translated it freely to me, he told the firman and the prime minister's officer, that it was Ramazan; that he should go to h—l; that he brought the Giaours here (meaning us well-behaved Christians), and if he did not leave, some terrible imprecation would fall on his head. He accompanied his words with blows from the cane over the firman's shoulders, who bowed and scraped, saying his "*salaam effendi*" (thanks, gentleman!); and not daring to drop the Nubian, for fear of the priests, five hundred of whom would have rushed out to help their slave. Quite a mob of Moslems had collected. We left rather incontinently. To-morrow, early, we try it again, I trust with better success.

It is our national birthday. Although we are now at the extremest point of our journey, and nearly 7,500 miles from our beloved land, yet the memory of its glad patriotism, bursting from millions of hearts in unison with our own, brings us closely home again. I will not devote my chapter to any raptures or gratulations over my native land. These would, however, come deeper and fuller from the heart of the *pilgrim*, than from the home-citizen. Our nation has so much to thank God for, that none but a traveller can feelingly and fully raise the orison.

We kept the 4th of July, by looking at the Sultan. We rowed across the Bosphorus, and were rejoiced to find ourselves in time to see him returning out of the mosque. He is obliged to show himself to the people every Friday, and always at fires, if the alarm does not cease within a certain time. To-day he was mounted on a splendid white charger, caparisoned in gold, and rode very languidly, yet not without the grace which betrays the Saracenic origin, between his files of soldiers and subjects. We were permitted by the officers to stand even before some pashas, as we were travellers; and saw him very well. His appearance is prepossessing. He has an unshorn face, rather pale, with mild, dark, and very small eyes. A sort of indolent dreaminess played about his lips and in his eye, indicating his character, which is that of a mild, kind-hearted prince, careless of politics and given up to pleasure. He devotes only some three hours a day to the affairs of his empire, and the rest of his time to his religious devotions, to the supervision of his palaces, which in modern European style are rising on the banks of the Bosphorus, to the society of his brother, mother and son, and no doubt a considerable time to the gallantries and attentions incumbent upon him as the head of a harem of four hundred ladies, into which no male is ever allowed to intrude, except the eunuchs, who number about seventy.

The Sultan is well beloved by the people, whose interests his government has favored. His manners are said to be unassuming and plain, and his disposition frank and amiable. He is not too good natured, however, to discriminate, for he always selects men of skill and science for the rewards and honors of the kingdom. His age is twenty-nine. A long life of usefulness may yet be his. His health was formerly precarious; and even now he appears effeminate and weak. He reminded me of the portraits I saw of Charles the Second of England. The distinguished part which Turkey has taken lately in the politics of Europe, has been owing to the ability and foresight of Reschid Pasha, the Prime Minister.

An Englishman remarked at our table, that "he always took off his hat to crowned heads, and that he must do it when the Sultan appeared." Oh! Spooneydom and Flunkeydom!—as Carlyle would say—are ye not dead yet? Did ye not die, poor wooden heads! when England turned off her vagabond Stuarts to spout to the winds their *divino jure?* No. I saw your embodiment to-day doff his beaver to the "crowned head;" and poor dunderbrain! he thought it was right loyal and good of him. I took off my poor straw hat, too; but it was on compulsion. Like Pickwick at the training, I was between two files of soldiers with fixed bayonets, and received admonition which I heeded, until I happened to think it was the 4th of July! and then I covered my republican pate, instanter.

It was quite antique and interesting to see the Sultan's train, led by a eunuch, whose lips would weigh less than ten pounds, (including teeth) and jetty dark, with a splendid robe and golden sword. Bringing up the rear came the petitioners, with their petitions in hand, following the Sultan to the palace, there to deliver them. It reminded me of what I had read of Orientalism, in its regal phases. It was one of those ancient customs, which the progressive spirit of the time has not eradicated. The changes which have been wrought in the Ottoman Empire and in the East generally, since Napoleon directed the genius of his Power hitherward, have been momentous. His enterprise was of little practical utility at the time; but it opened the richest portions of the earth to the eyes of the French, Russian, and English; and by their respective cupidity the Turkish power has been rendered less liable to aggression from either, and more formidable to all. Beside, steam has carried commerce to its primeval marts where Tyre and Sidon once flourished, and over these sacred spots where rove the Arab hordes. The reactionary influence of the west of Europe upon the East, rendered imperative by the possessions of England in India, of Russia in Circassia, and France in northern Africa, and by which the Oriental nations will be constantly aroused to improvement, is already evident in the augmentation of trade at Alexandria, Smyrna, in the Bosphorus, and in the Red Sea, and in the constant communication of travellers with the inhabitants of these most interesting countries. May we not hope that the new elements of our age, entering into the social organizations of the East, shall give again to this land that conspicuous greatness which God allotted to it when our world was young!

XVII.

A Lady's Verdict upon the Orient.

> "Charm'd magic casements, opening on the foam,
> Of perilous seas in faery lands."
>
> *Keats.*

PAINTERS have been known to confess that in copying one of Rembrandt's portraits, whose peculiarity is the darkness of the face silvered over with delicate lights, hundreds of the most exquisite lineaments were taken off, and still the likeness was not caught. The microscope was applied; and lo! another and yet another "gloomy light much like a shade" appeared, which being transferred to the copy, the expression came at once. So I think it is, in men's observation upon manners and things in travelling. *We* cannot reproduce the original as it gleams upon the eye. Hundreds of minute features may be trânscribed, but the original still lies in its *chiara obscura* like a Rembrandt, until you apply a woman's microscopic eye to the object, when the lineaments come forth, and the expression is happily transferred. Men lack that *circumstantialness* which women possess, and by which the latter picture with fidelity, if they do not color as highly. In our visit to the East, I have relied upon a lady-companion to apply the microscope, while my pen has been engaged in roving around from hill to hill and from sea to sea, from isle to isle and from shore to shore. The particularity of the description of the Seraglio, as well as of the visit to the Sweet Waters, will form a complement to my poor chapter, and complete its unity. Need I apologize for departing from the ordinary routine of book-making, by inserting the impressions of another? Will not the ladies at least give their sex a hearing? It is rare that a Buckeye daughter rambles amidst the camel-crowded streets of the mosque-adorned cities of the East; and her pencillings in familiar style;—well—well, they must speak for themselves, which they do, as follows:

Could I convey to the reader on paper a conversation which occurred this morning, it might somewhat account for this venturous chapter. I may, at least, confess thus much, that it is somewhat "on compulsion, Hal." My pages may, or may not, contain that which is novel; if not, they at least will be a novelty, journeying so far to greet you. Can it be possible that such a distance lies between us and our homes? We have seen so much, and yet have hastened hither with such incredible speed, that Time and Space have alike been annihilated.

The reader has, I think, been advised of our wanderings, so long as we were within the precincts of the European world. Shall it be my pleasure, now, to chat awhile of the Orient? We found the first touches of Orientalism in Greece—but it did not strike us so peculiarly as it has since, in cities farther east. Greece we visited for its ruins, and were amply repaid in the view from the Acropolis alone, with its surrounding Forum and Mars Hill, the temples and battle-scenes, and the whole spirit of the scenery which beams with delicacy, refinement and taste. I cannot leave Greece, however, without remembering the parting meal which we took with our kind friend Mr. Buel, the Baptist Missionary. After the fatigues of the day at Athens, we returned to his house at the Pireus, which, as well as the repast, impressed us so kindly and peculiarly, that I would fain remember them both in expression and thought; both were so Grecian, and yet so home-like. The house is a fine two-story one, with an entrance into a vestibule—a stairway on either side, leading to a common landing, half way up, which ends in a stairway turning to the centre of the room above. Folding doors open into a room large and airy, with walls and ceiling fitted up after the manner of those at Pompeii. A double window opens out upon a balcony; from which we viewed a charming sunset, all golden and radiant in beauty over the bay of Salamis, as well as the form of a lion couchant, cut out of the mountain against the distant sky. A bedroom opened on one side and a studio on the other; both having doors to the stairway. The three rooms consequently possessed a front view of one of the finest water scenes we have seen, always excepting Naples;—and that scene rendered doubly and thrillingly attractive, as the place where Themistocles triumphed and Greece was saved.

Mr. Buel had been distributing the ten commandments during a festival of the Greek church, and was thus the innocent cause of a mob at Corfu; and though he was under the protection of the authorities, yet the influence of the priests was so great that he was obliged to leave the island at short notice for Malta; from thence he came to Smyrna, and then to the Pireus; where he has been for the last six years subjected to much annoyance and vexation in various lawsuits connected with his mode of teaching and proclaiming Christianity in Greece. He is now firmly and successfully established in his post.

At dark, the servant called us to tea, where I had the honor of presiding, as Mrs. B. had been for some time, and was still absent in America, upon a visit. It was a charming, neat little table, and I shall remember it particularly, being desirous of emulating its simple elegance when *we* shall go to housekeeping. It pleased another. Tea, toast, bread and butter; a white acidified cream-dish, flavored and slightly resembling our Dutch cheese; the expressed quintessence of the heart of roses (a kind of eastern sweets,) and delicious sponge-cake;—What could have been more daintily delectable? Keats, in his "Eve of St. Agnes," hints at a similar regalia of viands. We enjoyed it finely as I fully demonstrated by my long delay thereat. But tea is past,—and we retire to the drawing-room, where in pleasant converse we hold the approaching night hours as in a spell, until it is time to be aboard. Mr. Buel escorted us thither. It was a pleasant sea-row; for the lightning's vivid flash lighted up sky and water with a strange glow; and the circling brilliants of lights that shone on the Pireus made earth rival heaven in its stellar splendor. But there was no rain with the lightning flash. Indeed, that would have been too much of a luxury. We have scarcely felt a shower since we left home, save the one of the arching prisms, beneath which we glided out of that dark and cavernous tunnel and into the gay city of Marseilles!

We reached our ship—rather an unpleasant change from so home-like a visit (how heartily tired I had become of the boat), although the officers greeted us with the kindly courtesy so peculiar to the French. How provoking not to know more fully their language. One half of the pleasure is thus lost through want of knowledge,—that is, the travelling part, for, when stationary, we can occupy ourselves sufficiently in sight-seeing.

The monotony of the voyage, however, was somewhat broken by the numerous isles,—some vine-clad and olive-colored, but mostly rocky and bleak, which are known as the Archipelago, and celebrated as the birthplaces and homes of the most gifted minds of ancient Greece. We awoke on the morning of the 30th of June in the harbor of Smyrna, Asia Minor. This is the point from which travellers start to see the seven churches of Asia, of which that at Smyrna is one. It lies along a slope of the hill-side. On the right hand is a large grove of cypress, pointing out the Moslem Cemetery. The roofs are brown,—from amidst which ascend the tall minarets and round domes of the mosques. The large castle sweeps, from the high hill above, the circular view. Deep shadows checker with warm sunlight the coast far around. From the green bay which curls all over with white-caps, the city lifts itself up, a dreamy, picturesque vision of truly Asiatic scenery! What a quaint old Orientalism it is!

We were early on shore, and went directly to a hotel; but, how unfortunate! they refused to give us breakfast until nine o'clock. This was not to be endured for a moment; and, as the ladies declared their willingness to resort to a café, we shook the dust off of our feet in a truly oriental style, and left with marked indignation! We had, by some queer turn of luck, been thrown into the way of an odd specimen for a guide,—a tall, gaunt Jew, bad-featured and bearded. His soiled garments and coarse brown Abrahamic tunic, gave him any thing but the appearance of a desirable cicerone to the ignorant and *respectable* stranger.

But a fine café soon brought us relief, in its large and airy proportions, its delightful water-view, and, what came more especially home to us, its substantial edibles. Chibouques and Hobble-gobbles (Turkish pipes) were plenteous. The bubbling water, curling smoke, and the indolent air of the smokers, indicated the luxurious East. As there was little to be seen here but the bazaars, it was only desirable to while away the time before the ship's departure; so bidding Abraham onward, we followed in close Indian file. The streets are quite narrow, and we could not do otherwise, considering the opposing stream of people to be met, and the single files of mules, camels, donkeys and horses, all to look out for. We threaded street and alley, turned corners innumerable, and finally entered upon the Bazaars. These are the marts of trade. They are low-roofed houses with projecting roofs, touching in the centre and forming a completely shaded arch. The little rooms on either side are some ten feet square. These furnish every thing that fancy can desire, from the richest Persian silks and cloth of gold to the veriest trifle or toy of a European city.

We stopped to purchase some Otto of Roses, and before we finished, we had collected quite a motley group around us; and what was worse, it did not leave us. Two of the group we had noticed at the boat; but all of them tarried where we tarried, and by skilful manœuvring contrived to reach each spot which we reached at the same time. Their aim was to forestall us in our purchases, adding twenty per cent. to the prices, or make the piastres out of us. Poor S——! it did not agree with his ideas at all—this numerous train—and he wielded his Vesuvius club with a still fiercer demonstration. As for P——, he seemed quite at ease, and considered it as adding to our importance, this truly oriental train. They might be taken for the train of some Grandee or Nabob!

As for Abraham, we tortured him incessantly with orders to send them back; and he, poor fellow, seeing our suspicions were already aroused, did his best, but in vain. One moment coming out upon a square, one old fellow would be seen quietly quaffing a draught from the fountain, no doubt out of breath with running round the corner,—another would pop out here, another there, and so on,—as if we possessed the ring of Aladdin upon which these genii waited. The Vesuvius club was no cause of fear. But it was becoming almost unendurable. "Good-bye," says S—— to one, "we can dispense with your farther company." "Oh! oh! never mind, I'm walking for pastime," was the provoking answer, as he swung his beads carelessly over his arm, and with most perverse air dogged on after us. Finally, oh! crowning thought, S—— bethinks him of the Janizary, and intimates that he will call one. Whereupon they quickly cried out, "Oh yes, we go, we go, give us four piastres." "No, you rascals, not one;" and away they vanished, as if Aladdin had lost his ring.

We passed a mosque, and on tiptoe took a peep within. It was quite plain and had a high gallery bounded by an iron railing. The gallery was to be occupied by the ladies. The ceiling was covered with innumerable suspended chains, to which were attached (they do say) any quantity of ostrich eggs and horse-tails, as well as lamps. We only saw the latter. A farther glimpse within, at the open door, showed us a floor covered with matting, nothing more. We were not permitted to enter unless the shoes were taken off, which was quite too much trouble. We saw the Turks perform their ablutions at the fountain in front. The fountain looked quaint enough surrounded by the stooping figures, with red turbans; each with his hands under the little water-spouts. When this ceremony is over, they enter the porch of the church, slip easily out of their shoes, and walk quietly within.

There were few ladies out during the daytime, and these few were shopping. They were enveloped in their mantles. A white piece of cloth covers the head like a nun's veil, from which drooped a black gauze covering. Nose and eyes were thus concealed from the gazer, but they themselves could see very easily. The white upper piece was connected with a white piece below, which hid the chin and lower part of the face. I had imagined that the concealment of the beauty of the Turkish ladies might be quite desirable in their own country. In some way I had been led to make the mistake, that a veil always hides something beautiful. The idea of mystery plays in the imagination and lends enchantment to every thing dim and forbidden. But when I came to see black Nubian damsels, darker than night, so dark that ebony might reflect a lily pallor beside them, veiled in the same way, I could but laugh outright. I wonder what possessed *them* to adopt that custom. And then the clumsy yellow boots that they manage to slide over the ground in; one can imagine nothing more cumbersome than their appearance. Indeed, the whole figure looks to us very ungainly and ungraceful. I have just read in some late papers, kindly handed to us by our consul, of the innovations at home in relation to ladies' dress, and of the introduction of these foreign costumes, among which the Turkish is mentioned. I should hope the latter will not be adopted; at least such as we have seen worn in the street. The costume for the house may be preferable. We have seen none in the street such as are spoken of in the American papers. Perhaps what is generally known in America as the Turkish dress, with the full pantaloons and jacket, is the Persian properly. If any innovation should be made on present fashions, *and there is room for improvement*, the Persian, somewhat contracted, would recommend itself for taste and comfort.

We passed on to the Caravansary bridge, supposing it to be

some grand sight, as our anxious Abraham seemed to think we must certainly see it. We found merely a stone bridge over a small yellow stream; but the cafés that lined the shore were a charming retreat for the weary or pleasure-seeking of the city. Jewish children huddled about us, to stare. We gave them some delicacies, whereat they were much pleased, kissing their little hands in token of thankfulness. Women negligent in attire, with hair dishevelled, were to be met with, unveiled. But these were Jewish. We sat beneath the shade of some noble old sycamores. These trees furnish grateful shade to the sun-oppressed pilgrims of the East. They seem placed here by Providence for this very beneficent end. The tall cypresses opposite kept their guardian watch over the white-turbaned tombs beneath. The cemetery was full—literally *full* of grave stones. Those for married men are capped with a turban cut in the white marble. A virgin's tomb bore a simple rose branch. I never saw the cypress attain to such a height, or so numerous as in these cemeteries; but soon I learned that, at the death of a dear friend or relative, it was formerly the custom to plant a cypress at the head of the grave; but which custom of late has fallen into disuse. Our guide proposed to ascend Castle Hill, but we declined, from fatigue, satisfied with the pleasant place we had already found.

These grounds are the nightly resort of all Smyrna. The ladies never make their appearance until after dinner at seven or eight o'clock (our evening), and then they are always dressed richly and gorgeously. They laugh, dance, sing, eat ices, and return to their homes at one, two, and three in the morning. Thus changing night into day, they become pale and sallow, in fact lose all freshness of color, and become any thing but the beauties we have always been taught to consider them. Sundays are their especial gala days.

How indolent these Orientals are! They si in front of their shops, smoke and take it easy. Their walk is very indolent. Indeed, it is said, that the only time that they are ever known to quicken their pace is in bearing a corpse to its grave, when they hurry fast enough. They believe that the agony commences as soon as death takes place, and this only ceases the moment when the body has been consigned to its final home. Singular belief!

Now and then an Arab would come sweeping by. The fierce look, turbaned head, wild roving air, and brace of pistols, betray the nation. They looked like the veriest banditti. Perhaps they were; for we have been told that there are many around Smyrna, and that they even venture into the town, through which they pass unmolested and untouched. Their spies are innumerable. They know every ship that lands, and every stranger that tarries. Murders and robberies are committed nightly, without and within the city. It is quite unsafe to venture on any of the excursions around the country. Only a few days ago two young sportsmen were out, and both were captured. The robbers sent one back with a message to the father of the other, that if a hundred pounds ransom were forthcoming for his son, he might be restored to him. If the next day passed without the ransom being received, one arm should be sent to his father; the second day, the second arm; and so on, quarter by quarter, until the money *was* paid. They keep advised of the wealth of each citizen, so as always to fall within bounds when naming the ransom. The soldiers are regular Falstaffians in character. Their European dress, which they are obliged to adopt, has quite unfitted them for anything like a display of courage. Six were sent for two robbers, and came back, after a skirmish, without them. What bravery? What a city, and what protectors? The troops number over a thousand, but should they leave the city in search of the robbers, they are not sure of those they leave behind—the population is so mixed.

Donkeys with huge burdens, camels with huger ones, and man a complete beast of burden, were sights that continually met our eyes. Large stones were carried on the backs of men, who almost bent double under their weight. Will it be believed when I say, that our Vice Consul at Constantinople saw one of these carriers bear over one thousand pounds on his back over two hundred yards?

Since arriving at Constantinople, so many sights of an Eastern cast have met my eye, that they have become almost too familiar to be depicted. Novelty always lends her aid in transcription. Constantinople presents a rich panorama, with its towers, domes, and minarets, as we glide up the Bosphorus into the noble harbor. But the beauty all lies *in the distance;* for when once the city is entered, the charm evanishes. The streets, bazaars, and throngs of strange costumes, are similar to those I have described at Smyrna.

But they tell me that there is one place where I shall not meet with disappointment. The Seraglio needs no distance to lend it enchantment. I had read Irving's Grenada and Alhambra, and pictured to myself, in imagination, the fountains and halls, minarets and groves, the varied and Oriental luxuriousness of that Moorish palace; and when they told me, that I might see in the Seraglio its resemblance, my heart bounded at the idea even of a partial fulfilment of that longing desire to see the original.

This far-famed palace occupies the spot of the ancient city of Byzantium, on the extreme eastern point of the promontory extending towards Asia, and forming the entrance to the Bosphorus. It is triangularly shaped, and nearly three miles in circumference. The palace has nothing to boast of in its outside appearance. The interior is a singular clustering of houses without order, which have been added from time to time at the caprice of the Sultanas.

Our party of twenty-five, English, French, Jews and Americans, sought the nearest point to the waters of the Golden Horn, entered a caïque, and crossed over to the Seraglio. We were detained for some time at the Café on the opposite shore, waiting for the firman. Then, with the officers, we entered upon our tour of inspection. The lower story consisted of a long hall, paved with tesselated gravel stones, and of servants' rooms surrounding and opening into it. At the far end was the stairway, upon reaching which we were obliged to glide into slippers. Such a slipping time as there was too! Imagine it—a lady's delicate slipper encased in the size furnished for a gentleman's boot. First one shoe and then another was left behind, in our vain efforts at this novel style of walking. Our guide was in constant requisition, bringing up the truants, who were obliged to resume their places again, to undergo the same penance. We reached the sacred precincts above, and made our entrance. That was a fine noble hall into which we were ushered, although it had a covering of matting on the floor. It at once completely initiated us into the whole mystery of Oriental luxuriousness.

I can but group the Seraglio, for it was one series of elegant apartments; marble basins, bagnios and gushing fountains. These gorgeous halls, the chaste cool baths and their attached rooms of reclining after bath-taking—formed a complete scene of deliciousness. They were somewhat similar to each other, with their ceilings of fretted gold—paintings of richest tracery, walls of landscapes, rounded and arched recesses overlooking the sea, windows with rich tapestry hangings, gilded clocks and miniature temples ornamenting the side places—divans and chairs of crimson figured damask, and gold cloths—and the coverings of white linen in which these latter were encased, giving a summery air to the whole,—all combined, made the Seraglio too enrapturing, entrancing, and unreal, almost to be conceived of—a place for reveries and dreams only,—the halls of poesy and sleep.

The floor and walls of the baths were of white marble, and the light from above entered through a honey-comb of white ceiling. Spigots turned the water out, which fell into white marble shells, or bath-basins ranged in perfect neatness. We walked down the long airy corridors where the ladies of the harem promenade and exercise. One side of the longest corridor was latticed with delicate net-work, through which the Odalisques could peep into gardens of every kind of fruit and flower; the other side being adorned with numerous paintings and engravings, representing every scene in nature to which they were denied.

The tea-room was a most delicious, cool retreat, close to the water's edge; and being a story or more below the others, it seemed half grotto-like. A fountain played in the centre, building its silvery dome with flakes of purple and ruby fire, glittering in the colors of the morning. Its basin, square and quite shallow, was fixed in the marble floor, in the midst of which swam shoals of golden fishes. A hundred pipes when playing, send the water and spray high up to the ceiling. Side fountains there were too, in which the water first plashing up to the height of the head, falls over into a marble shell. This, as it fills, runs over into its counterpart below, and so on successively like the little step water-falls we saw at Pompeii. At one end stood a triangular-shaped pyramid of honey-comb work. This also was a fountain, the water of which issued from innumerable honey-comb orifices. It was quite unique and quaint. But the rounded recess on the sea side was the favorite spot where the luxurious Ottoman and his Sultanas sat or reclined at their coffee-sipping. Was there ever so enchanting, so cool a grotto? The refreshing sea breeze, the balmy air of the playing fountains,—the soft music of their dashing, trembling, spraying waters,—the wavy plash of the Bosphorus without, against the walls, and the hum of the distant city borne across the Golden Horn,—the plying caïques with their arrowy points, darting by in graceful rapidity, the noble steamer and more lofty prow of the huge man-of-war cutting and parting the clear sea; in fine, the noble harbor of Constantinople with its busy mart, and the hills that rise in mellow distance above; all this—as well the scene without as the scene within,—glorious Nature and luxurious Art,—the spell of delight, the dream of enchantment; who can picture?—not we; and only those can *feel* it, who are there embathed in its enjoyments.

I wish I could peep in upon its occupants at some even tide, when the sun through leaves and lattice checkers in shadow the marble floor, to see if content and happiness dwell within,—to see how far such a life is fraught with pleasure and true content. They say the Sultanas are gay and happy. They have every thing to make them so, educated as they are only in their own Eastern customs. The Circassian beauty knows no higher desire or ambition than to become the Nourmahal—"Light of the Harem," to some Moslem chief. She possesses a charm for the senses. It is enough to make her the chosen one. Of course such an one, though beauteous as one of the Houri, can know nothing of that ideal delight of the soul which rises superior to the sense, or that longing for liberty which we should have under similar circumstances. Dr. Johnson, in his Rasselas, has represented this longing to be free, even though bound by golden chains in splendid palaces.

The gardens of the Seraglio are luxuriant in tree and shrub. The tall cypress waves ever green and fresh. The vine clings to the wall, and hides its bare face with the green tendril and leaf. Tender-eyed gazelles peep out of leafy coverts, while arches and pyramids of green bend and rise in every vista. A mimic lake occupies the centre, within which there is an island, and rustic bridges gracefully span the reach. The walks are of shells (some of which we gathered), margined with flowers of every kind, of which the Turks are not quite so selfish as the Europeans. Orange bowers are pendent with golden fruitage, and fragrance fills the air. These proclaim a perfection in the garniture of Nature, not as if it were imported or exotic, but as if it were at home in its own charming bower. But I cannot particularize farther; suffice it to say,

"No greener garden ever was known
Within the bounds of an earthly king."

The Armory, which we next visited, is one immense repository of arms. Multiplied stacks of long guns, short guns and pistols, were arranged in regular figures of squares and pyramids. Here was the ancient mail-clad knight, with his jointed armor and the long spear which the lancer poised mid air, before sending it to the heart. Here, too, was the sabre and kettle-drum. The room containing the keys to the different towns and cities owning the sway of the Sultan, was quite apart. The keys were gold and silver mounted, and were neatly arranged in a case. The key of Jerusalem, and that of Mecca, shone conspicuously. These keys in the armory finely symbolize the power of the Moslem, as it sweeps over the Orient, entering each city's portal, and controlling the wild Arabs of the desert.

The Sultan Mahmoud's tomb was a gorgeous affair, and peculiar as the home of the royal dead. Here it was necessary to go through the same formula of exchanging shoes, although the floor was covered with matting. The tomb is in the centre of the temple, surrounded by those of two sisters and three daughters. Each tomb is made in a sort of square pyramidical form, with a railing of most beautiful inlaid pearl-wood. Velvet cloths and elegant cashmere shawls were flung over these. Huge massive silver candelabras, and massive tapers of wax, stand at the head and foot of each, connected by a silver chain to the pillared corners. Over the taper was an extinguisher, figuring Death! The book-stands of inlaid white pearl, holding the richly bound Koran, and glistening in the sunlight, stood open near each tomb, with the gold embroidered cloth thrown lightly over them. This pearl work gave a brilliancy to the tomb more than I ever imagined could be displayed even by Oriental regality.

But our most charming visit, and the only ride we indulged in, was to the "Sweet waters of Europe." Our Consul's kind invitation had been accepted to ride thither in his carriage. The streets are horribly paved. A corduroy road at home would have been far preferable. Out of curiosity, I inquired the length of time a carriage would last here; the answer was two years. At the edge of the city we came upon the Sultan's favorite drive, which, consequently, is an open road, and as finely graded as any in England. We passed the writing school, the Polytechnic Institute, and the Barracks. The soldiers seem to have the most elegant residences, save the Sultan's palaces, and the villas. A long steep hill descended, led us into the valley, which is some two miles in length. The waters of this vale are quite sweet. The view is called finer than that of the sweet waters of Asia, on the Asiatic side. The road winds with the stream, and beneath the shade of numerous groves of sycamores, with a leaf like our oak, and elms, with leaves, looking like our maples. These groves are filled of a festal Friday, and upon every evening, when music and gayety prevail; but now in Ramazan, it was lone and deserted. No voice is heard, save that of the harsh croaking frog.

In this delightsome vale the Sultan has one of his summer residences; but we saw only the exterior. A marble Kiosk (summer-house) is just at the base of a dashing waterfall. The water plays all around it, while a bridge spans the stream below. The stream gradually widens, until it forms the Golden Horn, flowing through and dividing the city. As we ascended the hill, leaving the vale behind us, we came upon the Jews' burying ground, which is a sea of white stones, all plain, and lying flat or standing up, with not a tree or shrub to relieve the barenness of the spot. Our Consul remarked, that it was strange the Jews cared so little for the adornment of their cemeteries, and he wondered why it should be so. One of our party assigned as the reason, their strange belief, that the body did not rise where buried, but walked in agony underground to the Valley of Jehoshaphat, where it was judged; hence no associations of life and beauty clustered around the burial spot, and hence no adornment. When, Oh! shall I speak it? Yankeeism to the last, another suggests, "what a capital speculation it would be to run from this spot, an *underground railroad.*" Truly there would be no lack of passengers, judging by the infinity of stones, and the natural desire to finish so unpleasant a journey!

An old Greek priest came trotting by with great gravity, but as soon as he had passed us, spurred his horse into a wild gallop. How funny it looked—a priest playing mad John Gilpin over the grave-yard of the Jew, his full black robe and flying veil dancing at right angles before the wind.

As we neared the city, the sunlight played upon the windows in flames of living fire—no wonder when the houses are almost all windows.

How out of place a Cemetery would appear to us, as a resort for pleasure and promenade,—a place for eating, drinking, smoking, and musical performances. But so it is here, where Fatalism buries her dead without a tear, and the mourner, bowing to the blow, strokes his beard and ejaculates, "*God is great;*" "*God is great;*" and retires stoically to his ordinary pursuits. Chairs and tombstones furnish the seats, and the cypress tree the canopy, for these evening and midnight carousals, which are even more frequent during the Ramazan. We reached the Hotel at nine o'clock, two hours after the customary *dinner* time here.

Passing by our delightful sail over the Bosphorus, past villas and palaces—our lucky sight of Mahomet Ali, the Pasha of Egypt—of the prophet of Mecca with his strange, solemn countenance, and more than all, of the Sultan himself—a gorgeous Oriental pageantry; passing by the rich and ever-variant scenes of the streets, the busy bazaars and prayerful mosques,—I may not forget to mention one most especial peculiarity of this city, and that is its—*dogs.* They lie at every turn in mosque and market, in door and out, in the path of man and beast, and only answer to the tapping boot, trampling donkey, or nudging cane, by a squeak or growl. They are incorrigible, never moving for man or beast. They belong to no one; but each has his particular home-quarter, where he lives—a pauper on the public who hold him sacred.

But I think we have almost exhausted the city. As we pass out of the Golden Horn into the Bosphorus, we make our *Salaam* to the Orient. Farewell, old city! with your spires and domes glittering in the setting sun! It will be long ere we see thee again, for the pathway hither is over troublous seas, troublous for a man even, how much more troublous for one of the other sex.

XVIII.

The Turkish Body Politic in its Picturesque Dress.

"Know ye the land where the cypress and myrtle,
Are emblems of deeds that are done in their clime?"
Bride of Abydos.

WOULD that I had the magic bow of the Scythian Abaris to give it a twang, and that I could ride on the arrow with telegraphic velocity to our western clime, there to see what chances and changes have occurred since we left. We have not heard from home for two months. I suppose that Ohio has a new constitution adopted by this time. Constitutions—how different they are here from those in the States. Even Turkey has a constitution, adopted in 1840, by which certain rights are guarantied to all—Armenian and Jew, Christian as well as Turk. But like the other constitutions of Europe, it is just so much parchment, to be "dispensed" with by the government, just when it pleases. The *popular spirit* must constitute the last analysis of the State—the elemental organic law. .In the fire of the popular heart, lies the warm and the only healthy glow of the body politic. If this be extinguished or smothered, constitutions are but paper nothings. Now the constitution of Turkey was a voluntary renunciation of absolute power by the Sultan, for the purpose of reform and the happiness of all. It was called the *Hatti Sherif of Gulkenah*, or imperial charter. It was named after a kiosk called Gulkenah, the Runnymede of the Turkish Magna Charta, where, in presence of the principal Pashas and the diplomatic corps, Reschid Pasha read the constitution. It was drawn up by Reschid, who is the Grand Vizier. It mitigates many of the old punishments of the Turk, and thus conforms to the humane spirit of the Sultan, who has never been known to sanction an act of cruelty. It establishes boards and councils in the capital and principal towns, whose ordinances are, however, subject to the supervision of the Porte. It gives the privilege to the Armenian, Jew, and Christian, to sue and give testimony, and receive equal justice in the courts. But the Turkish kadis and muftis interpret justice and receive testimony just as they did before the constitution; judging all things by the Koran, and regarding all but Mussulmans as dogs and Giaours. The constitution is, in this respect, a complete dead letter. The blackest Nubian slave who believes in Mahomet can give testimony, but the most respectable Christian is not heard. The Ulemats of the law are permitted to plead and interpret the law as they please, which they do on paper, not orally; subject to the old contingency of being pounded to death in a mortar if they displease the government.

The Salique law is in full force in Turkey. Neither sons nor daughters under a certain age are raised to the throne, nor can a daughter transmit to a male offspring any claims to the succession. The brothers of the Sultan first succeed according to their age. The only brother of the present Sultan is kept close in the palace, and is seldom permitted to be seen. One of the tombs we saw was that of a Sultan. His brothers, murdered by him, to the number of nineteen, slumbered around him.—The object of their death was to avoid the law, so as to transmit the crown lineally to the Sultan's son. When the brothers fail, the son succeeds; hence the anxiety of Sultans about their brothers. The present Sultan, Abd-ul-Mejid has a son about ten years of age, of whom he is very fond, and to whom he is giving a fine education. He will succeed to the throne if the brother should happen to die.

The wives of the Sultan at present number thirteen. This does not include the harem, but only the Kadines, who alone have the privilege of producing an heir to the throne. They are chosen from the Odalisques, or females of the imperial harem.

There is no marriage ceremony performed, and the Sultan may divorce the marriage when he pleases. When the Sultan dies, the Kadines go into solitary retirement, still supported by the State. They never marry. The mother of the Sultan is more fortunate; she lives in a splendid palace, and is treated like the Queen Dowager of England. We saw the palace of the mother of the present Sultan at the head of the harbor—a splendid pile! She derives a large revenue from some of the isles of the empire.

The inheritance of property is regulated by laws dissimilar from that which regulates the succession to the throne. There are two kinds of property—*free* and *mortgage.* The first is transmitted to the children, male and female, share and share alike. The mortgage property becomes absolute in the mosque (to which alone mortgage is permitted) upon the death of the mortgagor. If a person wishes to borrow five thousand piastres, he goes to his mosque, and during life pays a small interest of about one-half per cent.; the condition of defeasance being, that the property, which must be worth double the amount loaned, shall become absolute in the mosque on the death of the borrower. The mosques do not accumulate, but immediately sell and reloan. In the time of the plague, the mosques make money in round numbers. This financial ecclesiastical feature will account for the number and the influence of the mosques in Constantinople. No wonder so many minarets glitter in the sun, and so many domes swell under the cloudless sky of the east, amidst the mean, dirty, wooden houses that line the filthy streets. No wonder the city gleams so grandly in the *distance*, and reposes so tranquilly beauteous, *far off!*

The influence of the Moslem priests is paramount to all law. There is no connection between the Church and State, for *they are one.* The religion of the people *is* the State. The Koran is the real Constitution. Every rule of private and public conduct is drawn from its page. Greater devotion to a religion could not be had. Prayer with the Turks is universal; and they do not seek the intervention of priests to commune with Allah. It is as common at night as in the day, at the feast as in Ramazan, in the field as in the chamber, in the mosque as in the cemetery. Last eve, at the fifth hour, the Moslems upon the steamer which is now bearing us westward, all bowed to the East, and simultaneously repeated their prayers, and performed their motions. At nightfall, the audible song went up from the deck, where cross-legged they sat; after which they enjoyed the pipe and their food, after the total abstinence of the day. The season of Ramazan is kept alike at every place.

We have two Pashas aboard, with whom I have been conversing in my usual manner by signs and a dictionary. Pleasant, dignified, and communicative, dressed in their ermine cloaks and red caps, and perfect gentlemen in all respects, except Christianity, they assume no airs, even over their own servants. Their salutation is tenderly symbolic of good will. They kiss the hand, touch the heart and forehead, and make a slight obeisance. They seem thus to unite the respect of the mind with the warmth of their hearts. They have the reputation of being honest, hospitable and truthful; and that is more than is said of the Greek and Armenian Christians, who live among them, and who *excuse* these characteristics by saying, "Oh! their religion commands these things." Beautiful Christians! The Turks drink no spirituous liquor, which accounts for their moral and physical health, as well as for the scarcity of beggars, and the absence of cripples. Opium is not used generally. Tobacco is as common as the turban or fez cap. A Turk without his chibouque, would be like a man without a nose. It is a part of himself, not to be severed. He gives it prominence above everything, except the Koran—above the feast, the bath, and the turban.

I think that the slavery of Turkey is not properly understood in America. I have taken some pains to learn about these social customs, and must acknowledge my obligation to our vice-consul, Mr. Daniese, who has furnished me with the information. The slave markets of Constantinople have drawn forth a great deal of sympathy, from the ladies especially. The idea of *white* women, almost naked, being sold in the public markets, has excited much horror. This is all superfluous. To be sure, slavery is bad enough in its best form. But the slave of the Turk is not the slave of the planter, by a good deal. Here, it signifies a person purchased to be the adopted son or daughter of the owner. The market for white slaves is alone open to Turks, who purchase two classes of persons; one for wives, the other for servants. The former are sent by the best families of Georgia and Circassia to the Commissioner, who takes . are that no insult of the slightest nature is offered. They are glad to go. All is voluntary. The females have the absolute right to refuse to be sold to any one whom they dislike. Ladies in America sometimes do not have as much accorded to them. Once bought, they become the wife of the Mussulman, just as fully as Miss Jones united to Mr. Smith, by Esq. Johnson, becomes Mrs. Smith. The law fixes their dowry; and if their husbands misuse them, it gives them redress in alimony and divorce. The alimony allowed is their whole dowry. The property in the servant-slaves inheres to the wife, and not to the husband. He is bound to protect them through life, and provide for their maintenance. But when there are several wives—what then? I imagine that there are very few who have more than *one* wife. Our acquaintance, the good Bey, only had one, as he said; perhaps he meant only one to whom he gave his heart. When the wives are many, the same rule as to dower and maintenance obtains. There is one redeeming feature in Turkish slavery, and that is, that the mother becomes free on the birth of a child, who is also free. There is no hereditary slavery.

The male slaves have every chance to rise in the world, because they rise with their masters. Merit and mind rise above the institution. The son-in-law of the late Sultan, Halil Pasha, was once the slave of Khrosref Pasha, himself once a Georgian slave. The mother of the present Sultan—a fine portly lady, living in luxury in her palace, was once a Circassian slave, sold for a price to Mahmoud II., the father of the present Emperor and is now the honored source of much of the power of the Sublime Porte. It is the religion which softens the harshness of the institution, and makes it a shadow. A day in Constantinople will convince the most unobserving that the Moslem faith recognizes no invidious distinction between the faithful. Indeed, the finest-looking man I saw was a dark but lofty-browed man, who, perhaps, was once a slave, but is now a chief prophet or priest of all Mahometanism. He presides at Mecca. I saw him under these circumstances. After leaving the gorgeous and splendid tomb of Mahmoud, the last Sultan, and while wondering at the perpetual freshness of grief which seemed to hover about the dead, caused by the rich shawls and mother-of-pearl work, as well as by the beautiful mosque around and over the tomb, and while admiring that appropriate symbol of the great wax candles, covered by the extinguisher, at the head of the tomb, we were disturbed and startled by the cries and bustle of the street. The soldiers were drawn up—the band played—the citizens rushed to see, and the word was—"*The Sultan, lo! he cometh over the Golden Horn!*"

We waited in the shadow of a shop, and soon the officers and Pashas rode along on their fine steeds, which were led by slaves on foot; next came an awe-inspiring man, dressed in a long sweeping green robe exquisitely wrought, and upon his broad and high brow he wore the finest turban of white, embound in red. He looked grave in his long and solemn face. He seemed a man of sorrow, and his face was thin and indented with grief. A great calm, dark eye looked out from beneath his heavy intellectual forehead. If Mahomet resembled this, his successor, I would no longer wonder at the spell of Islamism by which he thralled the East. You forget his gorgeous apparel and his dark countenance, in the great mind which speaks from the face. He sits upon his fine Arab horse, a picture to "witch the world," not as Hotspur did "in wondrous horsemanship," but by the priestly sanctity and intellectual composure of his appearance. If Carlyle could see him, he would perform a genuflexion of hero-worship in his praise, as he has already in praise of his predecessor.

His mien and grace forcibly remind me of that wonderful race, who combining in their characters, as in their language, the Tartar, Persian and Arabic elements, ruled the deserts, spread over the East, conquered the isles of the Mediterranean, and under the dominion of Sultan and Caliph, began new dynasties in the world. Religious fervor and strong arms,—what is able to resist their power? what;—save the stronger arm of God?

Following him, was a riderless barb, dressed in cloth of gold. No Sultan to-day. The crowds laugh at the disappointment, but I was well satisfied with seeing the prophet of Mecca. His portrait is daguerreotyped in my mind.

The Armenians form an important part of the population in Turkey. Forty thousand alone are to be found in Smyrna, and eighty thousand in Constantinople. They have become, by dint of enterprise and shrewdness, the brokers and bankers of the realm. They are the second estate. The Custom House and the taxes have been sold to them by the government for a number of years. The former was sold for fifty thousand pounds sterling. This is a novel way of raising funds. What is commendable about the matter is, that no extortion is resorted to. We found no unpleasant searching at the custom house.

These Armenians—where came they from? what are they? I was led to make the same inquiry; for in passing through the bazaars, my curiosity was excited by the singular black-eyed race who sat upon the couches and mats, ministering so dexterously to the buyers, pictures of lazy activity and patient enterprise! They excel the Jews in trading; and in singularity of custom and adhesiveness to their religion they resemble them. They are more easily distinguished from their turbaned neighbors than from the Jews. Perhaps they are one of the lost tribes.

The country of Armenia was situated in Asia, south of Georgia, somewhere in the vicinity of the garden of Eden. In the seventeenth century, it was laid waste by Shah Abbas, and its people distributed over the Turkish Empire and its adjacent countries, to the number of two millions. Many of them are in Hungary and Poland. Their religion is a sort of Christianity, with smoke enough about its altar to determine that some of the true fire is present. Eutychus was the founder of their peculiar creed, which was condemned as heresy in the fifth century. Their creed is not unlike that of the Greek church, but like near relations when they *do* differ, they hate each other cordially. Fifteen thousand acknowledge the Pope of Rome. The others are under the spiritual supervision of three patriarchs in Asia. Their monasteries, fasts, and superstitions resemble the Greek more than the Roman church. Their language is as hard to understand as the mysteries of the Cabala or the Rosicrucians. Few of themselves understand or speak it. They have a kind of *Knacker*, made up of French and Italian, which they use. You may perceive their cemetery, by the absence of the cypress, which is allowed to none but Moslems. Their tree is the terebinth or turpentine tree. Their idea of the future state of the soul is peculiar. They hold that it passes to a place of consciousness, where it is, however, quiescent, joyless and painless. Prayers are offered to deliver it from this purgatory of indifference. They would not have this deathless soul impaired in its immortal nature, but restored to its full and active energy.

How orderly those Mussulmans on deck perform their devotions. The cry of the leader just called me away to see the ceremony. While he sang, the others were discussing, as I judged by their gestures and laughing, the intricate question, "what direction is Mecca." Their shoes are all off. Their beards are washed. Their sleeves are rolled up. The leader has a white handkerchief over his head. The others all have on the red fez cap. They commence mumbling. The leader says something—they bend; something else—they bend lower with hands up, something still—their heads touch the deck. This process was repeated with closed eyes and devout faces, three times towards Mecca; when they performed "eyes right" and "eyes left," like a company of infantry in three sections, then arose, shook their mats, lit their pipes, and put on their shoes. A very simple and striking devotion.

I would like to have seen it upon a grander scale in Saint Sophia's mosque. I wrote of our abortive attempt to see the mosques, when a Nubian slave with his rattan drove our company away, although we had in it two English captains, one French navy captain, a French diplomatist, a German noble, an oaf of a Jew, and four Americans! We could not give it up; so, procuring our firman, we took an earlier start—while the Moslems, under the effects of the night's revel after Ramazan fast, should be asleep.—Our firman cautiously brought us around to an entrance less public. A cross-eyed Turk in priestly stole and endless turban opened the door. We put on our slippers, and winding up and around a long, dark gallery, found ourselves in the lofty hall of the great Mahomet. In every thing else but its size, we were disappointed, and with St. Peter's in our mind, even that lost its potency. The lofty columns of every species of granite, marble and porphyry, support a large gallery; while the dome is in the form of an ellipse. The circular dome is within this, and swells fearfully high and sublime. But where is the rich mosaic fresco of Genoa and Rome? Where are the forms of marble majesty and the breathing beauty of the canvass? Where is the soul of art and the genius of Italy? The eye swims restlessly about in unpeopled ether, with no graceful angel or bearded saint to buoy it upward into the celestial realm. Four large, bird looking, black colored, six winged, headless mosaic nondescripts, said to be angels, bespread their pinions at either corner of the dome.

It is said that the Persians seldom paint forms, fearful lest they will be required in the day of judgment to find *souls* for their creations, which it is very difficult to do. The artist will, on this principle, be condemned eternally for these creations These outré representations are intended for seraphim, who were companions of Mahomet—Gabriel, Michael, Raphael, and Israel. Near them are four large circular green signs, with Turkish calligraphy in golden letters, nearly as long as the name of the writer who has there displayed his genius. The name is Bitchiakdschisade Mustafa Techelebi! Phœbus, what a sounding for your trump! Nothing else strikes the beholder as very peculiar, unless it be a few fountains—a fine floor covered with ordinary matting; an altar turned towards Mecca; two flags from the pulpit, representing the triumph of Moslemism over Judaism and Christianity; some priests going about attending to the lamps, which are hung all around from strings alternating with ostrich eggs, flowers and tinsel, and which, when lighted, glimmer like cressets, and reflect bearded and tailed lights like comets. The lamps are curved-shaped; and when lit, as they are every night during this Ramazan season, seem like little fairy shallops floating in a sea of lustre, and among miniature starry islands. There is not so much gorgeousness as one would expect, after seeing what the Turk can display in the seraglio and palace. The shape of this temple is the Greek cross, and its dimensions are 200 feet by 275. The centre of the dome is 180 feet above the ground. Its vicissitudes have been remarkable, and its once glorious but now tarnished splendors lend a charm to it which apparently it has not. It is 1,500 years old—was dedicated to the divine wisdom, in the time of Constantine. It has been burned several times and rebuilt. Baalbec with its pillars of the temple of the Sun, Ephesus with its green columns of the temple of Diana, the temple of Pallas at Athens, of the Moon at Heliopolis, of Apollo at Delos, of Cybele at Cyzicus, of Isis and Osiris from Egypt, as well as the green, blue, black, white and parti-colored marbles of the world, are here represented in the 107 columns which support this splendid structure! This would amply repay us for the visit, were there no other points of interest. Tradition and history represent Saint

Sophia as having had angels for architects, and as the most remarkable temple of ancient Christendom. In it Chrysostom spoke with his lips of gold. Up to the time when Mahomet with his Osmans rode victoriously into the city, and even into this temple, and dismounting, leaped upon the altar exclaiming, *There is no* GOD *but* GOD, *and* MAHOMET *is his prophet!*"—up to the time when Sophia held her bloody carnival in these great walls, and while learning had here her chosen throne, this temple shone resplendent in Mosaic and gold, purple and marbles, with its silver doves and carved images, as the Church of the East and the glory of Christendom. It was only the other day when repairing some of the walls, that rich mosaics superior to any at Rome, were discovered beneath the plaster, representing saints and martyrs. The sultan ordered them (sensible soul!) to be covered again, not knowing but that they might come in play in some future age. It is a current belief among the Turks, that their authority will end in a century; and being Fatalists, it might prove a true prophecy; although, my firm belief is, that the Ottoman power is stronger now than it has been for half a century. The Mahometans have two or three miraculous objects in the church. One is a shining stone, said to be an onyx, which absorbs light, and when shone upon shines with intense glitter. Another is a sweating column, that emits a dampness, which is a panacea superior to Brandreth or the Life Bitters.

But most, Sophia will be remembered as the first home of the Christian: for the poet has truly sung that in

> "Sophia's far-famed dome,
> There first the faith in triumph was led home,
> Like some high bride, with banner and bright sign,
> And melody and flowers."

We saw places where the cross had been removed, and where images had been defaced. The crescent shone superior, however;

and from what we have observed in Constantinople generally, there is no present prospect of a wane of this symbol. The Sultan is building new palaces, the priests have their old powers, the Faith seems as firm, and the heart of the city throbs as warmly as ever. If these be indices of all Islamism, the Cross is not making much headway toward that Millennial point which we are assured it must attain even in these strong holds of the prophet.

The population of Constantinople is over 600,000 souls; and how many are in the surrounding cities I do not know. It is curious to see the unusual phases this population presents, not the least curious among which is that of a class called scribes, who sit cross-legged at their stands, and write letters and petitions for the people. The time is reckoned as at Rome, from sundown. The graveyards are the public promenades, where joy meets joy in gratulation. The muffled faces of the women, the odd costume of the men, the sacredness of the public dogs, the howling and dancing of the dervishes—a singular piece of madcapery—the easy air, grace, dignity and gorgeous apparel of the Pashas and Beys contrasted with the heavy-loaded, half bent and head-shaved carriers, are to be met with at every corner. But above all, is the unutterably grand panorama of the cities which form the margin of the Bosphorus, inclosed in walls which gleam as they wind over the distant hills—belted in from the waves of Marmora by a deep blue band, and the harbor interspersed with the heavy steamers and men-of-war, and light canoes by the thousand—and all this flooded by a sunlight, in which the orange and the acanthus bloom as no exotics, and the cypress points upward in rivalry of the gilded minarets and gleaming crescents, and where the transparent water repeats the enchanting scene, and waving, breaks it into myriad forms of glancing splendor. We left these scenes at sunset, and as we moved out of the harbor amidst schools of sportive porpoises and flocks of gulls (called condemned souls), soon bade the lovely scenes at distance farewell. "The sun of life will set" ere we forget thy luxurious people and gorgeous palaces, oh, Byzantium! Already to the memory thou risest like a vision of the night or a reverie of the evening, which painter never illustrated, and which Poetry alone has inwoven in

> "Dreams of many-colored light,
> Of golden towers and phantoms fair."

XIX.

Oriental Luxury and Classic Isles.

"Slow sinks more lovely ere his race be run,
Along Morea's hills, the setting sun,
Not as in Northern climes, obscurely bright,
But one unclouded blaze of living light."

Byron.

AFTER leaving the Dardanelles, we stopped again at Smyrna, where I took a Turkish bath, the seventh heaven of Orientalism. It is grateful enough for the traveller whose lungs have been shivered almost by the northern airs, or smothered by office confinement, just to breathe this delicious atmosphere under this rainless and cloudless sky. It is holy repose to the mind, vexed at home with business and pestered with care, only to look out through the calm eye upon these seas of beauteous blue (so blue that there is no expression for it), sleeping so calmly and tranquilly under a canopy of purple lustre, to watch the gloaming rise and die away along these coasts of Morea, and to recall in "clear dream and solemn vision," the mighty intellects who of old peopled these shores of Greece. Oh! it was delicious to float amidst the isles, upon this morning, around the promontory of Sunium, past the temple of Pallas upon its rocky crest, or amid the waves which wash Navarino; and which at a later day than that upon which they kissed the victorious prows of Themistocles at Salamis, bore the united fleets of Russia, England, and France, in array against the fleets of the Bosphorus and of Alexandria, and when in signal defeat the Turk was compelled to yield to Greece her dear-bought freedom. In fine, there is a delight which only belongs to dream-land and the Levant which we have experienced throughout these waters, where

Beauty loves to linger, and where crusading heroism roamed whilome; but after all, the apex of sensuous delight, the ultimate gratification of all the senses at once, lies in a Turkish bath. It laps the world of sense in a new Elysium.

The process consists simply of bath-rooms of heated air, in which, after becoming an embodied ooziness through perspiration, your attendant gently washes you in warm water, rubbing through many courses, including soaping and hair-glove processes (as many as a French table d'hôte), all the old Adam of clay out of you, leaving the original porcelain; when swathed in warm linen, turbaned and chibouqued, you are put away amidst pillowey ottomans to "sleep—perchance to dream;" and in that dream to be transported, in wavy motion, to new climes of softer skies and lovelier tintings, of mellower music and balmier fragrance. But —I wish I had leisure to tell you my dream as I sat all enveloped amidst a company of easy Greeks and luxurious Turks, in the baths of Smyrna. Two hours long it lasted. An American never experiences at home such an *indifferentism* to all sublunary things. He never loses his earnest consciousness of what he is—where he is—what he is born for. But this is a peculiarity of Orientalism. Such an abominable waste of time would never do in America. One's clients would go off in a huffy, and business would disappear completely. But one should not come to Turkey, unless he does as the Turks do, in some respects.

I never knew what it meant to "eat like a Turk," before I saw these Islam people in Ramazan time, when after fasting all day, at the sound of the sundown gun, they turn in with pipe and knife, and eat and smoke "till daylight does appear," when the gun calls a halt. If we Christians were one-tenth as observant of our religion as these benighted Mussulmans, one could reasonably speak of the Millennium. Mahometanism is an unceasing prayer. The very atmosphere of the East seems fitted for this most holy, solemn, and devout exercise. If Moslemism be untrue (and why should I write it conditionally)? what a condemnation awaits this Eastern world; not for its sins, *but for its devotion!*

But I have bid farewell to the Turks. The last one left us at Smyrna. Our deck jabbers with Greeks yet; who talk continually, ever moving their beads, rapidly or slowly according to the ardor of their heart and the interest of their theme. The presence of a Franciscan so frequently seen in Italy betokens our westward course. The Austrian steamer, the best boat we have yet had, dashes on as I write. Already she has passed the gulf of Navarino; and Zante just begins to look like a thin gauzy web in the distance. We shall run between that isle and the main land, when look out for Mount Olympus! By Jove! I will be on deck then, and if this visual orb cannot discern the gods upon its snowy top, I will resurrect the shade of Old Homer, and people imagination with the "powers imperial."

And now (enrapturing thought!) we sail the same watery way he sailed. His gods drank nectar upon that cloudy height. His Ulysses sought his home along these very shores, and we shall harbor in the same inlets which his crafty sagacity selected. Ithaca will meet our eye to-day, the most Homeric spot existing except Troy, and Leucadia's pale cliffs will shine to the eye as ever it has shone in classic light.

Our English captains have kindly invited us to break our fast ashore with them in their barracks to-morrow at Corfu, where we shall regret to part with them. Corfu is the ancient Corcyra, where Athenian greatness met a signal check. All around us throngs, without system or order, the spirit of the past. Botzarris sleeps where he fell upon the mainland near Missolonghi, where, too, Byron "chose his ground and took his rest," after his feverish, unhappy, yet not ungenerous life. What a land for the poet to die in? A land where each star in the lofty vault was a Deity, where each mount had its Oread, each river its Naiad, each fountain its Nymph, each woody copse its Dryad, and every scene its guardian angel! A land where no superstitious fear prevailed, such as the dark forests of the

North engendered; but where the rapture of Hope lit up the soul, until it saw in the trembling of the orange-tree, and the beauty of its bloom, in the spray of the cascade and the prism which arched it, a living presence of grace? A land, where harmony of thought and energy of action were equally illustrated, in the stirring representations of the drama, gliding from the masked actor with all the music of measured rhythm and a tuneful tongue; equally illustrated by the faithful eye and obedient hand of the artist, as his spirit caught a precision in delineation, which vanished imperceptibly into proportion, until there lived upon the rival canvas of Protogenes and Apelles, the charming creations of the ideal. A land where science and truth, even, yielded to the spirit of beauty; where stars and suns were compelled to move in harmony with a preconceived theory, in the unbroken circle, and not in the unharmonious ellipse; where the perfection of the standard would not allow the idea of beauty to be analyzed; although in its analysis the mind, like Newton, should separate its beam, clear, white, straight and dazzling, into the seven hues of the rainbow. Was it not a land for a poet to die in? Was it not a land wherein Byron, with his irrepressible poetic sensibility, should breathe his last wild note for the liberty of his adopted country?

We passed the ancient Arcadia within the hour. Although its coast has not so much of the beetling, craggy aspect as other parts of the Morea, yet in vain I looked for the green sward or vista of leafage, with Pan playing his lute upon the gnarled roots of the woodland. No pastoral repose softly swelled to the rising hill. The bleakness and harshness of the shore, spoke of the people who now indolently and sinfully draw out an ignoble existence, where once rural life joyed in her favorite haunt.

Yet we trust Greece has flung out the "banner with the strange device, Excelsior." Twenty years ago, Athens had not a house. Now it numbers 20,000 people. Missions and schools, colleges and archæological societies, are exhuming the ancient spirit. The zeal of the intelligent Greeks for their ancient literature is intense. In their schools are found little bright urchins, bearing the names of Leonidas, Aspasia, Demosthenes, and Miltiades.

The Morea can support five millions of people; yet there is not 900,000 within its borders, and among these not a farmer worth $1000. The government is poor, and it is as mean as poor. Greece is rich; how rich in its inheritance of greatness and in its future promise! It lacks the moral *stamina* which alone conserve the public weal, and which would send back to Bavaria the contemptible Otho and his truckling parasites, and scorn the influence of Russia, which even in this sunny clime is exercised to chill popular aspiration.

Well, we have arrived at Zante. As a sample of the Ionian isles, it is worth some notice. A rocky line, perpendicular and rough, forms the coast. A little art has been expended in making the harbor. On these heights are white houses irregularly distributed, which form a town. As our steamer rounds to, eager and crowded boats rush out of their coverts. Their steamers never land. They drop anchor, and the exit and entry are performed by little boats manned by jabbering Greeks. The scene which takes place at the gangway when these boats approach, is indescribable. Never did Hubbub hold a more Babel-revelry. The Greeks crawl up by chains and ropes, and though kicked off, manage to fall into a boat and again mount up. The water swarms with them to-day. An unusual number of Zanteotes, say 150, are going up to Corfu to attend a festival. These fètes number about 160 per annum, excluding Sunday, which is the biggest jollification of all. The Roman church has a goodly number of sacred days; but the Greek church overtops it. Why so many? Where can they find time? Bless you! Do you inquire after seeing these strutting dandies on deck, and those ladies dressed out and shivering with vanity like a pea-fowl on a chimney-top? They look and swell as if they were severally Presidents and Queens of these isles. But their fortune is on their back. Nice patent-leather boots, fur-lined coats and jewelry, adorn the men, and embroidered silk and satin, with enormous flounces, apparel the women; but if you go into their houses, you see nothing—absolutely nothing. They live on gayety and olives. They dance all the time except in olive season, when a few have been seen to dig the ground.

Now as I write we leave the isle, and the olive trees, ever green, embowering each mound and hill-slope, tell of the only riches (except the currant, which grows spontaneously) these idlers possess. The Olive requires little cultivation, and less soil. It grows almost upon the bare rocks, interweaving its roots like ivy; the trees thus supporting each other. There is no water, no manure, to assist them. They grow on the principle that Sam Weller's horse went on; he was too poor to pull, but once start the cart, and the shafts would keep him up and going while the impulse continued.

The Zanteotes, I said, were a pattern of the present Greeks, not alone in their gayety, but in their mendacity and cunning. They play the rascal as a matter of course; and have no respect for a man who does not. They live on little, are never in want, and keep their fêtes more to gratify their love of ease than any religious sentiment. What is singular too, is, that they have not changed, these islanders, since Homer's time. The Pagan has given way to the Christian(?) worship. That is all. Their moral character and pursuits, or rather lack of character and pursuits, are the same. The only pursuit they follow with perseverance is the dance, and it is the same miserable dance which frolicked under the olive shade when Ulysses came back and gave the natives a grand fandango. Their music is an old reed or pipe, precisely the same used by Pan, and a kind of a monotonous "tum! tum! tum!" made on a goat-skin spread over a wooden bowl. A slow drawling dance follows a slow drawling piping and thrumming; yet more than half the year these idlers thus pass the time. Well, the currant will grow and the olive will ripen, and the Zanteotes will enjoy life merrily behind their cliffs and peaks.

I learn from one of our English captains that he was Commandant of Ithaca, whose twin peaks lie off to the right, just as they did when Grecian song was young and Penelope watched (a pattern of a good wife, especially in her knitting!) for the coming of her lord. He informs me that there are many monuments there, Ulysses' castle and Arethusa's fountain, for instance, which bespeak its primitive greatness. Cephalonia we now approach. The only distinguishing point in that isle is, that the inhabitants do not allow their ladies ever to be seen. Our boat at last runs between Cephalonia or Samos ("Dash down that cup of Samian wine,"—*Byron*) and Ithaca. A curious phenomenon is seen upon the former. The water of the sea flows into the land in currents or rivulets, which descend and are lost in the bowels of the earth. Grist-mills have been erected on them. They pay, too. Ithaca has the form of the figure 8, and is in the middle about a half mile wide. It is just as it was in Ulysses' time, devoid of any level lawn. Captain Lowry informs me that there is not one hundred square feet of level. Well might the Chief Ulysses refuse the present of horses offered him by the Persian monarch, for neither mead nor plain can supply the horse with food or indulge his speed.

The sun had gone down when we entered the straits between these two isles. The dark mountains hung over in deep shadow, which the moon relieved by silvering their tops and revealing the old ruins of the Castle of Ulysses, as well as the sight of the old city, whence came the twenty-four suitors of Penelope. Only one little white house gleams out of the shadows below. Above are the famous sarcophagi, populous with human bones. The clear water shines with phosphorescent sparkle and milder moonlight, as we dart out into the open sea, with our prow toward Corfu. The coasts of Albania glide low and dim in the far-off East. The heavy breakers begin to tell upon my sensibilities, and I retire to wake up in the harbor of Corfu.

The Ionian islands have an organization which externally resembles somewhat our own federation. The states are, to be sure, under British influence and protection. Ionia was ceded to England by the treaty of Paris in 1815, and was thus rescued from the domination of Russia. The internal organization is regulated by a Parliament, consisting of a High Commissioner, a Senate, and a Legislative Assembly. The Commissioner, like our President, has a veto and is the executive, having under his control the police and foreign relations. He is represented by a President in each island, who stands in the relation of our Governors to our States. The Senate is elective. The four larger isles, Corfu, Zante, Cephalonia and St. Maura, send one member each. The lower house is elective, and consists of forty members, and meets every second year. These isles of the Adriatic are prospering under this form of government. The care of Great Britain is tutelage to their inexperience. The *Grecia mendax* is as common here as in other parts of Attica, unfitting, by its corrupt influence, the people from exercising in its purity the suffrages of honest freemen. Indeed, in Greece itself, where universal suffrage obtains, the government never fails to triumph, by means of false boxes for ballots and other fraudulent contrivances. Hence the Russian party is always dominant. The Liberal party must first reform the morals of the mass, so that they can feel an outrage upon their rights, and then they may be able to vindicate them. Shade of Demosthenes! If you could only fulminate over Greece, and awake the consciences of your degenerate countrymen, then Hope, winged like the image of Victory on the Acropolis, might visit each sacred haunt to revivify the glories of the past.

At Zante, there are three forts very strong and extensive. Several regiments are stationed here, to which belong our two Captain-companions. They were of our party, when the Nubian slave rattanned our firman, and drove us away from the mosque of St. Sophia, in Constantinople. Our ignoble retreat before a negro was a bond of sympathy which has united us ever since. The retreat of the ten thousand under Xenophon was nothing to ours. What was worse, we could not "knock *the negro* down," without danger of instant death in a Moslem mob.

Our captains sent their pleasure-boat for us, and escorted us around the forts, barracks, and esplanade, which make Corfu at once as formidable as it is beautiful. The isles of olive surrounding the harbor break the roughness of the sea, and give to the prospect a lake-appearance encircled by lofty hills. The coasts of Albania shut in the circle with their gateways of rock. The regiment of the Captains is the immortal 47th, celebrated by Harry Lorrequer, and was formerly that of General Wolfe. They stormed the heights of Abraham, and (what was better) were prisoners in Boston during the Revolution. The same plate and other appendages of the regiment have descended to the present "Mess." The Mess is a *quasi* incorporation, and holds some thousands of pounds worth of interesting relics. We shall never forget the cordial civility of these officers of the 47th. May they always be victorious, except when Uncle Sam is their enemy! Their courtesy did not end in showing us the Lord High Commissioner's palace, or the splendid intrenchments and forts. We found on our return a basket of fruitage, which could not have grown in any other isle than this, which rejoiced in the ancient gardens of Alcinous. Oranges large enough for cantelopes, bright and golden, with the green leaves and twigs still about them. Plums, purple outside, and sanguine within; cherries black as they were glossy; citrons losing their green in the silvery yellow; apples whose scarlet would put to blush our best horticulture, and mellow as the plums; apricots plump in their mealy lusciousness; figs fresh, and bursting their seams to show the glistening white and red that wooed the tooth; and by no means last or least, large peaches, emulating the color while rivalling the size of our red-cheeked melekatoons (spell it better if you can!)—all these on the first of July, and after we have exhausted the grape season of Smyrna. I would not omit the almonds, pears, and melons, so common I forgot them. The natives here, the year round, live on fruits and wine; and keep good health the mean time. Our health is by no means so bad, but that the above basket will vanish before we "tread water" in the limpid streets of Venice.

Before our steamer began to pant away from Corfu, our kind friends sailed by, on their way to Albania, boar-shooting; and stopped to say "good-bye." The last word of the gallant Captain Lowry, an Irishman by the way, was: "Mrs. C———, now don't forget to go to Killarney!" and as his boat careered away, there was borne on the breeze the words—"No more Mahometan niggers! ha! ha! ha!"

How kindly and warmly the words of friendship and courtesy fall upon the ear of the pilgrim. Not more musically sweet murmurs the fountain 'which shakes its loosened silver in the sun,' than the voice of a kindred spirit, in a far-off country beyond the sea. To hear a warm-hearted Englishman quote Longfellow with pride, and repeat Chatham's eloquent appeal for America with enthusiasm, were enough to banish 'squint suspicion,' and bid us hail him as our elder brother, had we no substantial evidence of genuine hospitality. If every English captain is as near like Sir Calidore in courtesy as Captain Fordyce or Lowry of the 47th, the army of England is nobly officered.

A fine veil of gossamer begins to invest the receding isles. We leave them in their unclouded canopy. But our memory of them—sweet is the balm which preserves it, as a sacred relic in life's pilgrimage. We leave them with tearful regret, clad as of yore in their azure vesture. Thus have they ever been; what Homer saw of them, they seemed to Byron; what Anacreon beheld in them, Shelley rejoiced to see. What Creation's dawn beheld, this day we see—enriched by the spoils of time and the associations of renown. Sleep on bright isles of Greece! Eternal summer gilds your sea; and ye sleep so tranquil under a sky

> "So cloudless, clear, and purely beautiful,
> That God is to be seen in Heaven."

We expected by this time to have been 'within thy gates, O Jerusalem.' But we learned at Athens that no steamer left for Joppa until the 25th of July. Too late that; for the Syrian sun has already all the heat, without the pleasure of a Turkish bath. To have been within ten days of the city which 'sits solitary'—the fulfilment of all prophecy; to have sailed within three days of the excellency and glory of the cedars of Lebanon; and not to have seen them, will it not be forever a drawback upon our retrospect? But suppose we had been in Zion, and surmounted Olivet, where David and a Greater than David went up sorrowfully; how could we have left Palestine without visiting the most beautiful of all cities—Damascus. Could we have had the continency of Mahomet and turned away from it as he did, saying, 'one Paradise is all that is allotted to man. I will take mine in the other world!' We fear not. But regrets are useless. Our face is set as a flint, no longer Zionward. The Adriatic is ploughed by our keel. As we turn homeward, the heart throbs more warmly; and when we are again in our native valley, we shall dwell in much content there, grateful to God if He shall permit us yet a few more years with our friends, and a resting spot at last amid our own Muskingum hills.

XX.

The City of the Sea.

Una Italum regina, altæ pulcherrimæ Romæ,
Æmula, quæ terris, quæ dominaris aquis.
O decus! O lux Ausoniæ!

WE are in Venice. For more than a week we have been tossing on the waters of the Mediterranean, straining in every plank to reach this point of the Adriatic. The isles have passed like unrealities before the mind; the East, with its many-shaped and colored costumes and scenery, has come and gone, leaving but its memory in dreamy outline floating in the soul. The unreality has not yet ceased; for we are again in the midst of wonders, not the least among which is the watery street that plays against our door, and the grotesque and unique architecture which is overlooked by the tower of St. Mark's.

Yesterday (Sunday) we arrived at Trieste, the only Austrian port of any consequence. It is remarkably clean, and handsomely built, at the head of the Adriatic. The streets are finely paved, and the promenades, green and enticing, lie along the harbor in grateful umbrage. It reminded us of New-York, except that each street was a Broadway in the regularity of the tall stone houses and solid paves. We drove about the city. On every side are groups and crowds of people in their Sunday best, laughing and listening to the music. The cafés are all thronged with eaters of ices and drinkers of wine. Our ride extended down between the two lofty hills, within whose scoop the city lies. We found a splendid café upon the side hill, with walks under oak groves winding up to the summit, and all crowded with people listening to music, and partaking of refreshment. We joined the throng much against our puritan principles. Waltzing whirled around in the houses of the poorer people as we passed. Sunday seemed absolutely sunk in the general joyousness. A few Russian soldiers reminded us of the union of Austria with her kindly ally, while numbers of the white-dressed soldiers of Austria spoke of the iron coercion which keeps down the spirit of the masses in the Lombardo-Venetian province of the Hapsburgs. And yet—why speak of their *spirit*, poor, contemptible, despot-fawning crowds; are they not enslaved by the very music and gayety which their masters have provided for them? And is it not the same sly expedient which now blows through brass, and beats on sheep skin in the piazza of St. Mark's, followed by eager thousands, totally absorbed in the pursuit? There are other chains than those of iron. Ignoble ease and oblivious gayety are worse than prisons of stone, and manacles of iron. They indicate a subjection of mind, and a meanness of spirit, wholly incompatible with the generous impulses and noble aims of freemen.

A heavy fort overlooks Trieste, from one of the hills—rather ominous. Similar forts *were* near Genoa and Rome, when the first of 1848 dawned. But they now lie in ruins—the expression of aroused popular indignation. Fine villas, embowered in green trees, and surrounded with vines and fruits, line the slopes of the hills around Trieste. Our star-spangled flag floats from two noble ships in port—the Independence and the Mississippi. They look a little saucy here, after Webster's letter. I wonder what business they have! They seem to say, "Just hang a spy, Sir Buzzard, an thou darest; but if you do, we will blow you to ——" I beg pardon—it is Sunday. One is apt to forget peace principles while abroad. The guns were firing, the music braying, and people hallooing, at a great rate. How could one think it was the Sabbath day?

There are daily steamers to Venice, small though they be. Indeed, owing to the wash of the Alpine rivers, which here empty, the Adriatic is not more than twelve fathoms deep, in and around these, her northern shores; hence these small boats. In coming into Venice, we had to sound with a long pole, as we wound between the piles driven to show the channel in the Lagoon. The sea is completely broken for eighty miles along the coast, by numerous isles, as well as by the noble rampart erected on the Lido di Palestrina, whose marble appearance and solid material unites beauty with utility, and forms a public monument not excelled by the Pireus, the mole of Ancona, or by any other similar work in the world. Venice itself is built upon seventy-two isles, in which piles are driven for the houses. Hence, such a city can sleep in comparative peace amidst the waters; though gondolas have been known to attend mass in St. Mark's! The mail from Alexandria and India is not carried by Venice, but by Trieste, in consequence of the shallowness of the waters.

For an hour before we reached Venice, the city was announced through its elegant cupolas and towers, rising out of the sea. The country around was flat, but now and then a silver thread of snow would glisten out of the Tyrol beyond, which rose under cloud-vestments, lofty and sublime. A few sail of colored canvas, peculiar to these shores, float by us. We pass around green isles, whereon are palaces. Orange groves and marble steps kiss the water's edge, and gondolas—floating hearses—begin to appear, but not trim and graceful, as the caïques of the Bosphorus. Sea-weed, as Rogers describes it, clings to the marble palaces. How variant is the verdure of the trees, ranging from the deep green of the cypress to the pale, yellowish green of the flowering locust. The Venetian Gothic, so nearly resembling the Byzantine style, rears its swelling domes from the sea. Soon watery alleys and streets begin to open, and little spanning bridges bend darkling far down the perspective. A few more dashes of the steamer, and we drop anchor in front of the Ducal Palace, at the mouth of the Grand Canal, and in view of the twin pillars, on one of which the authentic winged lion starts back with open mouth and snarling teeth; and upon the other, St. Theodore standing upon the crocodile, and, with an auriole around his brow, sheds his influence upon the magnificent temple of St. Mark, the fine Piazza, and this unique "City of the Sea." We do not long remain gazing at the unusual spectacle. A gondola plays the part of an omnibus, and drives us around to a hotel. We pull up at a by-door, ring a bell, and are welcomed at Doniella's. We found there five sovereigns—the Elector of Saxony and four Americans!

Being expeditious travellers, we immediately set about our work of sight-seeing. It is not easy labor by any means, and the best part of the pleasure lies in the review, during the expected hours of the winter fireside.

We found ourselves upon the Square of St. Mark. The grim and gloomy prison, connected by the Bridge of Sighs with the Ducal Palace—a place to freeze the soul with horror,—is passed before we reach the lesser piazza, in front of which our boat landed. The Venetian tower, brother to the ungainly-looking sentinel which clings to the Acropolis at Athens (where it is entirely out of place), springs out of the piazza some 300 or 400 feet high. A solemn and sweet bell rings in deep bass the hour of five. We gaze at the strange old vicissitudinous lion, which has so long presided over the destiny of the Venetian, and which some years ago paid a visit to Paris, exciting as much curiosity there as veneration here. This lion is the representative of St. Mark, the patron of the city. The king of beasts has been associated with that Evangelist, because the lion seen by Ezekiel in his mystic vision is supposed to be the prototype of St. Mark.

Around the corner to the left is the great Piazza. The columns of the café, covered with hangings, and the arcade of jewellers opposite, with the white marble palace, built by Napoleon at the west, and the Church of St. Mark at the east, form a large hollow square. wherein the joy-loving, mustering, trading, curious and devout citizens of Venice are wont to congregate.

St. Mark's, statued and niched, with its four bronze horses and lion, all glittering with mosaic and gilt, surmounted by its fine cupolas and pretty little domes above (how I like those domelets!), has a finer ground of vantage to display its singular style of beauty than any church, except St. Peter's, that we have seen. The first object after gazing above at the mosaics, in which St. Mark and his tomb play a prominent part, is the red lozenge stone, whereon the reconciliation between Pope Alexander III. and the Emperor Frederick Barbarossa took place, and where the former placed his foot upon the prostrate head of the latter, adding contempt to the abasement by saying, "*Thou shalt tread upon the lion and the adder.*" Oh! impotent foolery! Where are ye now, Alexander and Frederick? If ye are in Heaven, (?) little children are greater there than ye both!

The church within is dark. Golden mosaics give general tone to its appearance. Marbles of every kind, precious stones, among which I saw an agate six inches in diameter in the form of a dome, pillars from St. Sophia, which this church is said to resemble in its primitive adornments, transparent alabaster and exquisite jasper, meet the eye above, around, and below. Indeed, we tread upon the finest mosaic paves we have yet seen. The oozy foundation has broken the level, as well as many of the stones. While St. Mark's was in process of erection, each vessel was bound, upon every voyage, to bring home some piece of marble or precious stone to form a part of the structure. This will account for their abundant variety. To speak plainly, the church is made up of the results of petty larcenies in time of peace and under color of war. Even the body of St. Mark was stolen from Alexandria by some "wily Venetian," and is entombed in the centre of the church. The church is in the form of a Greek cross. There is not the freshness and brilliancy of St. Peter's in St. Mark's, but there is a greatness and antiquity about it which impresses it more solemnly on the mind. Massive doors, old inscriptions, bass-reliefs, fluted and spiral pillars, outré sculptures, together with a fine sacristy, constitute the inner adornment, over which the reflective golden light from the mosaics is poured in a dim, religious flood. But the outside is the most peculiar affair in Venice. Indeed, there is nothing like it any where. The four horses were brought, in the earlier eras, from the Hippodrome of Constantinople, and have played important parts upon numerous triumphal arches in Rome and Paris. Examine the entrance particularly. Prophets and Evangelists, allegorical figures of the months and of all trades, mystical figures of beasts and birds, many of them reminding you of "the half horse, half man, and the rest snapping-turtle," crockets and finials filled with statues, give the effect of a Gothic cathedral, intermingled with which is an Oriental style; and this combination has given to St. Mark's its *sui generis* character.

Was my reader at Cincinnati during the great rise of the Ohio, in the winter of 1848? Does he remember how the streets in the neighborhood of Lower Market looked in their watery garb? Just so,—with a difference in the color of the water and the kind of houses,—looked Venice when we caught its first impression between sun-down and moon-rise as we rowed up the grand canal to the Rialto. The impression of a flooded city, flattened houses, with desertion and desolation, could not be removed; although lamps gleamed at the door-ways, and marble steps were washed conveniently by the wave. Soon lights began to flicker and glance upon the gondola and bridge, which the water gave back with added brilliancy. We listened in vain for the songs of Tasso, sung under the rising moon by gondoliers,—in vain for serenading lovers with eyes upturned to the balconies, where we did see many a fair Desdemona; in vain for the Tobarro of the men and the Zendale of the women,—those national dresses of Venice in her proud days of independence. Austrian rule has robbed the home of Cassio and of *honest* Iago of that romance which has been associated with Venice, in the stage representation of Othello. The gondoliers near the Rialto made as much noise as the kind people who rapped up Brabantio to tell him that his daughter had ran off with the jealous blackamoor.

In default of foreign romance, we started a little of the Buckeye—some domestic songs from our gondola, and right sweetly sounded the voices of the songstresses, vibrating upon the silent water among the palaces of the merchant Kings. Their song echoed the scene ;

"'Tis midnight hour, the moon shines bright;
The dew-drops blaze beneath her rays;
The twinkling stars—their trembling light
Like Beauty's eyes display."

An hour upon the Piazza listening to other music, and enjoying the ices, and again we are housed for the night.

We had hardly been housed, before our sovereign cousin of Saxony, dressed in stately style, with a flaming retinue, departed to attend an evening party, to which we could not go, *owing to excessive fatigue.* Had we known, however, the rich treat which was afforded him, we certainly should have joined his train. Large gondolas of singers were arranged to precede him ; an hundred gondolas followed, each moving to the music with muffled oar ; lights glanced around from window and balcony. Boat answered boat in Venetian song, and all joined the chorus. When they reached the Rialto, a great blue light flashed forth, which displayed the whole scene, while the singers arranged under the swelling arch of the bridge made the welkin tremble with the freight of melody.

In some respects I am disappointed in Venice. I expected, or rather wished, to find it the Venice of the Doges. It is not so large as I expected. We have just returned from the summit of the great tower in the Piazza. It affords a fine view of the surrounding country, but not of the city. The city must be seen from the canals. The churches are distinguished by their domes and cupolas, from which there rolls up music from the sweetest toned bells we have yet heard. The isles and the royal garden near St. Mark's are the only green spots to break the sameness of the crockery tiles. The city seems like one isle out of the tower, from which the canals are unseen, connected with the main land by the bridge of the railroad (three miles long), leading to Milan. The hills of the west range up along the horizon, beyond which sleeps Ferrara. Odd looking chimneys, made apparently to catch rain, open their mouths in desperate yawns, while under and around them, upon the flat roofs, are frequently seen tables, chairs, and flowers, where resort at evening this air-loving people. The Adriatic is dotted with piles and gondolas, as well as with isles. To-day it is cloudy and gloomy. The breeze comes keen with driplets of rain. We take a glance at a few of the leaning towers of oozy Venice, and descend to visit the Ducal Palace.

The lion's mouth—*sans the mouth*—is at its old orifice of accusation. We enter superb stair-cases, passing the spot where Doge Marino Faliero was crowned and—hanged; and after looking until the eye aches at pictures of Venetians fighting Turks, and Doges being received and blessed by Popes, we find ourselves in the Great Council Chamber. It is a noble hall. At one end is a picture of Paradise, the largest oil painting in the world, being 85 by 35 feet. The room is 176 feet long and 185 broad, and is used as a library. How I love to enter a silent, solemn library, filled with the embound essence of the past, concentrated in words that 'live an immortality rather than a life.' Here, in this palace, lives have been strangled under the decree of the infernal Council of Ten; here the best blood of Venice was spilt at the beck of the cruel Decemvir; but in these alcoves the best compensation for blood is treasured up for a 'life beyond life.' How calmly, now, do these spirits rest in their bindings of white. Not more peacefully rests their dust in the cerements of the grave.

"Here all the rage of controversy ends
And rival zealots rest like bosom friends:
Socinians here with Calvinists abide,

> And thin partitions angry chiefs divide;
> Here wily Jesuits simple Quakers meet,
> And Bellarmine has rest at Luther's feet."

If these sectarian controversialists sleep not here, I am sure TASSO has repose in the bowers of his own muse, and DANTE feels no pang of exile in these hospitable shelves. All around are the forms of the Doges looking down upon their ancient hall. Only one portrait is wanting. A black curtain hangs over the place where Marino—the infamous—might have been.

The Venetian style of painting is admirable in more respects than having definitiveness of outline and clearness of expression, without which, whatever connoisseurs may say, painting is irksome to the eye, if not perplexing to the mind. Some persons make a merit of admiring paintings because they are dim and indefinite. The darker the outline, the more gloomy the figures—and the greater the visual effort to see what the artist may have designed, the more excellent, in their eye, is the painting. To all such, we would simply say, "look to the Transfiguration of Raphael—the mightiest effort of the pencil; and if you can find in it any dim, dark uncertainty, clinging about the forms or the idea which they embody, then hang your galleries full of blackish landscapes and shady forms, and call them—beautiful." How much more admirable in this regard is the painting of Venice than the school of Naples! But hurry is the word! The Council of Ten no longer close their mysterious door. The Council of Three have lost their guard. We enter each. Aye! even the deep, dark dungeons where the political prisoner received the rack, and the massive doors which lead to the Bridge of Sighs opens, and with spectral lamplight we view each den of horror, and gaze out of those bars where the sad prisoners looked last at the clear moonlight which was reflected from the Adriatic! The instruments of fiendish torture were in the Arsenal. We only saw its exterior.

How these sights speak of the cruel past! What a progress has man made even here, where Austria holds the key, since the golden days when the marriage ring was cast into the Adriatic! What a change could be marked upon that large globe in the library, where America in the sixteenth century is drawn in doubtful limning beyond the sea, and upon which I remarked the Florida Indians only as inhabiting the United States! Navigation has improved since the era when the Venetian ran to Crete and Byzantium, or planted the golden ball upon her mast as the symbol of her commercial glory.

In one respect the Venetians may boast. They have no dust to blind the eye of the passenger. Their streets are *well watered.* Another item is, that you hear no clatter of carriages or drays. No common council is troubled to death about paving the way. But as an offset, it must be confessed that pile-driving is troublesome, although bathing is handy. Water for drinking is carried about upon the shoulders by women and sold. It is drawn from the wells of bronze in the Ducal Piazza, into which it is poured for filtration after being boated into the city.

With dirt and sea-weed as her foundation, Venice has arisen from the sea, a city of might, and of wonderful duration in the course of time. For thirteen centuries, she continued independent and potent, unattacked by the scourges of the North, who overran the beautiful plains of Lombardy; and during that time extended her sway over great nations, from the Pireus—whose lions yet adorn her harbor—to Constantinople, where her towers yet bespeak her conquests!

XXI.

Lombardy,---The Garden of the World.

"Every tree, well from his fellow grew,
With branches broad, laden with leaves new,
That sprangen out against the sunny sheen."
Beaumont & Fletcher.

THE Austrian power is by no means to be contemned. One need not sojourn long even in Italy to ascertain that. This garden spot of the world, stretching from the Apennines and the Po to the Alps, has been sadly divided since our ancestral relatives, the Long Beards or Lombards, held it; and rejoiced to hold it under Queen Theolinda and the Iron Crown. A considerable portion of proud old Lombardy, including the Queen of the Adriatic, now owns the Austrian yoke. The treaty of Vienna, in 1814, which fixed, *temporarily*, the destiny of the Bonapartes (for the world is not yet done with them), also fixed in Austria all its former possessions, including Venice, which she had not before the revolutionary war. These possessions were erected into a distinct kingdom from that of Austria proper, and are known as the Lombardo-Venetian kingdom. There are two governments, Venice with 2,168,553 inhabitants, and Milan with some five thousand more than Venice.

These plains of Lombardy have ever been the theatre of ravages and wars. Long before Marengo, Lodi, and Arcoli were fought by Bonaparte, these fertile plains had attracted the eye of the savage Teutons, as they looked down through the Alpine passes. The best part of Italy, described by Virgil as the *ubere glebae et potens armis,*—the land of the mulberry and the worm, the vine and the olive—the realm of beautiful lakes mirroring lofty mountains,—the instructress of Christendom during the middle ages, in civil law and medicine,—now wears the badge of the Austrian, from the Northern to the Maritime Alps, stretching from the frontiers of Piedmont, where the Austrian in white uniform demanded our passports before we launched upon Maggiore, to the city of watery streets, which the reader has skimmed in my last chapter.

You may remember, that while at our hotel in Rome, one of the servants being a Republican, received a notice from Richard Roe, the government in possession, to quit the premises within a given time; and that we proposed to annex him to our confederacy. Well he met us, as agreed, in Venice, and by his knowledge of Italian, solved for us many difficulties. He bears the swelling and artistic name of Dominichino Pollano, and *loves* priests as do the other Republicans of 1848.

The Elector of Saxony, whom we shall ever respect as the successor to the great and good defender of Luther, was determined not to be left behind by us. We found him at the railroad station with his Queen, in the royal train, about to puff homeward. He seems always to beat us. We were behind him at the Venetian tower yesterday morn. We liked his homely and matter-of-fact air, but his aide-de-camp—Oh! mercy of me!

> "He had so tricked himself with Art,
> That of himself he was least part."

The Queen sat in her golden chair in the car, as it whizzed by the long stretched necks of prying Venetians, who seemed to snuff with eagerness the air of royalty. We were soon in full chase over the three-mile bridge, then out of the marshy land into the garden of gardens. On either side mulberries, festooned with and joined together by vines pendant with embryo clusters made vistas of exceeding loveliness. The trees were linked hand and hand by their green tendrils and branches, and as our cars dashed by, they danced jubilantly and gracefully. All nature was inwoven in one verdant texture; the ploughed fields, off of which the first crop had been taken, and which were now sowed for the second, of millet, lay between the linked arbors, alternating with the yellow and green fields. Southern Italy was luxuriant, but scorched and dusty; England was rural with comfort and beauty; France was clad in vineyards from the base of its swelling hills to their summits, but here,—*here, is the verdurous heart* of Nature, irrigated by Alpine showers and torrents, and throbbing with vegetable life to its minutest fibre. But why so many mulberries? Ah! do you ask, after looking into those halls, where roll a thousand reels, upon whose circuit the silken tomb of the worm is wound in glossy tenuity under the property of easiness which dwells in the fingers of the Italian women? And do you boast, Ohioan, that your State in a half century holds nearly two millions of souls supported by a vigorous agriculture? Listen to the story of progress in this Austrian dependency, in spite of exactions and insecurity, and be ready to confess that the man of industry and energy is not alone an American nor a Republican.

The white mulberry is a dwarfish thickly-leaved tree, and is the source of Lombard wealth. In thirty years, the production of silk from the fibre of this tree, and the spinning-worm feeding from it, has grown from a small value to the enormous sum of $50,000,000. In 1800, the Lombardo-Venetian kingdom did not exceed 1,800,000 lbs. of silk. In the dry and hilly parts of the country, the worm works to the best advantage; but throughout the whole of the kingdom, there is an activity in this branch, which furnishes to the people every comfort and convenience. Especially around Padua and Verona, to which our car is rapidly drawing near, is the silk culture prolific.

We had barely time to glance at Padua, renowned as the seat of the University, and of the Duomo of Michael Angelo. If I remember aright, it was from this queenly city of Padua that there came the 'second Daniel' to judge the case of the merchant of Venice, and she did judge it right learnedly for a 'timid female.' Vincenza, on a lofty hill, all beautified in leafiness, fortified and romantic, was soon lost to the eye, which wandered far over to the right, above the mountains of Tyrol, which in their coverings of cloud peeped out in a shower of rain. The hills toward Ferrara glistened in green. A slight breeze turned up the silvered willow leaves white to the view, while they rustled. Through the shower we looked very hard for the obelisk, and not in vain, which marks the desperate battle of Arcoli, fought upon a spot between the cities of Vincenza and Verona, upon the banks of the Adigo. Here Napoleon gave the best evidence on record of personal daring; here he was torn from his guards leading the forlorn hope, surrounded in the midst of the swamps, and protected only by the single arms of his aids, when the thrilling cry of "*Save the General!*" rang down the ranks of the disheartened French, and rallied them to victory! Here Lannes was wounded; and here the child of destiny himself received some of the first intuitions of the great calling which eventuated in his becoming the head of the empire. We entered Verona after dark, so that I could not see Shakspeare's "two gentlemen." Neither could I imagine any place in the dusky shade so completely romantic as the balcony of Juliet, nor observe any wall so provokingly high as to try the vigorous assault of the fond Romeo.

The cars stop here. Diligence is our next vehicle; and the morning found it tumbling into the famous city where the Chevalier Bayard displayed so much courage and gallantry,—I mean Brescia. We passed Lake Garda in the night. I have an indistinct notion of seeing a moon floating in a lucent wave, as we rattled along the margin of the lake, through a stony little town called Lugano. My consciousness was sufficiently restored to try a breakfast at Brescia.

Italy is no rank garden run to seed, or unweeded. Tidy and trim is each grape-vine and mulberry grove. At every turn we see women serving the reel and handling the cocoon, digging the ground and pruning the vines. Old fashioned, overshot wheels turn the machinery, and the same torrent which turns them, gives drink to the soil. The harvest was mostly in. A few gleaners were in the fields. The rivers along our way were all walled against the Alpine floods. Men were flailing like a band of Taluses, at the wheat, with women in high hats assisting the operation. A Yankee thrashing machine would scare these torrents to their sources. Shrines were plenty along the way, con taining rude pictures of the Madonna or some favorite Saint, hung with flowers. Heavy loaded two-wheeled wagons—having wine casks upon the top, and a human underneath in a hammock, swinging amid dust and sound asleep at the horses' heels, and rocks hanging fore or aft as ballast below to equalize the load —were drawn by five horses tandem, and not without the everlasting bell which must always jingle upon the highway. No beggars trot after us. The cars again receive us at Treviglio.

The arrangement at the station is even beautiful. You are introduced into an elegant room, awaiting your time to start. A bell taps! You start. "Nay—" says Dominichino; "that is for baggage." Another tap! "That is the first class, for fools and princes." Yet another! "Second class," and we find our door opened, and, without noise or confusion, are placed in our right seat. In a twinkling we were off for Milan between rows of locusts, which provokingly shut out the view, while they gave to our ride, umbrageousness.

We left Lodi and its gory honor on our south, crossed the Adra, and were soon knocking at the Posta gate of Milan, one of the most beautiful cities of the world. Our drive to the hotel is under a promenade, which constitutes the circumference of the city, and measures twelve miles! Travellers have rarely described Milan as it really is, in all the splendor of its views, and the greatness of its extent. Standing, as it does, between the gorgeous palaces of nature upon the North, and the temples of art and luxury upon the South, and sweeping, as its tributary, the blossom and fragrance of Italia's garden, Milan should not alone be spoken of for its Duomo and its Arena, its Arch and its "Last Supper," by De Vinci; but for its regal magnificence and commanding prospects. Lofty houses, elegant court-yards and fine paves, are not wanting to make an unbroken perspective of grandeur in the streets. But hold! miracle of wonder! what is that tall spire, sculptured and entablatured, rising from forth the sea of stone, "how silently," in its delicate and labyrinthine magic of art! Is it the phantasm of a dream, or the grotesque illusion of the clouds? The white statues, as you approach, people the slender pinnacles, and stand within the marble niches. This unparalleled Duomo has been likened to a river of marble shot into the air to a height of 500 feet, and then suddenly petrified while falling! Surely it must have arisen like an exhalation "to the sound of dulcet symphonies and voices sweet;" for it seems of the very air—airy in its frozen poetry.

We did not long tarry without. We entered its dark, high nave, branching like monster trees of some other world; and uplifted by octagon circular columns, so high, that they seem toppling to the upraised eye. The finest stained glass windows, perhaps, in the world, beautify the darksome aisles. The evening light slowly plays through every colored form of saint and prophet, flower and tracery.

While we stand spell-bound, the janitor, who spoke bad English, came up and politely offered to show us the top. After dropping a few sous for the church at the portal, we wound up a spiral inclined plane, and within the magic marble mountain. We are soon amid the mazes above. Solid as earth, it seems a fairy city of towers. One hundred and fifty-five pinnacles point upward; nearly 7,000 statues glance in the light, while niches stand waiting for 3,000 more! Fifteen thousand different points are lifted from the roofs—for there are more roofs than one, as we find by ascending staircase on staircase. Below us, on the last roof, is the *Botanic Garden!* What! is Italy so prodigal of its verdure, that the Cathedral's top should bud and blow like the hanging gardens of Old Assyria? It is only the marble which has sought, through genius and taste, manifold forms in the pointed spires. Fifteen thousand buds, flowers and

THE DUOMO AT MILAN.

fruits, each different, bloom perennially amid the upper air, and that without irrigation or pruning.

This immense pile, an imperfect idea of which may be gathered from the engraving, has been centuries in completing. Napoleon, whose mind was ever ready to build monuments to art and himself, added an immense addition. Architects have discussed the minutest points of this Duomo in lines of solid quarto. Nearly thirty hundred millions of francs have been expended upon it. An edifice as large as Grace Church, New-York, is upon its top as plainly as the Pantheon is upon St. Peter's.

The view from it, is incomparably fine. The eye may float over the scenery of Italy, and revel in its fairest bowers, discern the cities around for forty miles, and to the north see those everlasting Alps, which lock up the gateways of Europe. The beautiful hills of Como and Maggiore, surrounding the magic mirrors in which they are reflected; the Saint Gothard; farther west, the Simplon, through whose defiles we expect to pass; the Monte Rosa, white and radiant, except at sunset, when it illustrates its name in the sweetest of hues; Mount Cenis, to the direct west; and further around, the line of the Apennines; and to the southeast, the sweeping vale of the Po, with Cremoni and Crema—all can be viewed from this lofty spot! What a resplendent, magnificent, glorious creation is ours! How full of beauty and sublimity! Would that our distant friends could behold these splendid Alpine temples upon the north, from this marble observatory, and the great pleasure-grounds which lie around their feet in such luxuriance of vegetable life!

What are those scaffoldings, observable as we descend, erected far up to the topmost rose of the pinnacle? We are informed by the custodian, that ten men are constantly employed upon these scaffolds in cleaning the building, and that it takes them just twelve years to complete the circuit outside.

Can it be that the Great Father of all is pleased with such stately structures, erected for His worship? Does He delight rather in the marbles of Italy, than the rude churches of our land? Profitless inquisition; for the temple of His love is the upright heart and pure; and where that bows—whether under swelling dome or homely altar—whether under the light of stained splendors, or under the white radiance of an open sky, His presence appears more glorious than all else beside in heaven, or in earth!

We did not leave Milan without a drive around the city. The *Milaners* were still to be seen in their shops, with ribbons flaunting at the windows, and waxen images within, (horrible caricatures!)—just the same as when their taste gave name to the large class who now wear the badge of *Milaner*. We visited the arch of Peace, with her chariot and six horses upon the top, commenced by Napoleon, as an arch of Victory; and the great arena, where mimic naval battles were fought before Napoleon, and (the ring being changed into a more solid element by secret outlets) gladiatorial combats followed. From the front of the arena is seen the grand Piazza d'Armi, where Bonaparte, after his uninterrupted successes upon those garden spots, against the hosts of Austria, reviewed his Italian armies; and here, too, is seen the castle which has now 10,000 Austrians in it, and the Forum, around which walks are ranged in splendid style.

One cannot but mark, throughout Italy, that suppressed veneration for the memory of Napoleon, which speaks more of a *future*, than any other element. The old soldier who showed us the Arena, seemed full to the brim with admiration; but he expressed it in the eye and gesture, rather than with the tongue.

There is no unity of place regarded in the chapters of the Traveller, such as the drama demands, so that I have liberty to leap from the Duomo upon the boldest wing, into the clear air, and alight upon the bosom of the lake of Como. Above me is a circular range of living green, speckled with white palaces. Between the two gateways, wherein the Madonna is enshrined, small red steamers ply and cleave the placid waters. An old castle with broken towers, speaks eloquently of a feudal time from a forum of rock. Boats with fagots, *manned* by women, are putting into port, while a regiment of females are on their knees —washing clothes upon the stony brink. The air below is clear; but the green mountains have lost their tops in a cloud. Music floats across the lake from the Austrian fort, and every thing of beauty is here to fill the eye.

How tastefully has Nature decorated this valley of Como with landscapes of every variety of soft and sweet enchantment. Groves of myrtle and golden fruitage reflected in the glassy water, form terraces of green upon perpendicular strata. Como city seems sunk to the lake's level, in its setting of emerald, while out of the tower of the city there merrily rings the chime. By rowing, we reach a point, from which is visible the extreme of a perspective of hill after hill, dotted with shrines of wondrous charm, erratic granite blocks, (who knows whence they came?) and white villas. Houses cut in the solid rock appear high and aloof from the habitations of men. Truly, the genius of Bulwer was choice and rare, to a sense of deliciousness, when he made Claude Melnotte paint in fancy for the proud Pauline, the "Lady of Lyons," his palace of alabaster, and groves of myrtle amid these hills and this lake of Como!

Our ride to Como had been through a branch of the same picture gallery, of which Monza, the ancient capital of Lombardy, was the chief view, and where are the relics of Queen Theolinda and the Lombard crown of iron once worn by Charles V., and placed by no priestly hand on the brow of Napoleon.

A showery rain followed us across to Maggiore; but it only served to spread a transparent mist, like the veil we saw over the face of a marble nun in Rome, adorning a beauty it could not conceal.

We slept upon the shore of Maggiore at the base of a high dark mountain, unconscious until we were upon the lake, of its lofty presence. Levano was the town to which we were bound. Before we reached it, the jagged rocks, indicating our proximity to the Alps, gloomed terrifically black, as if about to be thunder-riven. Far above them a cloud hung its white linings to the eye, which curled and smoked as if out of the black mountain, like a furnace of Inferno. I had never before seen such sublimity of gloom and wildness. If these are but the shadows of the Alpine feet, what is the lofty head?

We are leaving the Paradise of Italy and entering the rough and broken land of Switzerland. The pass toward the Simplon was clear, an index, said our boatmen, of good weather. Lakes of white clouds wave between great mountain heights. Although we cannot see distinctly the lofty genii who guard the Simplon, yet we have before us still the magic of Beauty. The Borromean isles, owned by the Count Borromea, float in the crystal of Maggiore. Compelled to leave Milan with other noble families, on account of the Revolution of 1848, when he hoped to unite Italy in one grand union under Charles Albert, he has sought refuge in his Bella Isola. This isle looks out of the Piedmont into the Austrian line, near the shore, where an Austrian steamboat with three soldiers marks the extremity of her Italian power.

We persuaded our boatmen to make a deflection from the direct line, so as to run around these isles. The first one is a bower of trees, a quarter of a mile through; birds sing in it; an ivy-clad house appears, then a vista, showing a fine residence beyond. Flowers adorn the rocks which run up in strata, at an angle of 45 degrees from the clear water. But there is no one stirring at this early hour. Bella next appears, and well deserving the name. As we approach, a large white palace appears on the right, while on the left we pass a yellow octagonal tower, whose counterpart is on the other side. Between them rises a pyramid of green terraces, decked with urns of flowers, and surrounded with hundreds of figures of man and horse. Stone railings protect the rocky barriers of the isle. Arched grottoes, with every variety of tropical flowers and fruits growing in them, appear, and fill the air with a delicious aroma. Ten terraces there are, placed upon the slaty rock, warmed beneath by fires in winter, to protect these tropical flowers from the frost, which even in summer glistens from the tops of the mountains beyond. Magnolias in full bloom find sweet multiplication in the wave over which they hang. The soil upon which these rare flowers grow, is renewed every year by fresh imports from Italy. At the extreme end of the isle, there live about two hundred people, whose residences add nothing to the romance of the spot.

We pass the Fisher's isle, out of which the chapel bell sounds; in front is the mount whose sides have been wounded to build St. Paul's at Rome. The Ticino river empties the lake into the Mediterranean, with its freight of marble. The water of the lake is a clear green, answering to the emerald hills. The clouds part as we approach the shore, disclosing dark masses of mother Earth, like Mahomet's coffin suspended in mid air. The mist comes down on the bosom of the lake, as we land. Happily we have seen its beauties, and escaped its unpleasantness.

Under shadows of dark mountains, leading gradually up to the Alps from Italy; along immense quarries of marble; across torrents whose madness has torn away the bridges of the Simplon road; yet ever tending upward, we reach and rest at Domo d'Ossolo—the villa at the foot of the Simplon.

How gradually have we passed from the soft loveliness of Lombardy to the grandeur of Maggiore, and now to the rugged sublimity of the Alps. Doth not Nature, in these scenes of beauty and grandeur, speak warmly and closely to the heart of man? Doth she not "astonish him with her magnitude, appall him with her darkness, cheer him with her splendor and soothe him with her harmony?" God gave us faculties to enjoy these His mountains and flowers, torrents and tendrils, fields of verdure and of snow, lakes of crystal surrounding emerald and rocky islands. Let the heart, then, bound upward to His, as it swells in emotion at each passing glory!

If you will look with me at the raised globe I told you of in the Exhibition, you will observe a general elevation in the north of Italy, indented by torrent beds and peaked with snow points. Upon Lake Maggiore there frowns a ridge of mountains, stretching from St. Gothard, in the south-east of Switzerland, following the Rhone to the Simplon, bending at Mount Rosa, (what a hinge is Rosa!) to run due west where Mount Cervin frowns—St. Bernard opens, and Blanc—"every inch a king" —rules ever with his superior crown of snow, upon his sunless throne of rocks. The Maritime Alps, under the command of Mount Cenis—a brave subject of Blanc—turn south-westward, and march toward France, where we saw their white plumes and rough spears, as we journeyed to Marseilles; and then nearly right about, down the coast of Italy, where they meet with a heavy fire from Vesuvius and Etna; tearing them asunder at the Straits of Messina, which thus ends their career.

But we have now to do with but one of the great gaps which sportive nature has made in the chain—the Simplon—which we reserve for another chapter.

XXII.

Crossing the Alps.

"In the mountains he doth *feel* his faith,
All things responsive to the writing there
Breathed immortality———.
There littleness is not. The least of things
Seemed Infinite."

Wordsworth.

FROM the highly cultivated and sun-warmed plains of Italy to these Alpine peaks, snow-covered and wind-beaten, what a change?—How sudden! Can it be real? Yes; for the sough of the wind around this old stone auberge, and the chilly air without, are palpable proofs even on this 18th of July, that we are upon the summit of the Simplon, where winter lives under the open sky. Besides,—

"Small, busy flames play through the fresh laid coals,
And their faint crackling o'er our silence creeps
Like whispers of the household gods———

Two days ago and these fiery appendages would have been as superfluous as painting the lily, smoothing ice, or describing to one who had seen and felt them, the scenery and sensations which have followed our pathway up—up—some seven thousand feet above ordinary humanity and the sea-level. So much has been written of these passes through the Alps; so much that speaks to the eye, to the ear, to all the senses; so much has been told in every variety of style, by every variety of person, that I despair of uttering any thing that can convey, even partially, an adequate idea of their sublimities.

These Alpine scenes are not to be lightly passed. The impression they produce is not a theme for flimsy rapture or minute analysis. They seem born of the Great God, and within their august temples His presence becomes omnipotence, and His worship holy and awful!

The Simplon road is named after the snow-topped mount just above our hospice. It is the crowning peak of the pass. Over the pass the road is forty-five miles. It took six years to complete it, although 30,000 men were at work. It has 611 bridges, in addition to miles of solid masonry. It is twenty-five or thirty feet wide. The road was built by Bonaparte, and is one among the many monuments, other than warlike, by which his name will be heralded to posterity. The road begins properly at Milan and ends at Geneva. It is magnificent in its construction, and stupendous in its triumphs over the ruggedness and sinuosity of nature in her wildest and loftiest freaks. Where does not this road wind and venture? Over what fear-inspiring chasms; between what deep and terrific gorges; along what jutting and blackened granite, ever winding up through clouds, through cascades, among flowery meadows, along pine forests, until surmounting the jagged difficulties of the way, it leaves vegetation, yea, even the hardy lichen below, and descends with marble pathway, ever guarded at intervals with granite posts, into the valley of the Rhone!

Leaving behind us the lovely beauty of Lake Como; and the grandeur of her queenly sister Maggiore, we hurry by post to Domo D'Ossolo, the prominent place at the foot of the Simplon. Before reaching it, we had to cross by ferry, several wild torrents, where bridges had once been. Upon one of these ferries, there was a beautiful specimen of a chanticleer, with tiny bells in his gills and his comb; who, before we reached the opposite shore, rung his bells, crowed joyously, flapped his wings, and cleared the space between boat and shore. Perhaps that was his custom. I did not inquire. Our courier, Dominichino, was here at home, and rattled off his native Piedmontese idiom, with as much satisfaction to the host and postillions as to himself. The Piedmontese dislike the Austrians exceedingly, and take every occasion to show their contempt. Our republican courier was not behind in the national aversion. His passport arranged for Geneva, we began the ascent.

The vale of Domo D'Ossolo was soon spread out beneath, in its verdurous luxuriance, with mulberries and myrtles, figs and trellised vines, interspersed with lovely lawns. Suddenly we pass a bridge, and behold! in a hollow and awful abyss below, the torrent thundering in white spray over rocks—deep down in the creviced mountain!—Far up and around we again overlook the chasm and bridge. We turn to bid farewell to Italy, before we trace to its mountain source this Alpine torrent. By it, we are enabled to surmount the fastnesses; for its waters have torn out this Simplon pass. The bells of the city, ringing clearly, echoed from mountain to mountain, silverly, sweetly undulating in rare music, until they fill the ear with harmony. Blending the meanwhile therewith, was the angry undertone of the torrent Douvernia, making its way insanely and violently into its bolder-strewn bed of the vale; while far up and on every side, the slopes and perpendicular sides were vivacious with cascades fretting and shining, but ever singing. We have had rain for several days, so that the mountains all the way up hither were voiceful and nimble with fleecy waterfalls and bouncing cataracts. Out of cloud and out of chasm, skipping in gleeful bound, dashing into worn holes, and leaping upward in recoiling grace, to fall back hundreds of feet—sliding from mountain summit adown smooth marble paths, making thus exquisite lace-work, many-figured, wide and flowing, and white as milk, clear as air and musical as flutes—these fountain spirits seem to give life and activity to the massive, immovable, shattered, blackened, heaven-reaching, thunder-riven Alps. We were regretting, during our way from Como, that the rain cloud was constantly over us; but after the sun had chased it away this morning, and we found its result in such entrancing and soul-like sounds,

'So sweet we know not we are listening to them,

the regret was absorbed in the pervading joyousness and harmony.

I have been thus particular in my mention of these fountains and cascades, because they are so life-like. They peopled the solitudes. They laughed and glittered as they hung to the beetling crags, and sung in harmony with the greater torrent, along whose bewildering way we have been winding for so many hours.

To be sure, houses and people have not been wanting. Honest-looking masons were repairing the road; women with protuberances from their necks plainly telling of the goitre,—beggar-boys with no hands,—Piedmontese soldiers demanding passports,—postillions in glazed hats with silver band, in red-collared coats with bobby tails to them,—peasant girls washing clothes in the torrent, and now and then, a white-dressed chamois hunter, looking like a speck of snow against the sides of the cliffs, and firing away at Alpine venison in embryo, with what success we could not see,—these were the living people whom we met and saw. Farther down, the peasants were gathering in the golden grain from the pleasant vales between the frowning mounts; and farther up, they were discernible, clipping the harvest of grass even upon apparently inaccessible rocks, and attending the cattle. But Nature, not man and his puny works, is the great object of our view. How insignificant look the habitations of men here. Pigeon-boxes they seem, far up the perilous slopes. Nay, what are the grandest exhibitions of human art compared to that immense mountain which we passed just before we entered the first Gallery. Saint Sophia, the Duomo of Milan, St. Mark's, Nôtre Dame, St. Peter's—how minute, atomic, delicate, are ye all, compared to that one "moveless pillar of a mountain's weight." Cathedrals may be sliced off from its sides, temples taken from its tops; but its majestic *disproportionate proportions,* many-shaped minarets and domes, its coliseums and temples, its every-shaped structures peaking heavenward, still remain—the same for ever.

The mountain stream, whose valley forms the important Simplon, destroyed eight miles of the road in 1839. Every bridge of stone was swept away. Avalanches of stones, some huge enough to form islands, upon many of which are now cultivated gardens, and into many of which men have carved habitations, line the bed of the stream. They are scoured white and neat by the crystal cold water. Snow-drifts, under which arches are made by the torrents, lie in the bed of the stream, unmelted, and rivalling the frisky cascades in their pallid hue. Galleries are made at points along the road, under which we pass to emerge upon fearful heights above the stream, under other imminent craggy heights, jutting far over our heads.

The gallery of Gondo, and its surrounding scenery, I would select as a specimen of the majesty, terror, beauty, vivacity, awfulness, sublimity and glory of this celebrated pass. Artists have painted it upon the canvas, engineers have discussed it in mathematical equations, poets have sung of its manifold scenes and their correspondent emotions. Dare I intrude my vagrant pen in such goodly company? Just from the sublime spectacle, with the noise of its cascades still murmuring in my ear, and the glisten of its sun-bright snows yet dazzling the eye, my description may have the merit of freshness, if not any wonderful fidelity to the ineffable original.

The Gorge of Gondo is some fifteen miles from Domo D'Ossolo, just above a miserable village of the name of Gondo. The torrent Douveria furnishes a narrow but artificial bank for the road, which, winding under the smooth and almost treeless sides of the mountain, enters the gallery. The cut is 596 feet through the solid granite mountain. The granite was so hard, and the access so difficult, that it required the incessant labor of more than one hundred men, in gangs of eight, relieving each other, day and night, to pierce it through in eighteen months! And those side-galleries, looking out upon the deep-seething "hell of waters," far, deeply far, below—how think ye they were cut? The miners were suspended from the summit of the mountain by ropes, until they carved out a standing-place, when, simultaneously with the other miners, they formed these everlasting windows over the gorge. Opposite one of the windows can be read the inscription that tells of the energy which set this immense work in operation—"ÆRE ITALO 1805: NAP. IMP."

Close to this yawning cavern, on the right, there leaps out of a fissure which splits the mountain, and in which huge rocks, shattered and dark, lie in careless sublimity, the torrent of Frascinnone; less loud and hoarse in its brawling than the noisy Douveria, into which it empties, after splashing, spraying and fighting under us, hundreds of feet below the slender bridge leading into the gallery. The Douveria itself, across which one may leap at this point, is pressed into a narrow bed by the perpendicular rocks. It boils in mad, pallid fury, at its stony imprisonment; and at last bounds upward, and dashing into a cavern it has made, finds further vent in indignant eloquence, amidst a gigantic auditory of boulders, who line its current and cheer its impetuosity. The twin snow-peaks beyond and above the gallery, seen between the perpendicular walls, seem to sleep in quiet majesty, unmoved and frigid spectators of the scene. No wonder they are unmoved, for they are at least five thousand feet above the angry roar of the blended cataracts. The savage, grim horror which bristles up in the deep gloom of the abyss, is only equalled by the precipitous slate walls which, as high up as the eye can see, overhang the road. The torrent is squeezed into the narrow chasm,—the road into the narrow gorge, which seeks the gallery in relief. Scarcely any vegetation, not even the pine, clings to the sides. A little grass here and there peeps out of a crevice. The black figures on the rock are written over by millions of white specks, and imagination could easily find forms grotesque to image forth these gigantic drawings. Shattered fragments, loosened from the mountains, are piled all along, where a foothold may be had. The blue sky, with a fleecy cloud floating partly over it, like a flag from the peak, is seen up through the gorge. The old road, which once passed here on the other side, is barely discernible by the terraced stones lining the almost perpendicular side. It is wholly covered now. Amid this roar of waters, and this immensity, solitude, barrenness, and immovableness of granite masses, the little arched bridge for the road still spans the gorge; and there still winds upward the Simplon, with its marble way. The work of Man thus arises superior to the elements in their most terrific form. Yet these masses produce a stronger impression on the mind, than Man, with his infinitude of comprehension! In the whirl and buzz, the tinsel and superficialities of life, we forget that Man is a nobler substance than the mountains, and more eternal even than they! Their eternity is but the fiction of the brain; the eternity of the soul is a truth of God! Yet, in these mountains, one may best learn this truth; and, learning, ascend in view of its snow-white radiance, "seeking ever a higher object." Here best is taught that reverence which the Holy Word demands, and which Wordsworth, in the verses prefixed to this chapter, so feelingly embodies.

I could not refrain from repeating the solemn significance of the Bard of Rydal Mount, who was himself accustomed, like the eagle, to leave the impurpled hills of his own Cumberland, and among the mountains renew at evening his proud communication with the sun. I could not refrain, when gathering the little Alpine flowers, so beautifully delicate in petal and exquisite in aroma, so nicely stemmed and richly tinted—from pondering how *these* least of things seemed infinite. Nay, it is not mere poetry. Take your microscope and examine that world of germ and flower which, analogous to the out-budding constellations, is obeying the eternal order of growth;—and say, is there not an infinity in the tender petal of blue, bedropt with gold and specked with a love-light, growing under the mountain's shade? Come home to severe science, and you may learn, that the slightest alteration in the force of gravity which pervades the universe, would *alter the position of that blue Alpine flower*, peeping between its rock-ribbed home up to its kindred azure. An earth, greater or smaller, denser or rarer in the least, would require a change in the structure and strength of the stalks of every flower. There is something curious in considering the whole mass of the earth from pole to pole, from the centre to the circumference, as employed in keeping that blue flower bedropt with gold in its wild position, and the one most suitable to its vegetable health. If science thus demonstrates the infinitude of the relations of these tiny flowers, is there not a deep significance in the poetry of Wordsworth, that "littleness is not, the least of things seems infinite?" The highest poetry and the severest science will ever harmonize. Induction can never exhaust Castalia's fountain. Bacon was akin to Calliope, and Newton enjoyed her deepest confidence. Whewell and Wordsworth both agree, that in the humblest flower of the vale there is an infinity reposing as serenely as in the evolving nebulæ of the creation's bound! How I love, with such thoughts, to gather these little azure infinities. The meadows along the gushing streams are covered by them. They modestly peep up, almost with a shiver at the Lapland tops of the mountains. They seem like a dream of spring smiling around the icy features of winter. They contest the palm of beauty with the sliding and spraying cascades, which sporting around the chamois' home and eagle's nest, leap fearless out of cloud-land upon rock-land. But did the latter lose their vivacious loveliness, or the former their tender beauty, because of their frequent occurrence in our upward path? Ask the bird of song if her throat loses its sweetness upon that fairy isle of Maggiore, we passed yesterday, although her song is ever the same? Ask the cloud which reflects the dyes of evening over the Morea, if its glory is lost in the soul, because the same glow is continually around about us in splendid sun-settings?

We walk most of the way up, gathering strawberries as we walk. The cold air rushes down the valley as we near the hospice. Winter rules here. Hearken! how the wind howls, and the windows rattle! Seven thousand feet up in the earth's atmosphere, and yet so many other peaks above us! Why, I almost tremble for our earth's orbit. In wheeling around upon its soft axle, our pensile orb is in danger, with such tall protuberances into the sky. Thank Heaven! There are Andes, Himalehs and Alleghanies to balance the wheels, and make our earth dance to the tune of gravity, after the most precise method.

Ah! it was good to get to the Inn. It was better to feel the cheer of the fire. It was best to tickle the eager palate with mountain trout and chamois venison. The earth earthy will at times predominate. Cascades and lofty peaks were obliterated for a time, to play and pinnacle again in this poor page. All alone I sit at my table. My companions are recruiting themselves by sleep for the morrow, when we shall run down in three hours to Leuk, thence to Martigny and the Blanc. Seven hours is occupied in the ascent to this half-way spot.

The stars glisten in the windy air so fitfully bright; so cold yet lustrous. Never was I so near them before; never perhaps shall I be so near again; yet with all the sublimity of these mountains, the rolling clusters of constellations eclipse them all, even as Mont Blanc eclipses an Indian mound of our own valley. The bell of a convent near sounds wildly strange at this hour upon this height. The ghostly white mountains above gleam fearfully. A strange shudder comes over me, at the awful immensity of barrenness around. Truly has Byron written of these palaces of nature, pinnacled in clouds, throning eternity in their icy halls, and speeding on their mission of destruction the thunderbolt of snow:—

> "All that expands the spirit, yet appalls,
> Gather around their summits as to show,
> How Earth may soar to Heaven, yet leave vain man below."

How bracing is this upper air. Five hours of rest here is equivalent to ten in southern Italy. Midnight closed my last paragraph on the summit of the Simplon. A few hours of sleep, and we started on foot, ahead of the diligence, over the regions of uninhabited desolation. It seemed as if a great lake had once been upon this mountain, whose sides yet loom up in rugged grandeur. We passed the old and new Hospices erected for the safety of travellers—bid the monks "bon jour," bought mountain agates from the younkers on the mount, were overtaken by the rumbling vehicle, and at the word "monte !" we are in the coupé, rattling down the precipitous descent, overlooking valleys where the distant kine jingle their bells, and where the little chalêts are espied in the profound distance; and rushing through galleries of safety, serving at once as a bridge for waterfalls which roar over and under us and then plunge sheer into the air, and at the same time as a guard from the avalanches, whose scarring tracks are deeply trenched in the mountain sides. These galleries are cut in the solid rock, but drip with water or glitter with icicles like a grotto with stalactites. The pines are perpetually appearing wherever a moss fibre can crawl; and flowers—but I have said enough of them. Nature repeats her glories, but in every place how differently. At Boresa, where we stopped, the carol of the bird began to announce the vernal region. The outside, or rather the top of the diligence became my seat, as we ran down into the valley of the Rhone. It was a fearful seat at first. There were so many and such short curves, shaped like the letter S in the road, that at times I seemed about to be dashed with the diligence over precipices 2000 feet below, where torrents roared and rocks bristled. Around every point the downward serpentine of the road wound, cut out of the sides of the mountain, and absolutely suspended in the air. But what cared the driver for these glorious scenes or dangerous abysses? Halloo on, old glazed cap! "Hee! Hee! Yee-youp! Brabone!"—and snap! would go the lash at the lazy leader! For miles we wended downward, almost encircling Mount Eglise, whose five-and-twenty peaks, all joined in one Gothic spire, towered above the great snow-fields around, and pierced, as with a wedge, a dense cloud which seemed enamored of its untrodden pinnacles.

The vale of Brieg will long be remembered for its variety of rural beauty. It receives us as we run down the mountains. A magnificent vale it is, extending down the Simplon side of the mountains across the Rhone, whose whitish green waters rush over a bed enamelled with clean boulders, as far as the eye can see, and midway up the Bernese Alps. The drive down its valley was one of our finest. The way was a duplicate of sublimity—Vallais frowning upon one side with her angry mountain brows, glistening with Rosa and Moro; while Berne looked out gloomily from the Gemmi gorge at Leuk, so famous for its baths, and the immense perpendicularity of its mountain scenery.

Sion we reached before sunset. Its feudal towers rising before the city, revived the stories of barons bold and ladies fair; while in the city we found the warlike people crowding around a case of assault and battery, with two soldiers holding a man with a bloody nose, whom two loud-talking Sionians were pummelling under the soldiers' eyes. The shadow of the rural mountains kissed midway in the valley at sundown, and unitedly followed us into Martigny.

The fields along this part of the valley are mostly worked by women, coarse, robust, and gawky. Nearly every peasant woman has the swelling at the throat, known as the gôitre, so often referred to by travellers. It is the same disgusting execrescence which Juvenal refers to in the line—

> "Quis tumidum guttur miratur in Alpibus."

The swelling is of the thyroid gland or the parts adjoining, which grows with the growth of the person, until, as in some cases, which we saw, it becomes a huge bag, covering the breast, and rendering the person unable to walk under the burden. Various discussions as to its cause, have not as yet resulted in a remedy for the effect. The best sense of the medical profession has settled down upon the idea, that it is caused by a sort of malaria, owing to the confined air of the valleys, in the marshy places. Bad as it is, the women seem to care little for it. It is not nearly so disgusting as cretinism, which, from similar causes, prostrates the mind and deforms the body. How sad, that in such sublime and wonderful scenery, where physical Nature displays her utmost magnificence, poor human nature should be degraded and ruined by such a mysterious dispensation. Thank God for our own Ohio plains and undulations! where, if the ague does sometimes abound, it does not deform the body and shatter the mind!—But one can hardly wonder either at the dispensation, when it is considered to what a height these barriers rise above the low valleys. Disease will creep in, where the pure air of heaven cannot enter. Why! in one of the cantons near the Lauterbrünnen, which we passed, there lived, unknown by all their neighbors, a tribe of the most primitive heathens, until the twelfth century, when they were discovered by some daring cragsman, and converted to Christianity by the good Bishop of Constance! Could there be found a stronger illustration of the depths of these valleys, into and out of which even human curiosity failed to find its way?

XXIII.

Through the Tete Noir to Mont Blanc.

"Mont Blanc is the monarch of mountains,
They crowned him long ago,
On a throne of rocks, in a robe of clouds,
With his diadem of snow."

Byron's Manfred.

SUNDAY morning we awoke in Martigny. The chimes near our windows were playing—I verily believe—a waltz. It sounded so spirited and jocund. We are in the Catholic canton of Vallais, and of course every body goes to church. The women in tidy little hats surrounded with a broad silvered ribbon, and with prayer-book modestly folded in white handkerchief; with their high waists—but I am encroaching upon forbidden ground! It is enough, that their "bon jour, monsieur"—every where given smilingly and sweetly, to say nothing of their Sunday best attire—won our admiration. The smallest urchin made his obeisance to the stranger, and the oldest inhabitant removed his hat and bent his silvered head in respectful salutation. How pleasant to meet these kind-hearted Republicans.. God bless these descendants of Tell! The English, especially Murray, in his guide-book, have maligned the Swiss, most infamously. There is more true manhood and breeding in these simple-hearted people, than could be expressed out of all England, if she lay under the Alps for a century. Go to! Roast beef, go to! Hurrah for your Queen and spend your gold; but let unostentatious simplicity live unlibelled in its happy valley.

A novel mode of travel awaited us at Martigny. Mont Blanc must be seen from Chamouni, and the Tête Noir must be passed. Twenty miles inaccessible to the carriage, and traversible only by the mule, or upon foot, must be overcome. Our ladies are ready upon the sure-footed animals, and one mule is reserved for three of the other sex, wherewith to ride and tie. A Sabbath day's journey to the greatest temple in the universe, with Coleridge's hymn for our melody, and the roaring torrents for our diapason; who so Puritanic as to object to such an excursion? Well, we have a goodly calvacade up the mountain. Thirteen mules besides our own join us, and on we go, only stopping at the cool fountain or to fill our basket with strawberries. The way up was among pleasant apple orchards, and harvest fields. We had no dangers to encounter, or gôrges to tremble at; until we turned abruptly into the Tête Noir, or Black Head! Our mules then began to measure their steps cautiously, though they were evidently so familiar with the path as not to "snort suspicion."

The passes in the Alps have their grades of sublimity, terror, and beauty. The Simplon combines, in the greatest degree, all these qualities. The Splügen and the Gemmi have more of terror. The Tête Noir is deservedly celebrated, as well for its wildness, as for being the path to Mont Blanc. Within its savage gorges, the torrent thunders as if from lowest depths opening to devour. Dr. Cheever considered it a concentration, though somewhat in miniature, of the grand features of the Simplon, but at the same time rich and beautiful beyond description. I could not do better than to compress its scenery into the picture which he furnishes. "Abrupt precipices frowning at each other across the way like black thunder clouds, about to meet; enormous crags overhanging you so far, that you tremble to pass under them; savage cliffs looking down upon you, and watching you on the other side, as if waiting to see the mountain fall upon you; a torrent thundering beneath you, masses of the richest verdure flung in wild drapery over the gorge; galleries hewn in the rock, by which you pass the angular perpendicular cliffs, as in rocky hammocks swung in air; villages suspended above you, and looking sometimes as if floating in the clouds; snowy mountain ridges far above these; clusters of châlets almost as far below you, with the tinkling of bells, the hum of voices, and the war of the torrent, fitfully sweeping up to you on the wind; these are the combinations presented you in the Tête Noir." The picture is not exaggerated, nor unfaithful, save that we found but one gallery in the pass.

After passing a rude cross erected upon a fearful part of the road, to commemorate a young German who lost his life there in a storm by the falling of a pine, you perceive the "head," black and bushy with pines, rising out of the brown, twisted, craggy rocks. Turning toward Chamouni, and looking across the vale, not far from the Auberge, there appears a mount, less perpendicular, but higher than the "Tête," and a valley deeper! I counted seven silver cascades playing from its top, separating and uniting, bursting into spray, and floating in the air, then joining in a torrent. I could liken the scene to none other than a parliament or a congress of cascades, whose speeches were all to one point—the glory of the pass. One like an oily-tongued persuader, glides smoothly down the rock without splash or spray, and gains his end just as surely as the showy declaimer who raves and stamps, and tears a passion to tatters. Another spreads out his oratory in fine threads, every interruption fretting him into new points of grace and beauty, but uniting at the base in a torrent full and free, while his cogent neighbor, with continuity and unbrokenness of column, falls with all his force in one master apothegm upon the thread of his theme; and so they speak from their lofty tribune, illustrating their eloquence with flowers of sweetness, and rocks of truth. A villa of an hundred châlets listens demurely to their debate, and the torrent below unanimously carries the question down the vale with a glad shout of triumph. Well, metaphor will run mad in such a scene; so do not criticise my consistency. I wrote it on the spot, and give it as I wrote; interrupted now and then by the rapture of a lady-companion, who was filling her basket with flowers, and the shout of a gentleman, who had found high up in the rocks a Chamois nest (?) made of moss.

But why wreak one's thoughts upon expression, where there is so much to paint, and where words are not mountains, nor cascades, nor even the pictures of them? The monster back of that rock, breaking the vale in twain, but smiling in its shaggy grandeur with gardens along its sides, and lashed everlastingly by a torrent, at which it also smiles—where is the palette of wordy colors to paint that? Soon, through a perspective of snowy mounts, Mont Blanc, monarch of them all, lifts on high his blanched head. The view at first disappointed me. We were ourselves so high, that his 16,000 feet dwindled to half of that. The azure sky was unclouded, and the vast Gothic granite needles that pierce it around the monarch, were well defined and sharp. Far ahead of our party, I ran down through the Rouge and Verd mounts, leaving the Col de Balme behind—down—down—*down*—DOWN—past cattle feeding in the shadows which were creeping up the mountains on the east, and at last into the vale of Chamouni, with its lofty line of sublimities on either side. I knew the Arve—the bold brawler from the clouds and ice peaks, born amid thunder and storm, hastening by the humble cots from steep to steep,

> "Till mingling with the mighty Rhone
> It rests beneath Geneva's walls."

The Mer de Glace, and its outlet, the Glacier de Bois, hung over the vale under the everlasting pinnacles, threatening in aspect, while out of its hollow ice halls, rolled the "five wild torrents fiercely glad," which join to form the Aveiron. The vale lies north and south. The evening sun has left the valley, but lingers in a faint pink upon the great ice and snow fields of the monarch's head. The village of Chamouni, a pretty place enough, seems but a handful in these immensities of matter. Long after the shadows of night hung darkling over its roofs, the white light played on the top of the mountains. Perpetual layers of eternal whiteness, untracked and untainted by mortal tread, catch the last, and will gleam with the first light of heaven. The mind becomes oppressed with an overpowering sense of sublimity. There is the Hierarchy of Nature ministering between heaven and earth, in long white robes flowing down the enormous ravines, with a solemn silence which rebukes the noisy torrents at its feet, and the roar of the wavy pines midway up its sides. Dread ambassador! what a ministration between the Finite and Infinite is thine! Pomp of earthly kings!—how puerile and tame is your magnificence!

It is only a mighty mind like that of Coleridge, that could grasp and give expression to the *spirit* of this vale. I have read that he never visited this spot. It cannot be true. His hymn is the true worship of his lofty soul, uplifted through tears into this sublime serenity.

Raptures and exclamations are impotent and tame; the only style which befits the solemn significance of the scene at Chamouni, is that of the prophet who, wrapped in his mantle, bowed to the 'still small voice' in awe.

As I write now, the peaks and falls, glaciers and gorges, which surround me, have become familiar in name and position; but the spirit of the scene who can exhaust? Who can analyze its glories? Other travellers have essayed to do it as well beneath its shadow as upon the distant points of view. It is only to be felt by being seen. As I gazed upon it, while the day was departing, the lofty wish of the poet, seemed full of new meaning, when he prayed that he might grow more bright from commerce with the sun, at the approach of all involving night. And forgetful of the dear ones at home,—remembered ever upon all other occasions,—the wish started to the light, that here, beneath these hoar, high peaks of God's own majesty, we would love to live, and live to love, and at last sleep in the 'all involving night' of death, among the blossoms and flowers of this lovely vale.

I would like to take you up one more ascent—the Montanvert, which we ascended by mules, and from which the best view is to be had of the great granite peaks, and from which you may descend upon the Mer de Glace. Two hours and a half brought us to the Pavilion—a toilsome, rocky way, but rendered pleasant by the cool milk and and rich strawberries which the bright-eyed girls of the mountain offer us, at different points in the ascent. After a rest and a dish of strawberries, we descended upon the most wonderful phenomena of the Alps, the glacier. This glacier is the largest in the world, it being forty-five miles long, and in some places three wide. It was over a mile wide at the point where we were upon its moving mass. Rumble! crash! crack! boom! went the ice, as a huge granite rock in the midst tumbled into the cavernous profound. Hoarse and sepulchral, sharp and ear-piercing is the sound. Dare we venture upon the living sea,—peaked, hollow, roaring, trickling with water, quivering with life, and bursting its icy fetters? Before we venture, let us take one view of the magnificent spectacle, embosomed beneath in the vale, which is surrounded by the mounts and snow-peaks; pass not slightly over the minute beauties which are painted in the plain, with their coverlets of verdurous squares, triangular harvest-fields of yellow, mingled with the freshly plowed ground, lying between the belt of trees fringing the Arve and Aveiron, which, like two white ribbons inwrought with silver, dart with bright points of flashing, until they mingle to rave ceaselessly at the base of Blanc. These spots of rural beauty depend upon the melting glacier which feeds perpetual streams of irrigation. Do you ask why God hath placed the glacier here? Seek an answer in the well-filled granary and happy faces of the peasantry.

XXIV.

The Ice-Sea.

——— "He has seen the hoar
Glaciers of bleak Mont Blanc, both far and near,
And in Chamouni heard the thunder-hills of fear."

COULD you elevate your mental telescope sowewhat loftily, and turn it hitherward, you would perceive the Author in a situation at once extraordinary and peculiar. I do not know, but that my position is high enough to obviate the intervention of the 'thick rotundity' of the world, and the considerable distance between Ohio and Chamouni. I sit upon a granite boulder, in a sea of ice, called the Mer de Glace. My prospect in front is the great cathedral pinnacle of Dru; the point of Verdi, the highest of the needles, is in the rear; that of Bouchard is on the left, and on the right is the grand Horach, hid in snow; next to it is Charmoz, partly snow-covered. These points environ the glacier-bed with their spiry, rocky, snowy needles, rising out of the frigid green sea, jagged, terrific, and sublime!

We seize our Alpenstock, shod with iron, and under the lead of our excellent guides, who take charge of the ladies, we enter upon the icy bed even to its midst, and look down into some of the wildest gorges of the glacier, which shine with beautiful greenish blue. These gorges are deep and hollow. Within them the torrent's voice roars madly. Our guides threw large rocks into the chasm, and we stood breathless, listening to the reverberations beneath. Great granite rocks are upon the icebergs, and as the glacier moves, now and then they tumble into the gorges with thundering echo. The sound of the torrent and the progress of the immense mass make the place one of thrilling interest. Upon the opposite shore, under the peaks, there rise green pine forests, out of a sea of frost; and overhead, there float white clouds, like celestial navies sailing from point to point in the upper air. Surely this is the perfection of wild and gloomy desolation—overpowering and strange as a nether and an upper world, united in wild phantasy.

"What a dear little flower I have found just here upon the edge of the glacier; a little pink moss, or star-flower. Only look at it!"—breaks in a musical treble near by.

"Don't interrupt me, Madame; I am catching a likeness of Desolation himself in his own home?"

No wonder the Aveiron roars with such a perpetuity of music and continuity of stream, fed by such an interminable waste of ever trickling, but never melted ice. No wonder that the—

"Rose d'Alp?" inquires the same treble, upon the brink of the ice-sea, where its owner is plucking flowerets of most delicate hue and form.

"Oui, Madame," says the good guide; "il commence à fleurir."

"What's that mean, Dominichino? What kind of a flower does the guide call it?"

"It is not a flower yet, Madame. It's a begging to come out." Quite a poetical idea!

"Ah! a bud—yes, yes. How exquisite!"

See those other immense glaciers, high and away up the sea, miles off, branching out of the Mer, and each having its own great sluices. Hark! far up in their dreary profundities, the armies of ice are cannonading with sharp and thundering din!

"Come! come!" They are hallooing to us from above! "Let us go to the Englishman's rock!"

I cannot resist such persuasiveness; so picking up my ink horn and journal, and wondering how the poor fellow felt who fell into one of the icy gulfs and came out below in the torrent,

I left, to see the now broken granite rocks, under whose shelter Pococke and Windham, the first English adventurers into this valley in 1741, slept; and which has since then been moving down the ravine, "sloping amain," at the rate of one foot per day, sweeping an immense *moraine* of granite and earth along.

There is so much of the terrific and the peculiar connected with this Alpine phenomenon, that much scientific observation has been given to it. The deductions of scientific men are as remarkable as they are interesting, in relation to the origin, movement, former existence and effect of glaciers. The best information I can obtain is the following. It contains the eclecticism of the subject:

The summit of Mont Blanc, when its fused granitic mass rose up from the bowels of the earth, was for some time as bare as are the wasted peaks of the Aiguilles which surround it. The heat gradually subsided, an immense quantity of snow began to fall, as it now does, on the elevated rocks and valleys. In the highest regions, where rain is unknown, evaporation, proceeding from the extreme dryness of the atmosphere, causes these flakes to descend in particles somewhat resembling hail, whose loose dry grains, heaped on each other, are incoherent and form what is termed the neve. A great part of this is swept down on the lower stages of the mountain by those impetuous currents of air which almost constantly reign at great heights, at other times snow containing some portion of moisture is whirled up across the summit from the lower and warmer regions; during summer the solar rays, not having yet lost their calorific intensity by descent through the atmosphere, act with extraordinary force, avalanches are detached, and the moisture caused by the direct action of the heat on the exterior, as well as that arising from clouds which at times envelope the summit, is speedily absorbed by the remainder of the porous mass. To this succeeds nightly congelation and expansion, so that the neve descending gradually from this, combined with other causes, in the same manner as the low glacier, forms the reservoir of those vast ice streams which glide into the upper valleys of the Alps. Successive falls of snow, their thaws and congelations, are therefore the undoubted origin of the first glaciers.

Their movement is very differently explained. De Saussure attributes it to gravitation, which is improbable, because, if pressure *at ergo* were the sole cause, the entire body would slide down into the plains with gradually accelerated velocity. De Charpentier and Agassiz are partisans of the dilatation theory, supposing that daily thaw, constantly succeeded in the whole body by night frosts and expansion, causes the forward motion. This is refuted by the ascertained fact that congelation does not every where and always take place throughout the glacier, for the cold, except at its edges and thinner parts, penetrates no farther than into the earth when covered by a mantle of snow. Nocturnal cold merely suffices to dry up the streamlets at the exterior during summer, and the constant wasting of the glacier during that season proves that frost does not then exercise a dilating effect. While the prolonged winter season continues, it of course reaches a greater depth, but if entirely dependent on alternate thaw and frost the whole body would then freeze hard and not move at all.

Whoever examines the composition of the glacier will readily perceive it to be an eminently fragile body composed of a porous and plastic ice, different from that which forms on the surface of lakes and rivers. The manner in which it moulds and adapts itself to every bend and corner of a rocky valley proves its ductility. It is in short a semi-solid or viscous composition, urged downwards by its own weight and a mutual pressure of its coherent parts. The mass is detached from its bed of rock by the subterranean heat of the globe, the infiltration of rain-water, and of the moisture produced by exterior thaw. Being the outlet of the winter world it is fed in the upper regions by dilătation of the neve, the descent of avalanches, and by snow swept down on it from the summits.

Thus urged onwards, the daily waste below is replaced by

daily descent from above. Crevasses proceed from forcible separations caused by inequalities of the rock, its occasional swells, or abrupt descents, over which the viscous or half rigid mass strains forward. When an obstacle occurs, the glacier becomes transversely rent, its lower portion is separated, and proceeds, the fissure gradually enlarging, until closed up by pressure behind or accumulation of ice debris, to form afresh if the cause is renewed. Though the identical ice of which they, or the deep gully holes often seen on the glacier are composed, may, after a lapse of time, have advanced some hundred feet, the rents and fissures will always be found at the same spot like the eddies and deep pools in particular parts of a stream. Local conformations mould the ice; its centre advances more rapidly than the sides which it drags along; its upper surface more than the under one; the lower end more than the source or reservoir. The velocity is checked by cold but augmented by sunshine, thaw, or rain. The forward movement, through perpetual night and day, is irregular, and much greater in spring than summer, in summer than in autumn and winter. During the hot season the glacier wastes away in all its parts; during winter it is expanded upwards by frost and agglomeration to its former level, and, the progress being retarded, all its parts crowd together.

The abrasion of the diamond and the force of the lever give to the glacier an immense power. Hence the stupendous rocks found in places where no other agency could have borne them. Evidences are numerous in the vale of Chamouni, of this very glacier having torn away great portions of the mountain, and filled the vale to the height of five hundred feet or more. Indeed, when we consider the effect of this silent, slow, but resistless messenger from above, the fact that it overthrows or surmounts almost every opposition, and that a very slight depression of the present temperature of the earth would cause its increase ad infinitum, we must admit that such a mighty instrument may prove, in the hands of Providence, an agent more destructive of our globe than fire or water, since no effort can arrest, no obstacle prevent or divert its awful progress.

Ascending the Pavilion, we may discuss over a little Alp of strawberries, blanched with sugar, which quickly disappears under the keenness of the appetite—the science of this immense sea, more at leisure. While eating, however, I opened the register, and found that Montanvert had proved a Parnassus to some *genius incognitus*, who poured forth his sentiment right happily in the following

SONG OF THE MER DE GLACE.

"There ne'er was seen, on earth I ween,
A fairer sun than shone
On our Alpine pass of the Mer de Glace
This fourteenth day of June.

"Our feet have pressed the snowy crest
Of these wild waves deep and strange,
On whose strength of rock, writes the whirlwind's shock
Scarce the shadow of a change.

"And the mountains to-day, as they have alway
Since time began to be,
With reverend head guard the royal bed
Of that sleeping silver sea.

"And while ages fail, they'll tell the tale
To years—Time's laurels winning,—
Of ages that sleep in the awful deep
Beyond the great 'Beginning.'"

"Truly," says an annotation, "we forgot it was July—

'Which, remembered in time,
Would have spoiled the rhyme.'"

Other bards celebrate their drizzling days in Jeremiads and dripping lines, but there was no piece which struck me as worthy of a transcript, except the above.

We descended rapidly the *great highway*—my mule, like a gallant soldier, ever preferring the post of danger, and always provokingly hanging his ears over the most awful chasms, and eating grass just where one feared to be toppled headlong into the awful gorges. But it is great, to be high and aloof from the world and its vexations. For a lawyer to be 7,000 feet high, it is almost Paradise. No judge, jury or sheriff; no special pleading or demurring (save that of the mule) away up here. Chitty has no Precedent for the Dru; and Tidd, in all his "Practice," never drew so complex, yet so simple, a declaration as Mont Blanc draws against the serene azure. Never was I so near the great high Chancery, where all things are tested by the conscience, and not by the letter merely.

We bade adieu to Mont Blanc on Tuesday, to see his radiant face again from St. Martin's bridge, upon the road to Geneva, where it was said that one of the finest views could be had of him and his chain. St. Martin's is twelve miles from Mont Blanc. As you look up the valley of the furious Arve, there arises the Mount Foreclaze, covered with pines and pasturage; over these, the needles point around the Mer de Glace, and mingling with them, are the snow tops, consisting of great fields, which centuries have been piling, and which branch down the ravines in moving glaciers. The black pines gloom along the twelve mile perspective. It has been raining; the clouds are heavy, and hang around the mounts in variegated and wild gloominess. A great terraced point, swelling upward in cultivation, is upon our right, across the vale, while a stupendous castellated temple is upon our left. The birds sing, and the Arve roars. The mighty spirit of the spectacle glides along the walled ridges, and enters the soul, bedewing it with 'thanks and mute ecstasy.' Nature has many thoughts encased within, and flowing from, these rocky mounts, to be pondered with profit and delight. The reader who has not had the advantage of realizing the beauty and immensity of an Alpine scene, should at least turn back to our frontispiece, in which the talented artist, Hinshelwood, of New-York, has re-pictured to our memory the sublime view of Mont Blanc from St. Martin's bridge. The engraving is from a drawing upon the spot, and faithfully follows the hand of the great original. With such a pictured view, further description would be supererogation. The road to Geneva is alive with cascades of every variety of beauty; and it towers up with castellated mountains, into whose hearts large grottoes open. The fountain of Palerines, where there is a re coil in a parabolic curve of sixty feet, cannot be forgotten.

We passed, on going around a mountain, the exquisite cascade of Chede. The first jet is round and full, falling upon a rocky terrace, midway, where it divides into two other cascades, forming the shape of a heart, leaving a black rock within its silver setting. I cannot convey by language, nor by comparison, any adequate idea of the beauty of these cascades. We find them leaping like spirits from heaven out of clouds upon everlasting rocks, and detaining the eye with their grace, and the ear with their melody.

The cascade Nant d' Arpenaz was a joy for ever. Leaving our char, and bidding our courier and driver await, we wended our way over the meadows to its base. I leaped from rock to rock, until I sat under its spray, upon a boulder, my feet dangling amid flowers of loveliest blue. If you can imagine one of our ordinary Buckeye hills, say two hundred feet high, suddenly monstered into one of a thousand feet; one side perpendicular, with rocks standing on a horizontal basis; the middle point arching in great curved strata, and the other side an immense castellated mountain, which, unlike the other mounts, seemed serene amidst the primeval fire which once wildly interfused and intertwisted the granite ledges, you may have a faint idea of the mountain source of this cascade. All along are the results of the elder fires, scathing, melting, tearing, convulsing the mighty ribs of earth, and pitching them in defiance of heaven at its very portal; but this great castle-mount seems rather to have grown, so close and systematic is its gigantic masonry. Out of its arched granite heart there bursts a volume of whitest water, written full of beauteous characters, illuminated with prisms, fleecy as a nun's veil in the air, and buoyed up like powdery snow-flakes! So long is it in falling, that its points shoot out and burst like little rockets or miniature comets, with a nucleus and a streamer; or rather like the whitest steam puffs, curling and evanishing. The column, before it falls, bespreads itself wide and thin, but gathers into point below, where in a torrent it plays among rocks down the distance of thirty feet, then leaps in full column into a seething basin of hollow profundity, which roars and boils furiously.

The mind cannot find imagery for so beautiful an object, dashing out of so swelling an arch in so wild a spot. One likened it to a plume; another to a white pennon, floating feathery; another to Love, smiling in Hope and singing on the bosom of Might. Cheever likens it, or a similar fountain, to the fall of Divine grace into the Christian heart. Liken it to what you will, its serene undertone sung, and will ever sing to the soul of Memory—a radiant living thing amidst terrific immovableness. I leaped from rock to rock, plucked some flowers at its feet, felt its music thrill the heart, and was soon off again amidst the castles in the air, real and palpable, which line this Genevan road.

In the town of Bonneville, we saw a monument to a prince Carlo Felici, erected to his memory, because he—*dammed* the town (the old sinner!) to protect it against the torrent Arve which rushes along the valley.

With what trembling anxiety we approached Geneva, those only can tell who have been pilgrims for two months or more, without a word from home. At Geneva were our letters. The scenes grew less attractive as we neared the rural city. What chances and changes there had been among loved ones, we almost feared to know. We hoped, oh! how earnestly, that all were well and living as we left them. Can they be all well and living? Vain inquiry! Is not such a mournful blindness a part of that kind Providence, which is ever training the soul to rely upon the Almighty Word? Is it not a part of the lesson which GOD gives, to the weak and inconstant in faith?

With hearts painfully tremulous, we broke the seals, to find, alas! that one household near to us, was deprived of its happy children—that one hearth was no longer vocal with the merry twattling and play of the meek-eyed little ones. May God mercifully guard the living, is the prayer we waft from this home of Calvin, to our own dear Ohio!

XXV.

In and around Geneva.

——"The Rhone by Leman's waters washed,
Where mingled, yet separate, appears
The river from the lake, all bluely dashed
Through the serene and placid glassy deep."
Byron.

THERE is so much impressed, almost simultaneously, upon the mind in these mountain regions, that it staggers under the confused mass, in the very intoxication of bewilderment. One should have a subtle and pliant pen to picture, imperfectly even, these vicissitudes of sublimity and beauty upon lake and river, hill and mountain. At one time, you are called to view a place so desolate and wild, that you would think it was created for the last of human mould. Again you slide down almost insensibly into the loveliest pastures, by the most beautiful brooks, surrounded by the home-endearing châlets, the fragrance of new mown hay, and flowers of every hue. Again you shudder under imminent craggy heights, to gaze at which almost takes away your breath; to emerge upon a shore like that of Leman, whose pure water under the sun-ray, gleams like a bluish gem set in emerald, and sparkles with a light more diamond-like than even the bay at Naples, while its shelving green lawns, or vine-terraced margins, rise under an atmosphere of beauty where love *loved* to linger, and yet lingers in the pages of Rousseau, and the poetry of Byron. You have heard of Mont Blanc being seen sixty miles from the spot where he rears his high head, and being reflected in clear placid Leman lake near Geneva's walls at that distance: have you not? Were you now at my window at this hour of sunrise, you might well wonder, start and adore, at the revelation of splendors, dazzling and soul-entrancing, playing against the immovable masses of snow and ice which gild the sides and glitter in the crown of Blanc. Could my Buckeye reader look westward from Zanesville, and see an elevation of 16,000 feet, surrounded by others a few thousand less, through a perspective of mountains snow-blanched and pine-clad, robed everlastingly, and all so solemn, so still, so sublime—*rising out of Columbus*, and glaring down plainly to the eye; he would wonder, if this be our common world—would he not?

But too much of the descriptive wearies. You would prefer to hear of these republican cantons; how they sustain the lone banner (for France can hardly be called republican as yet), amidst the serried and surrounding ranks of absolutism. We Americans are apt to think Switzerland a place of little consequence—so deeply hid in the mountains that she cannot permeate Europe with any influence. We think of her as under a great shadow, cast out from communication with the 'rest of mankind.' Only enter Geneva, ride up the Lake Leman, whose banks are bedecked with homes of simple elegance, and through Vaud and Berne, whose fields are alive with the results of industry, and there will be found a civilization ripe and advanced, by no means circumscribed to the châlet of the peasant, or the hut of the cowherd. Wherever government assures man that he may enjoy the fruits of his labor, as it does here, where every one is industrious, comfort, and even elegance, will reign. How different are the people here from those in the south or middle of Italy. Here industry toils for ever, yet in perfect contentment. There is not the ostentatious gayety which dances under the festal garlands or surrounds the bedizened altars of the streets of Naples; but there is a quiet, substantial air of happiness, such as Goldsmith pictured in his 'Traveller,' when, from one of these mountain summits, he surveyed mankind in search of the true philosophy of life. Whether it be the tidy peasant girl in her white bodice, partly hid in dark velvet, knitting at dusk in the door of the cottage; whether it be the elderly dame who rears her top-knot of black gauze in the form of a cap of Elizabethan style, bidding you, with a smile, good-day; whether you are saluted in French or German, by Catholic or Protestant, whether by the cordial inn-keeper or the obliging vetturino-driver,—there is the same blandness of manner and kindness of spirit manifested and felt.

It would repay us but little to travel without seeing something besides material prospects. It is well to see the spirit of the people, in their every-day life and conversation. More glorious than snow-clad mounts, more harmonious than cascades, rises the soul of a people, informed with the true feeling of contentment, and conscious of their individual independence. This is our impression of the Swiss. When we saw inscribed over the quaint portal which led us into the confederation hall at Geneva, "The children of Tell shall ever be blessed!" when we saw the simple and unostentatious places for the meeting of *the people* and for the deposit of their suffrages; when we saw in their manly air the idea of personal liberty, embodied and expressed; when we looked upon the cultivated landscape, and into the busy workshops, then we felt that we were not in a land which is under the dominion of irresponsible powers, but breathing the air of republicans, who have an account with God, truth, and their country; and we felt too that there was a strange remissness on the part of the American Republic, in not providing an ambassador to this mountain sisterhood of states, whose presence and countenance should shine as an encouragement and a hope to the people amid the surrounding tyrannies. But when we listened to the lofty spirituality of D'Aubignè, the Homer to Luther, who was the Achilles of the Reformation; when we walked with him along the grassy marge of the placid lake, where he resides, and saw in his soul the reflection of the mountain thoughts which towered above the ordinary level of life's experience; when we caught the deep meaning which beamed from his expressive eye, as he talked of the Church and State, of the relations of the former to the latter, and of the abuses which spring from their union; when he spoke of Truth as superior to Protestantism, we felt that there was yet in Switzerland a something more excellent than all the hierarchies of the South and East, and even grander than the republicanism of the mass. I wondered not that Switzerland was a republic, and that from her emanated such powerful spiritual influences. Here, where John Knox lived, after being banished by a Stuart; here, where the Regicides, or many of them, lived after the Restoration; here, where *our* Puritanism imbibed its austere spirit of personal accountability, there lives in as noble forms as when Farel preached, Œcolampadius reasoned, or Calvin and Zwingle taught and ruled, the genuine spirit which ever protests against absorbing the individual in the State or in the hierarchy. Dr. Malan, and Merlè D'Aubignè are the truest embodiment of this spirit living; and that too without the intolerance which stained the name of Calvin, or the love of secular power which now weakens the Protestant Church as at present connected with the State in Geneva.

It seemed as if we were coming home when we started for Geneva. Here were our letters, and here were some friends to whom I had the kindest introductory letters from a classmate, who had sought in Geneva the fountain-head of Calvinism, and while quaffing its waters, had plucked an Alpine flower (a daughter of the celebrated Dr. Malan), and had borne it to America, where I saw him with his bride, full happy, at New Brunswick. To them we were indebted for so cordial a greeting from the venerable Doctor and his talented family.

Dr. Malan is one of the leaders of Protestantism in Europe, which has always found its front and lead in Geneva. I would refer the curious reader to Dr. Cheever for an animated and glowing eulogy upon his amiable character. It is not overwrought. How kind is his mien, with his bright eye and elastic step (though he is eighty), and flowing white hair. He seems like one of the Evangelists returned to earth. Since 1810, he has been a noble soldier amid the most trying crosses.

But most I enjoyed my visit to Dr. Merlê D'Aubignê, author of the History of the Reformation. His residence is upon the shores of clear placid Leman, which wooed Byron to 'leave life's troubled waters for a purer spring'—in vain. Our conversation was prolonged for more than an hour, walking (as is the hospitable custom here) under the shade-trees which line the water of the blue lake. He is like Dr. Wayland in feature, in energy of speech, and in character. There is such a pure spirituality in his presence, such a light of intelligence beaming in his black eye, under his long eye-brow, such a persuasiveness in his pure, though not perfectly pronounced English, that I listened with thrilling delight to his earnest conversation, as if it were an hour to be embalmed for ever. In speaking of the East, and the God-forsaken aspect of the old and favorite land of Deity, he changed his mournful tone into one of living energy as he said, "But—*the Spirit* of Almighty God knows no locality! For well saith Luther, (how he loves to quote the hero of his history,) they who do not cherish the seed when it is sown in their midst, it must—*must* die out. God ordains it!" Regretfully I left these choice men of the Protestant world, to feel, if not to see, their shadowy contrast at Ferney, where we visited the house, tomb, and old elm tree of Voltaire. We walked down the green arbor of beech (it is nearly 300 yards long), where the Infidel shrivelled and sneered, as he dictated his godless sentiments to his secretary. The arbor commands the view of Mont Blanc and his range. The house is being repaired, and the relics of Voltaire removed. The *church* he erected over his tomb, is now—a carriage house!

How infinite in its influence is the intellectual power which clustered in former times around Lake Leman. Not alone that infernal satanic sneer which lived on the lip and flashed in the antitheses of the arch infidel of Ferney; not alone the attractive sentimentality and social principles which were the seed of the French Revolution, and which filled the novels and imprinted the 'Social contract' of Rousseau, whose home, where he lived with Madame De Warens at the head of the lake near Vevay, we saw; not alone the learned and philosophic influence of Gibbon, who, amid the green bowers which shade the city of Lausanne, and along the delicious margin of the lake, turned over pages of Latin which none but the schoolmen of the middle ages had read, in order to write the decline of the Roman power, and to array his immense stores against the holiest of Religions; not alone, these elements of Revolution, Godliness, and Anarchy; but, thank God! the elements of construction and inspiration, more lasting than tomes of learning, more beautiful than sentiment, all invincible to satire, were here—mirrored in thy crystal waters, Oh Leman, even as Mont Blanc, with his summit of purity high reaching into heaven, is there reflected. Here was nursed and cultured that Puritanism, which was the chief cause of the American Revolution. Here that Protestantism grew which shook the Vatican; and here still, with Malan, Gaussen and D'Aubignè, grows the spirit of the Pilgrim Fathers, which, purer than that of Calvin, seeks to sever the State from the Church, and will never be ensanguined with the blood of a Servetus. Whole nations, constitutions, and revolutions, had their germs planted by the intellects who studied, wrote, and lived upon these beautiful shores.

We saw the house of John Calvin in Geneva, which (strange mutation!) now overlooks the theatre, which he so despised, and an ice-cream saloon, which in defiance of his sumptuary laws rises under his window. If the Genevese have not the stern religion of their ancestors, yet, as Dr. Malan remarked, God is shaking the sieve, and pearls are appearing, not mere Protestants, but true men.

Madame de Stäel at Coppet found a congenial place, and even yet it speaks of the taste and elegance of the author of Corinne. We walked down its leafy promenades by its bubbling brooks, around its time-honored Chateau, and even around the chapel where beside her father, the ill starred Minister, M. Neckar, her dust reposes. What a magnificent woman was she!

What a cotemporary of Napoleon! The widow of Baron de Stäel, one of her descendants, lives in the Chateau. She was in Paris, and the building was in process of repair.

Geneva and its beautiful environs constitute a complete rural city. Owing to its rurality, it scarcely seems circumscribed, as far up as the Castle of Chillon, out of whose gloomy prison Byron evoked such a genius of poetry, or bounded by the Jura upon the one side answering the Alps on the other.

While at Geneva, we drove to pay a visit to the junction of the Arve and Rhone, which Dr. Cheever vaunts upon the tallest stilts of his style. It was a very great disappointment. The furious Arve, which we had heard in the depths of the gorges, and which roared at the base of Blanc, timidly creeps along without mingling with the Rhone, which is a different river from that which empties its mud into Leman, in this, that it darts away clear and blue. It is an entire misnomer to call this the Rhone. How can any one discover the muddy mountain elf in the aerial sylph which glides through Lake Leman. It is owing to the presence of iodine, as Sir Humphrey Davy thought, that Leman is indebted for its poetical azure so transparently beautiful. Our ride up the Lake was in a little steamboat, which stopped at each village upon the banks. Mountain scenes still hung in the distant air, almost forgotten amidst the profusion of beauty which Art, the handmaiden of Nature, has strewn along the shore. Como has a half wild and rocky beauty; Maggiore is still wilder, answering as a preface to the Alps; Leman has all the softness and finish of loveliness. She is Beauty adorned, and wearing the adornment with a naturalness that Rousseau knew how to paint, and Byron, even in his roughest temper, to feel.

At the head of the Lake, near Vevay, the great St. Bernard shone in his cloud and snow garments, with a noble mien and a halo encircling his brow, bespeaking the first in command under Blanc! He rules the plains of Italy, as well as those of Switzerland, when the Monarch retires within his pavilion of clouds.

A curious bass-relief is that upon the Cathedral at Fribourg, which represents St. Peter and the Devil winnowing mankind from their several thrones. The latter personage also appears with a hog's head and a big basket on his back, chock full of sinners, whom he is turning into a seething caldron, stirred up by imps, and into a crocodile's mouth, opening wide. Again there is a pair of scales held up, with souls in it, and an imp hanging to one side, to make it kick the beam in favor of perdition. Surely John Bunyan has a rival in allegory in this artist. Rough in execution, it may be; but more expression than I can tell. Yet not more curious than the clock we saw to-day at Berne. Who would not have laughed to have seen us, with a dozen other travellers, German students, soldiers, English and French, waiting, with a pain in the neck, to see it strike? Well, the hour came. Up rises a rooster, flaps his wings, Cock-a-doodle-doo-oo-oo! Ha! ha! ha! ha! roar the astonished idlers. Out rush a company of bears, (the national brute of Berne; they keep several hundred at public expense; we saw their dens;) some on horseback, some with swords, all looking most quizzical and grotesque; when—pause—then an odd gentleman in knightly armor, a ghost of the middle ages, beats the hour in the tower above, while an old fellow who sits above the bears, opens his mouth and nods his head, as the stroke falls, and gradually turns over an hour-glass in his hands. Surely we are coming into Germany now. Indeed, the *yaw* and *nein* begin to announce the fact, had we no curious horologues to tell it.

None but a German, although a Swiss, could like a bear. Why? If the reader cannot tell, read on!—Every where,—on the coins, at the fountains, upon the crackers and gingerbread, stuffed in the Museum, and alive climbing trees and in their dens at Berne,—is Bruin, the pet of the people and the glory of art. The French carried off some two hundred bears to Paris, and put them in the Jardin des Plantes, in 1798; but they were demanded back with as much ceremony by Berne, as were franchises by other nations.

We may be said to have fairly entered German Switzerland, when we cross the great bridge at Fribourg. This bridge, by the way, deserves a notice. It spans the Saarine river, which runs into the Rhine below Schaffhausen. It is a wire-suspension, and has the longest single curve of any in the world, not even excepting Menai, near Liverpool. Menai is 580 feet long, 130 feet high; that of Fribourg is 941 feet long and 180 feet high. It commands a magnificent prospect; though we did not, on account of the drizzle, see much more than the beautiful vale.

We feared that we should leave Switzerland without a view of the Bernese Alps, with their Jungfrau and Wetterhorn, their Lauterbrünnen, and Grindenwald. But no! Scarcely had we left Berne, when a few minutes of sunshine cleared the sky, so as to permit us a farewell to this magnificent range, the scene of Manfred and William Tell; the glittering snow-peaks whose evening hues shine like the gates of heaven to which they everlastingly aspire. This view from a terrace near Berne, is its greatest charm. Although celebrated as the capital of the Cantons, whose Diet is now in session; although curious for its bears, and, like other Swiss towns, for its fountains; although celebrated for its fine streets with paves, roofed above for foot-passengers; yet nothing attracts the stranger so much as the distant Alps, with their robes of white and peaks of terror!

At all times fortunate, we enjoyed the vision. It well suffices for a closing view of these capital characters of the Creator—these 'unambiguous footsteps of the Deity'—written so clearly and boldly over these cantons of freedom. May the latter ever be as free from the footsteps of the despot, as Tell would have had them, and as the Alps themselves, in their lofty state of individual yet linked independence; and may they be as permanent, too, as those Alps upon their sunless pillars deep in earth!

XXVI.

Upon the Confines of Switzerland.

"Farewell, with thy glad dwellers, green vales among the rocks!"

Bryant.

UPON the evening of the 28th of July, the most ancient and walled city of Soleure, received us at its great gate, in feudal style, and regaled us with strawberries and cream, fountains that murmur, and promenades that please. As I write at the midnight hour, the sweetest of fountains, twins in melody and in beauty, burst near my window beneath the reverend forms of Moses smiting the rock, and Gideon wringing the fleece, sculptured in superb style, and guarding the steps which lead up to the Corinthian Cathedral before our hotel.

We visited the interior of the Cathedral. Noiselessly we walked under its white and chaste canopy of carved stone, and amid its silent worshippers. Nought was heard to break the religious stillness, save the whisper of the confessing and the suppressed bass of the priest in the gloomy confessional. The radiant images of the Virgin and of the Saviour beamed with mild love from the walls, and led our hearts away from the fastnesses and sublimities of nature, with which they had become so familiar, into the serener atmosphere of affection. The loved ones at home smiled so tearfully and happily, that, entranced in thoughts of them, we soon saw with the mental eye, only their invisible forms. After all, there are no forms we see while abroad, so enrapturing to behold as those which rise impurpled in love's own light, at the heart's warm bidding. Sculpture hath no such grace, painting no such warmth as that which moves and glows around the hearth-stone. We may visit the home where Calvin lived and died, as we did in Geneva, and claim him as a kindred spirit; we may see, as we did a few hours since, the house where Kosciusko lived, while an exile from the land he so loved, and revere his memory as connate with that of our own Washington; we may glow, while contemplating their excellencies, with kindred sparks; but at last, the mild and heavenly eye of a Madonna, from the minster-wall, will recall a mother's tenderness and care, and awaken the filial fear and love; while tearfully will go up the orison to Him who can guard, that he will protect from harm and woe, those to whom we are bound by the closest ties of earth.

Since writing the foregoing, we have traversed the remaining portion of Switzerland which lies between Soleure and Basle. This morning, we arrived at the latter place and found it—like Soleure,—well walled, with pepper-box towers around, and protcullises and the other paraphernalia of a free city of the middle ages, which it once was. Indeed it has not lost its character. This is the ancient city which furnished such convenient refuge to French Protestants, when to be one was to be burned. Farel, Anemand, Esch, Touissaint and their friends, here established the first general Evangelical Society. Hither fled those refugees of Lyons and Grenoble, which the good Margaret Valois, sister to Francis I., attempted in vain to shield. It was here that Luther's works and the Scriptures were first published in French, and here was the first Bible and Tract Society established. We had heard that so religiously strict were the descendants of these French refugees and of their protectors, that we could not obtain ingress within the walls, if the people were attending service. But we had not arrived within a half mile of the gate, before we saw a crowd of over two hundred collected around a circus, under the tent of which, a dozen hobby horses were flying around, mounted by youngsters with steels picking off rings as they passed a spot, to the great diversion of the elders. We had just left Soleure when the chimes were ringing the people to church, and a sawmill was cutting timber under the belfry's shadow; we had seen the stores all open there, and the peasants cutting their grain and working as usual all along the road; but we were not prepared for such impiety at Basle. Shade of Erasmus! where is your "praise of folly?" Your coterie of brilliants no longer shines around your witty board. Myconnis, Amberbach, Glarean—astute scholars and cordial spirits—where are they now? Have they no voice, to sting with satire the degeneracy of these Basle-folk? Alas! Erasmus lies in the old Cathedral, with the ungainly picture of St. George on horseback piercing the dragon as its frontispiece; and the noisy city rumbles by, unconscious of the Sabbath, intent on pleasure, and unwounded by the satire of the scholar.

We were down to see the Rhine. It was our first glance at this magician. I will not speak of him yet. The righteous people of ancient Basle were *not* on its bridge; and you cannot even truthfully repeat Longfellow's stanza,

> "There sat one day *in quiet*,
> By an ale-house on the Rhine,
> Four hale and hearty fellows,
> And drank the precious wine."

The fellows and the wine are not wanting; but the quiet—ah! one must go farther away from French neighborhood and into phlegmatic North-Germany, to find that—at least on a Sunday. Every body is out pitching quoits, rolling nine-pins, drinking wine, listening to music at cafés, and playing the noisy Diabolus generally.

In Switzerland, our mode of travel has been performed by means of vetturino—a hired carriage, for which we have a special contract, and which we can control as we please. Through a country sparkling with cascades and frowning with mountains, this *ad libitum* mode of conveyance is as convenient as it is pleasant. The roads every where are of the best quality, being in direct contrast with the roads at home, where, in wet weather, off of the turnpikes, ruts and mud prevail. Indeed, all the roads are elegantly McAdamized. The hotels, too, are of the most accommodating kind. At many of them we find some one who can speak English, and at all of them some one who can speak French. A little French to begin a tour with, is a great deal. The image of the rolling snowball was never more applicable than to the study of French by travelling: a basis is necessary to start with. It was humorous to see four Swiss citizens of Berne in our car going to Heidelberg, trying to practise the little English they were and had been studying. We were the target, and such fires as they made. The awkward squad, tipsy with the worst "old rye," never popped at a mark with such abominable inexactitude. We hope they will do better before they reach London, whither they are bound for the exhibition. We hope, too, that our primary efforts at French were not so convulsive to the hearer.

A goodly number from Germany and Switzerland, are *en route* for London. The exhibition will attract more the next month than it has during any other. Prints of it are in every window of every print-shop in all the places we pass through, gazed at with open-eyed wonder, by idlers. It is a constant topic of conversation. It is the theme of every inquiry. No one was so curious as the little lass, of bright eye and dimpled cheek, who waited on us at the summit of the Simplon pass. She had helped to make, as she told me, the mammoth cheese; and was extremely anxious to know if I had not noticed it in the palace. I told her, nay; but added that I would look it up on my return. A cheese from the milk of cows that eat the grass which grows on mounts snow-topped, and 8,000 feet above the flags of the glass palace, is a cheese that is not to be passed by indifferently. To some purpose the glacier melts to irrigate the valley—to some purpose doth the grass grow upon the heights of the Alps—to some purpose the cow-bell tinkles at evening in the vale. Cheese is one of the greatest of the products of Switzerland; and every nicety and care is taken to bring its manufacture to a high state of perfection. Among the most noticeable objects in a Swiss and German landscape, is the cottage, under whose ample straw roof, both the peasant and the kine are closely housed. As much care is taken of the cheese-producers as of the cheese-eaters. The proximity of the stable and house would not be agreeable to very refined olfactories.

It is interesting to move around these homes of the Reformers, to feel the struggle they felt, to recall the risk they ran, and to glory in their triumphs. Our way northward, will be amidst such scenes. And yet while possessed of a different faith, and belonging to a country where Protestantism preponderates, we should not forget that all-embracing toleration, which our Constitution embodies and our national spirit fosters. We have seen the rude images of the Saviour hanging to the cross, along the Valley of the Rhone; have seen in Malta the priest sitting at the church door under the sign "Plenaria Indulgenzia;" have seen the Roman people kissing the silver toe of the Madonna; and while shrinking from these modes of devotion so alien to our own education and faith, we know that God who seeth the heart is their judge, and He only.

XXVII.

Fatherland.

"Here I stand, I cannot otherwise. God help me! Amen!"
Luther before the Diet of Worms.

BETWEEN Basle and Heidelberg, which we ran on a railroad, at a cheap rate too, the country is well cultivated. Ploughed grounds, harvest fields, gardens of cabbages, and vines without measure, line the way. We begin to enter the region of castles. We stopped long enough at the capital of Baden, Carlsruhe, to admire the beautiful palace of the Grand Duke, in the centre of the city, from which all the streets run as the radii of a circle. The valley of the Rhine is wide and level until it reaches Heidelberg, where two mountains—rather small specimens after being in Chamouni—part to receive a respectable city, which, beginning in the plain, runs up between them along the Rhone. Heidelberg has associations not a few. Longfellow, in his Hyperion, has inwoven with the old castle which so majestically overlooks the enchanting scenery, some of the most pleasing sentiments; while the mediæval and reformatory ages march around its University halls and invincible ramparts, with banners of heroic and classic device. Here a chapter of the Augustine order met in 1518, which Luther attended, travelling from Wittenberg afoot, drinking in the scenery, disputing with Miger, and spreading abroad his bold and then heretical doctrines. Here his timid co-reformer, the gentle Philip Melancthon, studied before he began his labors. But most is Heidelberg interesting for *the* castle. We have seen none like it, in associations, in beauty, in situation, in environment. We rode down the valley, before we began to ascend its heights, and stopped at an enchanting spring called Wolfbrünnen, where an enchantress called Jetta, the Cassandra of the Palatinate, was torn in pieces by a wolf. A girl amused us by throwing minnows to fish of larger fry, who dashed about in the clear waters, where they are kept as pets. The speckled trout took my fancy, as they darted out of the shadow into the sunlight, snapped a little fellow-fish, turned a flip-flap, and evanished. But this wolfy place is small game, compared to the old red walls, with their carved armed knights filling the niches, and the heavy battlements surrounding the gardens, wherein the Electors Palatine once luxuriated. The castle is a perfect specimen of the middle-age architecture, strong with its portcullis, and beautiful in its archways and lawns. Statues of the family of the Electors are around. But the most interesting part is the English palace, built for Elizabeth, granddaughter of Mary, Queen of Scots, who married the Elector Frederick V. He built the noble arch of triumph which may be discerned among the shadows of the trees, entwined with heavy hangings of ivy, to celebrate the nuptials. It leads to a garden which was tastefully arranged for her pleasure. The reader of Mrs. Jameson will remember Elizabeth for a Stuart of the deepest dye, as proud and as arrogant as her degradation was beggarly and severe. A thick growth of glistening ivy clusters around each old wall, and enwraps with its trunk the stones of the ruins, as with bands of iron. The view of the country, of the Kaiser's Stuhl, of the three towers of Manheim down the vale, and of the tree-clad hills toward the Oberland, is bewitching under the red glow of the sinking sun. More especially is it fine after the dim eclipse which the orb has been suffering during the afternoon, and which we, with others at our hotel, through smoked glass, and in tubs of water, have curiously observed.

The height of the tower is near 1,500 feet. We passed through the prison, into the chapel, out upon the terraces of stone which overlook the vale, and afford a view of the magnificent front with its traceries of fruit and foliage, its statues and antique heads. The front rises in three portions, each capped with a statue.

I should not forget the wine casks of the cellar, the largest of which contains 800 hogsheads! It is 36 feet long and 24 feet high. When it is filled, the lads and lasses have a dance upon the platform on top. With so much wine under one's heels, one ought to trip it with wonderful vivacity, if not with grace. The cask is a wonder, only exceeding by a few feet its younger sister in the room hard by.

I have too much to write, and too little time to say it, to dwell long even in Heidelberg, with its students, its views, and its history. As a curious relic of the era, when Germany was united to the empire, and when the Palatinate had a large voice in the choice; of an era when chivalry poised its lance and lived in feudal towers, it stands unrivalled. An edifice, rivalling the castle in elegance, now stands in the city of Heidelberg, but it is a *vulgar* railroad station; and although its gardens display fine taste, its columns rise in harmony, and its rooms are decorated finer than ever was lady's bower in the feudal day—yet the soft twilight of antiquity is not on them. The coal smoke of the locomotive is not a very choice medium of beauty. A day and a half exhausted Heidelberg, and we were soon pushing onward through Darmstadt, a city situated among hills, studded with castles, where Charlemagne and his barons held their court.

The vine and tobacco; (oh! Fatherland, what oblivion dwells in these your staples!) peasant women harvesting wheat with small knives, and men cutting grass with scythes that gave no bend to the body; with alternation of green and golden fields, adorned with no stake or rider, indeed no fence at all—these in fast succession are passed, until the Maine, with Frankfort upon it, and a bridge leading over it, appeared.

This is a city that looks business-like. No lazy lazzaroni or sleepy Italians here. Bustle and industry indicate the old free town. Fine streets and houses indicate the presence of the Bankers and Ambassadors of Germany. We were not long in being hotelled, nor in seeking the curious. We found the latter in the Library, upon the Maine bank, a splendid structure containing twenty thousand books, together with the portraits of Luther, and his most excellent wife Katharine. The latter was so modest, and nun-like, so devout and simple-hearted in her appearance, compared to the gruff and harsh reformer, that we could not wonder at the docility of the latter under her gentle tuition, and the tender lamb-like letters he used to write her, when off from home, talking of indulgences and reformation. In the same glass case is shown his shoes—and rough ones too. The poorest American (if he has any) has a better pair than had the learned Doctor Martin. Not particularly fond of the beautiful material, but of the beautiful spiritual, was the brave old heart. His writings would indicate that, if his shoes had no meaning. We saw here his autograph, and two letters written by him, by the side of a letter of Melancthon, and one of Napoleon.

What momentous results have emanated from the bold action of the poor miner's son of Eisleben—the humble Augustine Friar Martin! With the world against him, empires threatening to devour him,—the thunders of the Vatican aimed at his destruction, he remained firm and invincible. We have placed his bold declaration at the head of our chapter on Germany; because he is the most German man in history. He had all the virtues and faults of the German nature. Dreamy in his mysticism, he was still an actor in the most severe trials of life. A fine scholar, he nevertheless was eminently social. His social disposition is one of the most beautiful traits in his character. It is said of him, that though he could scold like a fish-wife, he could be soft as a tender maiden; sometimes as wild as the storm that uproots the oak, and then as gentle as the zephyr that dallies with the violet. Nowhere is his kindly disposition so manifest as in his epistles to his good wife Katharine, while absent from home. I cannot refrain from referring to these, while gazing upon the portraits of the happy twain in the Library. One of his letters, and perhaps the one we saw, is addressed "to my Gracious Lady, Katharine Luther, of Bora and Zulsdorf, near Wittenberg; my Sweetheart. Grace and Peace, my dear maid and wife! Your grace shall know we are here, God be praised! fresh and sound; eat like Bohemians; yet not to excess—guzzle like Germans—yet not much; but are joyful." Another is addressed, "To the rich Lady at Zulsdorf, Lady Katharin Lutherin,—bodily resident at Wittenberg, and mentally wandering at Zulsdorf,—my beloved, for her own hands." Another still in reply to an anxious letter of his wife's; "To the deeply learned Katharin Lutherin, my Gracious Housewife at Wittenberg—Doctoress—Self-Martyress, my Gracious Lady for her hands and feet. Grace and Peace in the Lord, dear Kate! Do thou read John and the little catechism. For thou must needs care before thy God, just as if he were not Almighty and could not create ten Doctor Martins, if the single old one were to drown in the Soale, or the Ovenhole, or Wolf's Vogelhierd. Leave me in peace with thy anxiety. I have a better guardian than *thou and all the angels* are. Therefore be in peace! Amen!"

What a rough disguise is here for the most tender affection. The man of logic and fierce debate is seen playing with the heart-strings of home, and tinting with the rose the sober realities of his life and its mission; and who shall say that the Great Reformer does not appear more lovely in his life on account of this tenderness and affection? How demurely sweet his good nun-wife seems in the portrait, beside her fond yet rugged husband-Doctor. The first is dressed with a nun's veil in close folds enveloping her head; a dark fur mantle investing her person, except the open front, which is adorned with a white lace habit; ruffles encirling her neck; which together with the mantle are caught and fastened by cord and tassels, while her delicate little hands are meekly folded across her lap; and her whole appearance is in contrast with the burly Reformer, in his monkish hat and gown. These portraits are the only authentic ones known to exist, and in consequence are prized pricelessly.

The statue of Goethe, who lived and died here, which is seen in the vestibule to the library, is by Marchesi, and is so commanding in the intellectual sphere within which it sits like Jove enthroned amid the circle of Olympus, that it enthrals the beholder at the first glance. It is of Carrara marble. A larger image of the great poet is placed among the trees of a promenade, and is of bronze. It represents him as holding the wreath of literary fame, and dressed in the modern costume which appears beneath the ancient flowing toga. The bass-reliefs below are emblematic and appropriate. Well may Frankfort place prominently before her citizens the form of the great man of modern Germany. The intellectual power which commands your admiration, from the marble features of Goethe, is immense. The many-sided man of the world, knowing, restless, subtle, omitting no means or avenue to the human heart; at once sarcastic and facetious, thrilling and tender, wild and sublime,—Goethe, has embodied in language a spirit and an essence which has for ever imprinted its influence upon literature. Whether he seeks to exhibit all that is most terrific and demoniac in nature by the creation of Mephistophiles; or whether, like the demon, he assumes every phase of human nature,—he is still the peerless intellect,—the mental apex, having sixty millions of Germans for its base.

Busts of Goethe are to be seen in the shop windows, and representations of his genius are at every square. There is a fine emblem of his poetic inspiration in the library, where the poet is represented on the winged horse soaring above Olympus, sweeping the regions of the unknown, and visiting world after world by the might of his genius. Another statue, prized very much by the people of Frankfort, is that which illustrates the beautiful myth of Ariadne. It represents her at the culminating point of her history, when deserted by Theseus. Theseus was sent, with other Athenian prisoners, to be devoured by the centaur, in the midst of the labyrinth of Minos. He was enabled, by the aid of Ariadne, the daughter of Minos, to get into and out of the labyrinth by a thread; and promised, for his release, to wed and carry off the nymph as his bride. He wedded; then deserted her while she was sleeping. Bacchus became enamored of her, in the loveliness of her woe, and made her immortal. The statue represents her after she has been wedded to immortality in the person of the God of the Vineyard. She is seated upon the leopard of Bacchus, with proud and beautiful mien, conscious of the celestial ichor which now bounds in her veins! This statue is exhibited by its owner, Mr. Bethingen, at his princely residence, amidst a number of inferior marbles and casts.

But above all the results of German art, and incomparably superior to any painting we have yet seen in Europe (always excepting the Transfiguration), is the painting at the Museum by Lessing, known as "Huss before the Council of Constance." The ill-fated, but true-souled reformer, is represented amidst a group of sensual cardinals, priests and curious lookers on, some jeering, others intent upon his words of new life, others astounded at his boldness; but all yielding in effect to the superior air of Huss, who stands unappalled, with one hand upon his heart, the other upon the Word, and with the majesty and earnestness of a deep-seated persuasion, invincible as the soul itself to the threatenings of man, and lofty in the full consciousness of its immortal nature!

Huss was a light that beamed so brightly in the surrounding gloom, that it could not long remain. He leaped at once to the grandest truths. He did not, like Luther even, dally with old errors long after he had received new truths. When driven out of Prague into Bohemia, what said he? "I am no dreamer, but of this I am certain, that the image of Christ only will never be effaced. I, awakening from the dead, will leap with great joy." The artist has not made him a man of dreams, but of massive, wakeful mind, with pale high brow, a deep and mild, yet heavenly beaming eye, and sustained with the *conscia recti* of a lofty spiritual independence. There is a species of abstraction in the countenance that speaks of the mould of the man; and an air of superiority in his very humility, that almost awes you, as if it were a presence and a power. And is not the highest reach of art owing to the presence of powerful thought, seeking communion through the eye and mind with the deathless essence within? Does not Huss, from the canvas, tell us of trial, study, patience, opprobrium, and as the crown—glory, if not here, then hereafter?

His mournful history is a painful commentary upon the perjury of royal and ecclesiastical power, which had given him a solemn and written assurance of protection, and broke their promise, in order to rejoice around the crackling flames that consumed the body, but could not harm the soul of one of the noblest martyrs of Christendom.

The Cathedral in Frankfort has no merit as a structure. One of the Emperors reposes in it; and some fifty of them were therein crowned. We sat in the old chair in which their august majesties used to sit, but found no particular virtue in the operation. The Romer, or town-house, should never be omitted, especially by one who is fond of tracing back to its source in the German forests, the origin of that race which broke down the Roman power, united France, Germany, and Italy under one great head, penetrated Britain with its Saxon arm, and is fast rescuing the wilds of the western world from the dominion of Nature, and of the Spaniard. What an energy, a will, a steady unbroken perseverance burned in the old German tribes! You will find them all knit into the stalwart frames and proudly-rough bearing of Charlemagne and his successors, as they look down from their panels in the old Banqueting Hall of the town-house. The costumes are preserved, and underneath are the mottoes of each, in Latin, which speak much of justice and rectitude, but every where of boldness and decision in maintaining their right.

These portraits are by Lessing, Bendemann, and other eminent artists of Germany. The Hall is in the shape of a rhomboid, and is the place where the Emperors were waited upon by the kings and princes at the festivities. We went into the Election Chamber, where the senate of Frankfort now meets, and where of old the electors met to choose the Emperor. The honor of Emperor was long monopolized by the house of Hapsburg, now the ruling house of Austria. One among the many blessings which Napoleon conferred upon Europe, was the breaking up of this German Empire, with its hosts of Princes, Dukes, and Kings. There is now in the German mind an intense longing for a reünion, but not under the old rulers. The tie which so long gave unity to Germany grew weaker with time, in proportion as Prussia and Austria grew powerful and jealous of each other. Frederick the Great first suggested the idea of a separate union of Prussia with the other German States, except Austria. Ever since, Prussia has endeavored to render the policy of Austria impotent. Fear of Napoleon allayed for a time the hatred of Austria and Prussia; but in 1792 Prussia, by the treaty of Basle, secured for itself peace, while Austria was left to rejoice in such equivocal blessings as Marengo, Austerlitz, and Hohenlinden furnished. Prussia grew strong; Austria poor. In 1815, when Bonaparte fell, a German confederation, with Austria and Prussia for its head, and four free towns, of which Frankfort was one, at the other extremity, was formed, and regulated by a Diet which here assembled. It soon became the puppet of Austria and Russia. The fevers of 1848 disturbed somewhat this one-sided amicable game of princes; and a crisis was produced which called for constitutions and a union of the sixty millions of Germans under one great Nationality, with Liberty as its soul! But you know how things then eventuated. The King of Prussia might have made himself the Saviour of Germany; but the golden time culminated and set; and Liberty still remained—a dream of the Universities—a playmate of the ocean waves and wild winds, with no practical home in this splendid land. Weak, eccentric and reckless, showing at times excellent pluck, and again humiliating himself between

Russia and Austria—Frederick William, the King of Prussia, consented to be virtually crushed at Warsaw in the Schleswig difficulty, and at a time, too, when the people of Prussia were aroused with the finest spirit, and when absolutism again trembled for its power. Shall Germany ever reduce her ideal liberty to practical suffrages and legislatures, without this everlasting military and royal pageantry? We trust that *their* good day will dawn. How many Germans in America now pray for the same benison on their Fatherland?

Before leaving Frankfort, I should not forget the visit we made to Luther's house, which, with the portrait and the inscription, still remain over the doorway, near the town-house, and but a few steps from the two fountains, which, upon ancient coronation days, when the empire was at its zenith, ran with white and red wine for the populace. Neither should I forget the scarlet cloth at the Romer, which, upon the same day of rejoicing, the Emperor walked upon to the Cathedral, and which the people had the privilege of cutting off, piece by piece, as he passed, to the sad jeopardy of a royal pair of heels.

We leave Frankfort for the North in the morning. Our purchases of glass and pictures, our view of the city, with its odd houses, its scaly tiles, its mirrors before the windows reflecting the street in the room, its fine railroad stations, and its hearty, industrious, good-natured people, is finished, and we are off for Mayence, to take a boat for the Rhine beauties and Cologne.

XXVIII.

Down the Rhine, and across to Waterloo.

———"He through the armed files
Darts his experienced eye, and soon traverse
The whole battalion views; their order due;
Their numbers last he sums. And now his heart
Distends with pride, and, hardening in his strength,
Glories." *Milton.*

AS we shake hands at Frankfort, let us not imitate those old gentlemen we saw at the station, who embracing, kiss each other three or four times upon each cheek with all the enthusiastic smack of a girl just from her boarding-school. Let us not disturb either that life-and-death parting between the dragoon and his lady love, perhaps his wife, whose chubby cheeks hang in close proximity to an abyss of hair upon his upper and nether facial department. But in true American style, blow your whistle, not the horn as here, and under the supervision of one conductor, not six to a train as here, dash over the track to Mayence, at which we must most curiously look, and why? Because it was the home of the proud old electors? Pshaw! We are tired of such antiques. Nor of the luxurious canons either, who here, amid enormous revenues, returned to the Pope the ungracious and impudent answer, when reproved by him for their worldly habits, that they had more wine than was needed for mass, and not enough to turn their mills. No, no, for wines and vines are becoming common, very; but because it was the home of two great minds—Walpoden, who liberated trade from the duties which each robber in his feudal castle exacted from the merchant, by his active efforts in forming the Rhenish, afterwards the Hanseatic league; and Gutemberg the discoverer of printing—the 'Dermiurgus of the world,' the truc leveller of man. The people of Mayence have erected a statue to the latter, and in this age, when unfettered traffic is becoming appreciated, a suitable monument to the former might not be inappropriate.

It rained as we passed through Mayence, so that we barely got a glimpse of its towers before we were ushered into a Rhine steamer, and were plowing its yellow waters with arrowy rapidity.

Now, if you expect a panorama of the Rhine from my pen, you are doomed to be disappointed—agreeably; for I will not inflict a description. You should have seen our party alive—literally and emphatically, to this Rhine scenery. What makes it so attractive? Ah! there I am at a loss. It is not altogether the strange towns walled to the water's edge, and leading out to the river under old archways in ruin, with their quaintly painted houses; it is not altogether the shelving lawns and the harvest and green fields; not altogether the tall, terraced vineyards rising from the river among rocks to the altitude of fifteen hundred feet; although all these are beautiful indeed. It is not altogether the changing prospect ahead, by which the river widens into a magic lake seemingly without outlet, and crowned upon its margin with castles of the middle ages, which jut out, and point upward amid crags that seem hung in air, and twisted in every shape; it is not altogether the dim old traditions which haunt these spots, some purple with wild loves, others red with bloody hate, others black with devilish deeds; it is not alogether the nunneries, the palaces of kings and emperors, the green isles, and bridges of boats, nor the Gothic churches hid beneath the shadow of these Rhenish strongholds; it is not the dance of Bacchus, Ceres, and Pomona, from hill to hill; not the magic echo which is repeated fifteen times from the gun and horn of the shore; not the romantic prance of the steeds of the soldiers wending their way along the little road of the banks; not the spot where Blucher's army hailed the Rhine after they had drank themselves drunk with the blood of the retreating French at Waterloo; not the "two brothers," rival crags—the seven sisters, rocks once maidens; not the great rafts of the Rhine; not yon prison of torture, which betokens our approach to Coblentz, out of whose lofty but gloomy turrets the scream of agony upon the rack once burst upon the frighted air; not that range of towers embosomed in green, rising upon an eminent crag that hangs above the Rhine, in whose ancient halls the royal house of Prussia recently received Victoria; not Coblentz itself, the Rhenish Gibraltar, with the Drachenfels, and the other six mountains, whose battlements no iron shower could ever quell; not even the classic isle near Weissenthum, where the French crossed in 1797, and where Cæsar, as every school-boy well remembers, crossed upon his famous bridge, pictures of which Anthon has introduced into his edition to gratify the youthful curiosity, unsatisfied with the knotty text; not the 'banks of the blue Mozelle,' nor the rickety old ruin called the Devil's House; not all these severally, but all these collectively, form a complete scene, where romance struggles with industry, where beauty rises up into grandeur, and where a heritage of legendary lore floats around and above them all in strange, dreamy lustre. There is one spot nearly opposite the Drachenfels, around which romance has woven an entrancing story, as simple as it is touching. The artist has represented it in the beautiful vignette upon our title page. From the picture, the relative position of mountain, crags, river, isle, nunnery, and road may be seen; and thus the eye may aid the imagination in grouping a scene whose physical charm is enhanced by a legend, which, for the honor of our kind, we hope is not altogether the offspring of fiction. The spot is consecrated to the memory of a brave knight, Roland, who built upon the lofty crown of the mountain a tower which overlooks an isle to which his lady love retired. Bulwer thus tells the legend:—Roland goes to the wars. A false report of his death reaches his betrothed. She retires to the convent in the isle of

Nunnenworth, which yet exists as the vignette represents it, and takes the irrevocable veil. Roland returns home, flushed with glory and hope, to find that the very fidelity of his betrothed had placed an eternal barrier between them. He built the castle that bears his name, and which overlooks the monastery, and dwelt there till his death; happy in the power, at least to gaze, even to the last, upon the walls which held the treasure he had lost.

There is a mournful tenderness about the legend, which the scene seems to reflect. Indeed, the whole margin of the Rhine is instinct with a mournful influence, which the spirit in vain strives to repel.

The romance of the Rhine ends before you reach Cologne; and when you reach that city—Oh! spirit of Coleridge—what a mire! what a hole! We reached there in a drizzle, and left in a drizzle,—not very favorable circumstances under which to view a town, celebrated in the finest transcendental muse for its filth. The city looked well from the river, but when once in the streets, there was nothing but sloppiness, dirtiness, and muddiness, intolerable; splashed by boys, drays and horses, draggled by women's dresses, and odorous with every imaginable scent, prime and distinguishable among which is the—*eau de Cologne!* Oh! ye nymphs of Mud, and muses of Dirt! I distinctly call upon you to blot out from my mind the memory of Cologne. If a man wishes to insult me, let him revive that memory by putting a bottle of the *eau* under my nose—if he dares!

The city has a heritage of Roman renown. Many old monuments remain of the former rulers, and, until within a recent period, the 'better sort' were in the habit of calling themselves patricians, as descended from the Roman families. Napoleon disturbed these little fooleries, among a good many others. The unfinished Cathedral looms up from a great distance, as we dash away towards Aix-la-Chapelle—brilliant contrast of Cologne—which we reach by cars over a dead-level land, covered with Nature's richest gold-dust, viz., the golden wheat. Neat as wax-work, elegant and white, are the streets of this city. It is one of the magnificent bathing establishments of which Germany boasts. In some respects it should not boast. Curiosity led us to see its famous gambling-hell known as the Redoute. It was lit up in royal style. When we went in, a brilliant assemblage were in the conversation-room, listening to a concert of Italian music. In other rooms, the tinkling of the Napoleons and thalers resounded, while the deep silence was broken by the singsong tone of the bankers at the rouge-et-noir and roulette tables of the other rooms. We enter. There are loungers on elegant sofas. Lamps, shaded with green, light up an elegant table, at which a respectable gray head presides, and around which the assistants and betters are ranged. As the une, trois, cinque, turn up successfully or otherwise, the little rakes busily push around the gold, silver, and notes. Occasional betters stand up; the regulars are seated, with knit brows and trembling hands pricking their memoranda, in vain attempting to head the bank, which, however Fortune may smile, must ultimately, by a surety as demonstrable as Euclid, increase its revenues so much per cent. Ladies, finely dressed, were there, playing with more *sang-froid* than the men. One Yankee might be discerned, with a flush of good luck upon his cheek, and the marks of verdancy in his actions,—the observed of all observers. He had begun with a thaler; was lucky, doubled each time he won; and thus regaining all he lost, he continued to add to his store, until it became so cumbrous that he was obliged to, and did, in the flurry of excitement, occasionally use his hat as a reservoir. Some one observed, in a whisper, that he must soon stake his hat; but, shrewd to the last, he quit with a hat-full—enough to pay his way to a land where such gigantic splendors of Satan are not licensed by government nor patronized by the rich.

One cannot leave such a place without the reflection that here is a deeper sin than that which tinkles upon the ear and glitters upon the retina. To see so much money pass from hand to hand, grasped by the trembling fingers of age and the eager sweep of youth, or gathered into the coffers of the bankers,—to know that this is the representative of labor, wrung out of the soil and the husbandmen of Rhenish Prussia,—'must give us pause.' Comes it from the great estates of the German nobles, who flock here to the baths? Is it bled by the patient vine-dresser from the terraced hills of the Rhine? It matters not; whoever thus squanders, does man—suffering man—and avenging God, disservice and great wrong.

What a condemnation of this frivolity frowns from the old Cathedral and the town-house of Aix, where Charlemagne and the emperors once trod, with no soft and downy step, seeking pleasure.

We visited the Cathedral. Although heartily tired of seeing so many churches, we could not leave Aix without a sight of the bones of Charlemagne, which are kept here in great state, with many other relics—such as the sponge which held the vinegar at the crucifixion, the cord that bound our Saviour's hands, and portions of the Cross. In the Hotel de Ville, where Charlemagne resided, we saw the portraits of Napoleon and Josephine. They stand beside that of the great founder of the early empire.

In leaving Aix, you pass through a country once the abode of the Flemings, and even yet full of an enterprising manufacturing people, who worthily fill the places of those early pioneers to whom England owes her great manufacturing prosperity. Tall chimneys and glowing forges announce the appearance of the towns; wheat-fields divided off by roads shaded with trees like those of Lombardy, in long vistas—and pastures filled with cattle not confined by fences—attest a splendid agricultural country.

Was it Liege, or some other Belgium city, where the outraged people pitched seventeen of their magistrates out of the town-hall windows; for which they were banished the realm? They found refuge in England, and formed no unimportant link in the chain of her material progress. Liege was once a free city, and acted a daring part in the earlier eras. Occasionally, an old castle would leap up from the level, as we wound along the valley toward Brussels. The villages looked oddly enough in their dresses of pure white, with red roofs. We soon enter upon the fighting ground of Europe, where Marlborough, Wellington, and Napoleon led their armies, and where many a brave soldier fell under the iron sleet.

Busy Brussels—neat Brussels—beautiful Brussels,—why is it that I cannot dissociate your fine promenades and elegant residences from that field of blood? Land of laces,—Paris in miniature—place of palaces,—splendid Brussels, did ye not tremble at the roar of battle, when Europe hung in the balance, and Destiny for ever deserted her child?

No one can visit Brussels without seeing Waterloo; no one can see Waterloo without returning with the impression of awe and wonder at the almost superhuman ability and strategy of the —vanquished. True, we read on our way the English accounts of the battle, the despatches of Wellington, and of that bloody miscreant, Blucher; true, we know that Wellington, at least when the Prussian appeared through the woods on the left, pressed on to victory; true, that the English infantry, like dogged brutes that fear not death, stood solid at Hougoumont and La Haute Sainte, although Jerome Bonaparte stormed the former tremendously with twelve thousand men; and although attack after attack was made in quick succession, of which the broken walls and burned château yet give evidence; true, that the fiercest charge of the old guard, even when victorious, was rendered innoxious by the cool audacity of Wellington; yet, notwithstanding all, the impression remains, that the genius of man and the brunt of the fighting was with the French. The field of the dead—one-third of the allied army thereon lying, proclaimed the dreadful thunderbolt which Napoleon hurled upon that 18th of June. We visited each point, and saw the whole from the monument of the Belgian lion. There is nothing striking in the field itself. A crescent valley, with two hills, each occupied by the foe, within cannon range; the English having all the natural advantages, the French doing all the marching and manoeuvring—these are the features of the bloody field. The traveller treads curiously over spots where Victory waved her ensign, and Death reaped his sanguine harvest; where the hope of conquest glowed in the heart while life's last ebbing sands were running. The wheat grows finely now where thousands fell and mouldered; the flax, whose elegant warp and woof wrought into Brussels lace will adorn the lady in her parlor, springs out of the ground fructified by the blood of the brave. After the battle, the richest crops were taken from the fields; and nature even yet struggles on silently to redeem herself from the stains of a mighty murder by the kindest processes of vegetable growth. Man may struggle with his brother, and lie down upon his gory bed, and he may call it glorious; but God wipes away the evidences of such glory by the waving of beautiful plains. "Les hommes agitent, but Dieu les mene," says Bossuet. "Men agitate, but God rules." Never was there a bolder instrument of Providence than Napoleon. His history is written all over Europe. All the pages of English vituperation, from the most puerile penny-a-liner to the rankest old tory or gravest historian, cannot eradicate or tarnish the proud evidences of Napoleon's greatness. At Naples, in the roads and buildings; at Venice, in the improvements he there made; at Milan, where we were shown what Napoleon did; at Lisbon, where he turned out some eleven hundred lazy priests to clean the filthy city; along the Rhine, where he broke up nunneries by the hundred; in Paris, where I now write almost under the shadow of his splendid monuments, are the ineffaceable proofs of his utilitarian and exhaustless mind, as it projected works for the good of the people, and it must be confessed, for the glory of himself. His shadow, not himself, now rules here; yet his shadow is more powerful this day in France, than the sunlight of her brightest spirits.

XXIX.

The French Capital.

> "France, the staple of new modes,
> Where garbs and miens are current goods,
> Prescribes new garnitures and fashions,
> And how to drink and how to eat
> No out-of-fashion wine or meat,
> And to demonstrate with sufficient reason,
> What ribands, all the year, are in or out of season."
>
> *Butler.*

TWO months ago we left this city, to go, we knew not certainly whither, to return, Providence permitting, hither. We have completed the round,—from Brussels we ran over by cars to this centre of civilization and gayety, poodle dogs and grind organs, Boulevards and promenades, cafés and operas, military displays and Sunday fêtes,—every thing to divest the mind of gravity and invest it with the illusory, the transient and the mobile.

After having arrived here with such expeditious good luck, we felt like laying upon our oars and floating down the stream of Parisian life, without effort, amidst its ever-following margin of gayeties. Youth at the prow and pleasure at the helm, we *have* floated between promenades and gardens, flowers and temples, colors and melodies,—every object that excites the eye, ravishes the ear, and enfolds the senses in delight. This is surface work. It looks pretty and its novelty pleases. Beneath the surface of this gay world there lies moral filth and gross debasement. Content to fret the surface, we have not stirred the depths of the mysteries of Paris.

The Lord Mayor of London and his train have been here

the past week, feasted guests at the Hotel de Ville, invited visitors to Versailles upon Sunday, attendants upon splendid operatic performances, and wondering gazers at the sham battle in the Champ de Mars, on the 6th of August. The Circuses have brushed up their horses and added new features to their bills; the promenades have been newly trimmed and the palaces neatly swept; the manufactories of Gobelins tapestry, and Sevres porcelain, have been freely opened, and a general *entente cordiale* has been celebrated between the "perfidious Albionites," and the testy Gauls, in which the Juries of the World's Exhibition have taken part. In fine, Paris, always a fête to the stranger, especially to a Buckeye, has been in a perfect tip-top gala ever since the Lord Mayor arrived.

1. The great Sham Battle.

We have followed in the wake of the fête, seeing the ebullition and hearing the bubbling. A loud noise it made at the sham fight in the Field of Mars. Fortunately when we drove up to the field, we met the Commissary of the Police, who readily granted us, as strangers and Americans, a pass through the guards at the streets leading to the barriers. He even extended to us the courtesy of giving us a whiskered dragoon with a big hat, the specific gravity of which was very disproportionate to its bulk, by whom we were led through the crowd, and obtained a place high and aloof, commanding a view of the field.

The fight commenced with a thunder of artillery; then volleys of musketry; then parties dashed across the bridge and the fighting became close and severe,—very,—about our point. Soon the whole army, except the reserves, were in action. The artillery roared, the flame flashed amid rolling volumes of smoke, the bayonets glittered through it splendidly, the cavalry in long columns, with ensigns flying, charged hollow squares, after the party on one side had driven back the assailants, and had in their turn become the assailants. It was a magnificent sight to see the long winding trains of horsemen, forming into line and dashing off in glittering style through the cloud of dust they had raised; then, meeting a volley of cannon and guns, wheel about and take their old position. During the cavalry evolutions, the excitement of the crowd became intense. People below us in the street, were hiring fellows to let them have the use of their shoulders. Lemonade-men ceased their cries. Water-women held their breath; some of the Parisian "b'hoys," or blouses, had obtained boards and were scaling the terraces upon which the crowd, who had paid most liberally for them, were intently enjoying the spectacle. A real fight ensued; illustrating, in a twinkling, by the interest it created, how much more exciting is an atom of earnestness than an army of sham.

Stationed upon a fine terrace, overlooking the spot, we were in the midst of the roar, the smoke, the din, and the—*innocency* of the battle. Eighty thousand elegantly-dressed soldiers, glittering in the sun, marching in infantry, wheeling and curveting in cavalry, manœuvring with artillery, retreating, advancing, detouring, running, throwing bridges over the Seine, carrying forts, defending walls, in solid columns, in open order, in hollow squares, in videttes, in every imaginable figure and form known to the Art of Death, by powder and steel, with trumpets sounding, cannons flashing and thundering, musketry rolling, and pennons waving; all working out upon uneven ground, and finally upon the beautiful field of Mars, the problem of the day, and that, too, without any other catastrophe than a dragoon hors de combat, is a sight that stirs the spirit, while it does not disturb the ordinary flow of human sympathy. The idea of the battle was this: a hostile force from Passy and the Bois de Bologne, which was behind us, move on to take the Ecole Militaire, a strong fortress, having the Seine in front. The heights of Chaillôt was the spot where the contest waged hottest, where the most —powder was spilt. As the smoke rolled away toward the right, the assailants were seen to have encompassed by their cavalry the infantry, to have silenced by their cannon the opposing artillery; and to have occupied in beautiful array the field of Mars! Such enthusiasm, such a turn out, never could be found in any place but Paris. At least five hundred thousand people were on the grounds and heights, on the houses, columns, arches, woodpiles, and chimneys. The trees which lined the field of battle were full above, and under them was a long mass of people, stretching out at least a mile on either side. As the battle progressed, the barriers were removed, and the people rushed through in living floods to the scene. The fortress was at last taken; the troops filed off before Louis Napoleon and the Lord Mayor, the crowd broke through the barriers and inundated the Champs Elysées, where in great packed acres they stood awaiting the appearance of the President. He appeared under escort of the National Guard, when vivas long and loud went up to Napoleon! The blouses, as well as the better-dressed citizens, joined in the universal hurrah! Universal? Ah! there were a few brave fellows, who shouted "Viva la Republique!" I tell you that this great nation is not republican yet, save in name. There is no principle pervading the masses. Their enthusiasm is purely *personal.* There is no simplicity, nor love of independence in their movements. Parade, glitter, pomp, and hero-worship, is the idea of Parisian society. The government which can furnish the greatest quantity of gayety and glitter, in a given time, will be, at least for a time, the pet of the people. The revolution in manners must precede all other salutary revolutions.

2. Sabbath at Versailles.

Yesterday was Sunday here. I will avouch to its being the Sunday of the Calendar; but not our good old quiet Sunday. It was a Paris Sunday, with a few extras. Of course, you would not expect us to be so Puritanic as not to see a Parisian Sunday. You might as well attempt to go to Naples without seeing Vesuvius, Aix-la-Chapelle without seeing a gambling-hell, or

Venice without seeing the prisons of the Council of Ten. We heard there was *service* at Versailles—Parisian service—so we struck for that point. There were some sixty or seventy thousand bent in the same direction. As it was the first Sunday in the month, all the fountains were to play, and, as the fête was in progress, the Lord Mayor of London and the Exhibition Commissioners were to be there. A railroad dashed us past the far-famed palace and park of St. Cloud, into the town of Versailles. The town is of little account, though in the time of Louis XIV., when Royalty revelled so splendidly, it contained 100,000 people—one third of which number, only, are there at present. The grounds, with their green galleries and beautiful fountains, their innumerable statues, elegant orangery, interminable walks and flower-gardens, and the palaces,—these make Versailles the great resort of the pleasure-loving and the curious.

Of course, you would not expect, nor could I ever give, such a detailed description of Versailles as would reproduce it to the mind's eye. After seeing it, one should make his will. It caps the Seraglio, beats Hyde Park; the Luxembourg in Paris is tame beside it; the Brussels promenade *is* fine, and so is that of Naples; but where, in all our views, have we seen any thing comparable to Versailles? Whether it is the magnificent Place d'Armes, rivalling St. Peter's Piazza, guarded by the martial valor of France in the colossal statues of Condé, Turenne, and others, and all commanded by the majestic equestrian statue of Louis XIV., which is much more striking than that of Marcus Aurelius in the Capitol at Rome; whether it is the great and little Trianon, palaces famed in the history of the Queens of France, with their magnificent prospects of lawn and wood, water-sheets and water-jets, ranges of statuary, gardens of flowers and marble basins; whether it is the galleries of paintings shaming the Vatican in the richness and taste of their decoration (indeed Napoleon as King of Italy was as free in his appropriation of Italian art, as railroads are of real estate in Ohio), and illustrating in marble the scientific, literary and martial genius of the nation, and upon extensive canvas that military glory before which monarchs paled and the world trembled; wherever you go, whatever point of view you take, from palace window or upon the marble stairway, you are lost in the variety of objects, each one a chief in itself, but all arranged for one brilliant stroke of the vision over an expanse of area utterly inconceivable before by our unsophisticated mind. Addison has said, that the sight continues longest in service, affording for a longer time pleasure and delight, through its inlet to the soul, than any of the other senses. We found it true at Versailles. Without fatigue or cessation, it ranged from hall to hall; running through centuries, from Charlemagne and Pepin, down to Louis Philippe and Charles X., and in the mean time taking in all the splendid efforts of art from the reign of Louis XIV. and of the Empire. David's pictures of the Coronation of Napoleon, and of Napoleon giving the Eagles to the Army, fulfilled every anticipation concerning them; but the chapel, the frescoes, the landscape-paintings in which battle-scenes are introduced,—the wonderful effect of all these in developing, sustaining, and giving enthusiasm to *French*, purely French nationality, I had not before any adequate conception of.

It would require but a glance at the painting of the wounded Marshal Lannes, with Napoleon by his side, or of Austerlitz with the figure of Bonaparte proudly eminent, to give ésprit to the army of France, such as of old it possessed under its almost deified General.

This palace of Versailles was formerly a hunting-lodge for one of the earlier kings. Additions after additions were made, millions being expended in their construction, until the Revolution, after which it sunk into decay. Napoleon preferred to live at St. Germain or St. Cloud. He said that it would take forty millions of francs to put Versailles in repair. Louis Philippe had it in excellent order.

Our ladies were curious to see the Trianon, and especially the little Swiss cottage erected by order of Marie Antoinette;

but as I attempted to go by the soldier—a laughing, good-natured fellow, who marched under the signs "Propriété nationale," and "Liberté, Egalité et Fraternité"—he called out for a pass, which I had not provided, and I could effect no fraternization with him, by which to gain my end.

We saw a great crowd looking at the golden royal coach of Charles X., which is considerably laughed at just now. It may roll through these arbors and green lanes yet, with a Bourbon in it; who knows? But hurrah! here is a rush! what a crowd of Johnny Bulls; and there they go, after a fine-looking white-haired gentleman in very black, who is being led around into the orangery by the Prefect of the Seine. The English run after, like mad, women and men, fat and lean—mostly fat. Aha! now they are stopped. A French soldier, with ribbons on his coat, has run a rope across, and the soldiers are trying to guard the pass. In vain, fat Aldermen's fat wives, perspiring like the frogs in yonder fountain of Latona, dodge under, clamber over, escape outstretched arms, and caper away like kittens, after the Lord Mayor. At last the heft (to Yankee it) of the crowd is stopped. The rest present tickets, and talk *H*english quite *h*uselessly. The pageant has faded. And so has it been all day—a chase of English Aldermen, and their consorts, after the Mayor, who is hurried along by the Prefect at a good trot. It was a scene for Punch.

We returned home to see Paris by night, in the Champs Elysées, Boulevards, Luxembourg, and at the Cafés, where concerts, circuses, and amusements of every variety, keep a company of two hundred thousand, if not more, constantly on the *qui vive.* One does not know what that phrase means, until they see the sights here on Sunday. If there be any churches here, what were they built for? The question has been answered in a former chapter; they are but mausoleums over the buried great, or theatres for the display of festal and regal magnificence. They were built for man, not God.

3. Père La Chaise.

One of the most attractive places of resort in the environs of Paris is the Père La Chaise cemetery. There is a peculiarity in the tombs, and a beautiful custom connected with them, well worthy of mention and imitation. The cemetery lies to the northeast of the city.

We passed along the magnificent quays of the Seine, crossed the bridge, and stopped before the monument erected upon the spot where the Bastile of the old régime stood. It is built to the memory of those citizens who fell on the memorable three days of July, 1830, which dethroned the elder Bourbons, and made Louis Philippe "citizen king." The monument is elegantly surmounted with a gilded image of Victory winged, standing with one foot on tip-toe upon a globe, about 250 feet high. The image is exceedingly aerial and graceful. It is about the height of the majestic column to Napoleon in the Place Vendôme. The latter is modelled after that of Trajan at Rome, and moulded wholly out of the cannon and other metallic trophies taken in battle by the Emperor.

Through streets lined with marble stores, and shops where funereal wreaths are made, we pass up to the cemetery. Mourners stop to buy the wreaths of yellow and white. They are very touching, and expressive of kindly sympathy. Little images, too, of persons kneeling or mourning are bought, and all are placed upon the tombs, either within upon shrines, or without under little covers, to keep them from rain or sun. Almost every tomb was thus remembered. Very few were without some token. Many had flowers growing around and about them, most tastefully arranged. How good—how mindful are the French! was the exclamation, as we passed amid these emblems of life and decay. The tombs of La Place, of Volney, La Fontaine, and of David, the great painter, are here. Most eagerly we sought for the tomb of Heloïse and Abelard, so renowned in song and story. They flourished in the twelfth century, and were two of the most distinguished persons of their age in learning and beauty; but for nothing were they so famous, as for their unfortunate passion. After a long course of calamities, they retired each to a separate convent, and consecrated the remainder of their days to religion. Buried in life thus in divided graves, they were united in death in the same tomb; not, however, long to rest together, for ecclesiastical power followed their dust, and separated it, as it had their lives. But after many vicissitudes, they lie side by side, as is beautifully indicated by the sculptured images under the little Gothic temple which affection has reared. Wreaths there were not a few, upon their tomb,—touching tributes to that constancy and attachment which their lives, death and entombment, typified so beautifully. White roses grow plentifully within the inclosure, chaste symbols of a love which death has not quenched, but only purified. We plucked one rose as a souvenir of the spot, and, if any cemetery may be thus called, of this pleasant abode of the departed.

The Père la Chaise affords a fine view of Paris, which we were enjoying as the bell began to ring, and the watch of the cemetery began to cry the hour of departure from the different points. Taking a dish of berries and ices at a café (every body here lives at a café), our party went to the hotel, and I to the Theatre Comique, to see Paris in another phase and hear a funny opera.

Let not the lawyer who visits Paris fail to drive down to the Palais Justice, and observe the working of the courts. I spent very profitably a most interesting day in listening to the judges and lawyers. The latter are the most intelligent and best-looking gentlemen I have seen in Europe. I know that remark is superfluous. Dressed in their black gowns, and black caps shaped like the segment of a sugar loaf,—they move about from court to court with their briefs in hand, unincumbered with loads of authorities and ever ready to meet their cases. I heard a case tried by jury, and noticed many little improvements upon our present mode of practice. Their custom of questioning the accused shortens the trial, and it seems not at all inconsistent with fairness. The repartee even between prisoner and accuser, and prisoner and judge, while it excites from its dramatic character, generally shows where the blame or crime lies. Soldiers are always on hand to preserve order and protect the doors. It was a sufficient password to say that I was a stranger, in order to obtain admittance. There are some eight or ten judges in each of the courts. A good feature is, that the lawyers have a grand consultation every Saturday, when the poor may obtain gratuitous advice.

4. Parisian Medley.

Now I know that it is not the province of a transient traveller, to venture too far in generalizations upon national character and prospects. He is liable to make himself ridiculous. I only speak of what I have been informed. I have hardly seen enough for a respectable induction upon any subject. The proper subject of a traveller's pen is the superficial. Of that,—what an area has my eye covered! what multiform objects has it embraced! Can I enumerate! The Hotel des Invalides, where the veterans upon wooden legs and crutches line the fine walks, cultivate their little flower plots, and talk of Napoleon, whose remains are entombed within the chapel, where wave two hundred ensigns—trophies of his valor from the Pyramids to the Snows; the Louvre, that noble repertory of art, surpassing any of the galleries of Italy—being, in fact, the choice selection from them all—where Rubens and Vandyke vie with Raphael and Caracci for the palm of genius, where Salvator Rosa and Claude, the one in bold outline, the other in mellow lustre, reproduce nature in her loveliest aspect, where the holiest of beings beams benignly from the wall on the canvas of Murillo, and where the German Bacchanals drink beer with such a jollity, that the canvas fairly laughs; the Tuileries with its palace, where Louis Philippe once lived with his family, still preserved (with some few marks of popular fury) as it was in 1848, when Girardin recommended the abdication, which ended in an airing on horseback; and its gardens, which are only rivalled in tasteful walks, manifold flower-beds, beautiful fountains, and luxuriant orangeries by the Luxembourg,—where the taste of the Medici family is still preserved, notwithstanding Louis Blanc held socialist meetings there, and notwithstanding soldiers have rendezvoused in the gilded rooms; the museum of artillery, where the arms of France, from the invasion of Gaul down to the last revolution, are displayed, including the armor of Joan of Arc, and the delicate festoonery of the entrance hall, in the shape of the iron chain which the Turks used at the siege of Vienna, to construct a ponton bridge over the Danube; the Jardin des Plantes, where the roar of the beasts does not in the least disturb the silent putting forth of the fragrant flowers; where the cedar of Lebanon grows within sight of the anaconda's den; where the delicate tamarind tree and flowering magnolia are arranged in the same home with the gazelle and rhinoceros; where geology and botany have their halls, and the most disgusting lizard and snake their hiding-place; where all is scientifically arranged, and within whose centre is a bower and a summer-house overlooking the whole, and affording a splendid view of Paris;—and above all embracing a Sabbath evening, with its concerts in the open air, its crowded cafés, its immense promenades, a living and moving mass of blouses and monsieurs, fine ladies and mademoiselles in neat caps, the amusements, Punch and Judy, cross-bow firing at plasters, billiards, wooden-horse riding, circuses performing, music playing, cat and dog entertainments, children with little balloons, amidst glancing lights and spraying fountains, gardens of the rarest flowers, and shadows of arched trees, mingled with the everlasting jabber and gay laugh of the French; which latter is not the least wonderful phase of this city of wonders. But why enumerate, where there is so much to be seen? There is indeed " but one Paris." The world of science, politics, and of luxury, has here its heart. Its throbs are great, and penetrate the remotest part of Europe, aye, even extending world-wide.

Yet one cannot but feel that the jaw of destruction opens wide to ingulf this city. A few centuries more, and the curious traveller may wander along the ruined quays of the Seine, now adorned with so many bridges and walls, noting the piles where once stood the Hotel de Ville, from which Lamartine held the populace enchained by the beauty of his diction and the spell of his noble thoughts; or wondering at the brass column to Napoleon, eternal as his fame, towering up amidst decay; or at the despoiled gardens and palaces of this pleasure-maddened city. If the godlessness of a people is any indication of a future, imagination may revel in the ruins of the future Paris. May it not conceive yon Place de la Concorde, now glittering with lights, musical with fountains, and crowded with people,—where Louis XVI. and Marie Antoinette were beheaded,—as waving with the ripe corn, or chaotic in ruins, like the palace of the Cæsars? Or may we not rather hope that France, springing from the mire of moral degradation, shall rise in the newness of a civilization, in which republican simplicity shall walk hand in hand with Christian truth?

We yesterday visited the tombs of Voltaire and Rousseau, in the basement of the Pantheon. France venerates, at present, too highly their splendid intellects, to permit her to dissociate the effect of their genius from their glaring vices. On the tomb of Voltaire is the following: "Il combattit les athées et les fanatiques, inspira la tolerance et reclama les droits de l'homme contre la servitude de la feodalité." I thought the commentary of our refugee-republican-Roman courier most excellent. In his tolerable English he said, after reading it: "France built this Pantheon to her grand hommes, who wrote for liberty, and—she go to Rome to—kill Liberty;" and with a shrug of the shoulders, he turned away to read the inscription on Rousseau's tomb: "Here reposes the man of nature and of truth;" not knowing how significant of French fate was the sentiment thus graven upon the tomb of a man whose life gave the lie to all his beautiful raptures on truth and virtue.

The same thing is discernible now, in the public men of France. They talk political abstractions in pert, pithy, pretty, curt sentences; but when they undertake to *do*—Humph! Dominichino would shrug his shoulders again. France needs some such men as Lafayette—content to be useful, rather than splendid; practical, instead of brilliant.

5. Lafayette's Tomb.

We thought that we could not do better upon our second Sabbath, especially in Paris, than to visit Lafayette's grave. It is sought after by few, and these, I am proud to say, are Americans. The coachman could not find the street, without some difficulty. A long ride up the Faubourg de St. Antoine, brought us to the Rue de Picpus, upon the outskirts of the city. A convent, now occupied by the "Sisters of Charity," and an old chapel of Doric, surround the tomb of Lafayette. We walked through long arbors of grapes and flowers, amid the tidy-looking elderly dames—all dressed in their white dresses and whiter bonnets, until we turned into a narrow, treeless cemetery, where among the Montmorencies, Rosambos, and other noble families of France, reposes the friend of America and of Washington. A large slab covers the grave of himself and wife; and near by are the remains of George Washington Lafayette, his son, who died in 1849. The victims of the reign of terror lie around them. A few wreaths decorate the bare tomb. A deep and solemn quiet, in strange contrast to the ever-rushing tide of the streets, reigned within this sacred home. I loved this spot. It reminded me of our own simple American graveyards. No mark of nobility, no heraldic armor, was engraved upon the tomb. No old soldiers are here to guard it; no lofty column rises to the memory of the good and genial Lafayette. But he has a monument more durable than brass. It is in the heart of America. As time lapses, we should cherish more deeply, and care with nicer heed for, those revolutionary soldiers and patriots, who worked out so excellent a constitution, through so much difficulty and danger.

We have no long line of kings to emblazon in splendor the historic page, or palaces full of their pictures and trophies; we have no dim old cathedrals, hallowed with the footsteps of mighty cardinals and priests, and almost groaning with their weight of marble honors; we have no battles to boast of so scourging and bloody as Borodino and Austerlitz; but we have a history rich in spiritual independence, and eventuating in a government, which Lord Brougham has truly called, the highest refinement in civil polity which the world has ever seen. We have in our historic annals the name of at least the purest, if not the greatest of Frenchmen—Lafayette! His remains sleep quietly, sequestered among the kindly sisters of charity. No revolution will exhume them, as were exhumed the proud kings at St. Denis. Respect, if not enthusiasm, and never obloquy, will attend his memory. Americans will always delight to leave the din of the great city, to search out and honor his simple tomb.

XXX.

London,—in other Phases.

> "These struggling tides of life that seem
> In wayward, aimless course to tend,
> Are eddies of the mighty stream
> That rolls to its appointed end."
>
> *Bryant.*

WELL, it came over one right goodly, to reach a spot where one does not have to call our old homely Saxon words by such outré and unaccustomed terms. To say *breakfast*, instead of "déjeûné, monsieur;" to say "how much?" instead of that everlasting "combien?" to feel that you are understood and heeded without acting it out like a player, was indeed a relief.

On our ride up to London from Dover, the English country did not look so attractive as when we saw it in the beginning of June, all fresh and green in its primal garniture. Perhaps the scenes which Italy and the Alpine valleys had pencilled and laid away in memory's portfolio, detracted from the rural beauty; perhaps the fields bared of their grain, and wanting that rich, golden yellow which interlaced the fertile vales of the Rhone and of the Aar, have contributed to disparage the aspect of the country; and perhaps, our eyes have been sated with natural views. No matter, London—*London* has lost nothing of its attractions by our continental tour.

There is a kind of incredulity attaching itself to all the associations of ancient renown and power, which cling around the places we have visited upon the continent. We cannot more than half believe that the Doges of Venice ruled with such splendor and power; that Athens was the theatre of

16

such mighty deeds and noble thoughts; that Monza was the glittering capital of ancient Lombardy, with its kings and queens; that the Mediterranean was the scene of crusading thousands led by knightly prowess; that Charlemagne ruled along the Rhine with such pomp of empire, enacting deeds of high emprise,—all these and other relations of places to history, enter like shadows into the temple of faith, and, like shadows, soon depart. But when it comes to England—when it comes to London, with her bridges and her Whitehalls, her palaces and her Tower,—her historic incidents enter, with a stern, substantial, ringing step upon the portal, and challenge every form of doubt or overcome all incredulity. When to-day we entered the Tower, the dark and bloody history of England was turned over rapidly and tangibly by the wizard of the past, as each object aroused its familiar and undoubted chronicle.

The gateways we found crowded. Presently we purchased our tickets for the armory and jewel room. Then we were compelled to wait until the warder had collected a goodly number, when off we marched with him to inspect and wonder. These warders are numerous. They are dressed in their ancient costume—the same as that worn in the reign of Henry VII. It consists of a cap ribboned off gaudily, and a coat in the form of a blouse, gilded all over, with a crown on the breast and back boldly emblazoned. They are appointed from the army on account of their good character. The warder assigned us was a fine old Johnny Bull, who had a peculiar fondness for Americans. He lugged me out of the crowd at every turn, to display what he considered as much our history as England's. He said that he had no doubt that some of our ancestors had walked around these places. I hoped that they had not been *too* familiar with some parts of the premises. It made one feel quite antique to be guided about these old palaces and prisons by so odd a looking personage as our warder. Had it not been for the aspirate and the want of it in the wrong places, I could easily have transported our cockney warder at least into the age of Harry the

Eighth, or have placed him in charge of one of the Fairy Queen's castles.

Many persons wonder why England suffers the Tower to stand. Its darkness and gloom, to say nothing of its history, are in such bold contrast with the fine structures and elevated civilization of the present day, that it seems strange that it has not suffered the fate of the Bastile. Hallam has perhaps given the best image of the Tower as well as the best reason for its preservation, when he says, 'that it seems like a captive tyrant, reserved to grace the triumph of a glorious republic, and that it should teach us (Britons) to reflect in thankfulness, how highly we have been elevated in virtue and happiness above our forefathers.' Truly there is a lesson to be learned from its old stones, its murderous blocks, its manifold modifications of force, its solitary cells, its chivalric armors, and its costly regalias—a lesson of humility and of dependency upon an arm greater than that of flesh; the lesson taught by the text cut in the prison room occupied by Sir Walter Raleigh, which I read to-day—"*Be faithful unto the deth, and I wil give the a crowne of life!*"

The Tower dates from the Conqueror. Although some parts of it look new and lack gloom, yet there are others which have that streaked and blackened appearance which the oldest stone in northern climes always presents. We surveyed the interior; noted with interest the prison of the seven bishops, whose trial Macaulay graphically depicts, and upon whose acquittal, such a momentous change occurred in the British dynasty and constitution; looked curiously at the famous stone and mortar known as the White tower, which performed a star part in the drama of the great charter and King John, and which so many of the Plantagenets used as a palace and a prison; and more curiously still, and not without a shudder, at the Bloody Tower, which tradition and Shakspeare have rendered so horrible, as the scene of the suffocation of the young princes, nephews of the Duke of Gloster, Richard III. There is, however, considerable doubt as to the authenticity of the relation, which makes that part of the old pile so horrible. The underground compartments we did not see. It was enough to mark the Traitor's gate, with its portcullis, ready even yet to gnash its grim teeth upon the victim as he enters from the Thames, under the stone arch, and up the fatal steps; enough, to recall the great and good who have here suffered for popular freedom and religious faith.

We passed some time in gazing at the kings and celebrated men of England,—clad in their own identical armor, and mounted upon horseback. They were tastefully arranged in what is called the Horse Gallery. The most conspicuous among them all was the gross form of that rough brute, Henry VIII., and the despicably mean-looking visage of James II. Cromwell, Villiers, Stafford, and others whose names are a part of English history, were there. Above each king was arranged in stars, the peculiar arms of the period.

We enjoyed the visit to the Regalia room, where the crown jewels and crowns are kept. They are worth the enormous sum of fifteen millions of dollars—nearly equal to Ohio's state debt! The warder well remarked, that we would, in our country, hardly keep so much wealth idle. I told him, that we would apply it, perhaps, toward paying off the national debt, especially, if it amounted to eight hundred millions.

We were shown the block upon which Lady Jane Grey, Essex, and Raleigh suffered, as well as some horrible implements of torture. The latter were marked, "captured from the Spanish." I supposed that they were perfectly at home in the Tower, if we may rely upon history. Besides, what kind of a war trophy would be one of these engines of misery? What general would wish his triumph graced by such an instrument?

The crowning interest which belongs to the Tower, is, that it has been the prison of those who dared to assert the rights of Englishmen, who stood up, in the face of arrogant kings, to proclaim that the people alone had the *divine right* to control their own destiny. These brave spirits never suffered the house of Tudor or of Stuart to repose for a moment upon a couch of roses. Such men as Peter Wentworth in Elizabeth's time, and Coke and Selden in the time of James I., were the true forerunners of the Pyms, Hampdens, and Fiennes of a later day. They verified the French couplet,

> Le roi d'Angleterre
> Est le roi d'Enfer.

" The King of England is the king of hell." And although the Tower with its torments awaited them, still, like their transatlantic descendants upon similar great issues, they knew, and dared to maintain their privileges against the royal prerogative.

One cannot have an adequate idea of the immensity of the brick and mortar, known as London, without going up into some lofty point, such as the cupola of St. Paul's. Under the smoky obscurity there lies far—far around as the eye can see, one continuous, compact mass of buildings, interpersed with handsome spires, and divided by the Thames—upon which is seen, darting from pier to pier, the little steamers which ply from Chelsea to Greenwich. Paris is easily bounded, Constantinople you may take in at one large view, Naples lies along the bay, and in the clear air may be comprehended at a glance ; but London, and

> " The villas with which London stands begirt
> Like a swarth Indian, with his belt of beads,"

forms its own horizon of houses, while whole cities lie beyond. From St. Paul's, whence we viewed the city, the beautiful parks were scarcely discernible ; the new houses of Parliament and Westminster arose conspicuously, and the streets about St. Paul's, sent up their incessant hum and rattle.

We have visited the Tunnel of the Thames—a bazaar under a river—that is all. Indeed there are few sights worth a visit, which we have not seen. A promiscuous world is London, with its Zoological Gardens, where we saw the hippopotamus, " wallowing, unwieldy," and an orang-outang that looked more like a human being than some negroes I wot of; with its Northumberland House, where the lion of Percy faces the form of Nelson upon his column at Trafalgar Square; with its Kew Gardens, where the tamarind-tree and the bread-plant thrive beside the broad-leaved palm and the flowering magnolia, and where every vegetable production, from the cedar of Lebanon to the hyssop upon the wall, grows and creeps; with its ever polite policemen, its saucy cabmen, its jostling crowds in which rudeness is taken for manliness; with its great Brewery—how can I forget that, after the difficulty we had in attaining an insight—belonging to Barclay & Perkins, generally known in America as the place of Haynau's disgrace,—but better known as the reservoir of one-fourth of the ale and stout of the kingdom. We went through the establishment entire. I wondered somewhat at the wine cask of Heidelberg; but found here, one hundred and seventy-two larger beer kegs, each one of which holds not less than two thousand barrels, and the larger ones, three thousand five hundred. The other operations are on a similar extensive scale. Exeter Hall preaches temperance in vain, against such a monster. Bull must 'ave 'is hale.

The English are a credulous people. They will believe almost any thing of Americans. We took tea with a very respectable family the other day, and were amused to find how much of prejudice and misconception we could remove with ease. They believed that we all drank gin-slings and "Tom and Jerry;" that we were every day or so regaled with lynch-law, and that "life, liberty, and the pursuit of happiness," were very precarious franchises, especially in the west of America. A red-headed doctor, who attended me a while, gave as a reason for not going to America the following, after his peculiar style: "Suppose a man's robbed,—by a red-headed rascal; people mad—see my hair—get a rope—nearest tree—I swing—d'ye see?"

The manuscripts of Bacon, Pope, Newton and others, at the Museum, we looked at long and curiously. The original Magna Charta is preserved there. The Jerusalem Delivered of Tasso, is also there, in the handwriting of Tasso. There too are the relics of Nineveh, sent home by Layard, the indefatigable. English gold has been potent in drawing together such a fine collection.

You have heard of GOG, the Roman soldier, and MAGOG, the Ancient Briton, who preside over Guildhall, and have in their keeping the ancient municipality. Well, we saw the old genii, sure enough. Quaint and odd—painted in divers colors, and looking very grandly foolish, stuck up in their corners,—they constitute one of the sights of London, never to be omitted. As soon omit seeing the Bronze Wolf at the Roman Capitol, or the bears at Berne.

Rain and sunshine alternate here every other hour. The air is thus kept delightfully cool. The nights are beginning to grow cold. Indeed, we have had plain indications of the approaching fall. Driving through St. James's Park, we noticed the maples already shedding their leaves, and bestrewing the walks. Royal parks and American woods own a kindred nature, and together obey the great law of decay and growth. By analogy we would conclude that the same great law comprehends the royal occupants of St. James and the humblest tenant of our log cabins,—a simple truth which will bear pondering with profit. Death knows no distinction or rank. God knows none, save that which distinguishes the pure in heart from the vile.

What a home for crime and vice is London! To the traveller this does not appear so readily. A few hours' observation in the Mayor's court revealed more than I could have learned by going about the streets for a year. During those few hours, a crowd of tattered, miserable beings were lodging their complaints, or being tried for petty crimes. Police officers were bringing in offenders of high and low degree. They have curious and rapid modes of justice here. Immediately below the court-room are the prisons, which consist of little wicker cages. A trap-door opens, and after the manner of Banquo's ghost, there arises from below, the prisoner. By his side is the policeman. The attorney for the city states the charge. The judge requests the policeman to give evidence. He thus propels: "I found three and a half pounds of tobacco hid upon the prisoner's person, after I had asked him if he had any contraband goods, and after he had denied having any. There is a duty of nine shillings and threepence per pound, your honor."

Judge.—"What have you got to say to this?"

Prisoner.—"Please your honor, I gave three shillings for it, to send it down to my friends at Ramsgate."

Judge.—"Why did you conceal it?"

Prisoner—Mum.

Judge.—"You are sentenced to fourteen days' imprisonment, or to pay a fine of twenty shillings."

The trap door opens; exit prisoner, saying, "I gave my last shilling for the tobacco; I can't pay the fine, zur."

I would have liked exceedingly to have had the privilege of visiting the courts of Westminster, but they will not be in session till November. The Old Bailey must repay in part for the disappointment.

I visited the 'Old Bailey' to see that famous criminal-mill grind out a batch of offenders. My friend, the City Solicitor, was on hand at the indictment office, preparing his indictments for the Grand Jury; but he found time to give me a prominent place from which to observe the operations. In the first court, they were arraigning the newly indicted, which was done in droves, classified according to their crimes. The other court was more interesting. It moved like clockwork. The court-rooms are not so fine as those of the Palais Justice; and I missed the beautiful painting of the Saviour upon the cross, which always hangs over the heads of the French judges. Neither does the judge demean himself so attentively and sympathetically. I did not look for much sympathy in the Old Bailey. I would as soon have looked for pearls in a pudding-stone. The lawyers sat on circular benches, in whitish curly wigs, and gowns. I had no idea that so respectable a profession could be dressed up so as to look so assinine. Of course they are used to the absurdity; but is it always to continue? Now it does not look so ridiculous to see the officer of the court in a great blue cloak-dress, fringed with furs, and the crier (I believe it was) with his sword dangling about a pair of spindle-shanks, dressed in tights, while his head was queued and ribboned in gala style; for these officers "have no discretion;" they are executive—machines. Lawyers are supposed to be thinking men, not fantastic harlequins. But there I sat, almost choking because I could not laugh, at the grave and gay wigs (some looked in the face to be not more than twenty-one years of age) which surrounded me. A gentleman thief was on trial for stealing a box of silver. He was standing in the dock, counterfeiting a tremble, and using a handkerchief to brush away imaginary tears. An old wig (I have no respect for men who place themselves in such a guise) was trying his best to bamboozle a jury that seemed utterly indifferent to every thing. If you remember a sketch of the jury that tried Bardell *vs.* Pickwick, by Cruikshank, you will have an idea of this jury. Pretty soon the old wig, after having disposed of each tittle of testimony, calling it nothing, multiplied them together, and produced nothing—against his client, and sat down to his infinite satisfaction.

"My lord," the judge, summed up in a few words: the jury leaned over the bench, and without going out (they never go out in the Old Bailey), returned a verdict of guilty, almost as soon as I can write this sentence; the judge immediately sentenced the prisoner to ten year's transportation. The prisoner asked if he could be permitted to use spectacles. A voice (female) from the gallery, "My lord, he's blind." "Silence!" growls an officer. That was all the attention shown to the request. Previous to sentence, two policemen swear to the prisoner as one of the "swell-mob" (genteelly dressed thieves), which did not mitigate the sentence. And so they go on. I suppose an ordinary case is tried in ten minutes, on which a man's whole life and reputation is staked. The court has no more soul than a threshing machine, and the bar no more sympathy than is in their wigs.

What a relief—a contrast, to turn from this harsh home of justice, to the silent homes of the great, who are buried in the Poet's Corner of Westminster. With what fear and awe are we inspired, as we pass over the graves where Campbell and Sheridan sleep, to see the monument of Shakspeare—so gentle, so meek, so graceful, as he stands upon it, with a scroll of his own verses about the cloud-capped towers and gorgeous palaces of human greatness, that fade, how unlike his own name, and leave not a rack behind!

All about him are names familiar to us as those of our own family, Rowe, Addison, Goldsmith, ("poor Goldy!") Southey, Dryden, "rare Ben," and rarer Samuel Johnson; but why name them? Is not this the repository of England's most precious dust? What a spirit speaks from the urns of these princes and kings of song! How silently, through the mighty medium of type, does it bear on its pinion the elements of beauty, humor, truth and goodness, to make the world purer and holier! How kindly does it bear down to future ages and to the extremest parts of the earth, the riches of our noble Anglo-Saxon language! And even now, in the polished poetry of Longfellow, and the graceful prose of Irving, is verified, but not to its splendid fulfilment, the prophetic rapture of an old English bard, Daniels, as he speaks of that language which these mouldering forms spoke and wrote:

"And who in time knows whither he may vent
The treasures of our tongue? To what strange shores
This gain of our best glory shall be sent
T' enrich unknowing nations with our stores?
What worlds in th' yet unformed Occident
May come refined with th' accents which are ours."

XXXI.

The Great Exhibition Revisited.

"I would rather believe all the fables of the Talmud, the Legend and the Alcoran, than that this universal frame is without MIND!"

Lord Bacon.

IT is utterly impossible for me even to essay any further expression about the Exhibition, which will in the least degree reflect its great and little wonders. As I entered it again, the same bright and glittering array and the same multiform variety marched before me in sections, regiments and battalions, completely capturing my senses and depriving my pen of its ordinary volubility. I entered with the intention of studying closely certain branches, say that of agricultural implements (having an intelligent farmer friend, Mr. Buckingham, along), but the shortness of my stay here and the immensity of the objects to be studied, admonished me not to undertake so hopeless a work. Upon each entrance to the different departments, I have found some new modification of a familiar thing, some new principle of mechanics, and some additional beauty in Art. The most useful things that I have seen have been the most beautifully finished; and in this, is confirmed a very pleasant truth. Even the locomotive which is marked with a ribbon around its pipe, and a card of the prize medal, is a piece of exquisite beauty, dazzling as a mirror in its steel and brass, and carved into grace at every point where ornament may give grace without detracting from strength. Is it not ever thus in the mental world? Are the sterling and strong metals of thought, any worse for being wrought into rich and elegant figures? Ask Milton, or

Dante, or Bacon, or Shakspeare? The rich colorings of the papier maché, or the exquisitely wrought mosaics of the circular tables, lose none of their elegant proportions, because they are colored. But the most refined beauty is not that of form or color. It lies in the *object* of the thing judged, and the adaptation to attain that object. The closer and more facile that relation, the more beautiful will be the instrument. A churn, simple and unostentatious, worked by a little hand-wheel, but partaking of three motions, rotary, horizontal and perpendicular, combining at once several forces, including atmospheric pressure, and making butter in five minutes with ease, was an object of intrinsic beauty, to be looked at with as much pleasure as any of those splendid silver-wrought ornaments.

A steam plough may be mentioned in the same category. Behind the locomotive are the rotary ploughs. The resistance of the earth they meet with, propels the machine, as the steamboat is propelled by the resistance of the water to the wheel. Of course, such an instrument would be entirely useless in the greatest part of Ohio, where stumps and roots are yet plenty, and where the land is not so light and level, as it is in the greater part of England.

I went through the agricultural implement department, examined what I could, and always left,—wondering at the simplicity and the immense labor-saving property of the instrument studied.

But there is nothing superior to McCormick's reaping machine. I had seen it tried before in Muskingum; knew its peculiarities, and was not astonished that the discerning commissioners awarded McCormick the great prize medal. He bears his honor meekly; says that it will sell much better here than in America; because, 1st, it will save more labor here, since five men sickle in one day what one man in America would cradle in the same time; and 2d, because the ground is more even, and better fitted for its operation. The wages here are less by about a half; so that *that* will make a difference. The reaper has had a good trial and a successful one. Never was the God-given genius of invention better used, than in furnishing for man such beautiful appliances for the farm. It helps to wipe away the elder curse. It dries the sweating brow of the harvest-man, in the moment of golden fruition, when haste, anxiety, care, and more than ordinary labor are called into requisition to save his grain. If America has not been represented in the exhibition by the flaunting silks, embroideries, paintings, glass and marbles which other nations so vauntingly display, she has much to show of the solid, substantial, and useful. Her objects will bear study and scrutiny. It cannot be expected of her, that she should send over cloths of gold, like India and Tunis, nor coronets of diamonds, like Russia. She is young in the finer arts.

> "A Satyr that comes staring from the woods,
> Cannot at first speak like an orator."

But it can speak some rough, shaggy, natural truths, whose virtue lies not in the husk but in the kernel, and which, when examined, will show that *activity of mind toward beneficent ends*, which is the highest reach of all arts.

America has had her own absolutely necessary work to do since she whipped her mother. She has been at home doing it, like a good housewife. She has not been gadding about, peeping into this keyhole, and stealing into that corner, in order to enrich her industrial designs. She has been

> ——— "struggling with the oak
> In search of *bread and home*, has learned to rive
> Its stubborn boughs, till limbs, once lightly strung,
> Might mate in cordage with its infant stems."

And, as in the young Hercules the astrologers read the lines of after-strength, so in the lineaments of America may now be read those of Empire. God has written them, in great mountains, rivers, lakes, men and energies, all over the face of the Union.

It seemed to me as if I could read them, in epitome, in the bust of Webster, which since I was last here has been added, with good taste, to the American department. Spirit of Phidias! would you not take it for a loftier god than your own Jove? How massive the brow, how full of will are the lines around the mouth—how commanding, all! An American, not a partisan, is Webster abroad. There was some sting, but great truth, in the remark, that Webster was the greatest animal and the greatest man in America. His brain, even in its contour of marble, tell both.

By his side is a lifelike model of Oliver Twist, from America. It is much looked at. I stood by, watching alternately the little wo-begone victim of a peculiar state or crust of English society, in his tatters and troubles, and the sympathetic old women who came up to see and remark upon little Oliver. "What a pity, to be sure! I suppose he has a history, poor boy!" He has, old lady, and perhaps part of it has been under your own nose. "I wonder if he is not some rich man's son, strayed off or stolen by the gipsies?" and with such-like commentaries upon the image of him whose history is far more familiar in America than in England, they pass unreflectingly by.

I examined with great care the Chinese rooms. They reward the care. Specimens of rare jars and paintings, together with most elaborate ivory carvings, do the Chinese justice, I trust. They are a large nation, and should be well represented. Besides, they have begun to fight and bestir themselves lately; and who knows but that the Celestial feet may, under destiny, be leading silently towards the temple of the Union, for that annexation which their friends across the Pacific enjoy? Some of their maxims, which are blazoned boldly in their rooms, bespoke for them a worldly wisdom worthy of annexation and Poor Richard. For instance:

"1. Let every man sweep the snow from before his own

door, and not busy himself about the frost on his neighbor's tiles." Confucius! how that hits some men!

"2. The ripest fruit will not fall into your mouth." Franklin! how that meets *your* approval!

"3. Dig a well before you are thirsty." The Spartan's brevity, and Solomon's wisdom!

"4. Water does not remain on mountains, nor vengeance in a great mind." A lofty thought gushing down a mountain mind!

In going through the Exhibition, there attaches to many departments an added interest, because we have seen the natives at home in their workshops, attaining the results here so magnificently alluring. At Brussels, for instance, we saw the Flemish girls making their fingers fly, as they leaned over the pillow upon their laps, with the pattern pricked into black paper, tacked to the pillow, and the paper full of pins, around and across which they were passing, with rapid skill, the numerous little linen spools of thread, to form the elegant figures and delicate tracery of the richest laces. At Gobelins we saw the tapestries slowly evolving from the massive loom. At Rome, we saw the mosaics grow into beauty and life under the patient hand of the artist. At Genoa, we beheld the filigree-goldsmiths educing forms of light grace out of the silver. At every turn we see objects that we have seen in bazaars for sale, and forms and figures whose prime originals dwell in everlasting freshness upon the marbles of the Acropolis or the walls of Pompeii.

But in seeing all here in one vast repertory, we possess the pleasure of *comparison*, which is the greatest provocative to remembrance, and the greatest hindrance to intolerance; for where there is so much to be seen and studied, spurs to memory are needed, and intolerance has been as virulent, at times, in art and science, as in politics and religion. The great object of this exhibition has been to break down the contracted barriers of intolerance and nationality, so that industry may fraternize and the people be elevated. England will receive an immense pecuniary benefit from the Exhibition, no doubt; but this was not the primary intention. Her artists and artisans will glean much from these displays wherewith to enrich her future. This was one of the professed objects of the Palace, but not its highest. The highest object was the cultivation of international good-will. The people of Europe cannot lose by this. The despots may. Foreign wars have been often used by tyrants to inflame national prejudices, so as to repress the better feelings of independence and liberty. The foreigners who visit England must go home with new ideas of their own about civic wants and oppressions. And although there is nothing in war I do not detest, yet when begun by a people against old, irresponsible, hereditary powers, the heart would desire its bloody continuance until every symbol, form, and official instrument of power were exterminated, root and branch. I pray God that such a war may come. It is the *only way*—steel and powder—the only way of unloosing the gripe of the Austrian and Russian, and I may add of the French, upon the liberties of Europe. Peace-societies may preach and sing psalms till doomsday; but the arch-scoundrel of Naples and the petty princes of Germany will laugh and hold on. International wars may Heaven avert, and turn the bayonet and cannon against the palaces, castles, and forts, built by robbing tyrants to intimidate, so as better to prey upon, their own people.

They talk of turning the Crystal Palace into a Winter Garden. The plan is disapproved of by many, but approved of by more. Its image has become so familiar that it can be illy spared. It has been infinitely reproduced. Boys cry it in the streets: "'Ere's the Crystal Palace on a medal, or on a breast-pin, or on a card, *h*only a penny—'ave one, sir?" All the print-shops show it, in every size and color and mode of art. It has had a long season, and meanwhile it has taught many a severe, many a delightful lesson. This one truth it teaches above all others, that the effluence of Deity—the subtle mind of man—has powers of insight and apprehension that can never cease to mould its images and produce its results. Immortality must be the goal of such creative power, and shall not that immortality find repose at last in HIS presence, who delighted in the works of His own hands, when he saw that they were good, and whose Palace, from everlasting to everlasting more crystalline than light, is eternal in the heavens!

XXXII.

Windsor Scenes and Sports.

> " There is an old tale goes, that Herne, the Hunter,
> Sometime a keeper here in Windsor forest,
> Doth all the winter time, in still midnight
> Walk round about an oak, with great ragged horns."
>
> *Shakspeare.*

I MUCH prefer the railroad route up the valley of the Thames, past Richmond to Windsor, to any other ride in the environs of London. A whole day must be given to it at the least. Cars leave Waterloo bridge station almost hourly, and before you are aware of it, you are ushered, by the unpoetical steam-car, through Windsor Forest, where Herne the Hunter took his round, and where the fairies danced in the jocund moonlight to plague Falstaff for his sins.

The railroad station is under the shadow of the Castle ; which is a congregation of towers and buildings of stone somewhat ancient—some of them even dating back to Cæsar, but fitted up with every comfort for the residence of the Queen, who delights, it is said, to retire here.

We easily obtained admission to the halls and reception rooms of the Castle. The portraits of the Stuarts, especially of the unfortunate Charles I., and his family, by Vandyke, are fine artistic pieces, more admirable than their power-besotted originals. The line of heavy Dutchmen (always excepting the bright and manly form of William III.), who followed the Stuarts, hung upon the walls of the splendid dining halls. Elegance, taste, and richness, beyond comparison with any thing except Versailles, are displayed throughout the apartments. The object of all, the Queen herself, had just left Windsor for the Isle of Wight, where the yatching season is opening.

We rode up in the cars, with the India-rubber man to the Queen. He was visiting the riding-school to line the riding-rings with India-rubber. "Why?" do you ask? As an Englishman would say—"Don't you zee,—Hif an 'orse kicks and makes a sound, he kicks again. Hif he kicks hindia-rubber, don't you zee, he makes no sound. He don't kick again. The 'orses are spirited and high kept. They never kick twice at hindia-rubber. Don't you zee, zur?" The transcendentalism of the above, I would love to enlarge upon. The Queen and her children practise daily in the riding-rings at Windsor, and extend their drives through the adjacent parks.

From the towers or from the terrace there is one of the grandest views in England. Twelve counties can be seen. Eton, in neat Gothic, and white compared to the buildings of the metroplis, the nursery of the greatest and best of England, lies immediately below. Slough, where Gray is buried, and the churchyard in which he composed his elegy, are plainly discernible. There is intervening and every where filling up the view, the greenest, goodliest English landscapes we have yet admired. The Royal relatives, including the Queen's mother, whose wealth has been unsparingly bestowed to decorate these vales and hills, reside in the precincts of Windsor.

But what immense area is that, stretching over 6,000 acres, measuring a circuit of 48 miles, interspersed with the lime, chestnut, beech, holly, fir, and oak?—None other than the Windsor Forest, upon whose domain we intrenched when we entered the tower below. Look down the green lane, miles long, known as Queen Anne's walk, and terminated by a colossal statue of George III.,—with its triple roads, and you will see a part of our magnificent drive to the Virginia Waters. These waters lie on the other side of the forest; consequently we shall have a ride through the fairy-haunted greenwood.

But before we go, let us give a few thoughts to that dim elder day, which arose with Chaucer, and beamed upon these leafy walks and gray battlements. It was here that our Helicon's first stream gushed in its own native and rugged simplicity. Irving visited here in the genial month of May, when the birds twittered musically in the groves, and wrote his sketch of the Royal poet—James I. of Scotland—who was imprisoned for many years of his youth, by Henry IV. in the castle. While a prisoner, he fell in love with one of the maidens of the court, and poured forth his plaint like a caged nightingale. But *his* song is but a tiny voice in that grand choral harmony of English bards, whose leader, Chaucer, trod these very paths, and attuned his lyre under these gnarled oaks. Well has Campbell sung of Windsor and Chaucer:—

"Should thy bowers in ivied ruin rot,
There's one, thine inmate once, whose strain renowned
Would interdict thy name to be forgot.
———He led the way
To welcome the long after-coming beam
Of Spenser's light and Shakspeare's perfect day!"

To read the quaint old bard, somewhat grimly smiling, as it were, through a rusty visor,—to catch the genuine humor and natural poetry of his soul, as he tells his tales of Canterbury,—to do this, without visiting Windsor, is a rare joy; but to re-read Chaucer, after having seen his haunts,—well, wait till the bright fire snaps in the winter evening, when we have our gown and slippers on, with the wind whistling bleakly; methinks, then, these scenes of to-day will help to open the chambers of fancy, light the flame of imagination, and bid the Old Muse sing with heartiest song.

These grounds of Windsor were the favorite residences of the Georges—kings of England. How much time, care and money has been bestowed by them in introducing Virginia Water into the park! It was formed when the Duke of Cumberland, the hero of Culloden, resided in the large red maze of building, wherein the hounds of Prince Albert were baying deep-mouthed when we passed; and it is the largest artificial piece of water in the realm. The streams of the neighborhood are collected into a basin, which is adorned and margined in its winding picturesqueness with leafy copses, and a velvet sward. Our grassplots do not give one the idea at all of that velvety, spongy smoothness which I mean, when I speak of the English lawn. A dark glen or ravine receives the water—after it falls in a cascade of some twenty feet. Around are by-paths, inviting the foot to wander at pleasure, through every variety of shade. The trees are none of them so high as our best forest trees, but they have the tough old venerableness that Chaucer loved, and the neat trim of architectural beauty. Where clusters of them occur, they are arranged so as to form one top, with happy effect. Deer in great herds crop the grass or sleep under the shade. But their timidity has been long lost. The approach of the stranger excites no attention—no quivering nostril, wild glance or swift bound into the covert. Six thousand deer people the park, to say nothing of other game—plenty as blackberries, kept for Prince Albert's peculiar pastime.

It was one of the finest walks conceivable to leave the carriage and stray along Virginia Water. A man-of-war, flaunting the flags of all nations, lay upon its tranquil bosom—a present to the late Queen Adelaide. Lovers were sauntering most lovingly, and as Yellowplush would say, 'Oh! 'ow 'appily,' along the sward. Swans were swimming along the verdant margin. A little distance from the bank we found the Grecian temple in ruins; an excellent imitation of the temple of Jupiter at Athens. Shelley loved to meditate amidst these witching spots, and perhaps here drank in the spirit of that Beauty which informed his Muse. He resided in the little village of Bishopsgate near by, itself surrounded by every allurement of rural loveliness.

The royal Conservatory is in the midst of the forest, still kept in royal style, affording a resting-place for the Queen when she airs in these woods. Prince Albert has a farm of 500 acres in the midst. It looked as neat as a model. The hay was put up as smoothly as if it were to remain for ever. The stock consisted of a large variety. I should venture out of my sphere if I undertook to tell about farms and their appendages. Silence is discretion. There is a horticultural phenomenon in the forest at the Belvidere worth naming. It consists of one grapevine, off of which was gathered last year over twenty-three hundred pounds of grapes. But under cover. Oh! bless you—if Apollo had not had a glass medium he could not have hit, with his quiver of beams, old Bacchus so plump in the eye,—not in England at any rate.

One may ride 101 miles in this park over the most beautiful road, and surrounded by the most grateful prospect. Yet of the 6000 acres here, only 500 answers God's law. Five thousand five hundred acres will have a poor account to render in their day of judgment. It will not do then to say, "Poetry and beauty required of us our service and our shades. Royalty wished to press our smooth velvet sward, excluded from the vulgar gaze. Aristocrats delighted to drive down our green lanes in fine coaches with arms on them, to indulge flimsy raptures upon the scenes they could not comprehend in their deeper significance. Fairies had their favorite resorts upon

—— "The bank whereon the wild thyme blows,
Where cowslips and the nodding violet grows,
Quite over-canopied with luscious woodbine,
With sweet musk roses, and with eglantine,
Where slept Titania."———

Inquisition will be made for the English poor, and the inquiry will be, Why were these, His own image, famished, while a few —in His eye—no better, are suffered to lord it over such an immense area of bread-growing soil, in search of an antidote to ennui? I believe with Emerson, in the idea of compensation, and would carry it somewhat into the after-life.

The Merry Wives of Windsor, as Shakspeare draws their characters, were never great favorites of mine. I should not put them down as patterns of domestic sobriety, nor of delicate refinement. They would have been unfaithful to the idea of the comedy, had they been so. They would, according to my observation, have belied their locality, had they been otherwise. The day we visited Windsor happened (how fortunate !) to be the anniversary *revel* of the Bachelors of Windsor. Of course, I had a fine chance to see the merry wives. Indeed, I did not see a soul that was not a little cracked with the glee of the day, except those who had been stupefied with too much "sack."

I looked into, it may have been, the Garter Inn, to see where Sir Jack drank sack, and Dame Quickly gossiped; but I only saw a crowd of revellers dancing to a fiddle; the young fellows with long clay pipes in their mouths, shuffling the sandy floor, with red-cheeked, flaxen-haired country damsels.

The revel was established many years ago, by a rich lady, who bequeathed a sum of money and the ground, in the very midst of the town, for the sports. These consist of the old English games, and they are conducted on the old principles. When we went on the ground, some such scene as the following was presented. About twenty thousand people were standing in and around the side hills, overlooking the rings, stage and booths. The folk in our vicinage were holding mugs of ale and stout, with a noisy hilarity as gross as that of the ugliest *villein* in the time of the Conqueror. Soldiers and policemen were numerously interspersed.

Flaxen heads were uncovered in dishevelled riot. The "merry wives" are by no means idle or unconcerned. They were moving among the crowd, enjoying the rude brutality of the hour. The stage was the great object of interest. Two flaxen heads upon it were woolling each other, and trying to trip. A shout announced the result in a fall. Another shout announced a tumble of both off the stage. Again they are at it; the tall one, who is a Northumberland man (says our driver, who knows the peculiarities of skill), gives the lesser one a jerk, which flings his coat over his head, and while blinded, he gives him the soundest fall, amid shouts of merriment. In the mean while, wooden horses, circular boats, and other riding establishments, in the shape of overshot wheels, are gyrating. Dancing, and Punch and Judy, with other entertainments, enliven the booths. Chimney-sweeps are climbing the three greased poles near the stage, in vain—the oily lubricity of the poles is too much for them; and amid derisive cries, they slide down. At last one skilful fellow attained the top, and the noise became deafening. Next came the game of whipping the ball out of the hole. A half dozen are blindfolded. They have long whips with sharp crackers. When the ball came out, the signal was given by an officer, when the blindfolded began most severely to whip each other. Ha! *ha!* HAW! in hearty great guffaws, rung from side to side. The damsels, all crimson, left their partners in the rustic dance, and rushed out to see. The mugs were dropped —the stupid, beer-besotted fellows in white overshirts, open their eyes. "Gad! Tommy! 'ow the little one catches it! Don't they lay it on right soundly, man? Hoorah!" This brutal game of the ball is repeated. It seemed to be one of the most approved sports. We had been too late to see the cricket, and other matches. But we saw enough to know that it was rightly named the Windsor revel.

The corporation of Windsor, to their honor, have tried every means in their power, which included a strong litigation, to get rid of this revel. They have tried to build roads over the place. They are gradually encroaching on the spot. But the Bachelors, who belong to a most ancient order, take great pride in these sports, and have resisted successfully every encroachment upon their prescriptive rights. Besides, the Queen gives ten pounds for it, and her mother a considerable sum.

In passing out of Windsor, we drove by a magnificent equipage, with liveried servants, within which was seated a maiden lady named Miss Harvey Bonnell, the owner of a large estate in the vicinage, with an annual income of $150,000. She was dressed in the style of Queen Anne, consisting of a great white ruff, and a black hat with black ostrich plumes, which waved finely as she bowed to us from her carriage. The lady from whom she inherited the immense estate wore the same costume, and her devisors had the same habit. We would commend the style to the attention of our countrywomen, as we understand that novel modes of dress are in quest among them. The reputation of Miss Bonnell is that of a sane, charitable, noble lady. She is a peculiarity worth notice. Her residence is beautifully situated amidst her elegant grounds, and is a peer even among the royal abodes.

But we must hasten to London; congratulating ourselves on having seen so much of the present and the past, and on our way drawing conclusions not at all unfavorable to the decency, good sense and humanity of the American yeomanry, compared to the "revellers" of Windsor.

XXXIII

Avon---Shakspeare's Home.

> "What needs my Shakspeare for his honor'd bones?
> The labor of an age in piled stones;
> Or that his hallowed relics should be hid
> Under a starry-pointing pyramid?
> ——— Thou our fancy, of itself bereaving,
> Dost make us *marble* with too much conceiving;
> And so sepulchred, in such pomp dost lie,
> That kings for such a tomb would wish to die."
>
> *Milton's Sonnet.*

MORE than a week had we been at London, studying it from the little boats which fret the Thames; from the top of the omnibuses that meander through its winding streets; from St. Paul's cupola; from amid its gardens and parks, its palaces and courts of justice; endeavoring to see every phase of that stirring life called London, and of that strangely industrious and perseveringly active race from which we derive our habits, our laws, and ourselves. Of all the people I have yet seen, if I had to have an ancestry (which is exceedingly uncomfortable sometimes to some people, especially if it happens to run back into a shoemaker or a tailor), I would prefer our own Anglo-Saxon stock. It is a shaggy old oak, rough, intertwisted and stubborn; but it spreads a large and gracious umbrage, and is destined to spread still, a larger and a better shade. The French are too much like their own tall, military-looking, top-plumed poplars, constantly bending to the lightest breeze of fickleness, and only affording slim lumber with the best of sawing.

One thing noticeable among the English is, that they care

more for their physical frames than their descendants in America. We are worn-out, when they are fully matured. Climate has much to do with this, but habit more. An Englishman hardly ever dies. I went down into Hampshire to look after the estate of an old gentleman, whose friends in America thought that he ought to have been dead long ago. On making inquiry, everybody knew him, he had lived so long, and asked me, in return, if he was not the "great cricketer." That is the secret. Manly exercise and constant care had rendered his old age as vigorous as a man in our country would hardly be at forty-five.

We bid London good-bye yesterday morning, and are here in Shakspeare's home, by thy willowy marge—Oh! Avon! Running to Coventry, famous for some of Falstaff's military operations, if I remember rightly, we left the main trunk of the railway and glided into Kenilworth, whose castle Scott has saved from ruin by his incomparable novel; then to Warwick, where the old earls of that name, the "King Makers," in the earliest eras of English history, resided, and where an earl of the same title now lives. We stopped to see its exterior; and taking a fly, ran over a fine road commanding an excellent view of the rolling fields of Avon vale. The harvesting was almost over. Poor women were gleaning the fields, and farmers and their men were getting in their wheat. The Avon is not much larger than one of our creeks. Its banks are low and shaded with willows, which mark its course as it winds through the green meadows, until it passes through Stratford.

Our first visit was to the house where Shakspeare was born; a rude, half-cottage, upon one of the principal streets of the town, easily discernible by its unique and aged appearance. It bears an antique sign—"THE IMMORTAL SHAKSPEARE WAS BORN IN THIS HOUSE."

A tidy old lady, who takes care of it for the Shakspearean Society, to whom it belongs, welcomed us; and showed us the room where the immortal Bard first caught the light and breath of life. It is a little room with low ceiling, all scribbled over, black with names, among which is the autograph of Schiller. The name of Walter Scott is also shown, cut by himself upon the glass window.

Not a descendant of the Bard remains. It was enough to have had such offspring as Macbeth, Lear and Othello. His dust reposes in a church of the town, which we reached under a canopy of green trees. The original bust in stones said to have been taken from the Bard himself, is there. There is no question about its being a likeness, not a fancy-piece. It was originally colored and painted, so as to resemble Shakspeare; but Malone, the commentator, had it painted over white, for which meddlesome work he has been greatly censured,—and to have punished whom Charles Lamb longed to have been a contemporaneous justice of the peace in Warwickshire. Underneath an old slab lies the body, which has never been removed; mankind kindly heeding the spirit of the inscription, composed by the poet himself;

"GOOD FRIEND FOR JESUS' SAKE FORBEAR
TO DIG THE DUST INCLOSED HEARE,
BLEST BE YE MAN YT SPARES THES STONES
AND CURST BE HE YT MOVES MY BONES."

His family reside in their narrow homes near him. His daughter Susannah, has this quaint inscription upon her slab:

"Witty above her sexe, but that's not all
Wise to Salvation was good Mistris Hall,
Something of Shakspeare was in that, but this
Wholy of him with whom she's now in blisse.
Then, passenger ha'st ne'er a tear,
To weep with her that wept with all?
That wept, yet set herself to cheer
Them up with comforts cordiall,
Her love shall live, her mercy spread,
When thou ha'st ne'er a teare to shed.

Right touching and gentle—is it not?

But we must leave these sacred precincts, to wander forth into the green lanes where the youthful poet wandered, and where he developed that faculty divine, by which he swept the realm of song with an all-potent sceptre. Through pleasant ways by thatched cottages, along hill-sides and down vales, we reached the spot where Shakspeare's young heart thrilled and trembled many a time and oft; for near that cottage by the road-side, where the peas and corn now grow within the hedge, he was wont to see his Anne Hatheway. Within lived old John Hatheway, whose beautiful daughter the poet espoused. Imagination could run wild in picturing scenes hereabout, with Shakspeare for the hero; but most, it loves in this rural spot to paint him as the *gentle* Shakspeare,

> ——— ——— "Fancy's child
> Warbling his native wood-notes wild."

Nine miles from Warwick are these localities which are so rich in memory. Over a lovely landscape winds the large and shaded road—a landscape, ever fringed with green hedges and yellow with the abundant harvest. The people of this region I liked. They seemed affable and gentle, compared to the ordinary rude and rough people to be met with around London and Windsor. An Englishman generally acts as if he thought it extremely feminine to move out of the road or show a civility. Ladies are to him, apparently, objects upon which he may exhibit his characteristic rudeness. Of course there are exceptions to this; but we have found them rare. In Italy or France we have never known an incivility. But here, from the porters of public places, the drivers of omnibuses, and from the officers of the railroads, we have received a nameless gruffness, which may be accounted manliness, but which is certainly ill-breeding and gross impudence. The policemen are conspicuous exceptions. From them one may learn every direction, with the utmost blandness and good nature. In Turkey, in Greece, in Italy and France, and especially in Switzerland, we have found our guides and waiters always pervious to good humor, and exceedingly apt at joking and pleasant conversation—ever ready to understand and join heartily in a laugh. Not so in England. There is a sort of pseudo-dignity which renders each good-humored sympathy as much feared as poison. Sam Wellers are *raræ aves.* Honest, credulous, pompous Pickwicks are common. They are ever ready to receive with implicitness the most improbable story, if it is out of their sphere, which consists of an experience in English breakfasts and dinners, and reading the Times. Far better informed about England is our population, than the population of England about America. The ordinary people want to know if we have telegraphs and railroads; and when informed of their extent in our country, receive the information with the amazement and the implicit reliance which a revelation from Heaven would engender. Several times we have been the object of special wonder because we spoke English like one of themselves, and because we were —white!

It is no uncommon subject of merriment among Americans, that even well-educated Englishmen have frequently asked the most unsophisticated questions in relation to our society, its language and customs.

XXXIV.

A Glance at Ireland.

"The grave abound in pleasantries, the dull in repartees and points of wit."
Addison.

IT would be ungracious in the extreme to suffer the fatigues of a voyage from America, and return without a glimpse, at least, of Ireland. We have devoted, therefore, the last ten days of our stay to a circuit which includes Dublin and Belfast, and extends into Scotland.

We awoke at Kingstown, Ireland, this morning, the 24th of August. Hurriedly dressing, we rushed out of the boat, for the Dublin cars. It was raining. Not being perfectly awake, I did not perceive the state of the weather, until some broth of a boy, with a carriage, shouted, 'Sure, and is it the likes of you that will let your leddies walk in the rain?' while another, a porter, suggested to my companion: 'An it's you that's so well dressed, that you will not carry your own portmanteau?' I felt sure that I was in Ireland.

Dublin town is remarkable for nothing, unless it be a fine park, wide straight streets, an elegant custom-house, brick houses, and a monument or so. The shoeless women and tattered children to be seen in the streets bespeak the truth, that Ireland is indeed wedded to poverty. A great many persons from too much zeal in Protestantism, attribute all the misery of Ireland to her peculiar religion. The mischief lies deeper,—in the tenure of the soil. No one can travel through the Catholic countries which we have seen, especially those in Switzerland, and conclude that Catholicism, in and of itself, tends to produce poverty, or that it is not favorable, when left free and pure, unconnected with politics, to the growth of manliness and virtue. A more generous and a nobler people never lived than some of those Alpine Catholics. The same may be said of some parts of Germany. At Heidelberg, we found the pleasing anomaly of Catholic and Protestant simultaneously worshipping in the same church. The people there seem pervaded with the gentle tolerance of Melancthon, who was educated at Heidelberg University. What a shame it is, that the people of Ireland are not permitted to enjoy their own religion with the same freedom with which the Protestants of England enjoy theirs.

Catholicism is as much the religion of the Irish *people* as Protestantism is that of England. For years its enjoyment, under such officers and in such modes as they might see fit, has been guaranteed. Even the English Lord-lieutenant has addressed the Catholic primates, by the titles which they have here assumed, and has sent soldiers to guard their assemblies from disturbance; when, all at once, on the pretext afforded by Cardinal Wiseman's case, these titles are declared illegal, as well in Ireland as in England; and penalties enacted against those who wear them, as if they were in a horrible conspiracy against the majesty of Victoria. How magnanimous, this, most truly! What if the Roman cardinals be corrupt, as no doubt they are; what if English Protestant worship be hardly tolerated at Rome; what if the good-hearted Pope issues his rescript? Is there any danger herein to the English hierarchy? and if there were, shall the Irish clergy be placed under ban and penalty therefor, especially after so long an encouragement? Into what dilemmas and absurdities will not a nation run, that does not strictly adhere to the most unlimited toleration, or that connects its civil with its religious establishment. A great meeting of Irish clergymen and people, has lately been held. There is but one spirit breathing throughout their proceedings,—united resistance to this unexampled aggression. England could not render Ireland more ungovernable by any other act than that of the last session about the ecclesiastical titles, for it strikes at her religion—the most sensitive part of every society. Let resistance, strong and steadfast, be made; and let the American people, Catholic and Protestant, sympathize in a movement, whose object is to resist the most miserable intolerance that has disgraced the English statute-book since the time when Dissenters and Catholics alike, were at the mercy of Jeffries, and when conformity to the established church, was a principle and a practice, at once repugnant to reason and humanity.

The Church of England can gain nothing, but must lose much, by its coercive measures towards the Catholics. Persecution will do its old work, by creating devotees around the altars of the persecuted.

It is Sunday in Dublin. They call it a "walking Sunday," because there are no festivities or glees on hand, but every one *walks* about soberly and decently; a prelude to the uproariousness of the coming Fair week. To-morrow the grand fair begins at Donnybrook, a little streamlet, upon whose banks the Irish gather in crowds, to spend and lose all they have, in gaming, drinking and dancing. We took a car, an outside one, and visited the spot, in company with Mr. Mowatt, a friend in Dublin, whose humor was as amusing as his attentions were kind. The car is peculiar in itself, and peculiar to, as well as common in, Dublin. It is a sulky, with low wheels, and seats directly over the wheels. The passengers ride sideways, their feet resting outside the wheels on a footboard, and the driver sits aloft upon a seat in front, full of wit, which, like his whip, is constantly on the crack. Six can ride on the outside. It is like an omnibus on two wheels, with all the top off, and the seats back to back—very light, and a convenient observatory of men and manners in the streets. We arrived at Donnybrook, and found many thousands gathered in the green fields, looking at the erection of the booths, preparatory for the morrow. Already the houses and taverns about were full of revellers. Scotch whiskey, bagpipes and fiddling, were going, in conjunction with pattering feet upon sanded floors. Pipes and apples, toys and cakes, were being vended by witty rogues. But every thing was decent, and in order. The "bating the police with shillelaghs," and the bloody noses, do not become dramatic, until the fair is fairly opened. Then look out!

Passing fine houses, and through airy streets, enjoying the humorous repartees of our driver, we drove by Nelson's column, and penetrated the Park. It is an extremely large area, full of deer and game, and specially kept for the recreation of the Lord-lieutenant. A fine monument to Wellington, not unlike that of Bunker Hill, is in the midst, overlooking the hills of green upon the south, and the city with its river Anne Liffey (named after a King's daughter who was drowned in it whilome), over whose waters are numerous handsome bridges, connecting the city. Nelson and Wellington! England's proudest boast; the hero of the sea, and the hero of the land. Why should they be so conspicuously honored by Ireland? Why? Because they remembered England's glory, and not Irish ruth? The Duke has been indeed "iron," so far as Ireland claimed his sympathy. He has none of the impetuous open-heartedness which ever marks the true son of Erin.

To-day we have experienced very cold weather. It may be accounted for here in this wise. It is the 24th of August, St. Bartholomew's day. The Irish have a maxim,

"St. Bartholomew
Brings the cold dew."

Upon this day he puts a stone into the waters, which turns the river-water all cold, and the well-water all warm; and this continues until St. Patrick's day, 17th of March, when that clever old saint turns the stone, and renders the wells cold, and the rivers warm. How many scientific disquisitions and meteorological observations are saved by such a simple tradition!

There are two extensive poor-houses here, with over ten thousand in each; and yet the beggars of Dublin are as thick as leaves at Vallambrosa. The country looks finely, the harvests are heavy, and the large park, eight miles around, seems to smile derisively at the poverty of the people. Land owners live in England, and their agents remain here to rob both them and the tenants. Here is the capital defect of the social system. It needs an axe at the root.

We took but a glance of Northern Ireland, and this portion of the isle is almost a Paradise, compared to the southern portion, where starvation ever cowers and shivers. And yet no part of any land that we have seen, reveals so much destitution, rags and beggary, as the north of Ireland. Of Belfast I can but say, that no American city of the same size presents so much activity and commercial life; while, at the same time, it is laid out with an elegance which betokens foresight and grace. Belfast is the seat of the linen manufacture. The fields in and around it were snow white with linen blanching in the sun; while the country between Drogheda and Belfast waved with the flax, some of which was in process of pulling. But the towns between Dublin and Belfast, including Drogheda—what a picture of poverty did they present! The women, in tatters, hung around our vehicle, and when it drove off, boys by the dozen ran after us, turning somersets, and using every insinuation which native Irish wit could suggest, to obtain alms. "*Will you! will you!—gentlemon, throw me a ha'penny?*" and with other exclamations, they followed until the ha'penny was thrown, when a young Irish melée occurred in a scramble for the copper, which generally issued in some bloody noses, that required additional coppers to stanch. It was no better, if bread was thrown. A company of famished wolves could not dart with more singleness, or less ferocity of purpose, after the bread. And yet in this depth of poverty the gleams of an invincible humor flashed from the laughing lips of the little starveling imps; as it were, gleams of sunshine in bright cheerful bars, irradiating a dungeon's darkness.

How kindly is that Providence distributed, which thus lightens the fetters of circumstance. Who knows what genius lives, waiting development, in these elfish urchins, that emit such sparkles of fun, as they run after the traveller for the penny? The atmosphere of gross earthliness encircles and taints the clear beams of that soul which God has created with such subtle yet latent apprehension. It is solid truth, that there are hidden energies under the clouds of ignorance. This is the seminal principle of our educational systems—the germ of that hopeful ness, from which the stability of the future, as well as the pro gressiveness of the race, spring. Would that these young blos soming energies, only blooming to be nipped by "the eager air" of poverty and crime, could be early transplanted to a more genial soil!

The country looks as if already deserted by its working people. Houses are empty, fields look neglected, and hedges are untrimmed. True, there is a heavy harvest; but it is gathered by hands that work slowly, and that lack the impulse which proprietorship and enjoyment ever bestow. We understood that those who were gathering the crop of wheat, and of flax, received but a ha'penny per day! To be sure they were found—but a cent a day for harvest hands! Some index of the prevailing destitution may be found in the signs so common, "Licensed to sell spirits," and the crowd of idlers which such signs always collect. This may, in part, account for the mud-houses, where filth and poverty are the presiding Penates. But where are the gilded flies that fatten on this corruption? Where are the landlords who dole out their ha'pennies per diem to these images of God, for the use of their muscles and energies? Oh! living in England most sumptuously. They heed not the shriek of penury for bread. They affect to believe that no faces are sallow, that no sunken eyes peer out of their tenant mud-houses. The curses of the destitute muttered in secret, give them a sullen joy, that their lot is not like that of the ungovernable, untractable, and whiskey-drinking Irish.

Even Belfast, so beautiful and prosperous, is not wanting

in illustrations of Irish destitution. They crowd around the hotels, and besiege the landings. The heart grows sad and heavy to see so much of the same wretchedness. Would to God that some relief could be discerned for Ireland! England will only learn how to treat her, when she finds the green isle depopulated by emigration.

XXX..

Scotch Scenery and Genius.

"Rear high thy bleak majestic hills,
Thy sheltered valleys proudly spread,
And, Scotia, pour thy thousand rills,
And wave thy heaths with blossoms red."
Roscoe.

HOW different is Scotland in its social appearance from impoverished Ireland! We hear the same peculiar intonations of voice, called the brogue, and this, with the peat beds, is about all that resembles Ireland. You may remember, however, that the north of Ireland was originally settled by the Scotch. This will account for the similarity of brogue.

We left Belfast at sundown, and arrived at Ayr, not very far from the mouth of bonnie Doon, by sunrise. Here, where Burns used to walk and sing, we met the first genuine Scotchmen on their native heaths, and heard the musical cadences of

"That tongue which Godlike heroes spoke,
Which Oram, Ullin, Ossian, sung;
The tongue which spurned the Roman yoke,
When thraldom o'er the world was flung."

But since we landed at Ayr, we have heard it in the Highlands, where Sandy spoke the unquestioned Gaelic drawn from an undefiled well, and where scawns and oaten-meal cakes were eaten, and the descendants of the clans prided themselves upon their brave ancestry.

Our ride to Glasgow by rail from Ayr upon a rainy morning, was without incident. The great commercial metropolis of Scotland, I had almost said of Great Britain, for it is the third city of the realm, has a noble history, as well as numerous points of local interest. The reader of Scotch history and literature will need no refreshing, as to the scenes here enacted, when the Covenant was a matter of life and death; or when Bailie Nichol Jarvie here lived and gossipped. The Clyde has formed many associations with the minds of the gifted in its ebbing and flowing; and none stronger than that with the poet Campbell, who was born at Glasgow; and who, after a long absence from his native stream and city, found the nineteenth century at work, with its coal and iron elements, destroying much of the poetry of the spot. He found it *improved* as we in America would say; and lamented in verse,

> "That it no more through pastoral scenes should glide,
> My Wallace's own stream, and once romantic Clyde."

On going up the Clyde, we found it full of craft. Iron steamers were plying up and down its muddy waters. Thousands of workmen were repairing and building other iron steamers. The clink of hammers resounded on every side. Energy never lags or slackens here. No wonder, with such calls as the world makes for Scotch iron and Scotch machinery.

Material prosperity walks abreast with charity and education in Glasgow. You may see this, without examining statistics, in the bright benevolent faces which pass you on the pave. My time will not permit me to speak of the monuments, edifices and institutions of this city. I would love to do so, for there is a close similitude between the American and Scotch character in all its developments, which is worthy of a Plutarch's parallel. The "*perfervidum ingenium Scotorum*" or, as the French term it, "*Fier comme Ecossais*," by which they manage to accumulate—to "get along" in the world, is so peculiarly Yankee, as to have attracted the attention of writers and travellers very frequently. There is no stupidity or slowness in a Scotchman's look or movement. Besides, the Scotch have the logic—the intellect of

Great Britain, that is, the superior mind, the commanding mind of the island. Edinburgh has ruled for a half century from her throne of rocks, the realms of politics, taste, and philosophy, with a potency that Bonaparte feared, even though it was exercised by 'paper pellets of the brain.' And does she not deserve the epithet of modern Athens? Is she not the "eye" of Great Britain? Was it not by a son of Caledonia, that the great, vital and universal principles of political economy received enunciation, an enunciation which time has not bettered—only confirmed? Is this not the home of Hume, Browne, Stuart, Scott, and Chalmers? But why dwell on these elements of greatness.

Farewell to the sooty exhalations of Glasgow—the mud boats of the Clyde—the monuments of Scott and Sir John Moore, and the Necropolis. Ho! for the Highlands! where the air of romance weaves its spell of enchantment, where nature paints the heather and makes musical the rill, where the Lochs reflect the Bens, and the old bare-headed Bens are peopled with cloud shadows and clouds themselves; where the clansmen once fought in the close defiles, and the misty heroes of Ossian came and went like the unresting shadows which lie 'in bright uncertainty,' upon the moving lake.

How had I longed to see Lomond and Katrine, with their isles and glens, their mountains and moors! Leaving Glasgow in the steamer in the afternoon, we reach Dumbarton, whose rock at the junction of the Leven and Clyde rises to the height of nearly 600 feet, measuring a mile in circumference at its base, terminating in two sharp points, studded with houses and battlements. Here, in one of the towers of Wallace's seat was the prison of that warrior, after his base betrayal by Sir John Monteith. A goodly number of heroic adventures, among which is the taking of the castle at its most formidable point, are connected with Dumbarton. A Captain Crawford, during one of those relentless wars which desolated Scotland in Queen Mary's time, contrived by scaling ladders to reach the summit of the crags; and was proceeding with the men to enter the battlements, when one of them, while climbing, was struck with apoplexy, probably induced by excessive terror. He could neither go up nor down. To have slain him would have been cruel; besides, his fall would have created alarm. What was to be done? Invincible to the last, Crawford tied him to the ladder, then turned it over, and with his men gained the summit, by mounting the other side from that to which the apoplectic soldier was tied, slew the sentinel, and accomplished one of the most daring feats ever achieved, even in this wild Scottish warfare.

The town of Dumbarton has nothing in itself worthy of notice. The old ruin upon the opposite side of the Clyde is the Castle of Cardross, where Robert Bruce (whose crown we saw to-day in the Castle of Edinburgh) breathed his last. But if we should undertake to tell of all the renowned castles and battle-fields we have seen, during the last few days, a volume would be necessary to contain them.

Let us at once take cars, and hurry up to Balloch, where the little steamer is awaiting us. The rain will hardly permit us five minutes at a time upon the deck. Clouds, dark and lowering, roll over the highlands, and are succeeded by sunshine. Rainbows and mountain-tops,—the purple heather of the isles and hills,—the baldness of old Ben Lomond, his head silvered with a cloud, sunlit and beautiful,—the darkish waters of the lake, vexed and whitened,—together with an original, *sui generis* wildness, that only belongs to Scottish scenery,—made up a view, our admiration for which could not be dampened by any rain nor enlivened by any sunshine.

The lake is full of green, rocky isles. Indeed, Lomond signifies "many-isled." As we approach our destination, Invernsnaid, the loch grows more narrow, until it seems lost among mountains of mist. While going along, gazing upon islet and shore, ever and anon turning to see the reverend form of Ben Lomond, we should not forget that the fierce clan of the Mac Gregors were once here, in their pride and power; that it was while rowing down this loch, that the song for the gathering of the clan was sung:

> "The moon 's on the lake, and the mist 's on the brae,
> And the clan has a name that is nameless by day,
> Then gather, gather, gather, Gregalich!"

It is pleasant, too, to think, as we step on shore at Invernsnaid, that Wordsworth has been here before us, and that his Muse, ever seeking the covert beauties and sympathies of nature, had rendered classic the spot and cascade by his exquisite poem called "The Highland Girl." We rested all night near the cascade, within sight and hearing of its wild foaming and music. From the top of the mountain, over which we go toward Katrine, it rushes, with many interpositions of rock and tree, bristling and white, until it plunges, sheer and broken, out of a clump of pines into a boiling basin, where it hisses and steams until it finds placidity in the Loch Lomond below. It was right grand to clamber up from crag to crag, leaping from rock to rock, and at last finding solid foothold under the flashing, foaming mass, and near the trembling, spraying abyss,—to sit beneath the 'sweat of great agony' wrung from out this Highland Phlegethon that swayed in the wind which roared madly up the glen and amid the brae. True, it was not Niagara; nor are Lomond, Ben Ledi, Ben Ann, and their associates, like the Alps. They are but an abridged edition of them, with many of the finest figures and loftiest sentiments omitted; yet how much is here for the finest capacity to grasp and mould into mirrors "radiant with fair images." Wonder not that Fingal, and those children of the mist, waked by Ossian, here had their local habitation. Wonder not that Scott has inwoven such a rich and weird web of romance around

> All the fairy crowds
> Of islands that together lie
> As quietly as spots of sky
> Among the evening clouds.

Well have the people of Edinburgh erected the Gothic monument to Scott—rising so solidly, yet so lightly, in such fair proportions, looming so loftily in the shadow of their Acropolis! Well have they honored Burns too, whose heart and soul sung a song for Scotia's sake, and whose genius has rendered more immortal than the Alps the mountains of Caledonia. Scott and Burns!—noble duümvirate! They have monuments—not alone in Edinburgh, but every peak and castled crag form monuments to their undying fame!

Why—what is that wild Loch Katrine, with its green gem called Ellen's Isle—its Rob Roy's prison; its Rhoderick Dhu's watchtower,—and its Ben Venue; its groves vocal with the music of birds; its hundred white mountain streams, its bleached sand silvered by the wash of the clear wave; its wild goats climbing where no other feet, save those of the bird, can venture; its clumps of wood and ample fields, and, near by, its Trossachs, so wildly beautiful; what is all this without the creative genius which has peopled the isle, the moor, the mountain and the glen with the Lady of the Lake, the Douglass, the merry roaming King Fitz James, and the wild Roderick!

We found a tiny steamer ready to ply toward the Trossachs, and there we found an open carriage and an understanding driver, who talked queerly in the Gælic, as he gave us the legend which clung to each spot to beautify and embalm.

A few hours' ride and we were in sight of Stirling Castle. The superior attraction of this brave old rocky seat of power, drowns the associations of the Highlands. We cannot stop to paint the scene where Roderick and Fitz James fought, nor where the latter lost his gallant gray; for we are surmounting at Stirling the very seat of James V. himself; around which the sports and games of the olden time were enacted. We enter the halls of the kings—look at each old memento, not forgetting the big tarpaulin-looking hat worn by Cromwell. I am no hero-worshipper, but there are some peculiarities which Old Noll had that tickle my fancy, if they do not engage my worship, such as praying with a lot of solemn Scotchmen from six in the afternoon till three in the morning, in order to lull suspicion, and create the impression that he was quite godly.

The view from Stirling Castle is magnificent, only surpassed in Scotland by the view we enjoyed to-day from the Castle of Edinburgh. Below are the garden spots once laid out by the mother of Queen Mary, and to the north is a small castle, where so many executions took place, and where the death axe sounded so frequently.

Not far, is the scene of one of Sir William Wallace's most splendid engagements, where he disputed the passage of the Forth by the English army under Cressingham. The Highlands stretch with a bold sweep upon the distant horizon. From Stirling towers, where often the spectator of many a bloody fray stood poised betwixt hope and fear, we took our final view of those homes of song and story,—those Highlands, where the mist seems continually to hover, and the hardy heather seems ever to bloom.

The railroad whirls us past many a scene renowned, prime among which is that famous field of Bannockburn, where Bruce won the day against more than double his number.

We have spent two days in Edinburgh, never ceasing to admire its architectural elegance, both in church and mansion, in castle and monument. But most is the city to be remembered for its Acropolis—that feature which makes it akin to Athens. The view from it is inspiriting and noble, expanding the soul, and almost fitting it with wings "wherewith to scorn the earth." But wherever we go, whether to Scott's monument, to the Old Parliament House, to St. Giles, where Knox talked gospel, where Regent Stuart lies, and Napier the author of the Logarithms reposes, and where the Covenant was signed, to Calton Hill, where monuments and a fragmentary temple mark it prominently; whether to the old Tolbooth or down Canonsgate; in old town or new; whether we enter the old room where Queen Mary slept, in the castle, or look at the palace of Holyrood,—the talk and the cry is "the Queen! the Queen!!" and sure enough, at three o'clock all Edinburgh, and the adjacent country had assembled near the ancient Holyrood, and under the shadow and upon the green sides of Salisbury crags, to see Victoria and her handsome husband. We mingled with the mass, saw the royal folk (plainly dressed people, and really human), and can avouch that no ostentation was displayed by royalty on this occasion. The Queen wore a very ordinary bonnet, without ribbons, shading a reddish ordinary countenance; while Prince Albert looked like a sensible, good-natured, honest German gentleman, as he undoubtedly is. Had we no other evidence of the latter fact, we might find it in the model house which he invented and caused to be erected near the Exhibition Palace, for the purpose of showing how comfortably the poor might be provided for, with little expense.

There was great excitement in the city. The Provost was knighted by a tap on the shoulder from the little Regina; Holyrood smoked and gleamed with life; the people were in groups about it; the railroad cars stood crowned and garlanded near; for the Queen was there in that old home of power, about to leave; and Loyalty stood without, ready to hurrah and throw up its hat!

From Edinburgh our course was over the Border; not omitting, by the way, a visit to Melrose Abbey, the delicate beauty of whose ruins, Poetry has for ever enshrined; to Dryburgh Abbey, the place of sepulture of Sir Walter Scott, and rich in an old Druidical umbrage and in its ivied hangings; to Abbotsford, the repository of the Antiquary's curiosities, and the home of the Author of Waverly; to Fountain Abbey, in North England, —an immense ruin in the noble park of Earl Grey, with all the relics of the monastic age still clustering about tower and transept, nave and prison, kitchen and cloister; and not omitting either the castles, gray and black, which frowned in early days defiant at each other across the Border, now in the decrepitude of age, but, like old soldiers, still vaunting their wounds and strength even in decay. Such visits were not made, be it ever remembered, without crossing thy stream, rushing, romantic Tweed! nor without admiring the select diversity of pastoral beauty, majestic hills, arching bridges, splendid palaces, and the wizard enchantment which dwell in thy sweet valley, Teviotdale!

XXXVI.

Crossing the Border, and the Old Abbeys.

"Within the quiet of the convent cell,
The well-fed inmates pattered prayer, and slept,
And sinned, and liked their penance well."
Bryant.

THIS last day of summer has met us with a most delightful sunshine in this capital of North England, the ancient city of York. It comes, too, upon the holy day, when the air is hushed. A quietude of unaccustomed delight seems showered upon field and grove, minster and wall, as the sunlight glances upon the earth. The cool air, which has so long followed us through Scotland, and down to this city, gently gives way before the warming radiance. The influence woos one from the fireside.

Through manifold turnings, the ancient walls of the city are gained, and easily ascended. How exhilarating is the Sabbath-morning walk along the gray battlements! Spring hath come again in seeming. The birds in the apple-trees below are almost as numerous as the fruitage, and twitter with so transporting a melody, that Silence herself seemeth to listen. It is indeed a 'merry, merry sunshine.' The green hedges glisten with the freshening morning. The lowing of the kine, ever and anon, is borne toward the walls from the country beyond; while, as I turn, the city appears to rest solemnly and still as the gray walls themselves. Chimney-stacks no longer stream with smoke. Their week-day work is done. They join the spires in their silent gesture upward. The Minster—that old York Minster, so celebrated in annals, and so glorious in structure—stands out prominently in the glistening air, with its lofty tower of solid masonry, companioned by two other towers, 'with spiry turrets crowned,' high above the Gothic arches and niches which grace the body of the immense pile. The eye glances at many an old and humble church, with stained windows and blackened stone, half hid in the green copses and red-tiled houses which, intermingling, give the city a rural aspect. The slate roofs here and there may be seen by the dazzling glance of the sun upon them, which, upon this last summer day, makes all nature shimmer in the grateful sheen. The chimes begin their morning hymn, inundating the glittering landscape with viewless waves of sound.

This is a scene that awakens many a memory which the English classics have implanted by their faithful delineations of English town and country. Cowper and Thomson are beneath my eye in their placid, bright, original features. How blessed is that country which can boast so glorious a landscape—so green, so goodly, so pleasing, 'that the harp of Orpheus is not more charming!' How doubly blessed is that country whose native genius hath painted, in undying language, the quiet beauty and cheerful spirit that brood over field and city, dale and hill!

There is a similar pensive beauty clinging to the country throughout the North of England and the South of Scotland—and which may be called 'the Border'—that pleases, and engenders a deep devotional spirit while it pleases. Was it not this peculiarity which led to the erection of such piles as Melrose Abbey, Dryburgh Abbey, and Fountain Abbey? But of these by and by, when we take the reader over the border.

The tramp of many feet upon the pavements indicates the church-going crowd. We have been too long absent from worship not to wish for an hour's communion in the house of God. A stranger need not inquire the way to York Minster; for it is its own great guide to its own great temple. It cannot be surveyed with as much effect from any other point as from the large green upon the north. Buildings surround it upon the other sides, which forbid a view commensurate with its extent and grandeur. Its form is that of a cross; and its appearance, except in a small portion, is rather new, compared with other minsters of England.

We spent some time under an ivy shade, upon a seat of stone, busying the eye in climbing from point to point, and unravelling the Gothic complexity which binds the whole. If you take it apart, you may form numerous large churches and chapels, each one a marvel; each one having its Gothic arches and niches, with windows whose dull colors from the outside inadequately foretell the resplendent beauties which are revealed within. Flowers and leaves, obdurate to frost, bedeck each pinnacle; while spire after spire rise around like a petrified forest. Festoons of stone, richly carved, grace the different arches, while in the niches stand the forms of prophet and saint. Quaint, grim, and humorous heads are protruded at different points. Together, the immense structure constitutes a maze, in which the sight may wander and in grateful variety be lost.

There can be no question but that the Gothic sprung from the green alleys and branching trunks which beautify nature. If we go within, and note the lofty vault, with its intertwisted and adorning branches and foliage, the idea of a forest of giant trees interlaced, cannot be repressed. But as we enter, other thoughts are ours. The organ swells in grand symphony, filling the large temple with a harmonious complexity of music, which well befits such a Gothic pile. Service has begun. The choir is full of worshippers. The chanting floats mildly "upon the easy bosom of the air." The bishop enters the chancel with two other ecclesiastics, preceded by an usher bearing a silver rod. I am a novice in these ceremonies, having been reared in "Dissent," and cannot call things by their right names. But that does not prevent an appreciation of the beautiful service in choice *English*, which issues from the lips of the venerable prelate, and finds reponse in the choir, from the lips of a score of youths in white dresses, whose tenor voices, under some master-tone, rise and fall sweetly in unison with the organ's swell and cadence. Near by, the unresting eye discovers a saintly and martial company, wholly unmoved by this discourse of praise. In stony immovableness they repose upon, and kneel over their own graves—these abbots and bishops in strange uncouth dress, and those soldiers and knights invested with mail and uniform. The light, colored by the stained glass, irradiates their fixed features, fills the air with its purple hue, rests against the huge pillars, and tips the canopies of carved wood which overhang so fitly the Gothic seats.

I noticed here, as at Westminster, that much of the old manner and form is preserved. The ceremony which we heard and saw at Rome was here translated into English, and pruned of many of its formulas; but to us it appeared *ceremony* still. The tendency at present in the English church is decidedly toward the formal, and, consequently, from the spiritual. The good Archbishop of Canterbury has given notice to many of those who minister under his charge, that he will summon them into his court, unless they cease certain practices not "set down" in the Book of Common Prayer: to wit, lighting candles at the altar, turning from the congregation, chanting certain parts of the service, *et cætera*. Well, let the prelates fix the forms of their church as best they may. We simple-worshipping Puritans can only hope that in the form they will ever enshrine, as they have often enshrined, the sincere spirit; and that we may never be ashamed of our plain service and plain meeting-houses, wherein the GREAT OBJECT of all worship is as accessible as in Gothic minsters or Italian basilicas. Nay, have we not what our ancestry had, and what all mankind in common have, that temple which no human art can adorn, where no exclusiveness reigns, and where no intercessor intervenes between GOD and the soul except the SAVIOR? Have we not the temple of Nature? "What a structure is it; and what a glorious adorning is put upon it, to touch the springs of imagination and feeling, and to excite the principles of devotion! What painted or gilded dome is like that arch of blue that swells above us! What blaze of clustered lamps, or even burning tapers, is like the lamp of day hung in the heavens, or the silent and mysterious lights that burn for ever in the far-off depths of the evening sky! And what are the splendid curtains with which the churches of Rome are clothed for festal occasions, to the gorgeous clouds that float around the pavilion of morning or the tabernacle of the setting sun! And what mighty pavement of tessellated marble can compare with the green valleys, the enamelled plains, the whole variegated, broad and boundless pavement of this world's surface, on which the mighty congregation of the children of men are standing! What, too, are altars reared by human hands, compared with the everlasting mountains—those altars in the temple of nature; and what incense ever arose from human altars like the bright and beautiful mountain mists that float around those eternal heights, and then rise above them and are dissolved into the pure and transparent ether, like the fast-fading shadows of human imperfection, losing themselves in the splendor of heaven! And what voice ever spoke from human altar like the voice of the thunder from its cloudy tabernacle on those sublime heights of the creation! And what anthem or pæan ever rolled from organ or orchestra, or from the voice of a countless multitude, like the dread and deafening roar of ocean, with all its "swelling multitude of waves!"

For the last few days we have been visiting the ruins of other temples, those made with human hands, in the middle ages. We have been admiring the elegance of art, as it sprung from the hands of the old freemasons, and the spots where burned the singular devotion of those early scholars and monks whose power evoked such beautiful structures. We look at them more curiously than at the great temple of Nature. Why?

Because human, fraternal sympathies draw us thither. We feel that hearts once beat to impulses kindred with our own, within those cloisters, where now the tenacious ivy clings; that the intellects of the patient schoolmen here pondered the classic tomes their hands preserved, and delved into dialectics more abstruse than any we now have, and formed systems of philosophy as wonderful as they were fruitless; and that here, hospitality once gathered the wayfarers around its ample board in the old abbey, where now the velvet grassplot grows, and the traveller wanders. It is these kindred sympathies which make Melrose, Dryburgh and Fountain Abbeys, such pleasing resorts for the traveller. May I not herein weave an episode of our pilgrimage to these ancient shrines?

Edinburgh was in a tremor of excitement the morning we left for Melrose. A crowd as great as that which gathered the evening before to greet the Queen, now hung darkling about the gates of Holyrood, impatient to see her Majesty enter the crowned and garlanded car, which was awaiting her appearance as we leisurely moved by in our own unostentatious conveyance. Arthur's Seat and Salisbury Crags soon shut out the classic city of the North. The tall castle and ever-beauteous monument to Scott have fixed Edinburgh in our mind as deeply as the Acropolis and the Theseum have fixed Athens. Around them arise the many-storied dwellings and black old churches which give a peculiar air of antiquity to Old Town, and the neatly-pillared fabrics which adorn the vicinage of Queen-street and Crescent-place in New Town.

Thirty-seven miles from these spots, in the fertile valley of the Tweed, where nature is so richly diversified with pastoral slope and majestic hill, we found the finest specimen of Gothic architecture ever reared to the honor of man or the service of God in Great Britain. Its peculiarity consists not in its size, nor its stone, nor its form; but more especially in the perfection of its minute ornaments every where profusely carved, and its elegant proportions on every sides till traceable. Its form was that of the Latin cross, with a square tower in the centre. The choir and the transept yet remain. Our guide led us into them, and up between the masonry, by narrow stairways, upon the walls. The west gable is in ruin. Over the richly-moulded Gothic portal in the south transept is a magnificent window, the great attraction of Melrose. It is twenty-four feet by sixteen, divided by four bars, which interlace at the top in various curves. The stone-work of the window is as perfect as when the colored light first beamed in upon the vocal choir. Nine niches are above this window, and two on each buttress, for images of CHRIST and HIS apostles. Various images yet remain in their places. Sculptured forms of plant and animal adorn pedestal, canopy, and buttress. The leafy tracery is yet to be seen, so delicate and light that straws may pierce, and just pierce, their minute orifices. The eastern window is particularly beautiful, and has been the theme of Sir Walter Scott's poetry. He recommends the visitor to see it when the oriel, the corbeils, grotesque and grim, and the pillars, like bundles of lances bound with garlands, are all silvered with the mild moonlight. We can well imagine that, under so magic an enchantment, when the silver light edges the imagery, giving the semblance of ebony and ivory to the delicately-wrought material, Melrose would enchain the beholder, as it were some fairy creation, and would justify the verse of Sir Walter.

> "Thou wouldst have thought some fairy's hand
> 'Twixt poplars straight the osier wand
> In many a freakish knot had twined;
> Then framed a spell when the work was done,
> And changed the willow wreaths to stone."

Many of the Douglas family, as well as other noted persons in Scotch annals, including Alexander II., are buried in this abbey. The heart of Bruce lies beneath a broken stone. Douglas tried unsuccessfully to bear it to the Holy Land. It reposes in more congenial soil. Around it the grass and alders grow, and plentiful hangings of ivy climb. Around it there repose, in the graveyard, generation after generation of those who have named the name of Bruce with thrilling pride; and nearer, within the abbey, lie numerous abbots and monks who once ruled, and, if tradition be true, revelled right jollily, in these sacred walls. We walked about the ruins over the mounds—a silent company. We felt, in truth, that "never was scene so sad, so fair." Scott has breathed the immortality of his poetry upon the scene, and has given it added interest by weaving the "Lay of the Last Minstrel" around it. Could we do better, after seeing Melrose, than to visit the home of him, whose pen had imparted so much interest to the old abbey, and indeed to almost every spot which we have visited in Scotland?

I wish that I could forget one thing about Abbotsford, and only remember what we saw, and not what we heard. From Melrose we drove through hedged lanes and turnpike gates, until we reached the portal of Abbotsford. We met there a party of Americans who had been waiting some time for entrance. Under their direction, and being advised that it was proper, we took a path leading down to the stream, and enjoyed the view of the houses, which, taken together, and with as much unity as they can muster, constitute Sir Walter's seat. They have no particular style or comeliness; but they have a fine prospect of water and hill, mead and wood. A grassy lawn spreads its green carpet between the stream and house. Additions are being built, which cannot adorn the house more, nor add a single leaf to its volume of associations.

We returned to the portal just in time to see a queer old English housewife dancing along, with a crowd after her, and scolding with a virago's tongue. She unlocked the gate. Now came our turn: "So, so! you're the party that have been wandering over the grounds, where you've no business—none at all!" I did not like to spoil our visit, so kept my teeth clenched, and my tongue in prison; and we all marched in like whipped and naughty children, smothering revenge enough to have cannibalized the old Xantippe, and sauce enough for the meal. With a consequential, snappish air, and a lachrymose sniffle, (rare combination!) she led us into a hall, or armory, where, amidst the tasteful arrangement of guns, pistols and swords, many of them once carried by kings and Highland chieftains (including Rob Roy), were hung, as primary in interest, the iron keys of the Tolbooth, which the reader of the Heart of Mid-Lothian need not be reminded, once turned the lock on deluded Effie Deans. A glass case contained the last suit of clothes worn by Sir Walter. Presents from Byron, among which was a silver urn of rare workmanship, containing some human bones from Athens, were distributed around among the canes, hatchets and other instruments which the novelist had used. We were ushered into his study; saw the old arm-chair in which he received the airy servitors of his brain; his books and furniture, all just as they were when he died. A good-natured Louisianian asked if he might sit in the chair.

'No, sir—*noh!* never have heard such presumption before—never!'

'Oh! but it couldn't hurt it, and it would be quite a pleasure to remember.'

The old lady flushed, while she replied: 'I don't admire such taste as yours, sir. We hold that chair too sacred for any one to sit in. This way, sir. Oblige me by not delaying, *you*—Miss! If I allowed every body to sit in it, it would soon be dirty and ragged. Pass on, sir.'

And so, with tantalizing haste and unwomanly pertness, she posted us from room to room, until all the sanctity of the place began to ooze out in vexation, which finally found relief in the humorous. Would not Sir Walter himself chuckle to see such a specimen showing off his mementoes?

The library gave us most satisfaction. The portraits of the family hung around. Sir Walter's picture did not impress me so peculiarly as the statue in Edinburgh, in the Gothic monument. Neither has it the intellectual vigor which speaks from the marble bust by Chantrey, which is in the library. A bay-window and recess hung with crimson damask, occupied the side of the room next to the stream. The window opened to one of the finest views of nature that ever inspired an author. Before the fire-place a dog was quietly snugged in the deep wool of the rug, which gave a peculiarly Scott-air to the chamber. Sir Walter was always accompanied by his dog, and is so represented in his portraits. His famous dog cut in stone stands before the outer door, under the shadow of the stag-antlers.

We would not dwell too much upon the minute; but such an arrangement as we saw at Abbotsford is worth a study. It indicates a chaste and superlative refinement, and connects the idea of literary ease with worldly comfort so deliciously, that we would fain have lingered, but for: 'The door's open, sir; don't you see?' from Mrs. Xantippe. Taking one glance at the portrait of Lockhart, another at the odd sketches, illustrating Sir Walter's characters, which hung on the wall, and still another, despite Mrs. Xantippe, at a sketch of Queen Elizabeth dancing in full costume, frills, ruffs, high head-dress (all in admirable caricature), which was a pet of Sir Walter's, and is an unique and striking crotchet from the brain of Art, I left the library to enter into another room, in which time only was allowed to see Napoleon's pistols, which I wickedly wished might spontaneously go off at Mrs. Xantippe.

One of the party ventured to inquire something about the family who reside at Abbotsford (a gentleman who married his granddaughter—I forget his name—lives there), when our splenetic madam put a clapper on his interrogation by saying: 'It's not very polite, sir, to ask such questions when the people are in the house. They might hear you. I wish nothing of the kind mentioned. There's the court: a sixpence each. Come! no loitering!'

And thus we passed by the rare collection of curiosities which the antiquary had gathered. A glance at the shield spoken of in Waverley; a stride past the writing-desk presented by George IV.; a retina confused, and a tympanum fretted with the petulance of the guide; a few maledictions on the shameful and disgusting manner in which so much that could inspire respect for the memory of the wonderful 'Wizard of the North' is displayed; and we are *en route* for a more delightful and a holier spot—the burial-place of the great bard and novelist at Dryburgh Abbey.

Ettrick and Yarrow, made known far and wide as the English tongue travels, by the songs of Hogg and the sonnets of Wordsworth, lie contiguous with their wild hills, and are plainly seen from Abbotsford. Before we reach Dryburgh, the Tweed, which is here a trout stream, swift and clear, must be crossed. As we rowed over, we observed an odd anchor in the midst of the stream, staying by its human grip a skiff, in which a nobleman who owned the fishery was standing, swishing his pole and letting out his gossamer line after the most approved custom of Izaak Walton, and totally unconscious of the shivering servant, nearly up to his arms in the cold water, who moved the boat at the pleasure of his lord. But did not that servant watch anxiously for glorious nibbles or sundown?

The abbey at Dryburgh is hid in a wood, and is approached through an orchard. It is very ancient, having been founded during the reign of David I., by the Lord of Lauderdale. The spot was once a worship-grove of the Druids. Lying near the border, it has been subject to the harshest vicissitudes of border war. Its ruins are very extensive. It has one charm which no other ruin possesses: a large star-window perfectly preserved, high up in a wall which is entirely clad in ivy, and leaving only this gem of stone and sky, like a sapphire brooch, clasping the glistening drapery of green investing the ruin, all too beautiful for the corrosion of Time.

On the twenty-sixth of September, 1832, a solemn procession moved over this eminently beautiful spot, and under these verdurous arches, bearing the remains of the greatest of the name which appears so frequently upon the grave-stones of the abbey. Mourning no common loss, they heavily carry the bier down the grassy aisle of St. Mary; and soon, with holy rite and sad hearts, the body of WALTER SCOTT is committed to the earth to mingle with the common mould, surrounded by his ancestry and the ancient proprietors of the abbey. But Marmion, Waverley, Ivanhoe and Old Mortality were not interred in Dryburgh upon that day. They form a part of the deathless spirit and creative mind of him who shed at once so much lustre upon his country's legends and history, and so much benignity upon mankind. We gathered a twig of ivy near his tomb, and added one more link to the chain of kindred thoughts, which already contains the resting-places of Shelley, Keats, Virgil, and the kings and princes of song who rule from the urns of Westminster Abbey.

The ruins of Dryburgh are fast decaying. But the granite slab which covers the remains of Sir Walter looks fresh and new. On either side are his wife and only son, and the tombs of all three are inclosed in an iron railing. They are ivy-clad, and deeply embowered in a shade which is worthy of its Druidical dedication in the olden time.

Dryburgh was the refuge of Edward II., after his unsuccessful invasion of Scotland. The vault once haunted by the familiar spirit known as Fatlips, that attended the female wanderer who once sought refuge here, is still shown. She had made a vow that she never would see the light of day until her lover returned. She only left her vault by night to procure the means of subsistence. A statue of Wallace occupies a prominent spot in the wood above the abbey. As we cross the stream again, the fine monument on the battle-field of Penuelheugh appears, which, like the triple-topped mountain cleft by the wizard Michael Scott, follows us far toward Kelso. Our ride down sweet Teviotdale during the setting of the sun (and a lustrous setting it was, gorgeous in cloud-gold!) was by many ancient seats of power and pleasure, and over many spots rich in legendary lore and historic interest. The meagre remnant of Roxburgh castle, upon a commanding hill near the road, overlooked the romantic river. A holly tree near, still marks the spot where James II. was killed, while besieging the castle. The Duke of Roxburgh resides in the splendid palace of Fleurs, a stately specimen of the Tudor style, which rises from a sloping lawn that runs up from the opposite bank of the stream, not far from where the Teviot mingles with the Tweed.

Castles and abbeys become common before we reach Berwick, and even after we leave it for Newcastle, upon the 'coaly Tyne.' Between Newcastle and Thirsk, amid the country of coal-pits, an apparition strange, yet beautiful, appeared upon a distant hill. It was a Grecian temple, not far from Aycliffe. How finely its rounded columns and proportionate entablature rested against the sky! An extended ride still kept its classic elegance in view; and it will be a long, long time before the vision of that temple will fade from our memory of northern England. That temple in the smoky landscape became a reminder of the classic lands. It was like—what was it like? A jewel in an Ethiop's ear; an hexameter from Virgil in the dry black-letter of an old law tome.

We have unavoidably omitted much of the descriptive belonging to the valley of the Tweed, which cultivated hills and dimpled lawns, great bridges and time-gnarled forests, combine to diversify and grace. The railroad hurries us to Ripon, through a country where monuments to England's material greatness arise in the form of tall chimneys, and locomotives dash, with a white scarf floating behind, almost at every point of the compass. We frequently counted six or eight playing over the land at once. What will not iron and coal do for a little island? Our object in coming to Ripon was to see the most extensive abbey-ruin in Great Britain. It is upon the property of Earl Grey, and accessible to strangers. It is like those I have described, but with a difference. It is approached through an extensive park, in which profuse art has adorned nature, by changing her trees into vaulted aisles, her waters into swan-peopled lakes, and her lawns into spreads of loveliest verdure. Statues are seen ranged through vistas. Laurel banks, neatly trimmed, line the paths. Water-falls murmur in the quiet air. Soon the extensive ruins are seen, of course ivy-garlanded, with towers of immense size and altitude, and arches under ground, between which the stream sullenly complains. Dungeons with iron fastenings are visible, not far from the long range of cloisters where the monks studied and walked. It requires no heavy draft on the imagination, to evoke from the tombs over which we tread, the forms of those monkish clerks and copyists, whose enthusiastic zeal led to such manual dexterity, that the art of printing has not been able, with all its refinement, to excel their manuscripts. The ancient Bibles which were shown to us in Rome, and the snowy vellum missals in the British Museum, illustrated with gold, blue, and carmine, with their shining black letters,—each one able to bear a microscopic scrutiny,—speak of a quietude and seriousness which must have reigned in these walls where so much study and care were given. The forms of the Venerable Bede, of Friar Bacon, Theodore of Canterbury, and others who loved to reproduce and pore over the select and precious gems of the monkish library, rise with solemn air, and read us lessons of patience and perseverance which our age, with its acquisitiveness and hurry cannot teach.

Why is it that all religions have had a system of asceti cism? Is it consistent with the ordination of God, that His ministers should be set apart from the world, which they ought to teach? Yet, Mahometanism had, and has even yet, its Soofies and Dervishes, from the Mediterranean to the Ganges; the Jews had their Essenes, who lived in the desert and held their property in common, and their Therapeuts, who sought happiness in solitary contemplation of the Divine essence; the religions of the East, Boodhism and Braminism, have had their monastic orders, their Yooges and Fakirs; the Pythagoreans in Greece, imitating the sects of Egypt, from which they learned their mysteries, dwelt apart from the haunts of men; and Catholicism has had its monasticism, under various names and forms, Anchorets, Cenobites, Benedictines, Carthusians, Cistercians, Mendicants; and these had their subdivisions. It must be confessed that much good has emanated from these recluses. Giant minds have been nursed in the solitary cell. Civilization in its intellectual and industrious phases, received advancement from these holy orders; and even yet, if there be a spot where the light *cannot* be kept burning in the fitful gusts of human passion and ignorance, these sequestered homes of thought and piety might be of service. But in this century, when light has gone forth among the nations, no one can praise a fugitive and cloistered virtue, that shuns the dust and heat of active life.

Other parts of Fountain Abbey bear evidence of other employments besides the intellectual and devotional. The great chimneys and fireplaces, yet showing marks of the culinary caloric, are to be seen; while near by, upon a portal stone, are carved the arms of the abbey, which are three horseshoes—emblems of good luck, and talismanic to keep the witches away. The nave and transept were very extensive, and finely preserved. But every where the hand of sacrilegious decay is at work, despoiling window and niche of figure and strength; while time has sown his grass-seed gently over the tessellated floor, which now yields to the traveller's tread, as he passes through this great home of the monkish multitude, and in fancy re-peoples it with singing choir and praying priests, all ruled by the baronial abbot and his men-at-arms.

By Knaresborough, and the Dropping Well, we seek this capital of Yorkshire, and have spent our Sabbath in enjoying its repose and pencilling our journeyings. We are ready once more to gather our robes about us, and trudge on to other scenes. But the three abbeys, and Abbotsford, must ever be our landmarks by which to tell the high tide of our pleasure and our progress through the Borders.

What is the influence which remains, now that our eyes have

feasted upon ruin and landscape, and our minds have recalled the associations with which they are fraught? Now that the pleasure-loving and curious propensity has been gratified, what permanent good has been ingrafted upon the immortal soul, by thus moving amid the beauties of nature and of art, under the twilight of antiquity? Are these objects but the chance scribblings and frolicksome creations of the dead past, meaningless and indifferent in this present time? Is there no lesson of beauty to be learned from a perception and a study of these Gothic piles, in the witchery of their ruins? Comes there no admonition to patience and devotion, as we recall from their graves the form of monk and friar, and think how, day after day, and night after night, they fought within the cloister the logomachies of Aristotle, under the command of Scotus or Aquinas? Oh, yes! Here, in these homes of the studious and learned, there burned altars to truth and goodness, although their fires were dim and sepulchral. When all else was ignorance profound, with vestal vigilance the light was kept bright, until it burst into the full radiance of a better civilization. When baronial insolence ruled its serfs with iron sway, and ran riot in the worst passions of our sinful nature, there was found in these abbeys a refuge, where peace and good-will hedged the innocent round about with protection, and where the religion of Jesus kindled its hope of celestial beatitude, high and aloof from the troubles and turmoils of the world.

XXXVII.

English Husbandry, and the Beauty of Chatsworth.

"Each one contends, with all her might and main,
Each day a higher verdant crown to gain."
COWLEY'S *Poem on Plants.*

THIS northern part of England, around York, is checkered with railroads so completely, that it is impossible to look out upon the landscape without seeing the swift-rushing car. From Newburg to Sheffield, at all angles,—obtuse, acute, and right,—these vehicles are every moment darting, freighted with coal and coke, iron and humanity. The country after night seems alive with fires from furnaces and coke-ovens; while by day, deep, dark holes, 'into which the mild sunbeam hath not power to pierce,' and into which only the lightning could dart illumination, open on every side like entrances to Hades, out of which machinery is shelling coal by the ton. And yet here, as in every arable part of Great Britain that we have seen, Agriculture seems to gather as rich a harvest, and to take as nice a heed in the cultivation of the soil, as in other less manufacturing districts. The harvest-time was just at its middle point. Two months later than in Ohio, they gather their wheat. It is mostly done by Irish, who come up from Liverpool, and even across the Channel, thus to reap their little harvest of shillings. We saw them at York, these laborers, packed by twenties and fifties, into unventilated cars (used for cattle on ordinary occasions), all somewhat intoxicated, all armed with scythe and sickle, but so closely packed, that in the biggest hullabaloo imaginable, they could hardly use their 'gougers,' much less their instruments of husbandry. One poor fellow was, by some fatality, placed in our car. He had his bundle, his sickle, and the never-failing resource of an Irishman, his pipe. He told me that he received from eight to ten shillings an acre, and "that it took him four days to cut an acre, and right heavy crops they were too." When assured that an American swung a *cradle* to the tune of five acres a day, he took a long whiff, and opened his eyes, while his mouth, too, opened to exclaim in consternation, "that he would like to see one of them—(is it creedles ye call thim?) at work." He thought that if a company of Americans should come over here, with their "creedles," that they would make a good harvest of shillings, at ten per acre. In very deed, it would pay almost as well as working in a Sacramento digging. Ten dollars a day and found; what do our farmers think of that? They would not, however, wonder at it, if they could go into an English harvest-field, and observe the women and men lazily gathering the straws and cutting them by handfulls! Why, an ox with any thing like a tongue could clip a field about as soon as one of these sickles. No wonder McCormick's reaper created such delightful surprise among farmers here, where even the cradle was unknown. No wonder that he has made an arrangement, by which $25,000 for the first year is guarantied to him for the privilege of selling five hundred of his reapers, with a proportionate increase on an increased number sold. No wonder the London Times claimed the Reaper as an equivalent to *Protection.*

But one thing must be said in commendation of the English farming. There is a completeness and cleanliness in the way a field is attended to, whether pasture, woodland or wheat field, that leaves nothing to be done. Ruth would have found scanty gleanings in the wake of an English husbandman. So with regard to the hay-stack and the straw-stack. They are all laid up with the precision of architecture, and nicely thatched. Not a straw is out of place. The wheat is stacked upon frames some feet above the ground, so as to preserve the grain from mice

Nothing is wasted. The manure is cared for as sedulously as if it were wheat. Yet with all this nicety and completeness of cultivation, Ohio flour can be seen, (I can tell its brand as the face of an old friend), at any hour, unloading at Liverpool, swinging upward to its high-storied wareroom, or being waggoned through the streets for the depôt, there to be distributed among these very districts where the fields are heavy with a better than placer gold.

An English *farmer* generally rents of the landed proprietor. The latter is called a gentleman in England, the farmer is not. Gentility is here dependent on the relation of the person to the Earth, whether it be as freeholder, or leaseholder. These proprietors number only thirty thousand in all England. The rent paid is from five to ten dollars per acre, according to the quality of the soil. In addition, there is the tithe and poor-rate. The farmer is not allowed to cultivate in wheat each year, more than a third or a quarter of the land rented; because the soil must be kept up; and to this end, there must be a rotation of crops. The first crop taken after the ground is manured, consists of some root, as the beet or turnip; and is called the hoed crop. After this, comes barley, oats, and beans; and then the wheat. Almost every thing raised is fed to stock (of which a farm is rarely without), except the wheat and barley. In the case of a grazing farm, this rotation would not apply. When a part of it is sown in grass, it is suffered to remain in pasture for three years, more or less, which supersedes artificial manuring. Our farmers cannot realize, without an inspection of English farming, the immense outlay of expenditure, and the capital required to carry on a farm here. The manures are the largest item. They are mostly manufactured near London. Bone dust is a principal article. It is nothing unusual to put upon one acre twenty-five dollars worth of manure. The amount of capital actually required to carry on a farm cannot fall short of fifty dollars an acre, by which I mean the expense of stock, implements, manure, and labor required to keep the land in good cultivable condition. A farmer with one thousand acres, must be worth fifty thousand dollars, in order to carry on his farm as it is here carried on.

Whatever may be the expense attending agriculture in England compared to America, there is one regard in which England may claim the palm of excellence. It is in the tasteful and even elegant mode in which the fields, parks, and gardens are arranged and displayed. God never intended that man should for ever sweat over the furrow and in the harvest field, to obtain his daily bread. By creating the beauty of flowers which enamel the meads, the trees which waver in the wind and give charm to the landscape, the waters which plash in fountains and circle in eddies, the varieties of hill and dale, rocky eminences and green lawns; by bending over all this regalia of Nature, His Empyrean of azure, does He not teach, that there is an inner spirit which is not gratified, and cannot be satisfied merely with utilities; but which looks out inquiringly through the senses, for the objects of admiration and love? Life would be an uneasy and desperate thraldom, unless Beauty enfranchised its activities, and led it along its own 'primrose path of dalliance.'

How little do we in America, especially in Ohio, think of these sentiments practically! How rarely do we find around our log-cabins and country residences any thing to attract, except its genial hospitality! Yet how much does prodigal nature lay at the feet of our people, which, with little pruning and care, would displace the few flag-stones, the wood-pile, the mud-puddle and cow-resort before the threshold, and array our residences in fragrant vines, surround them with trees and flowers native to our woods, and make home sweeter and dearer by these ministrations to Beauty! Would the young man just out of his teens be looking after a quarter section in Illinois and Iowa, if the roof-tree of home thus blossomed? In England it is otherwise. Time hath here left legacy after legacy of garniture to each cot tage and hall. Her people prize the boon, and transmit to posterity the landscape, with new features of loveliness.

The highest refinement of rural beauty in England, and even, it was said, in the world, was to be found at Chatsworth, the prime country-seat, among seven others, belonging to the Duke of Devonshire. To have left England without having seen Chatsworth, would have argued us insensible to the voice of undisputed rumor, which located the modern Paradise over the moors beyond Sheffield, whither upon yesterday we were bound. It was our last sight in the Old World, and anticipation made it the culminating point of our voyaging. The reputation of the Duke's manager, who is none other than Paxton, the designer of the Crystal Palace, added a zest to anticipation: while the leisure of a complete day was dedicated to its fruition.

Sheffield has little to attract. Its smoky factories almost darkened our hopefulness as we drove down its streets. But in the beautiful environs we found compensation for the coaly effluence. Chatsworth was 17 miles from Sheffield, and the luxury of an open carriage enabled us to enjoy the intervening scenes. We drove by the residence of the cutlers, among which was that of Rogers, the King Cutler, whose steel is as famous as that of Damascus. In the valley were distributed different manufactories for cutlery, which, before fit for the market, undergoes various processes in different establishments, from the smelting of the metal up to its grinding, tempering, and polishing.

As we approached Chatsworth, the view became enchanting. The moors appeared in the hazy distance covered and colored with the purple heather, or ling, as it is called in England, which gives the aspect of a blooming garden to these wastes. We had not expected to see such extensive wastes near the great marts of Sheffield and Manchester, in a county more densely populated than any other part of the island. But so it was. Why? The Duke of Rutland owned the range for hunting. The Duke of Devonshire yonder heath for the same.

Grouse hide under the ferns, and feed upon the blossom of the heather. The land is let by the thousand acres, at $250 for that area for hunting, besides which the lessee has a large outlay for preserving the game. We saw lazy fellows sitting near the bars preserving the game from the poachers, and we saw, too, 'chaps' with their phaeton in the road, *innocently* looking over the walls, while a man with setters was starting up the game, which the 'chap' from the road would as innocently fire at as it rose. This is what is called, taking it 'on the sly.' Grouse were rising on all sides. Huntsmen were on the distant hills. The smoke and flash were visible—otherwise all was desolate. Bleak rocks, scattered about like those at Vesuvius, but unlike them adorned with ferns and ling, are upon the summit of the moor, which looks over a vast range of country, taking in Chatsworth, with its palace and park, where we soon arrived.

We went first to the kitchen gardens, and found ingress. Long ranges of walls and hot-houses, as far as the eye could reach, met our view, with neat grass and flower-plots between. A machine was at work, used by the hand, which clipped the grass while it rolled it smoothly and carried the clippings along. I wondered no more at the velvet elegance of the English lawn. On the larger lawns, we saw larger machines drawn by horses, which performed the same function. We entered the principal hot-house, where tropical plants flowered in every hue of the chromatic scale, and in every form which an Infinite Creator moulds. The Paxonian hung its rich pink pendants beside the large straw-colored alamander which crept upon the ceiling, over beds of exotics perfumed to a sense of faintness. In another green-house, water-lilies alone were kept in a mimic lake, which was not suffered to stagnate; for little water-wheels fretted it continually. Lilies, did I say? There was but *one* lily, called the Victoria Regia, from which twenty large leaves, as 'round as my shield,' and five feet in diameter, were spread upon the surface. These leaves seemed like green tables, supported, for all that I could see, by water-nymphs. A large lily was in flower; while another, ghostly pale, was bursting its verdant cerements. I always loved the lily; so pure, so stainless, so emblematic of innocence. It is a quaint myth, which accounts for its origin. Jupiter, in order to make Hercules immortal, clapped him to the breast of Juno, when she was asleep. The young embodiment of Strength drew so hard that, too great a gush of milk coming down, some slipped upon the sky, which made the Galaxy, or Milky Way, and out of some which fell upon the earth, rose the lily. A queenly origin hath the proud white flower! The Regia of Chatsworth does no discredit to its celestial lineage. A curious flower, called the stanopia, which grows out below instead of above the root, was in full bloom. Tall futia in red, great cup and pitcher flowers; indeed, every style of vegetable beauty, in hues which the sea-shell can never rival, warmed into life in the heated air.

Without, the arrangement was simple in its elegance. Each class of flowers had its own plot. The kith and kin all lived neighborly, and smiled happily as they bent to each other or looked up into the sky. The walls were warmed with subterranean flues, and clad with peach and apricot, flatly trimmed against them. The pine-apples were growing under glass, finer than I ever saw them at home. The grapes, purple and white, larger than—no matter; it is too toothsomely luscious to talk about, as it was too tempting to the larcenously inclined fingers. What Elia says of roast pig (oh! reader, forgive the savory illusion in this unnatural connection), may I not say of those clusters, that they produced a premonitory moistening—or overflowing of the nether lip, and the idea of tasting them created a delight—if not sinful, yet so like to sinning, that a tender-conscienced person would do well to pause. We paused.

We walk out again to hear the bees hum from flower to flower, and see them at work in their straw hives. Large beds of vegetables of the largest development are ranged near. This smacked of the kitchen; all else might well become seraglios and palaces.

As we move through the great gate, we are conducted into the palace, which is a superb structure, topped with figures and urns, and rich in bass-reliefs and carvings. We pass through halls of paintings by masters, through apartments where were the coronation chairs of England's royalty, through rooms where the presents of the Emperor Nicholas to the Duke were arranged, and through others, where the greatest collection of sketchings in the world is exhibited. From the windows, in each of which there is but one pane, we have prospects of the hills and woods; of the Derwent water, in which hundreds of Durhams are wading or ruminating; of the Park, where sheep and deer together nip the herbage; of sheets of water, glancing under the sun, reminding us of the water-views down the leafy avenues of Versailles, and of fountain-jets, playing out of manifold forms of Triton and God. Not another fabric is to be seen on the premises—not one. Nothing, upon the whole sixteen hundred acres, appears to mar the complete diversity of rural loveliness. There is no point which has not contributed its portion to the manifest unity of Beauty, which embraces so much variety in its magic zone.

The hall of statuary has not a fragment nor a blotch. Every piece is a gem. The pure Parian glistens in tasteful array and graceful form. A door opens, and a conservatory, with elegant and costly vases, filled with oranges and flowers, is presented; out of which, as from an enchanter's realm, we walk upon paths of pulverized spar, shining like diamonds, and surrounded by lawns spongy to the foot and as neatly trimmed as tapestry. Here another guide meets us, and leading us by pillars vine-clad, by temples copied from classic models, and by statuary, guarding the old trees under whose shade they stand, gives us a vantage ground from which to see the glory of Chatsworth. See!—Far up in a woody mountain, from natural springs, whose supply is exhaustless, there leaps the live water-falls; so high and distant, you may not hear their music. These gather to a head and fall over a temple's dome, from which they leap, but to rebound into fountains, where they are bespread in veils of fleecy whiteness, and hasten down a succession of steps, some three hundred yards long and fifteen feet wide. As we reclined on the soft turf, at the foot of these steps, the guide let on a full volume of water, which leaped, gushed and sprung, danced, sang and glittered, until at our feet it disappeared under ground, to emerge, perhaps at lower points in other capacities. How much has *motion* to do with the loveliness of a landscape!

Passing under copses of shaggy-trunked trees, which we did very leisurely, we are invited to enter cool, rocky retreats, artificially arranged, and not without their fern and heather. Here the genius of Paxton is seen, in those huge masses of rock which apparently block up our path, but yield to a gentle push as they swing upon their pivots. Rocking stones of immense weight are around, mobile to a child's strength. Among the roots of pine trees and out of rocky fissures, little rills played, and laughed as they ran around stones and through moss, as if at the theatrical imposition which the artificial was acting for our admiration. Birds hopped and chirruped as unconsciously as if Nature and not Paxton had given them their bowers. But the cunning carollers,—we did not see any of them alight on a certain tree, which deceived my perception, if it could not their instinct. A New Haven gentleman—a wag, by the way—wished me just to examine its bark; it was so very odd. I was going up for that purpose, when I observed the tree bleeding water-drops; and before I could look again, to be sure it was no phantasy, every point and pore of twig and branch spurted its jet, and the turf under my feet became suddenly alive with subtle fountains! Of course, I retired. Of course, I was food for merriment. Of course, invidious remarks, comparing my verdancy with the curious vegetable production, were made. Of course, I had to join the roar of laughter. 'New Haven' had procured the guide to say the 'Open Sesame' to a rock, behind which he touched a spring, whose magic proved my discomfiture and his fun.

It was by this rocky path that we went to see the Crystal

Palace,—not the one at London, but its progenitor, the original, built by Paxton, and from which he designed the great Exhibition Palace. This looked crystalline; it had no painted col umns, by scores and hundreds, and no drapery; but a concave without these, of clearest glass, so arranged as scarcely to show the sash, and all strong. Terraces, hedges, and flowers surround it; while, in the lake near, a fountain plays two hundred and eighty feet high! We entered, and saw the same beautiful arrangement which distinguishes the transept of the Great Palace; large palms and blooming creepers, flowers of every clime, dressed in their gala colors, and rocks streaming with tendrils! Some idea of its extent may be had, when it is considered that there are in the building seven miles of six-inch heated piping.

Is it strange that such magnificence exists where there are one hundred and twenty-seven gardeners alone engaged? Or, with such an immense revenue as belongs to the duke, and with such a manager as Paxton? Before leaving the domain, you may survey it from a tower, so erected as to comprehend all its beauty. There is no smoke to obscure the view. It is all carried off to a great distance, by underground flues. The very coal used by so many hot-houses, is conveyed by a subterranean railway. The farming arrangements and the village without the domain, are a complement to what I have faintly pictured. The village is the model of England. All the cottages were either Gothic or Swiss—of stone, exact and elegant, with grass and flower-plots. Surrounding church and school-house were linden-trees. trimmed neatly and inwoven as one, meeting and arching. Could there be scandal, or gossip, or backbiting, or aught but harmony in such a paragon of a town? Sir Thomas Moore, in the picture he has drawn of the towns of Utopia, so precise and perfect, might have given grace to the drawing, had a Chatsworth been contemporaneous with his time.

The owner of all this paradise is a bachelor. Hold! Not so fast, ladies! A confirmed bachelor, a bachelor bound hand

and foot! Some difficulty as to the title of the duke was started; which was hushed by an arrangement between the contending families. The duke agreed to live and die unmarried; so that Lord Mortington, the claimant, should be his heir. The duke is old and infirm. He is liberal in the use which he makes of his wealth. His fruitage and venison load the tables of his friends; and he has freely opened to the public these grounds and this palace, where, in its consummate perfection, the luxury of the East and the arts of Italy vie with the tasteful elegance of France and the natural beauties of Switzerland and Scotland; and where all combine to render Chatsworth one of the most attractive spots for the traveller in Great Britain, if not in Europe.

Such spots are needed, to show man from what a beautiful estate he has fallen. If immense fortunes must be entailed, let them thus be transformed into the poetry and music of nature, that they may allay or divert the passions and perturbations of our sinful state. Sir William Temple says, that human life is at the best and greatest but like a froward child, that must be played with and humored a little to keep it quiet, till it falls asleep, and then the care is over. Then why not please it with such charms as Chatsworth displays, until it reposes on the bosom of its mother earth? It was our last—may not I say—greatest pleasure, in this land of our ancestors. It will not be forgotten, until we repose in that sleep that knows no waking. Will it then? Not if a thing of beauty be a joy *forever*.

From Sheffield, through Manchester, a huge, compact, black and busy city—we have returned to Liverpool, where all the day we have been reading letters from home—thinking of home, and what is better, packing for home, whither we will be soon going.

XXXVIII.

The Buckeye for Home.

"Ever drifting, drifting, drifting,
On the shifting,
Currents of the restless heart;
Till at length in books recorded,
They like hoarded
Household words, no more depart."

Longfellow.

IT was with unwonted alacrity that we packed our luggage, and called our last cab on transatlantic shores. By noon of the 3d of September, we were down upon the Mersey's brink, awaiting the return of the tender, which was to bear us to the vessel's side. Nearly two hundred Americans were with us upon that tender, and they now float with us as I write. We did not feel much reluctance in leaving England. With our faces turned westward, where could our hearts be, but westward—in our own blessed home! The perils of the great sea are forgotten; or what is worse, its disagreeableness is joyfully encountered; for through all, we see smiling the faces of those who wait to welcome our return. Liverpool is not noted; its superb customhouse and miles of docks receive no encomium. When the heart bounds so warmly, the eye is blind to external things. The Mersey's green banks scarcely are thought of; for there comes the greeting of friend with friend. Old companions in voyaging shake hands, laugh, and talk over scenes that they have viewed since separation, and of their gladness in anticipating their return to America. A few there were who were leaving dear friends in England. The wave of the handkerchief from steamer and shore, the hand-kissing, the tear-dropping, the stifled sobbing; did they not bring to mind our own parting, when the Asia cleft the waves of New-York harbor?

The mails were aboard, the guns fired, the cheers given and answered; and the noble "Pacific" bore away with as hopeful a cargo of humanity as ever trod a steamer's deck,—hopeful in that sense which antedates the joy of the future with large and generous impulses.

Our first two days out were pleasant in the extreme. I began to think myself quite a sailor. True, the channel was not rough; but then there were two days gone, and not a sign of mine ancient enemy. Not even his advanced guard was visible. I began to tread the deck proudly—looked people in the face, as if I were an old salt—perfectly accustomed to nautical experiences. Complacency sat serenely on my front like 'Halcyon on the wave.' Besides, was not the Pacific a larger boat, with less rocking and rolling than the Asia? Bravely I marched down to dinner; called the waiter with a confidence which solid earth might have inspired; had no misgivings but that travelling had indurated the system; in fine, conducted myself as if I were already a triumphant champion over the insidious foe. The sequel is plain. Pride fell with the Son of the Morning; why not with fallible humanity? I felt, rather than saw my enemy approach. He came upon a tall wave, with a white ensign, and a sparkling lance. His first blow was aimed at the very point of the system, where the Ancients seated courage. If the citadel itself was beseiged, where were the outposts? Not without a struggle did I yield. With Sir Jack, I may now say, 'that had I known he was so cunning o'fence, I would have seen him d—d, ere I had fought him.' I marched the deck with determination, pursed up my lip, perked up my eyebrows, and assumed that serio-careless air which seemed to say: ''tis a little disturbance of the animal economy—soon be right—good ship—rather like the sea—it's so bracing—ahem!' But it would not do. I walked stoutly, did not look at any other object than the wheel-house, made imaginary speeches to evanescent juries, tried every abstraction and even my best expedient, viz., hummed 'Scot's wha ha,' and whistled that air, known in Buckeyedom, as the 'big muster tune,' to whose inspiring music the corn-stalk militia of the Miami, Sciota, and Muskingum valleys were wont to march in disorganized and timeless array, in the good old days when training was the duty of Ohio's citizenry. All would not do. A large billow gave the vessel a lurch and a twist, I changed my tune, struck my colors, and with more precipitation than grace, retired below. In the piteous strain of an old bard, let me ask,

"Was ever mortal wight in such a woeful case?"

Ask me not to renew the *infandum dolorem* of the six subsequent days, during which without intermission we have had tempestuous weather. How the winds raved, the boat snapped and creaked, the waters roared and the rains came; these are a part of the malignant triumphings of my enemy, which I would fain forget. Yesterday the fog enveloped us; but the sun soon shone through, the Newfoundland banks were near; the sea was calm; and it was said by a few tough old fellows without stomach or sympathy, who had been on deck for eight days, that we had stopped on the banks to *wood*, when there mysteriously appeared on deck over 150 strange passengers!

Ours is a stanch steamer. She has braved the continuous storms nobly. True we have lost about a day on account of the weather; but on our worst day we ran two hundred and thirty miles, and in a good sea we can run three hundred and thirty. I will not undertake to compare her with the Cunard steamers; comparisons are odious; but for elegant saloons, comfortable berths, an excellent table and speed, the Pacific has no superior, if any equal. She has made the four best trips ever made over the Ocean, except the one great great trip of the Baltic, which Capt. Nye will not suffer long to eclipse his fame.

American superiority in yatching, whatever may be said of steaming, was fully illustrated last month at Cowes, by the saucy little America, who ran away with all the prizes, while she upset the English idea of naval superiority in a manner which was only equalled, let me in justice say, by the manly courtesy and civility of the English gentlemen who afforded her so fair an opportunity of beating all their aristocratic craft. We were constantly congratulated in England, on the America's success. It did much to relieve the barren aspect of our part of the Great Exhibition; for at one swoop, it threw down all the models of naval architecture which adorned the west end of the British department.

The line of coast, which begins to grow plainer, indicates that we are in sight of our own continent. It does not strike us as our own country. Bare, bleak and uninhabited, it presents its cheerless, rocky edge of slanting strata, to the pitiless peltings of the sea. Shoals of black fish darken the water, and the spouting of whales in the horizon present more attractions than this inhospitable shore of Newfoundland.

But that shore tells me that we shall soon be home, and leads me to review, before I conclude these sketches. I confess that there has been a pleasure imparted, if not to others at least to myself, in recording this pilgrimage and *currente calamo*, gossiping about its incidents. There is now to my mind new meaning in Wordsworth's verse:

"Minds that have nothing to confer,
Find little to perceive."———

It is a truth, though a paradox in mental philosophy, that by sharing your spiritual spoil, you add to it; for you instil the prompture which moves to acquisition. These fugitive pages have been a constant prompture, a pleasant spur to observation. There was opportunity for conference with friends and kindred minds, and I looked with closer perception for the best subjects of communion.

In this delightful employment, over five months have been passed. What a season of ineffable enjoyment has it been! What a life—a novel life has been compressed into these months! What sacrifices could adequately measure the rich ingathering of their experience. A business temporarily left; the results of three years of professional labor expended in a summer; not alone for my own gratification, but for that of a companion, who will life-long share it; the aggravations of homelessness encountered upon steamboat, at hotel, in coach and car, contention with strange languages, disagreeableness upon the sea and the hazards of travel, the deprivation from worship at home and at church, the absence of friends and relations whose life is bound up with our own; all these are the sacrifices we have made, not the least among which is that constant call for cash, which the bag Peter Schlemil sold his shadow for, could hardly supply. What have we in return? Memories, eternal as our nature. Of what? Ruins which are histories; temples which are chronicles; seas and shores where Crusader and Corsair, Christian and Infidel, fought and gloried; the silence of deserted and exhumed cities, and of desolate solitudes in the mountain passes and heights; the magnificence of Art in her present phases, and as she appears in the vestiges of Antiquity; the recondite springs of the world's activity, developing forms of every use and variety, enshrined in the Palace of Industry; the splendid seats of Power, the fields of blood and valor; and the beautiful and unadorned scenes of nature; all instinct with their past pageantry, or with the busy energies of our own day. Upon the hot pavements of the Southern city, in the narrow streets of the Eastern, through the shady promenades of the gay capitals of Europe, over the mountain and moor, the lake and river, we have sought out the evidences of buried civilization, and witnessed the results of the living. We have stood by the tombs of the great and the gifted, whose names were a terror or an honor to their kind; have witnessed the ceremonies and devotions of different religions in their splendid structures, and have lingered around localities which the warm breath of enthusiasm, like that of spring, hath bid to blossom with the flower and perfume of Poetry. Who says that the earth is cold and pulseless? Let him take the pilgrim staff, and trace upon its surface its letters, legible with the stories of human Passion and Love. Within its rocky bosom there throbs the heart of Humanity, and every pulsation plays its part in that economy of Providence, which is the key to all revolutions, and to all philosophy, which reconciles every contradiction in morals and physics, and is the fulfilment of every prophecy.

What new significance will we find in the poetry, the romance, the philosophy and history of the world! What rivets for recollection have been forged by these journeyings! What lessons have we conned of the relations of man to man in society! How flimsy and meaningless seem the distinctions of wealth, which some draw even in America, when we reflect upon the riches that we have seen adorning nature by art, calling every luxury upon the sumptuous board, and every decoration around the tomb of the departed! How much more do we love to contemplate man, *as man*, undisguised by the frippery of rank, and ennobled by his native dignity! As, in passing, we have realized the existence of place after place, and object after object, of which we had read, and which slept in the twilight of uncertainty, a deeper confidence in human veracity has been inspired, and a firmer faith in the Invisible and Eternal established!

And yet travelling has its drawbacks in social cultivation. Where so much want and beggary is seen, and which not even Fortunatus, with his purse, could relieve, the heart is apt to grow callous to misery. Oh! it is not in the broad gairish sunshine of the world that the gentler affections flourish best, but in the security and seclusion of home. The sweetest and tenderest flowers are the offspring of the shade. Under the domestic roof, the primal duties are best observed. From the window of home they are seen "to shine aloft like stars."

Some people estimate the attraction of an object by the distance from which it may draw the beholder (a truth in science, if not in travelling), without regard to its intrinsic merit. So do not I. In this age of steam locomotion, in which even so unsophisticated a traveller as the writer has travelled over fourteen thousand miles in five months, the fashion is becoming stale of judging beauty by its latitude, or sublimity by its longitude. As well judge of the sublimity of Niagara by its furlongs from Columbus, or the glory of Waterloo by its acres. We have endeavored to detect the natural and artificial beauty, or recall the classic allusion and historic association of the locality, and thus present it for your eye. We were the more inclined to observe this rule, from some excellent strictures of an Edinburgh Reviewer, which we perused last spring. He said, that the tourist just returned from Switzerland, looked down with a superior air on the visitor of the Rhine; that he who had reached Rome was subdued into silence before him who had scaled Vesuvius; while the few who had actually seen the East, were marked men, and excited a kind of envy among the holiday herd of wanderers whom their presence reduced to insignificance. He says well, that there is no real distinction in having measured thousands of miles, pent up with mobs of fellow creatures in steamers and inns; for the smartest young Oxonian scarcely ventures, in mixed society, to open his budget of stories about the new hotel at Constantinople, or the old guide to Jerusalem, when the odds are, that some one of the company is fresh from California, or the trans-Himalayan regions. The importance attached to long journeys merely is thus dying away.

If I should ever open my little budget too vauntingly, let some friend remind me of an acquaintance I made going into Smyrna. He was a Greek, and the only model of the age of Pericles I had seen—a very Alcibiades in the elegance of his person, and the accomplishment of his manners. He was a black-eyed, black-haired gentleman, with a face hirsute, yet beaming with intelligence. He had been educated in some Italian University, and was a thorough scholar, especially in the classic

Greek. He had left his parents fourteen years before, for his travels, and was just returning. He spoke French like a Parisian, German very well, Russian well, English tolerably, and also the Turkish and his vernacular Greek. He was not illy versed in the language of the Arab, and some others of the Asiatic tribes.

No wonder that he was such an encyclopedian linguist. He had travelled from Asia, through Italy, France, Germany, England, and into Russia, where, having engaged in Caucasian and Siberian expeditions, he was led into Asia again. He had traversed the most inaccessible parts of Caucasia and Georgia, had roved among the Tartars, and exchanged hyperboles with the Persian. The most inhospitable races in the world, as well as the most difficult places to enter, may be found in the mountains of Asia; yet these races he had lived with, and these difficulties surmounted. He had not travelled without an object. With a pocket edition of Xenophon, he had followed that martial scholar in his retreat with the "ten thousand;" and had verified the account given, parasang by parasang, and object after object. He had gone with Jason to Colchis—a perilous journey even yet (although Colonel Doniphan's march during the Mexican war is far more wonderful than either Xenophon's or Jason's adventure), in search of the Argonautic fleece of gold. With perils among snows and deserts, from poniards, starvation and war, he had at last reached his home, where he proposed remaining, in order to reduce his experience to writing, and publish it in French at Paris. But I doubt if such a nomad remain long in Smyrna. His eye was already wandering over the ruins of Central America and Peru, which he wished to see, in order to verify some favorite hypotheses in relation to the Asiatic and American races. I gave him a list of American books which treat upon the subject. These will but fan the sparks into a blaze; in which he will go off, perhaps in search of the Hesperides, or Isles of the Blest, beyond the setting sun, of which his favorite Grecian poets so rapturously sing.

With such an adventurer yet alive on the earth, would it not be wise to be chary of displaying one's limited travelling experience, and to adopt the best, as well as the true touchstone, which ever tests the objects seen by their intrinsic, and not by any adventitious merit.

By this touchstone I would desire to test my native country; and would call upon the census returns, just taken, for my facts and figures. By the same touchstone, I would desire to test my native Buckeye State. She has not a long line of heraldry—renowned in war, and great in council; but she has yet in her midst many of her own pioneers—honest, hardy and true—who have seen her grow in a half century from a wilderness, supporting a few Indians by its game, into a State with nearly two millions of free people, and outgrowing her old constitution, and within that time forced by the expansive spirit, and the increased prosperity of her people, to adopt a new organic law! She has not ruins and temples, basilicas and minsters; but she has great cities rising in the might of sleepless energy; and all the product of a few years. Well may the philosopher and economist wonder at the results attained by the Republic of the New World. Her progress, her civilization, her polity, her comforts and amenities of life, and her prosperity, have no parallel in the history of nations. Those who are in her midst are not conscious of this supremacy. From the shores of the Old World one can gaze at the United States, with a full appreciation of its truth, and return to its bosom to mingle with her masses, with a citizen's pride, that no display of royalty, or glitter of rank, no monuments of past glory or evidences of present power, from the Bosphorus to the Thames, can mortify or humble. If more of our young men could see the nations of the Old World, as to whose enfranchisement from galling tyrannies the heart almost ceases to hope; if they could breathe the stifled air, which must not hear a whisper of liberalism; and then contemplate our own free country, rising in the greatness of her strength and instinct with the prompting of Destiny; would there not be instilled into the heart a warmer love and purer devotion to their own native land?

The "Buckeye abroad," will soon be a Buckeye at HOME. The kindly air is blowing from the 'sweet South.' The fogs are left upon the banks. The sun shines pleasantly. Boston is on our west. To-morrow morning, and we are in New-York! But within the last few days, time has not hung so heavily. We have on board a songstress, Miss Hayes and troupe, going to New-York to rival Jenny Lind. Yesterday a concert came off for the benefit of the gallant tars and firemen, who brought us safely out of the gales. Nearly two hundred dollars were raised; Miss Hayes warbled and Braham sang, with a potency that calmed the sea; and it was said, drew shoals of fish after our steamer, which, considering that we were in the midst of the great fisheries, was not so remarkable a phenomenon. As to our dinner speeches, our hurrahs, our cheerful inventions to pass time; as to these minor matters, I need not now speak. Pardon me, that occasionally I have indulged in the light, where there is so much of the serious to be written about. I fear to attempt the profound; lest it turn into the heavy, which even the inspiration of the old world, with its thronging multitude of interests, could not relieve. But my readers will do me the justice to say, that where Antiquity was present as a power, and God was visible in the grandeur of his works, I have not indulged in the frivolous. There is one part of the tourist's record, which has not regaled my readers. Have I made mouths over meals, called on the reader to condole with my boiled egg or pudding, or to swear at Boots while I stood in stocking feet bawling in bad French? Have I dilated upon the want of water in my pitcher, or grumbled like John Bull at the infamous charges of landlords? Content to eat what I could, and surprised to find the world so much more honest than it has credit for—I have endeavored to realize my childhood's dream and boyhood's wonder, by finding in the scenes of the Old World an enchantment and a Presence, which in the repose of home, Memory will 'not willingly let die.'

The cry is that Rhode Island is in sight! Oh! but that sounds like home! Little Rhody; in whose University so many months were passed conning over scenes which the last summer has realized—next to Ohio, she seems my own native State. May not the pilgrim now conclude his wanderings, in the language of Sir John Mandeville, that *veracious* and quaint old traveller, whose marvels he read in the old halls upon that shore: 'I have passed manye landes and manye yles and contrees, and cherched (found) manye fulle straunge places, and have ben in manye fulle gode honourable companye. Now I am comen home to reste. And thus have I recorded the tyme passed.'

THE END.

www.ingramcontent.com/pod-product-compliance
Lightning Source LLC
LaVergne TN
LVHW090545110826
845146LV00001B/26

* 9 7 8 1 4 2 5 5 5 1 2 2 3 *